STAR WARS™

WAR OF THE BOUNTY HUNTERS

STAR WARS™
WAR OF THE BOUNTY HUNTERS

Writer
CHARLES SOULE

Artist
RAMON ROSANAS

Color Artist
RACHELLE ROSENBERG

Letterer
VC's CLAYTON COWLES

Cover Art
CARLO PAGULAYAN, JASON PAZ & RAIN BEREDO

Assistant Editors
TOM GRONEMAN & DANNY KHAZEM

Editor
MARK PANICCIA

Collection Editor	JENNIFER GRÜNWALD
Assistant Editor	DANIEL KIRCHHOFFER
Assistant Managing Editor	MAIA LOY
Assistant Managing Editor	LISA MONTALBANO
VP Production & Special Projects	JEFF YOUNGQUIST
Book Designer	ADAM DEL RE
SVP Print, Sales & Marketing	DAVID GABRIEL
Editor in Chief	C.B. CEBULSKI

For Lucasfilm:

Senior Editor	ROBERT SIMPSON
Creative Director	MICHAEL SIGLAIN
Art Director	TROY ALDERS
Lucasfilm Story Group	MATT MARTIN
	PABLO HIDALGO
	EMILY SHKOUKANI
Creative Art Manager	PHIL SZOSTAK

STAR WARS VOL. 3: WAR OF THE BOUNTY HUNTERS. Contains material originally published in magazine form as STAR WARS (2020) #12-18. First printing 2021. ISBN 978-1-302-92080-7. Published by MARVEL WORLDWIDE, INC., a subsidiary of MARVEL ENTERTAINMENT, LLC. OFFICE OF PUBLICATION: 1290 Avenue of the Americas, New York, NY 10104.

Printed in Canada. KEVIN FEIGE, Chief Creative Officer; DAN BUCKLEY, President, Marvel Entertainment; JOE QUESADA, EVP & Creative Director; DAVID BOGART, Associate Publisher & SVP of Talent Affairs; TOM BREVOORT, VP, Executive Editor; NICK LOWE, Executive Editor, VP of Content, Digital Publishing; DAVID GABRIEL, VP of Print & Digital Publishing; JEFF YOUNGQUIST, VP of Production & Special Projects; ALEX MORALES, Director of Publishing Operations; DAN EDINGTON, Managing Editor; RICKEY PURDIN, Director of Talent Relations; JENNIFER GRÜNWALD, Senior Editor, Special Projects; SUSAN CRESPI, Production Manager; STAN LEE, Chairman Emeritus. For information regarding advertising in Marvel Comics or on Marvel.com, please contact Vit DeBellis, Custom Solutions & Integrated Advertising Manager, at vdebellis@marvel.com. For Marvel subscription inquiries, please call 888-511-5480. **Manufactured between 10/15/2021 and 11/16/2021 by SOLISCO PRINTERS, SCOTT, QC, CANADA.**

10 9 8 7 6 5 4 3 2 1

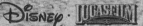

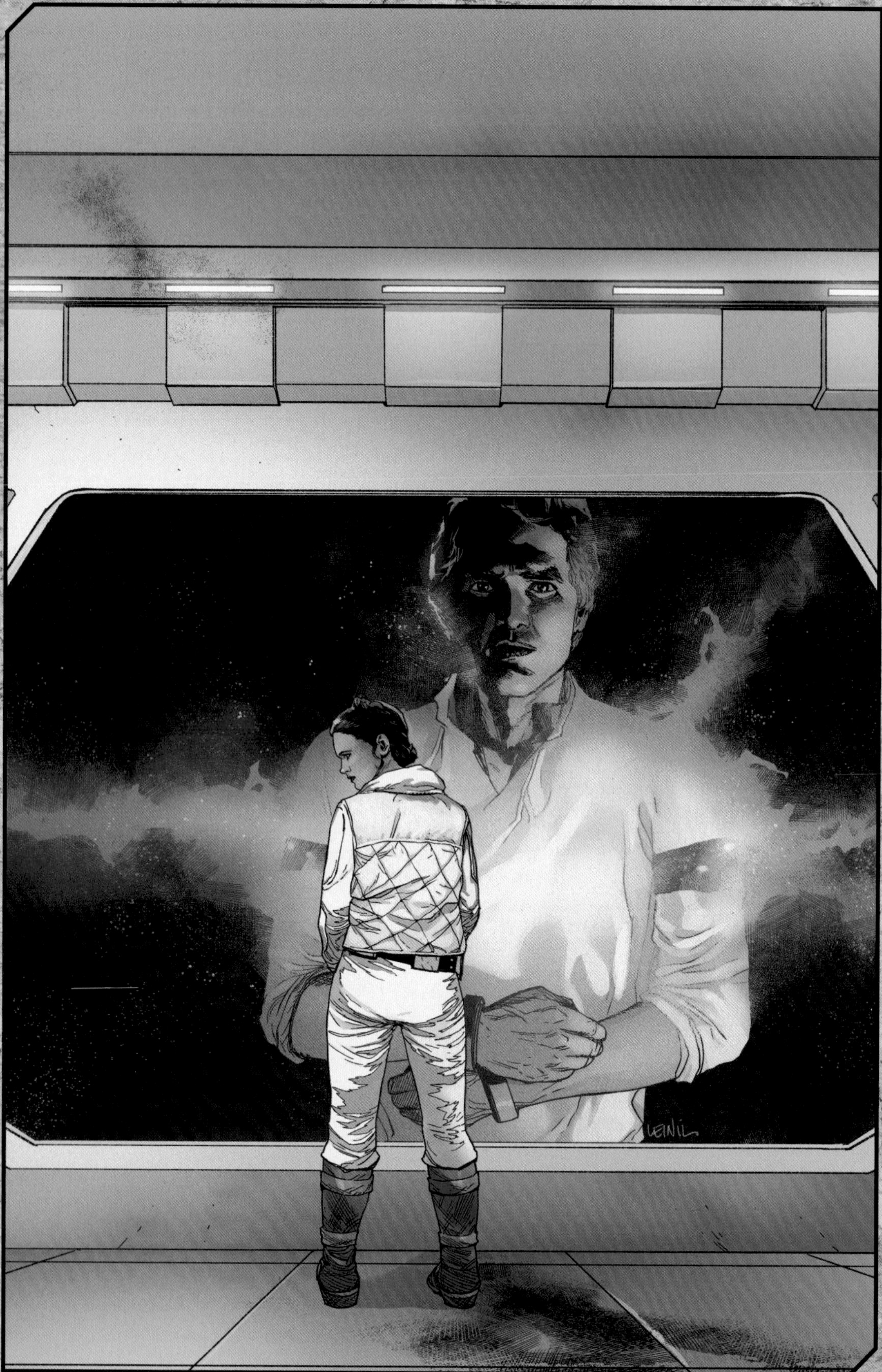
LEINIL

#12 Variant by
LEINIL FRANCIS YU & SUNNY GHO

12 – REFLECTIONS OF THE LOST

Starlight Squadron's first mission ends in disaster.

Commander Zahra, eager to destroy the scattered rebel fleet, sprung a trap that cost the squadron their leader, Shara Bey.

The rest of Starlight escaped with their lives, carrying crucial Imperial data that could give the Rebellion the edge they need to finally defeat the Empire. . . .

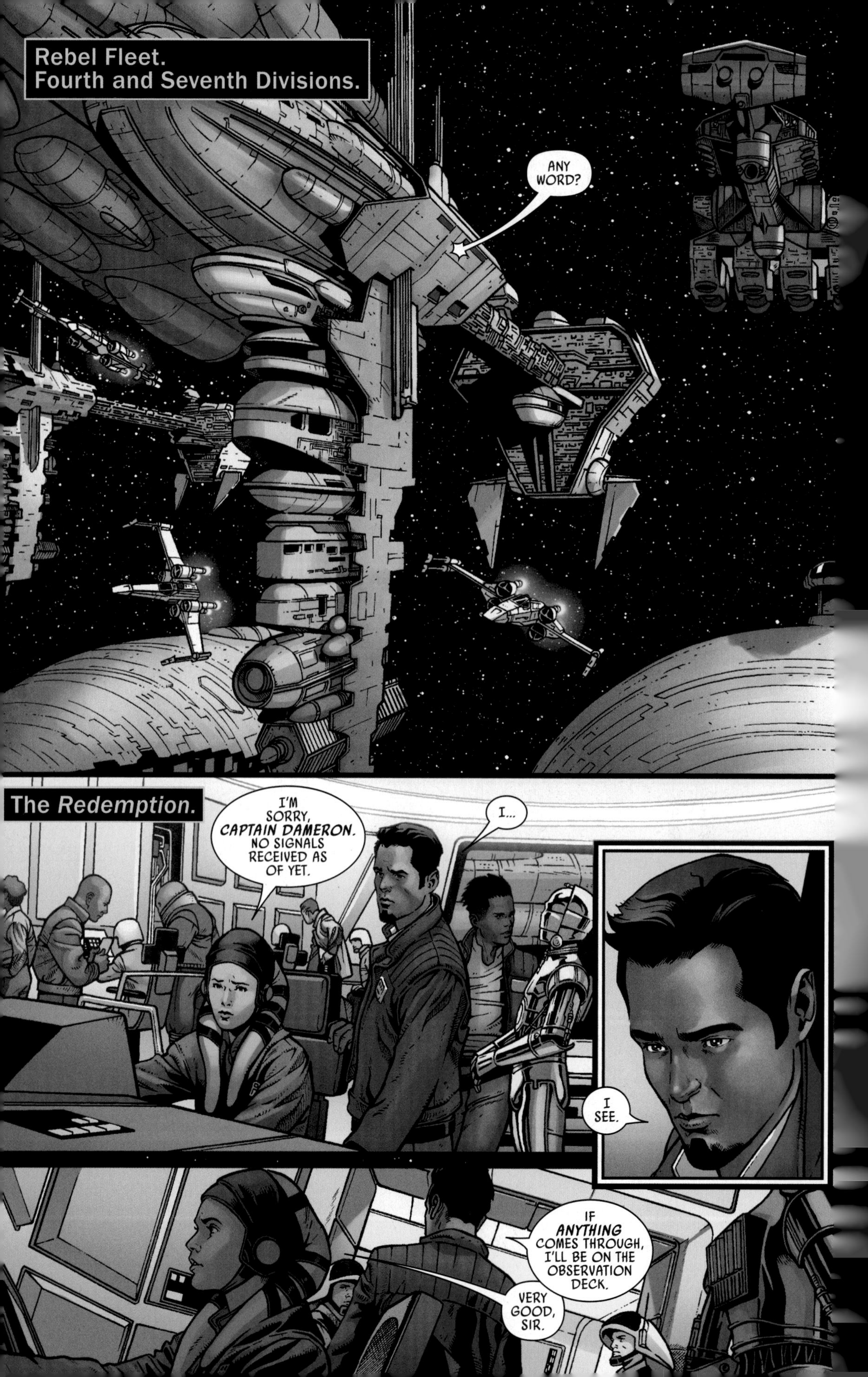
Rebel Fleet.
Fourth and Seventh Divisions.
ANY WORD?
The Redemption.
I'M SORRY, CAPTAIN DAMERON. NO SIGNALS RECEIVED AS OF YET.
I...
I SEE.
IF ANYTHING COMES THROUGH, I'LL BE ON THE OBSERVATION DECK.
VERY GOOD, SIR.

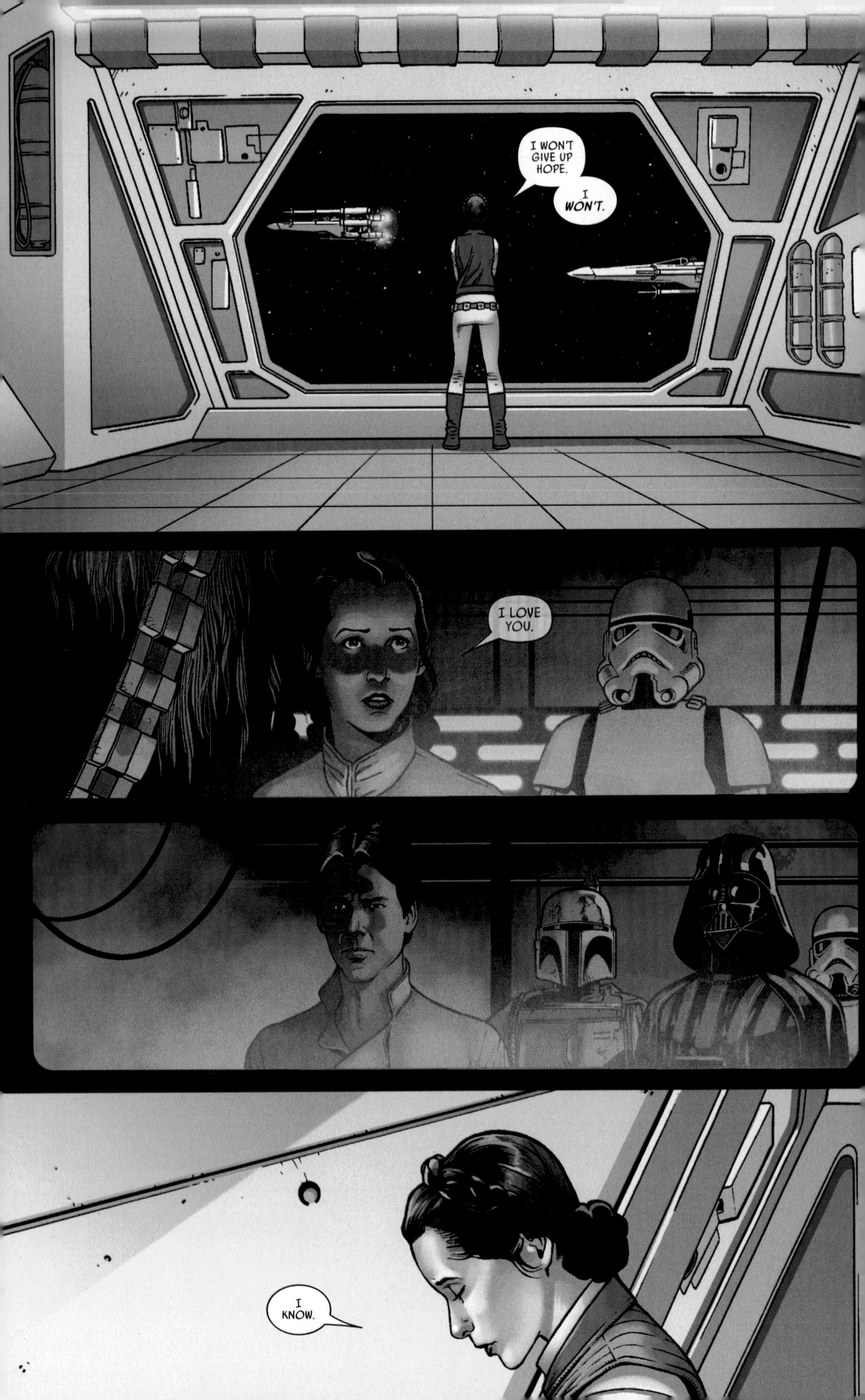
I WON'T GIVE UP HOPE.
I WON'T.
I LOVE YOU.
I KNOW.

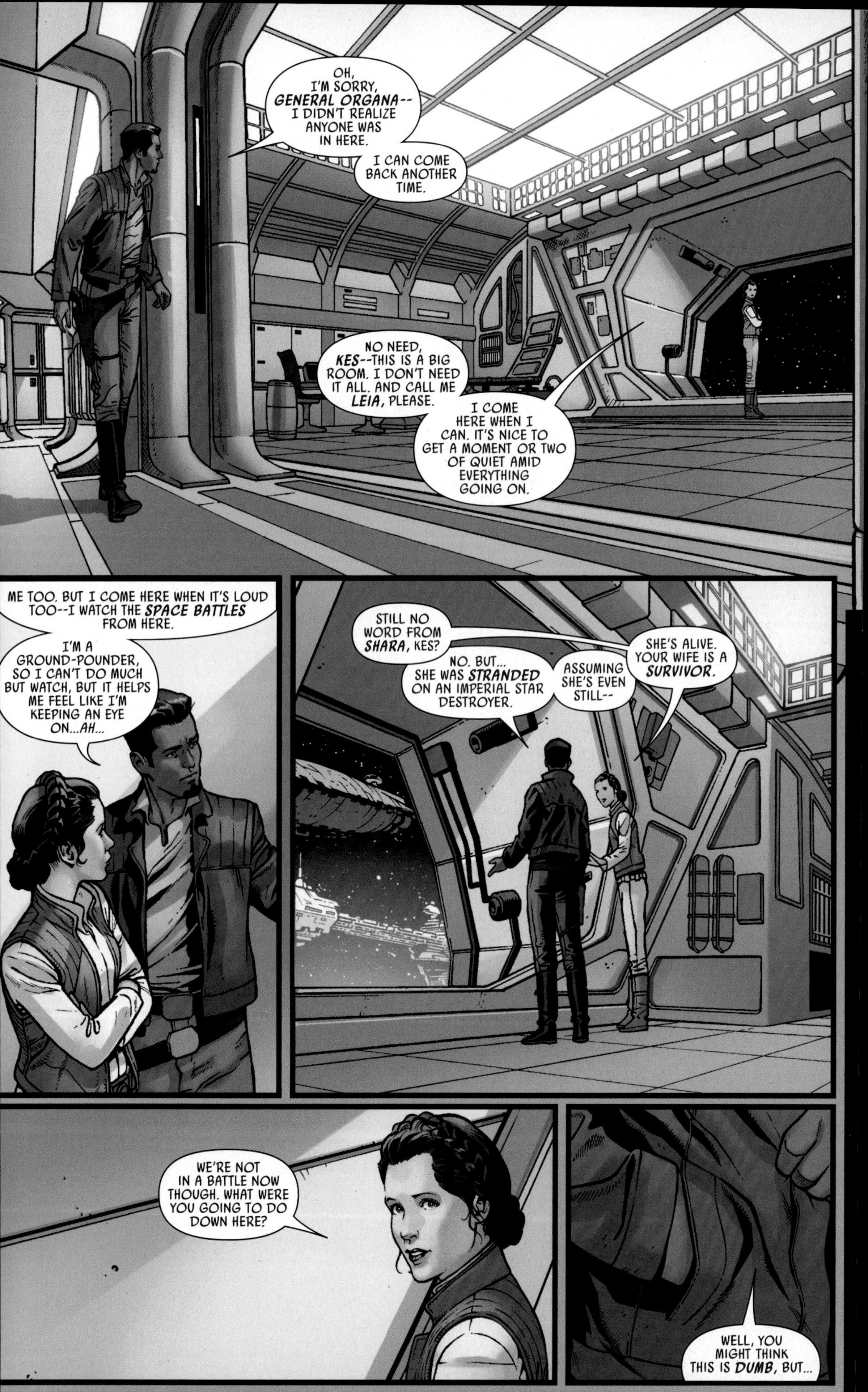
OH, I'M SORRY, GENERAL ORGANA-- I DIDN'T REALIZE ANYONE WAS IN HERE.
I CAN COME BACK ANOTHER TIME.
NO NEED, KES--THIS IS A BIG ROOM. I DON'T NEED IT ALL. AND CALL ME LEIA, PLEASE.
I COME HERE WHEN I CAN. IT'S NICE TO GET A MOMENT OR TWO OF QUIET AMID EVERYTHING GOING ON.
ME TOO. BUT I COME HERE WHEN IT'S LOUD TOO--I WATCH THE SPACE BATTLES FROM HERE.
I'M A GROUND-POUNDER, SO I CAN'T DO MUCH BUT WATCH, BUT IT HELPS ME FEEL LIKE I'M KEEPING AN EYE ON...AH...
STILL NO WORD FROM SHARA, KES?
NO. BUT... SHE WAS STRANDED ON AN IMPERIAL STAR DESTROYER.
ASSUMING SHE'S EVEN STILL--
SHE'S ALIVE. YOUR WIFE IS A SURVIVOR.
WE'RE NOT IN A BATTLE NOW THOUGH. WHAT WERE YOU GOING TO DO DOWN HERE?
WELL, YOU MIGHT THINK THIS IS DUMB, BUT...

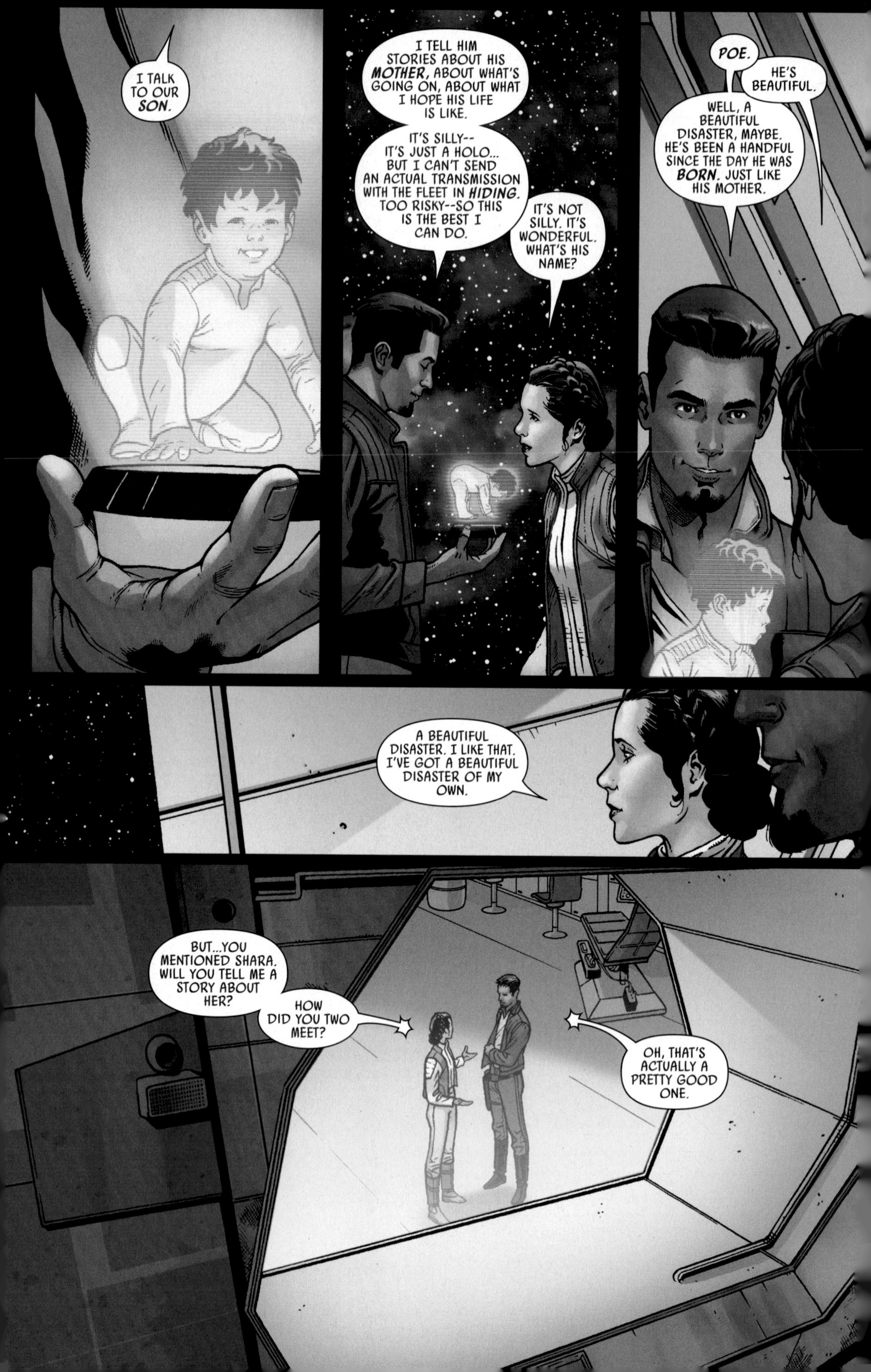
I TALK TO OUR *SON*.
I TELL HIM STORIES ABOUT HIS *MOTHER*, ABOUT WHAT'S GOING ON, ABOUT WHAT I HOPE HIS LIFE IS LIKE.
IT'S SILLY-- IT'S JUST A HOLO... BUT I CAN'T SEND AN ACTUAL TRANSMISSION WITH THE FLEET IN *HIDING*. TOO RISKY--SO THIS IS THE BEST I CAN DO.
IT'S NOT SILLY. IT'S WONDERFUL. WHAT'S HIS NAME?
POE.
WELL, A BEAUTIFUL DISASTER, MAYBE. HE'S BEEN A HANDFUL SINCE THE DAY HE WAS *BORN*. JUST LIKE HIS MOTHER.
HE'S BEAUTIFUL.
A BEAUTIFUL DISASTER. I LIKE THAT. I'VE GOT A BEAUTIFUL DISASTER OF MY OWN.
BUT...YOU MENTIONED SHARA. WILL YOU TELL ME A STORY ABOUT HER?
HOW DID YOU TWO MEET?
OH, THAT'S ACTUALLY A PRETTY GOOD ONE.

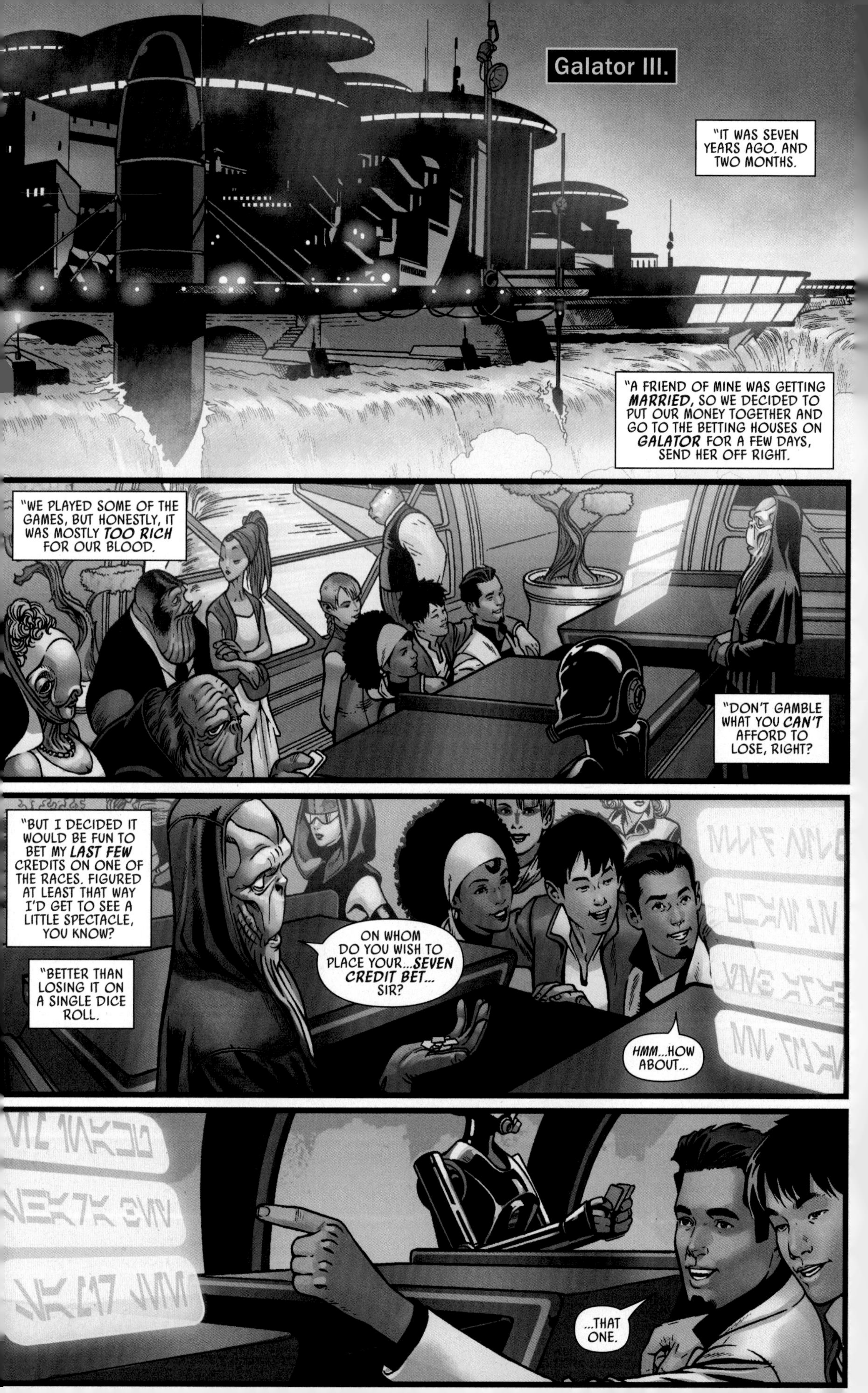
Galator III.
"IT WAS SEVEN YEARS AGO. AND TWO MONTHS.
"A FRIEND OF MINE WAS GETTING MARRIED, SO WE DECIDED TO PUT OUR MONEY TOGETHER AND GO TO THE BETTING HOUSES ON GALATOR FOR A FEW DAYS, SEND HER OFF RIGHT.
"WE PLAYED SOME OF THE GAMES, BUT HONESTLY, IT WAS MOSTLY TOO RICH FOR OUR BLOOD.
"DON'T GAMBLE WHAT YOU CAN'T AFFORD TO LOSE, RIGHT?
"BUT I DECIDED IT WOULD BE FUN TO BET MY LAST FEW CREDITS ON ONE OF THE RACES. FIGURED AT LEAST THAT WAY I'D GET TO SEE A LITTLE SPECTACLE, YOU KNOW?
"BETTER THAN LOSING IT ON A SINGLE DICE ROLL.
ON WHOM DO YOU WISH TO PLACE YOUR...SEVEN CREDIT BET... SIR?
HMM...HOW ABOUT...
...THAT ONE.

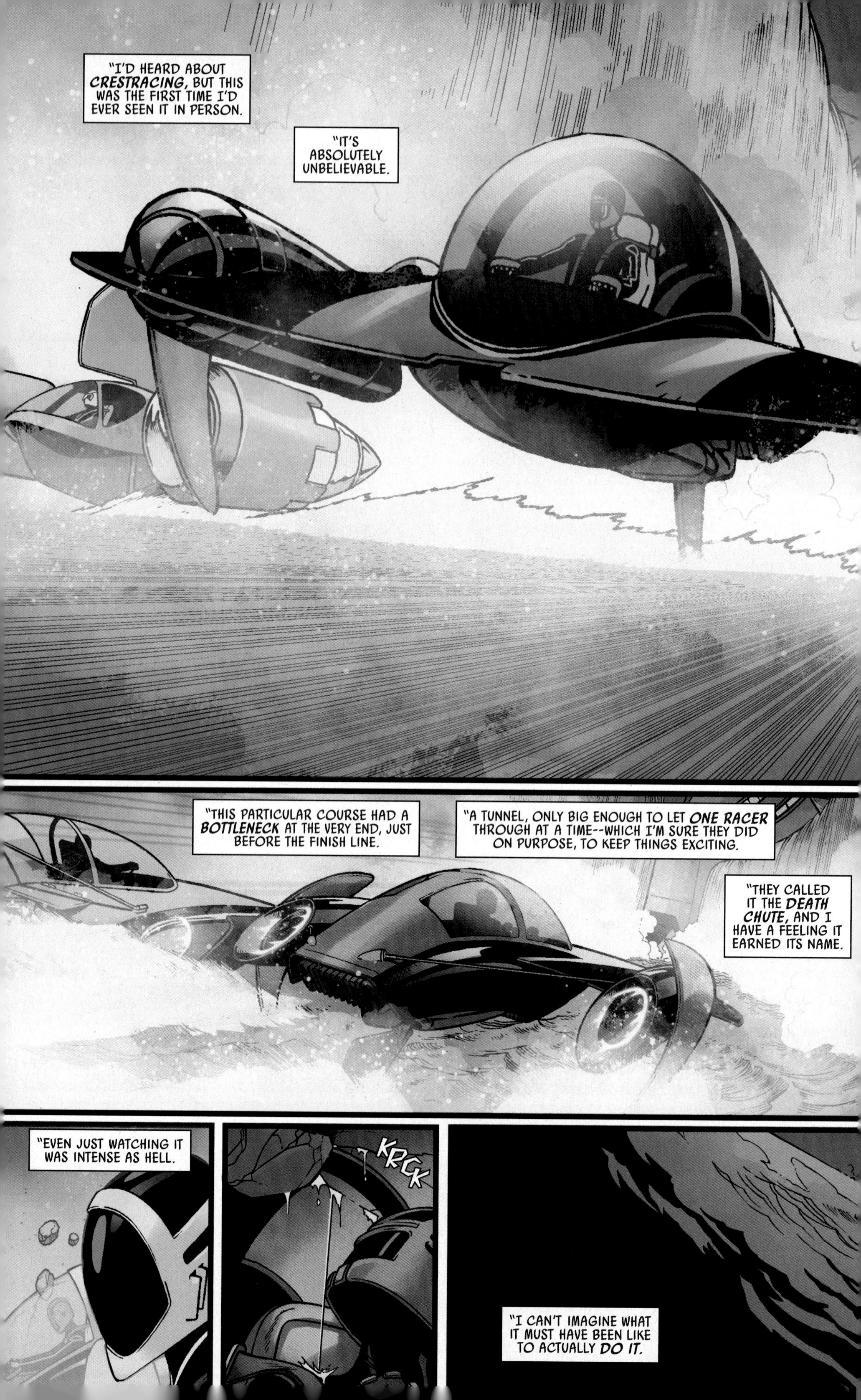
"I'D HEARD ABOUT CRESTRACING, BUT THIS WAS THE FIRST TIME I'D EVER SEEN IT IN PERSON.
"IT'S ABSOLUTELY UNBELIEVABLE.
"THIS PARTICULAR COURSE HAD A BOTTLENECK AT THE VERY END, JUST BEFORE THE FINISH LINE.
"A TUNNEL, ONLY BIG ENOUGH TO LET ONE RACER THROUGH AT A TIME--WHICH I'M SURE THEY DID ON PURPOSE, TO KEEP THINGS EXCITING.
"THEY CALLED IT THE DEATH CHUTE, AND I HAVE A FEELING IT EARNED ITS NAME.
"EVEN JUST WATCHING IT WAS INTENSE AS HELL.
KRCK
"I CAN'T IMAGINE WHAT IT MUST HAVE BEEN LIKE TO ACTUALLY DO IT.

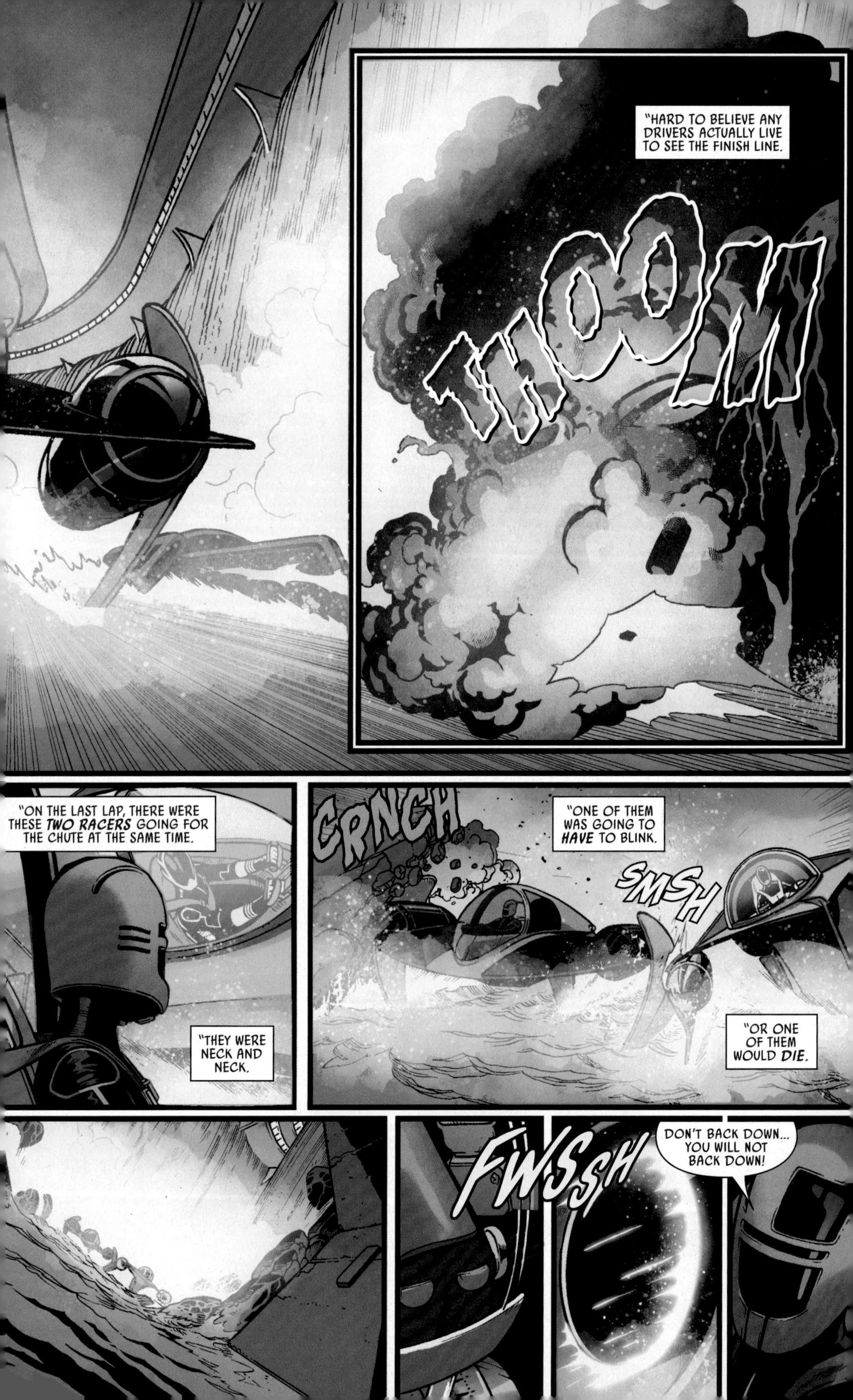
"HARD TO BELIEVE ANY DRIVERS ACTUALLY LIVE TO SEE THE FINISH LINE.
THOOM
"ON THE LAST LAP, THERE WERE THESE TWO RACERS GOING FOR THE CHUTE AT THE SAME TIME.
"THEY WERE NECK AND NECK.
CRNCH
"ONE OF THEM WAS GOING TO HAVE TO BLINK.
SMSH
"OR ONE OF THEM WOULD DIE.
FWSSH
DON'T BACK DOWN... YOU WILL NOT BACK DOWN!

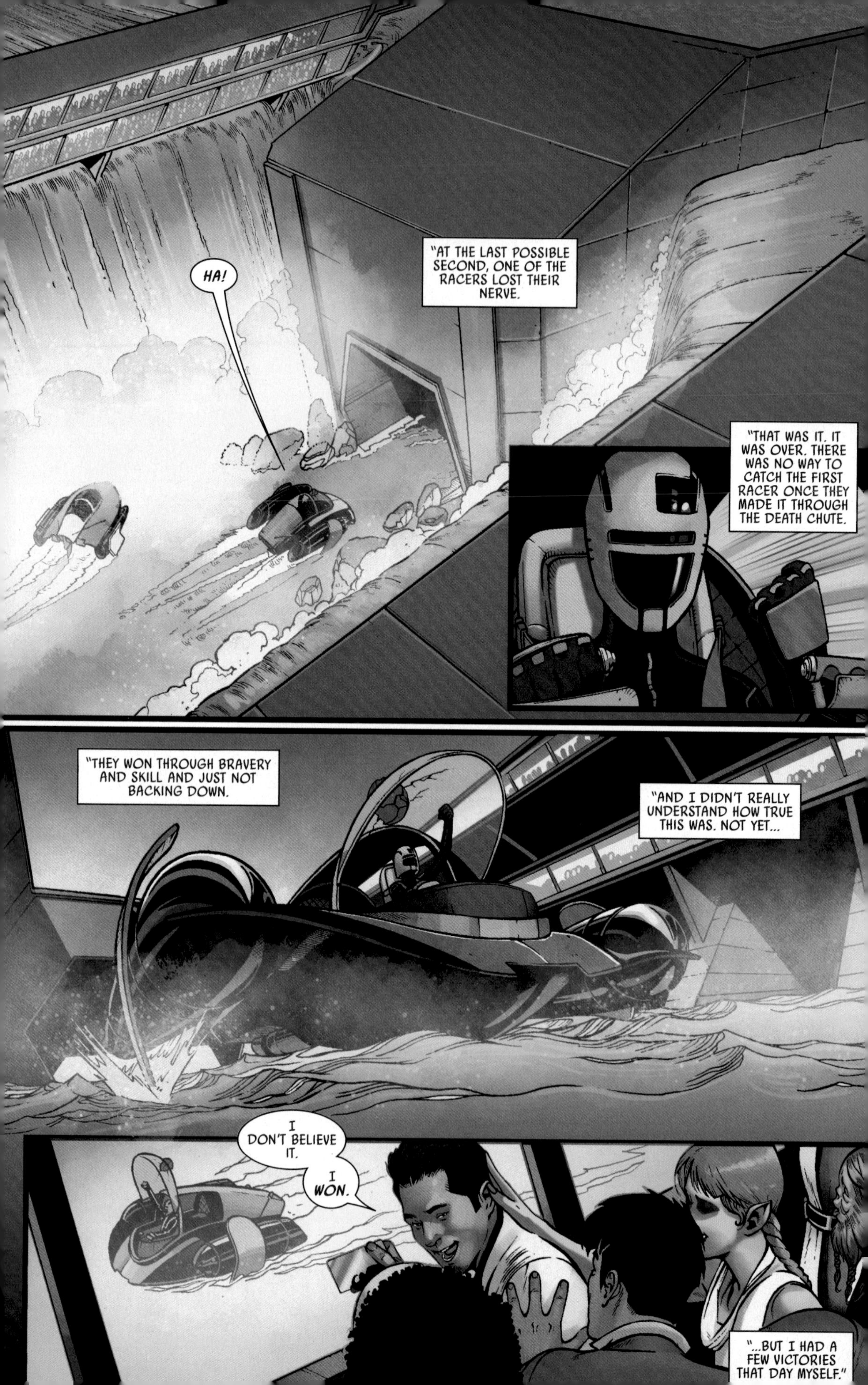
"AT THE LAST POSSIBLE SECOND, ONE OF THE RACERS LOST THEIR NERVE.
HA!
"THAT WAS IT. IT WAS OVER. THERE WAS NO WAY TO CATCH THE FIRST RACER ONCE THEY MADE IT THROUGH THE DEATH CHUTE.
"THEY WON THROUGH BRAVERY AND SKILL AND JUST NOT BACKING DOWN.
"AND I DIDN'T REALLY UNDERSTAND HOW TRUE THIS WAS. NOT YET...
I DON'T BELIEVE IT.
I WON.
"...BUT I HAD A FEW VICTORIES THAT DAY MYSELF."

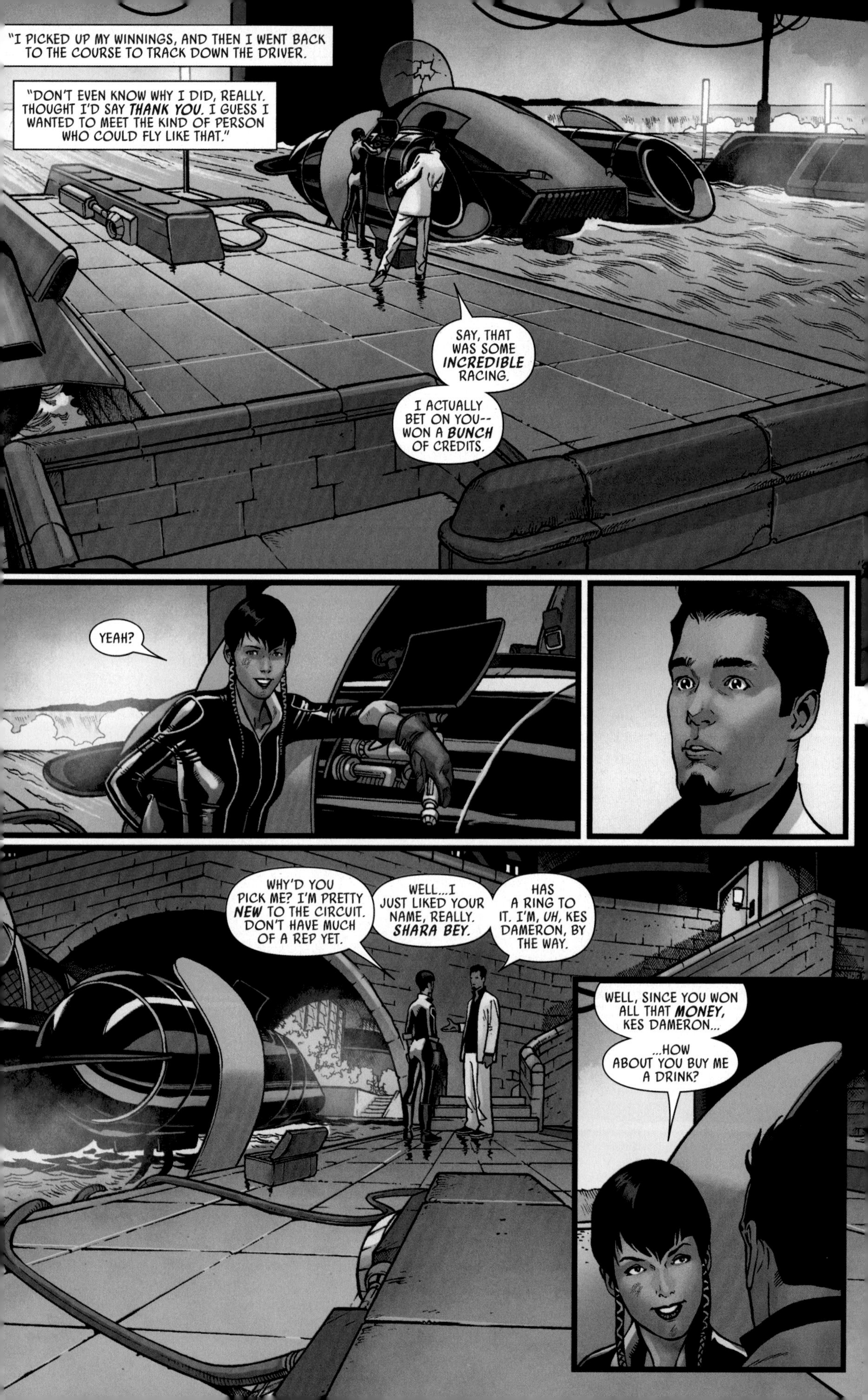
"I PICKED UP MY WINNINGS, AND THEN I WENT BACK TO THE COURSE TO TRACK DOWN THE DRIVER.
"DON'T EVEN KNOW WHY I DID, REALLY. THOUGHT I'D SAY *THANK YOU.* I GUESS I WANTED TO MEET THE KIND OF PERSON WHO COULD FLY LIKE THAT."
SAY, THAT WAS SOME *INCREDIBLE* RACING.
I ACTUALLY BET ON YOU-- WON A *BUNCH* OF CREDITS.
YEAH?
WHY'D YOU PICK ME? I'M PRETTY *NEW* TO THE CIRCUIT. DON'T HAVE MUCH OF A REP YET.
WELL...I JUST LIKED YOUR NAME, REALLY. *SHARA BEY.*
HAS A RING TO IT. I'M, *UH,* KES DAMERON, BY THE WAY.
WELL, SINCE YOU WON ALL THAT *MONEY,* KES DAMERON...
...HOW ABOUT YOU BUY ME A DRINK?

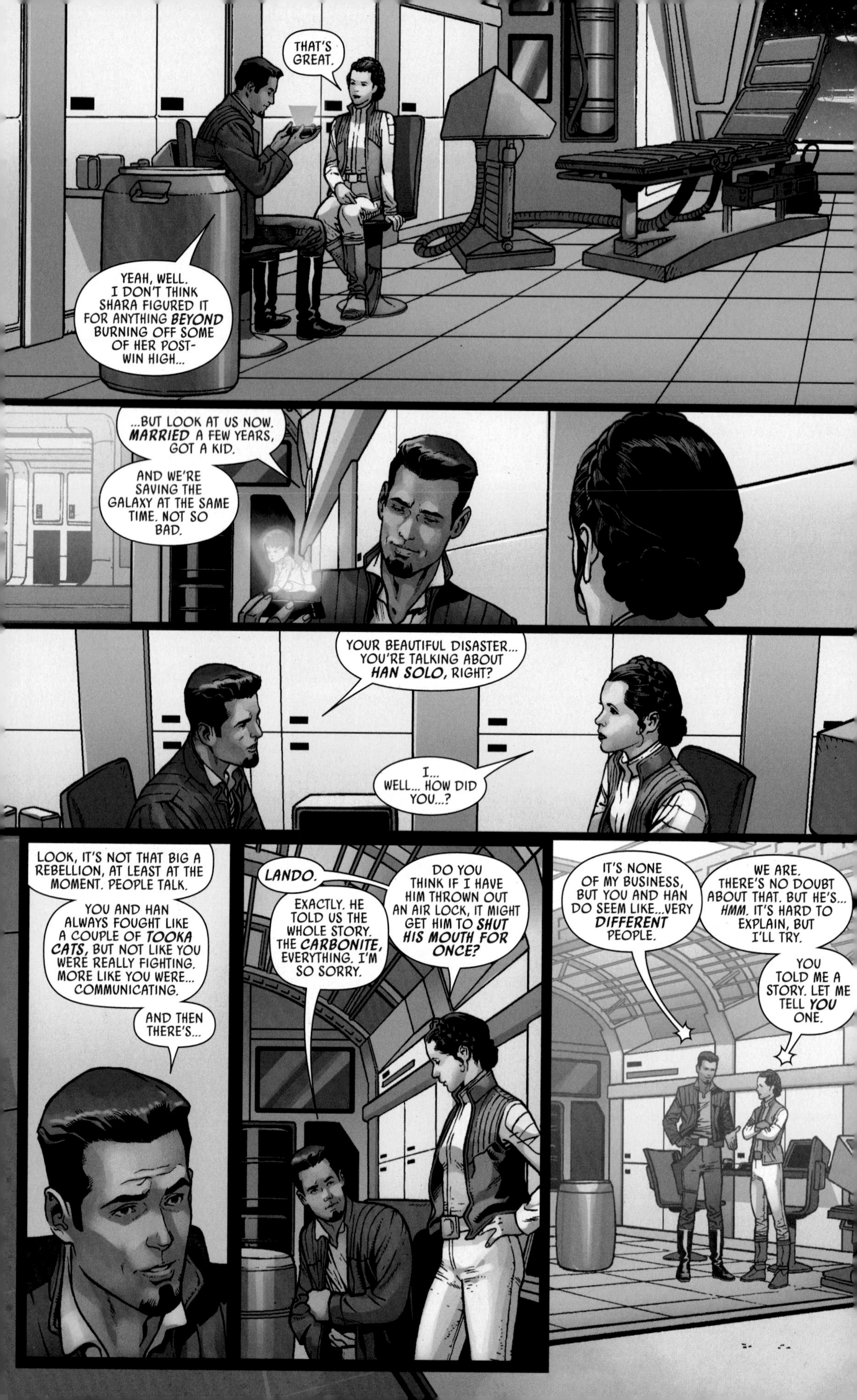
THAT'S GREAT.
YEAH, WELL. I DON'T THINK SHARA FIGURED IT FOR ANYTHING BEYOND BURNING OFF SOME OF HER POST-WIN HIGH...
...BUT LOOK AT US NOW. MARRIED A FEW YEARS, GOT A KID.
AND WE'RE SAVING THE GALAXY AT THE SAME TIME. NOT SO BAD.
YOUR BEAUTIFUL DISASTER... YOU'RE TALKING ABOUT HAN SOLO, RIGHT?
I... WELL... HOW DID YOU...?
LOOK, IT'S NOT THAT BIG A REBELLION, AT LEAST AT THE MOMENT. PEOPLE TALK.
YOU AND HAN ALWAYS FOUGHT LIKE A COUPLE OF TOOKA CATS, BUT NOT LIKE YOU WERE REALLY FIGHTING. MORE LIKE YOU WERE... COMMUNICATING.
AND THEN THERE'S...
LANDO.
EXACTLY. HE TOLD US THE WHOLE STORY. THE CARBONITE, EVERYTHING. I'M SO SORRY.
DO YOU THINK IF I HAVE HIM THROWN OUT AN AIR LOCK, IT MIGHT GET HIM TO SHUT HIS MOUTH FOR ONCE?
IT'S NONE OF MY BUSINESS, BUT YOU AND HAN DO SEEM LIKE...VERY DIFFERENT PEOPLE.
WE ARE. THERE'S NO DOUBT ABOUT THAT. BUT HE'S... HMM. IT'S HARD TO EXPLAIN, BUT I'LL TRY.
YOU TOLD ME A STORY. LET ME TELL YOU ONE.

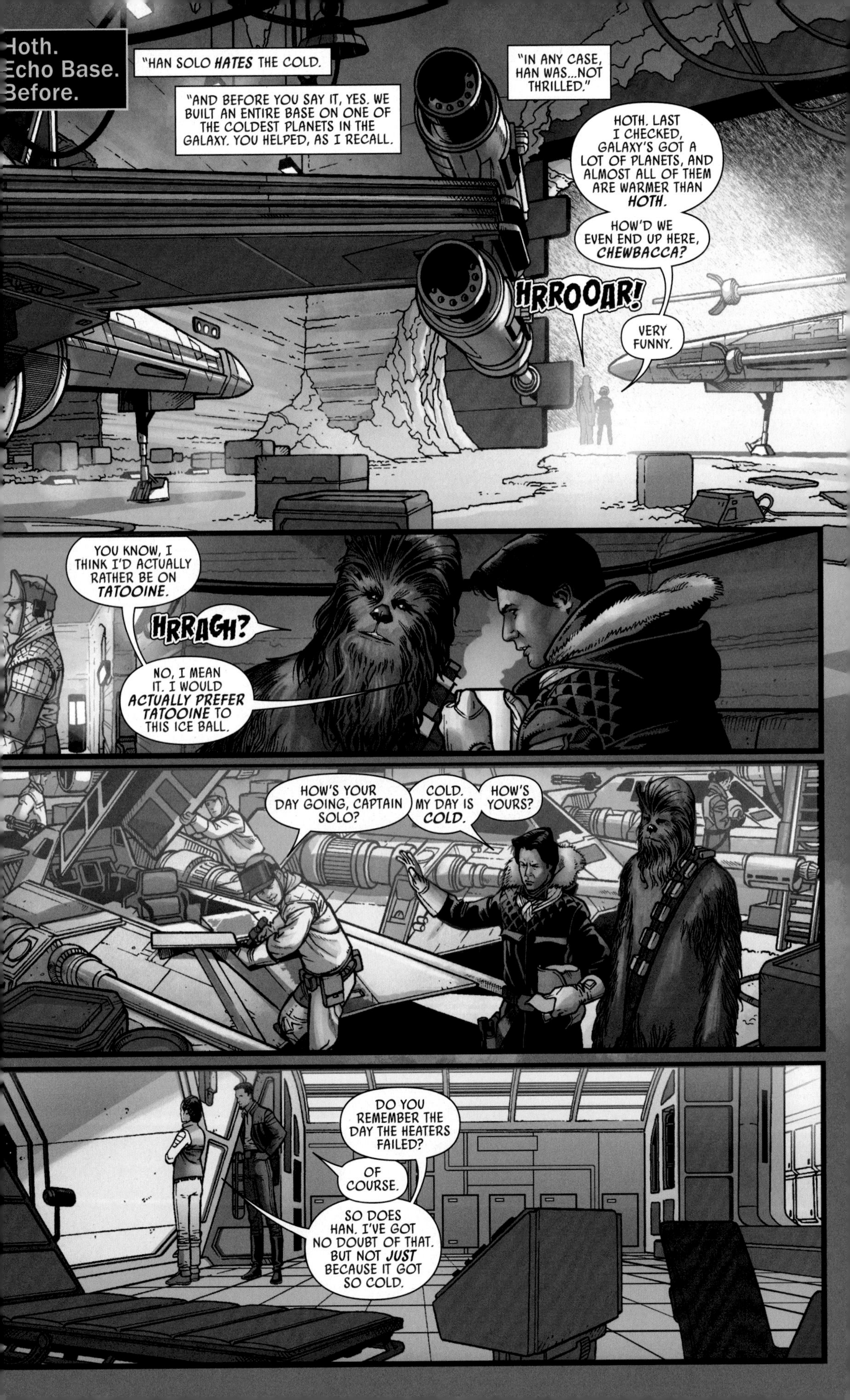
Hoth.
Echo Base.
Before.
"HAN SOLO HATES THE COLD.
"AND BEFORE YOU SAY IT, YES. WE BUILT AN ENTIRE BASE ON ONE OF THE COLDEST PLANETS IN THE GALAXY. YOU HELPED, AS I RECALL.
"IN ANY CASE, HAN WAS...NOT THRILLED."
HOTH. LAST I CHECKED, GALAXY'S GOT A LOT OF PLANETS, AND ALMOST ALL OF THEM ARE WARMER THAN HOTH.
HOW'D WE EVEN END UP HERE, CHEWBACCA?
HRROOAR!
VERY FUNNY.
YOU KNOW, I THINK I'D ACTUALLY RATHER BE ON TATOOINE.
HRRAGH?
NO, I MEAN IT. I WOULD ACTUALLY PREFER TATOOINE TO THIS ICE BALL.
HOW'S YOUR DAY GOING, CAPTAIN SOLO?
COLD. MY DAY IS COLD.
HOW'S YOURS?
DO YOU REMEMBER THE DAY THE HEATERS FAILED?
OF COURSE.
SO DOES HAN. I'VE GOT NO DOUBT OF THAT. BUT NOT JUST BECAUSE IT GOT SO COLD.

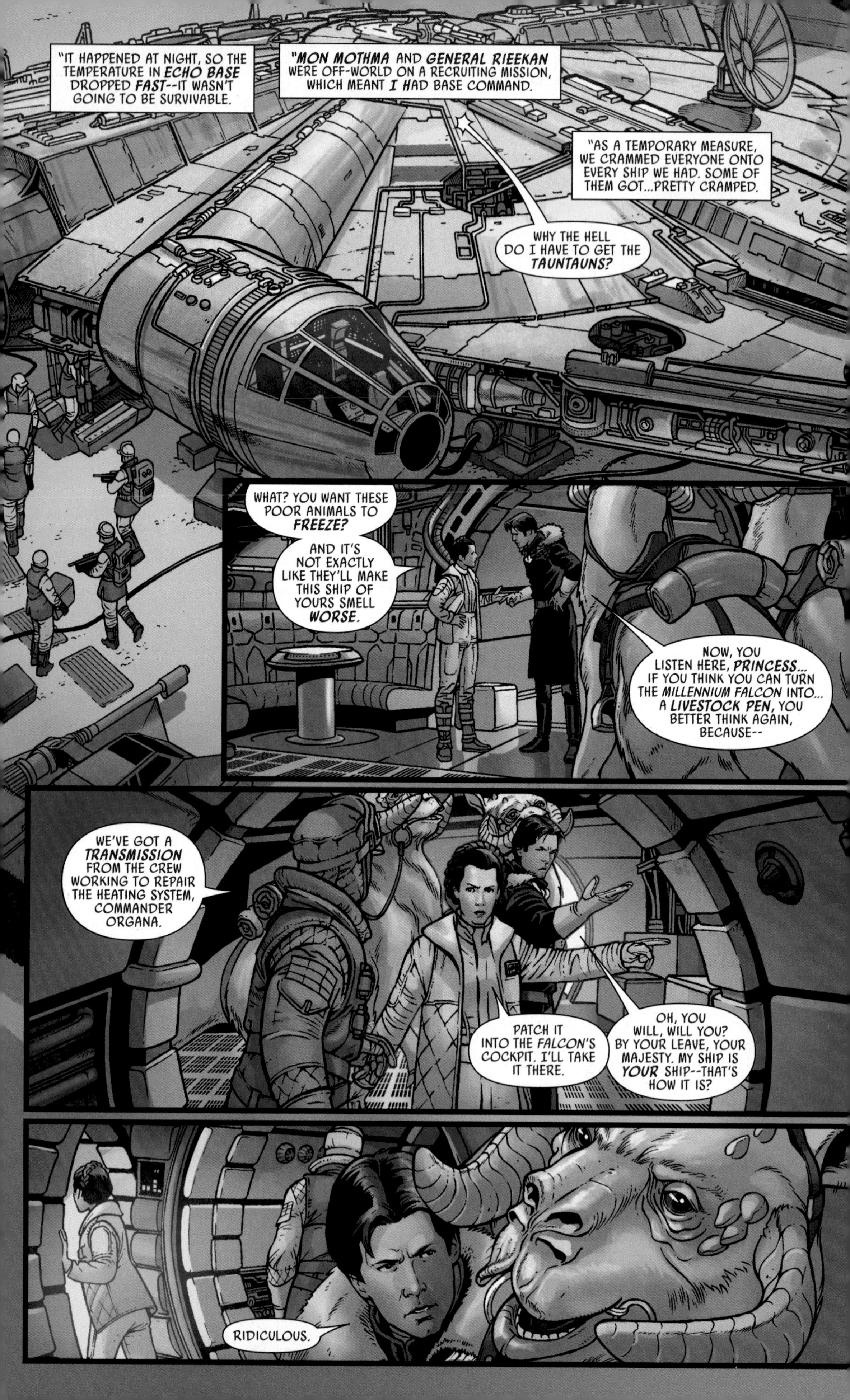
"IT HAPPENED AT NIGHT, SO THE TEMPERATURE IN ECHO BASE DROPPED FAST--IT WASN'T GOING TO BE SURVIVABLE.
"MON MOTHMA AND GENERAL RIEEKAN WERE OFF-WORLD ON A RECRUITING MISSION, WHICH MEANT I HAD BASE COMMAND.
"AS A TEMPORARY MEASURE, WE CRAMMED EVERYONE ONTO EVERY SHIP WE HAD. SOME OF THEM GOT...PRETTY CRAMPED.
WHY THE HELL DO I HAVE TO GET THE TAUNTAUNS?
WHAT? YOU WANT THESE POOR ANIMALS TO FREEZE?
AND IT'S NOT EXACTLY LIKE THEY'LL MAKE THIS SHIP OF YOURS SMELL WORSE.
NOW, YOU LISTEN HERE, PRINCESS... IF YOU THINK YOU CAN TURN THE MILLENNIUM FALCON INTO... A LIVESTOCK PEN, YOU BETTER THINK AGAIN, BECAUSE--
WE'VE GOT A TRANSMISSION FROM THE CREW WORKING TO REPAIR THE HEATING SYSTEM, COMMANDER ORGANA.
PATCH IT INTO THE FALCON'S COCKPIT. I'LL TAKE IT THERE.
OH, YOU WILL, WILL YOU? BY YOUR LEAVE, YOUR MAJESTY. MY SHIP IS YOUR SHIP--THAT'S HOW IT IS?
RIDICULOUS.

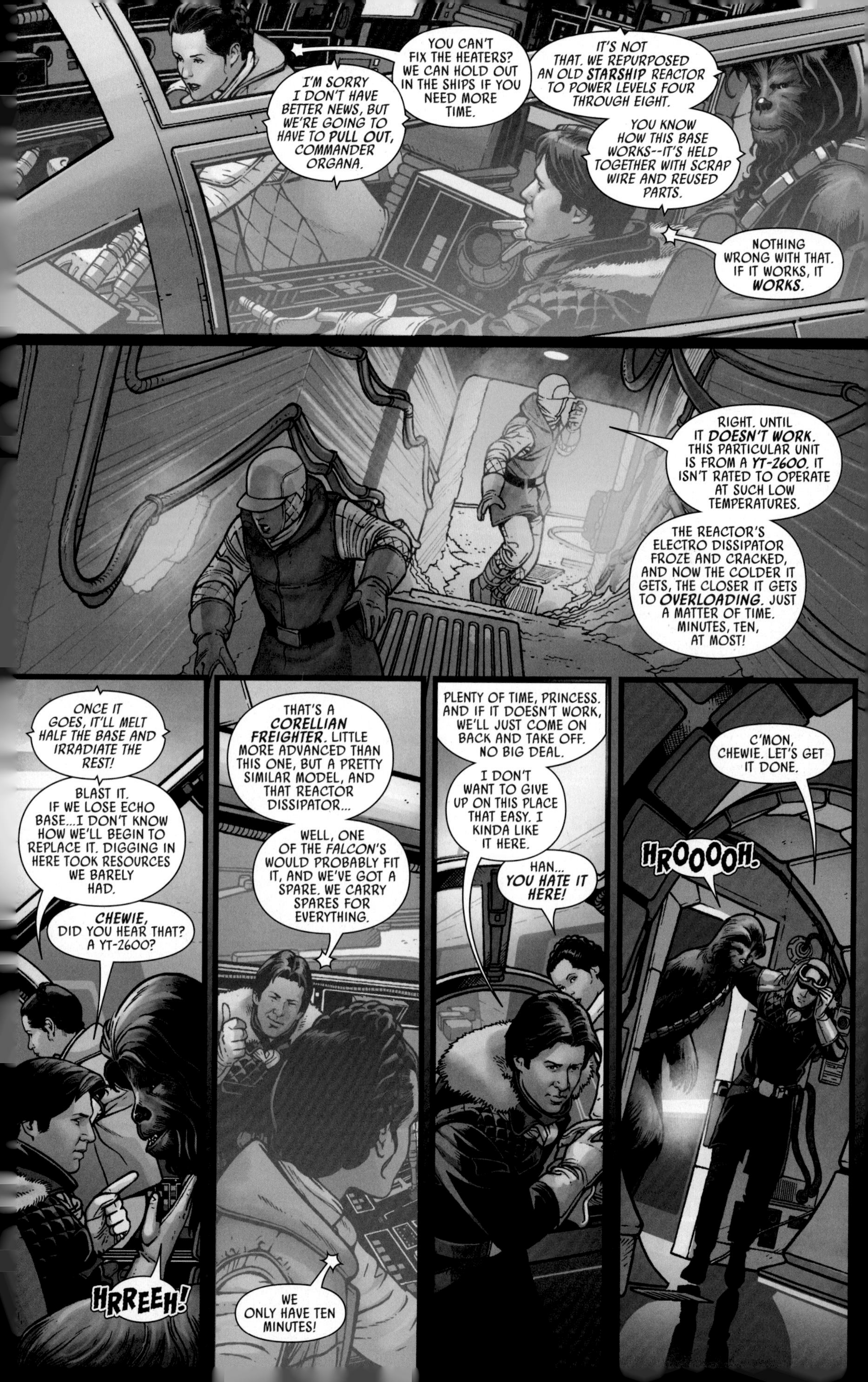
I'M SORRY I DON'T HAVE BETTER NEWS, BUT WE'RE GOING TO HAVE TO **PULL OUT**, COMMANDER ORGANA.
YOU CAN'T FIX THE HEATERS? WE CAN HOLD OUT IN THE SHIPS IF YOU NEED MORE TIME.
IT'S NOT THAT. WE REPURPOSED AN OLD **STARSHIP** REACTOR TO POWER LEVELS FOUR THROUGH EIGHT.
YOU KNOW HOW THIS BASE WORKS--IT'S HELD TOGETHER WITH SCRAP WIRE AND REUSED PARTS.
NOTHING WRONG WITH THAT. IF IT WORKS, IT **WORKS.**
RIGHT. UNTIL IT **DOESN'T WORK.** THIS PARTICULAR UNIT IS FROM A **YT-2600.** IT ISN'T RATED TO OPERATE AT SUCH LOW TEMPERATURES.
THE REACTOR'S ELECTRO DISSIPATOR FROZE AND CRACKED, AND NOW THE COLDER IT GETS, THE CLOSER IT GETS TO **OVERLOADING.** JUST A MATTER OF TIME. MINUTES. TEN, AT MOST!
ONCE IT GOES, IT'LL MELT HALF THE BASE AND IRRADIATE THE REST!
BLAST IT. IF WE LOSE ECHO BASE...I DON'T KNOW HOW WE'LL BEGIN TO REPLACE IT. DIGGING IN HERE TOOK RESOURCES WE BARELY HAD.
CHEWIE, DID YOU HEAR THAT? A YT-2600?
HRREEH!
THAT'S A **CORELLIAN FREIGHTER.** LITTLE MORE ADVANCED THAN THIS ONE, BUT A PRETTY SIMILAR MODEL, AND THAT REACTOR DISSIPATOR...
WELL, ONE OF THE *FALCON'S* WOULD PROBABLY FIT IT, AND WE'VE GOT A SPARE. WE CARRY SPARES FOR EVERYTHING.
WE ONLY HAVE TEN MINUTES!
PLENTY OF TIME, PRINCESS. AND IF IT DOESN'T WORK, WE'LL JUST COME ON BACK AND TAKE OFF. NO BIG DEAL.
I DON'T WANT TO GIVE UP ON THIS PLACE THAT EASY. I KINDA LIKE IT HERE.
HAN... **YOU HATE IT HERE!**
C'MON, CHEWIE. LET'S GET IT DONE.
HROOOOH.

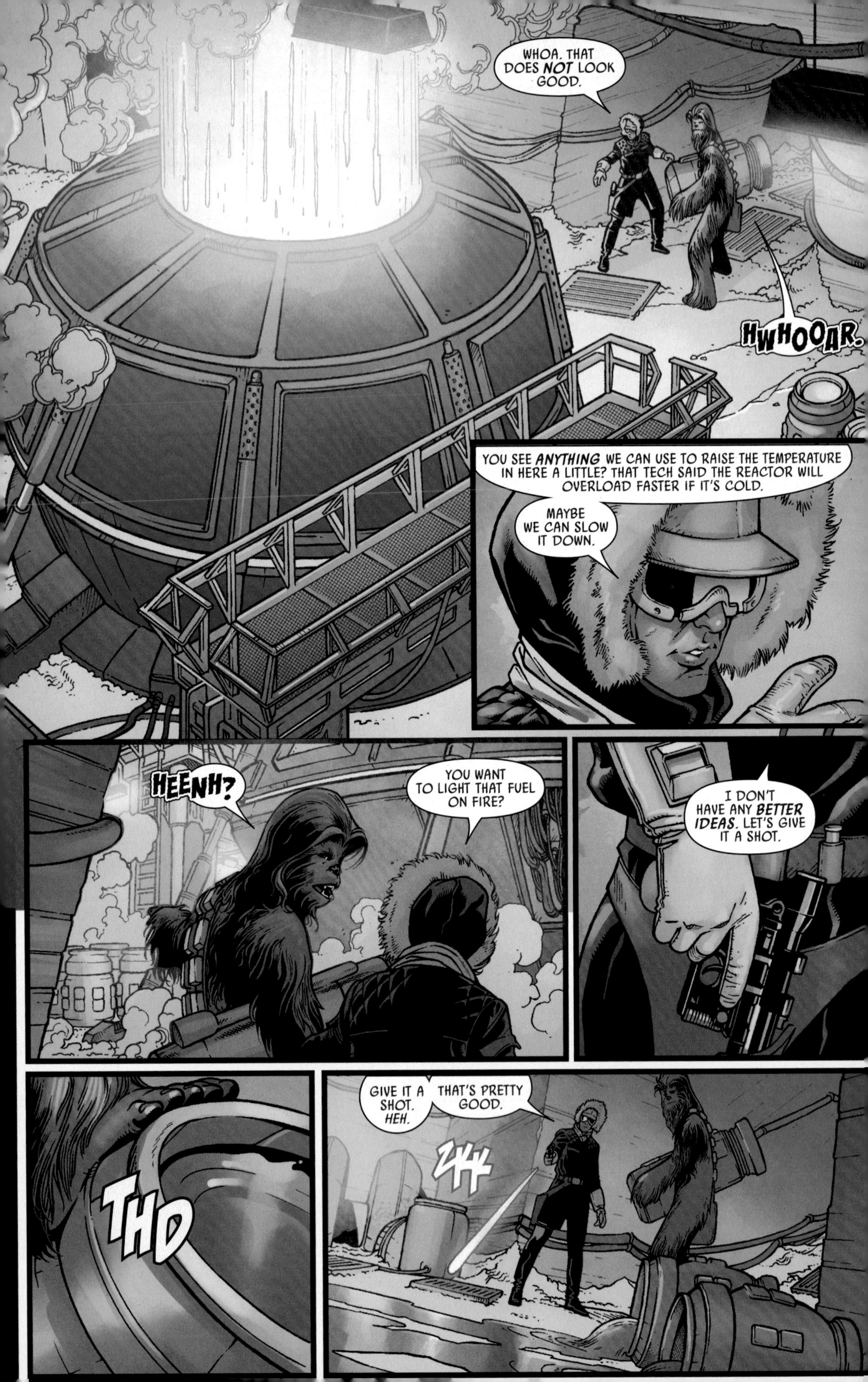
WHOA. THAT DOES NOT LOOK GOOD.
HWHOOAR.
YOU SEE ANYTHING WE CAN USE TO RAISE THE TEMPERATURE IN HERE A LITTLE? THAT TECH SAID THE REACTOR WILL OVERLOAD FASTER IF IT'S COLD.
MAYBE WE CAN SLOW IT DOWN.
HEENH?
YOU WANT TO LIGHT THAT FUEL ON FIRE?
I DON'T HAVE ANY BETTER IDEAS. LET'S GIVE IT A SHOT.
THD
GIVE IT A SHOT. HEH.
THAT'S PRETTY GOOD.
ZKK

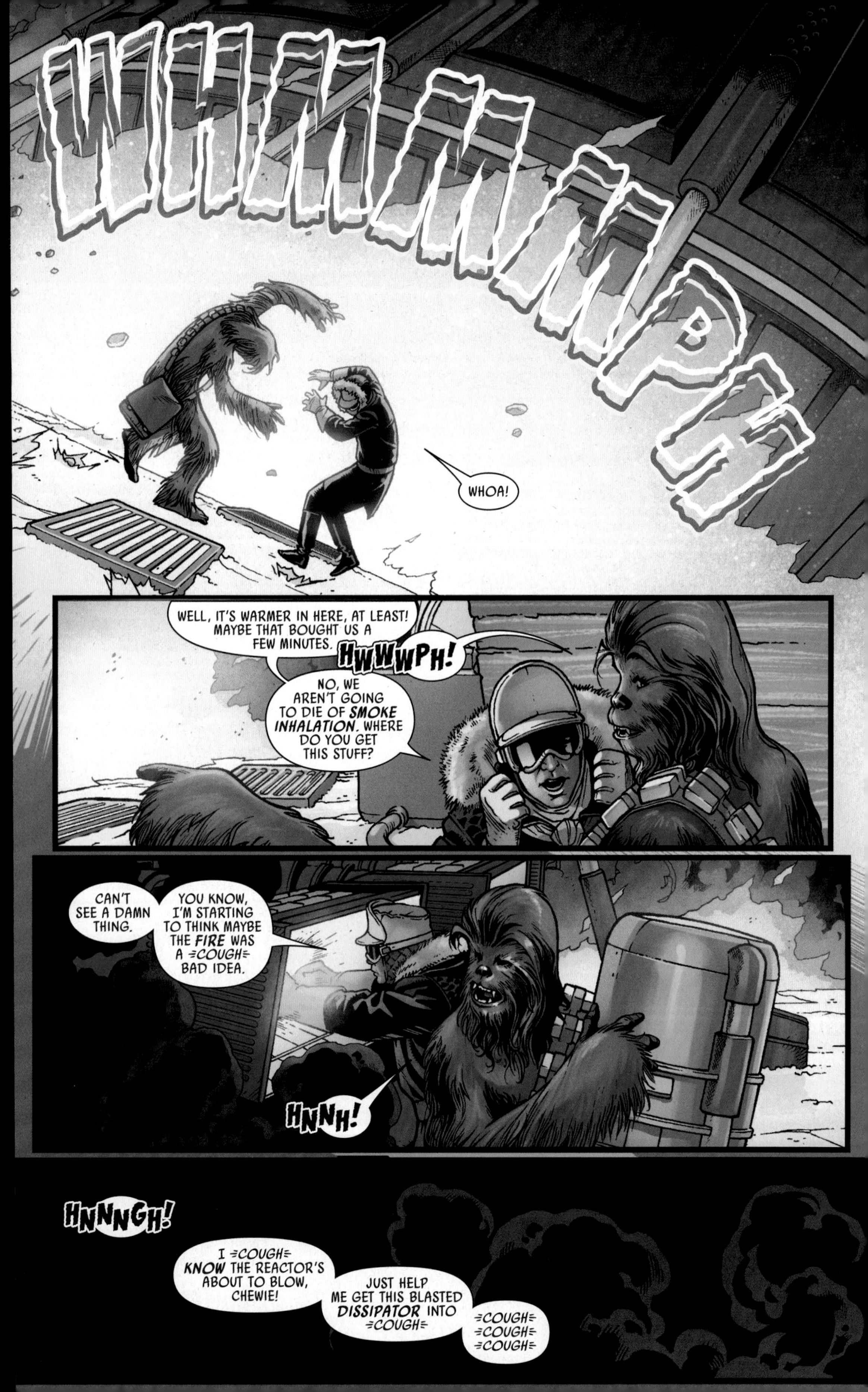
WHAMMPH
WHOA!
WELL, IT'S WARMER IN HERE, AT LEAST! MAYBE THAT BOUGHT US A FEW MINUTES.
HWWWPH!
NO, WE AREN'T GOING TO DIE OF SMOKE INHALATION. WHERE DO YOU GET THIS STUFF?
CAN'T SEE A DAMN THING.
YOU KNOW, I'M STARTING TO THINK MAYBE THE FIRE WAS A =COUGH= BAD IDEA.
HNNH!
HNNNGH!
I =COUGH= KNOW THE REACTOR'S ABOUT TO BLOW, CHEWIE!
JUST HELP ME GET THIS BLASTED DISSIPATOR INTO =COUGH=
=COUGH= =COUGH= =COUGH=

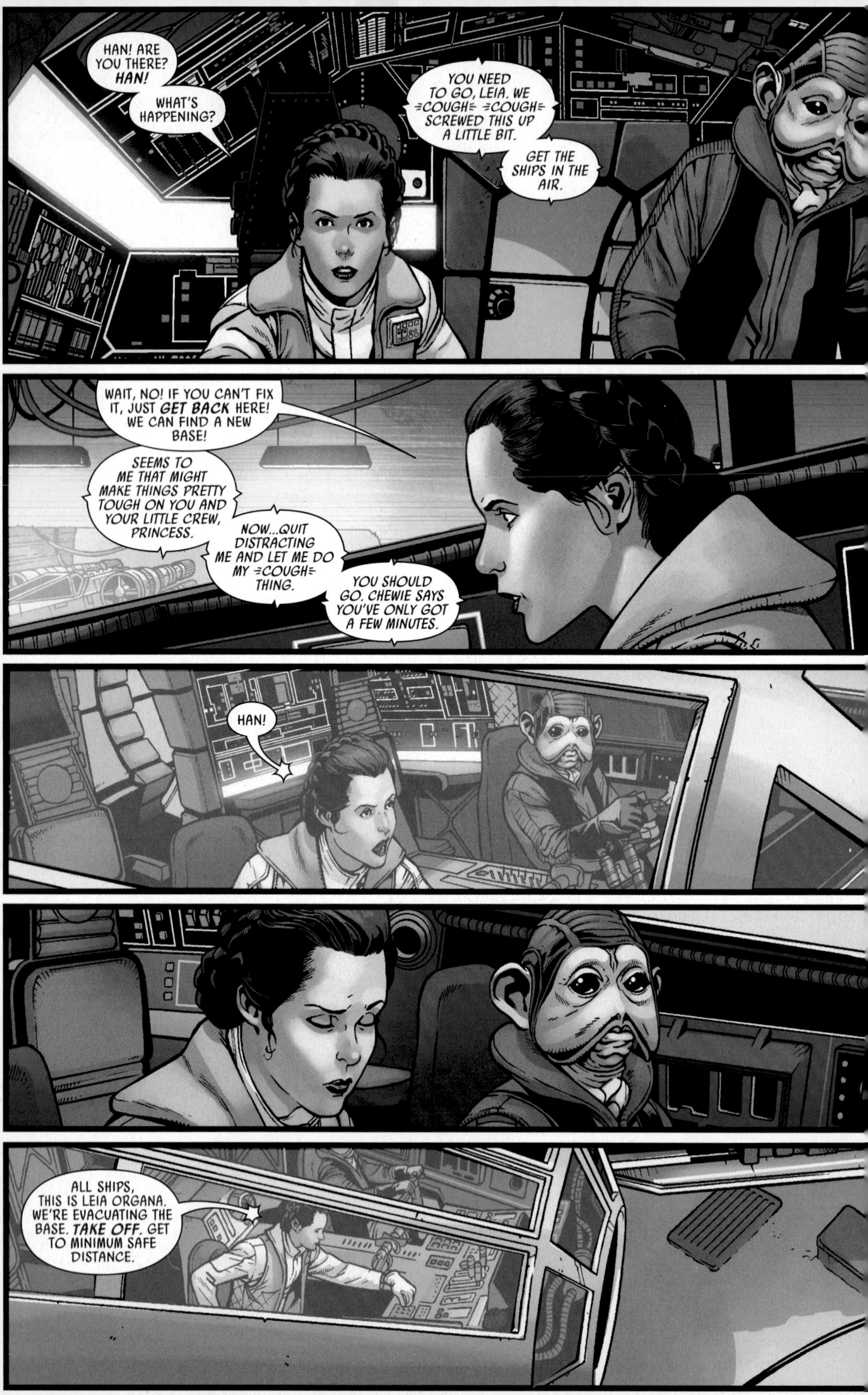
HAN! ARE YOU THERE? HAN!
WHAT'S HAPPENING?
YOU NEED TO GO, LEIA. WE =COUGH= =COUGH= SCREWED THIS UP A LITTLE BIT.
GET THE SHIPS IN THE AIR.
WAIT, NO! IF YOU CAN'T FIX IT, JUST GET BACK HERE! WE CAN FIND A NEW BASE!
SEEMS TO ME THAT MIGHT MAKE THINGS PRETTY TOUGH ON YOU AND YOUR LITTLE CREW, PRINCESS.
NOW...QUIT DISTRACTING ME AND LET ME DO MY =COUGH= THING.
YOU SHOULD GO. CHEWIE SAYS YOU'VE ONLY GOT A FEW MINUTES.
HAN!
ALL SHIPS, THIS IS LEIA ORGANA. WE'RE EVACUATING THE BASE. TAKE OFF. GET TO MINIMUM SAFE DISTANCE.

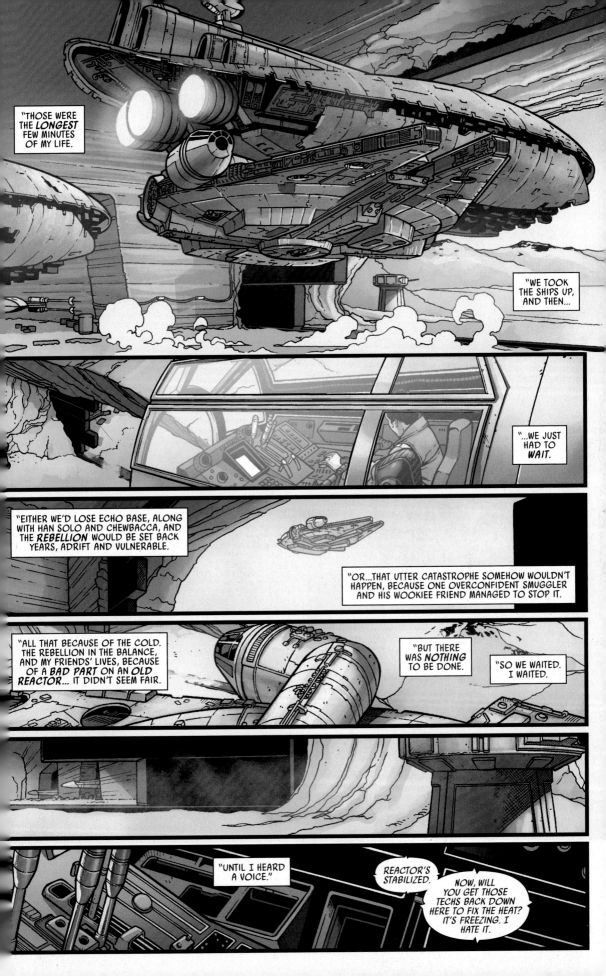

"THOSE WERE THE *LONGEST* FEW MINUTES OF MY LIFE.

"WE TOOK THE SHIPS UP, AND THEN...

"...WE JUST HAD TO *WAIT*.

"EITHER WE'D LOSE ECHO BASE, ALONG WITH HAN SOLO AND CHEWBACCA, AND THE *REBELLION* WOULD BE SET BACK YEARS, ADRIFT AND VULNERABLE.

"OR...THAT UTTER CATASTROPHE SOMEHOW WOULDN'T HAPPEN, BECAUSE ONE OVERCONFIDENT SMUGGLER AND HIS WOOKIEE FRIEND MANAGED TO STOP IT.

"ALL THAT BECAUSE OF THE COLD. THE REBELLION IN THE BALANCE, AND MY FRIENDS' LIVES, BECAUSE OF A *BAD PART* ON AN *OLD REACTOR*... IT DIDN'T SEEM FAIR.

"BUT THERE WAS *NOTHING* TO BE DONE.

"SO WE WAITED. I WAITED.

"UNTIL I HEARD A VOICE."

REACTOR'S STABILIZED. NOW, WILL YOU GET THOSE TECHS BACK DOWN HERE TO FIX THE HEAT? IT'S FREEZING. I HATE IT.

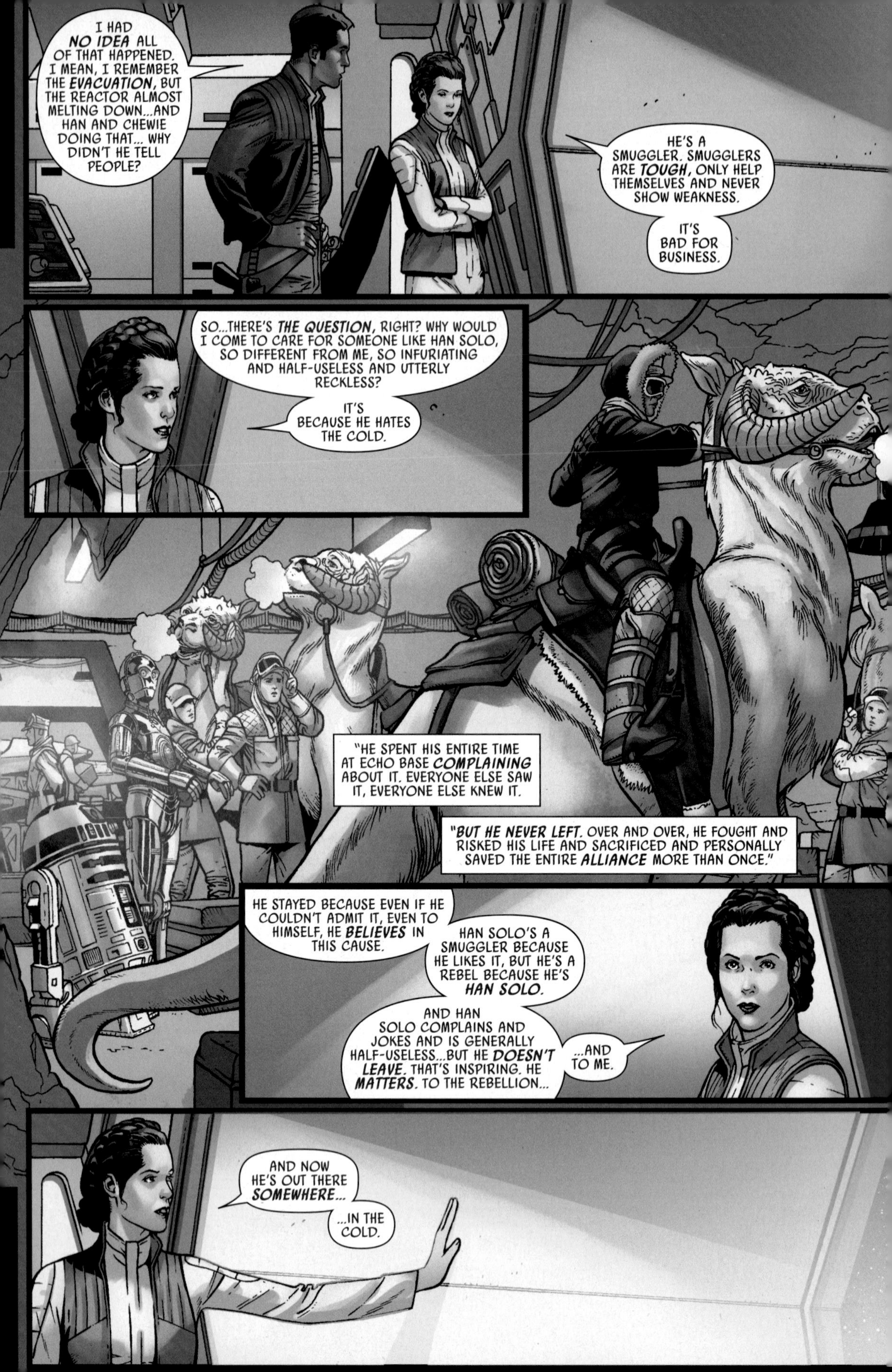
I HAD NO IDEA ALL OF THAT HAPPENED. I MEAN, I REMEMBER THE EVACUATION, BUT THE REACTOR ALMOST MELTING DOWN...AND HAN AND CHEWIE DOING THAT... WHY DIDN'T HE TELL PEOPLE?
HE'S A SMUGGLER. SMUGGLERS ARE TOUGH, ONLY HELP THEMSELVES AND NEVER SHOW WEAKNESS.
IT'S BAD FOR BUSINESS.
SO...THERE'S THE QUESTION, RIGHT? WHY WOULD I COME TO CARE FOR SOMEONE LIKE HAN SOLO, SO DIFFERENT FROM ME, SO INFURIATING AND HALF-USELESS AND UTTERLY RECKLESS?
IT'S BECAUSE HE HATES THE COLD.
"HE SPENT HIS ENTIRE TIME AT ECHO BASE COMPLAINING ABOUT IT. EVERYONE ELSE SAW IT, EVERYONE ELSE KNEW IT.
"BUT HE NEVER LEFT. OVER AND OVER, HE FOUGHT AND RISKED HIS LIFE AND SACRIFICED AND PERSONALLY SAVED THE ENTIRE ALLIANCE MORE THAN ONCE."
HE STAYED BECAUSE EVEN IF HE COULDN'T ADMIT IT, EVEN TO HIMSELF, HE BELIEVES IN THIS CAUSE.
HAN SOLO'S A SMUGGLER BECAUSE HE LIKES IT, BUT HE'S A REBEL BECAUSE HE'S HAN SOLO.
AND HAN SOLO COMPLAINS AND JOKES AND IS GENERALLY HALF-USELESS...BUT HE DOESN'T LEAVE. THAT'S INSPIRING. HE MATTERS. TO THE REBELLION...
...AND TO ME.
AND NOW HE'S OUT THERE SOMEWHERE...
...IN THE COLD.

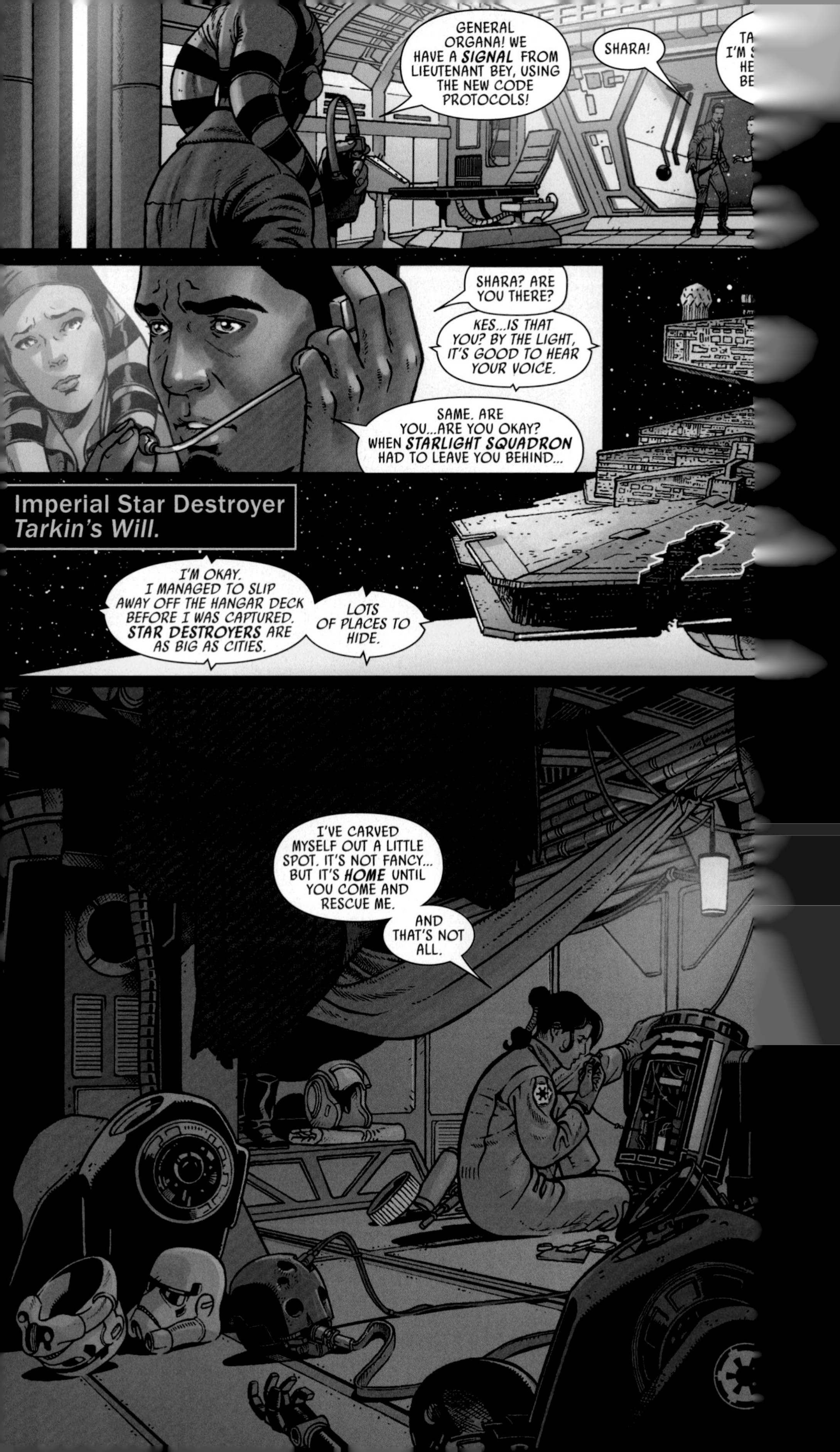
GENERAL ORGANA! WE HAVE A SIGNAL FROM LIEUTENANT BEY, USING THE NEW CODE PROTOCOLS!
SHARA!
SHARA? ARE YOU THERE?
KES...IS THAT YOU? BY THE LIGHT, IT'S GOOD TO HEAR YOUR VOICE.
SAME. ARE YOU...ARE YOU OKAY? WHEN STARLIGHT SQUADRON HAD TO LEAVE YOU BEHIND...
Imperial Star Destroyer Tarkin's Will.
I'M OKAY. I MANAGED TO SLIP AWAY OFF THE HANGAR DECK BEFORE I WAS CAPTURED. STAR DESTROYERS ARE AS BIG AS CITIES.
LOTS OF PLACES TO HIDE.
I'VE CARVED MYSELF OUT A LITTLE SPOT. IT'S NOT FANCY... BUT IT'S HOME UNTIL YOU COME AND RESCUE ME.
AND THAT'S NOT ALL.

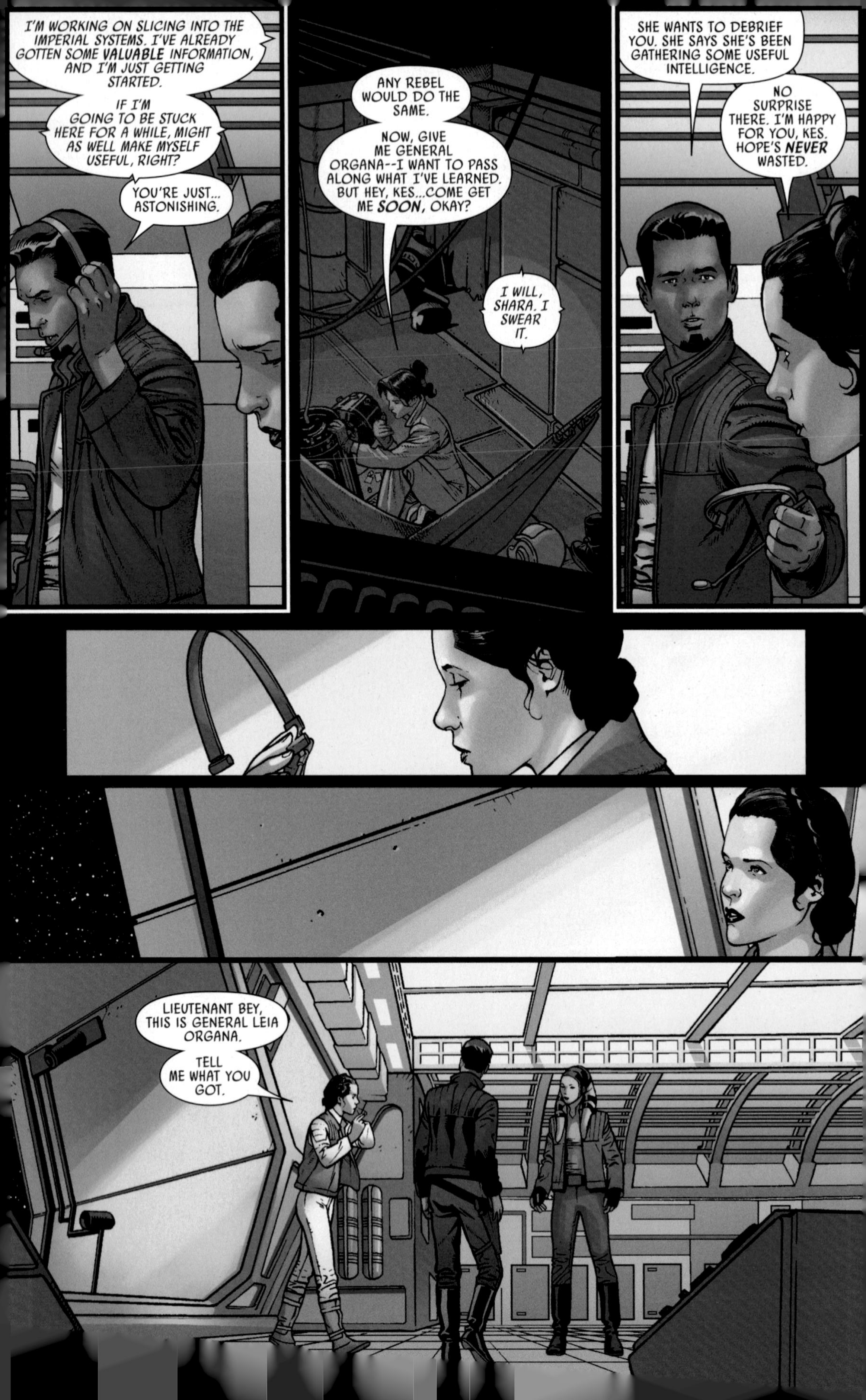
I'M WORKING ON SLICING INTO THE IMPERIAL SYSTEMS. I'VE ALREADY GOTTEN SOME VALUABLE INFORMATION, AND I'M JUST GETTING STARTED.
IF I'M GOING TO BE STUCK HERE FOR A WHILE, MIGHT AS WELL MAKE MYSELF USEFUL, RIGHT?
YOU'RE JUST... ASTONISHING.
ANY REBEL WOULD DO THE SAME.
NOW, GIVE ME GENERAL ORGANA--I WANT TO PASS ALONG WHAT I'VE LEARNED. BUT HEY, KES...COME GET ME SOON, OKAY?
I WILL, SHARA. I SWEAR IT.
SHE WANTS TO DEBRIEF YOU. SHE SAYS SHE'S BEEN GATHERING SOME USEFUL INTELLIGENCE.
NO SURPRISE THERE. I'M HAPPY FOR YOU, KES. HOPE'S NEVER WASTED.
LIEUTENANT BEY, THIS IS GENERAL LEIA ORGANA.
TELL ME WHAT YOU GOT.

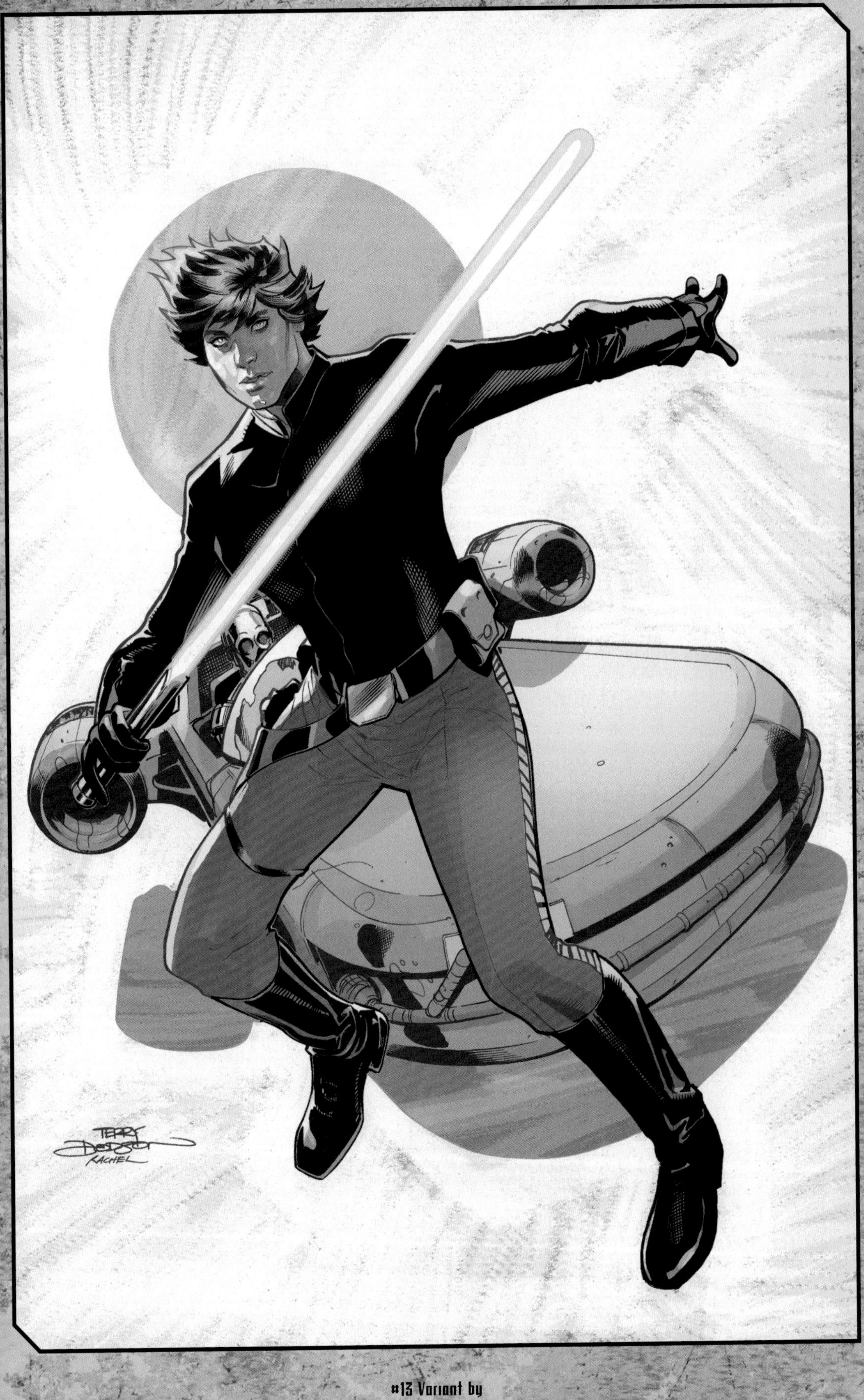

TERRY
DODSON
RACHEL

#13 Variant by
TERRY DODSON & RACHEL DODSON

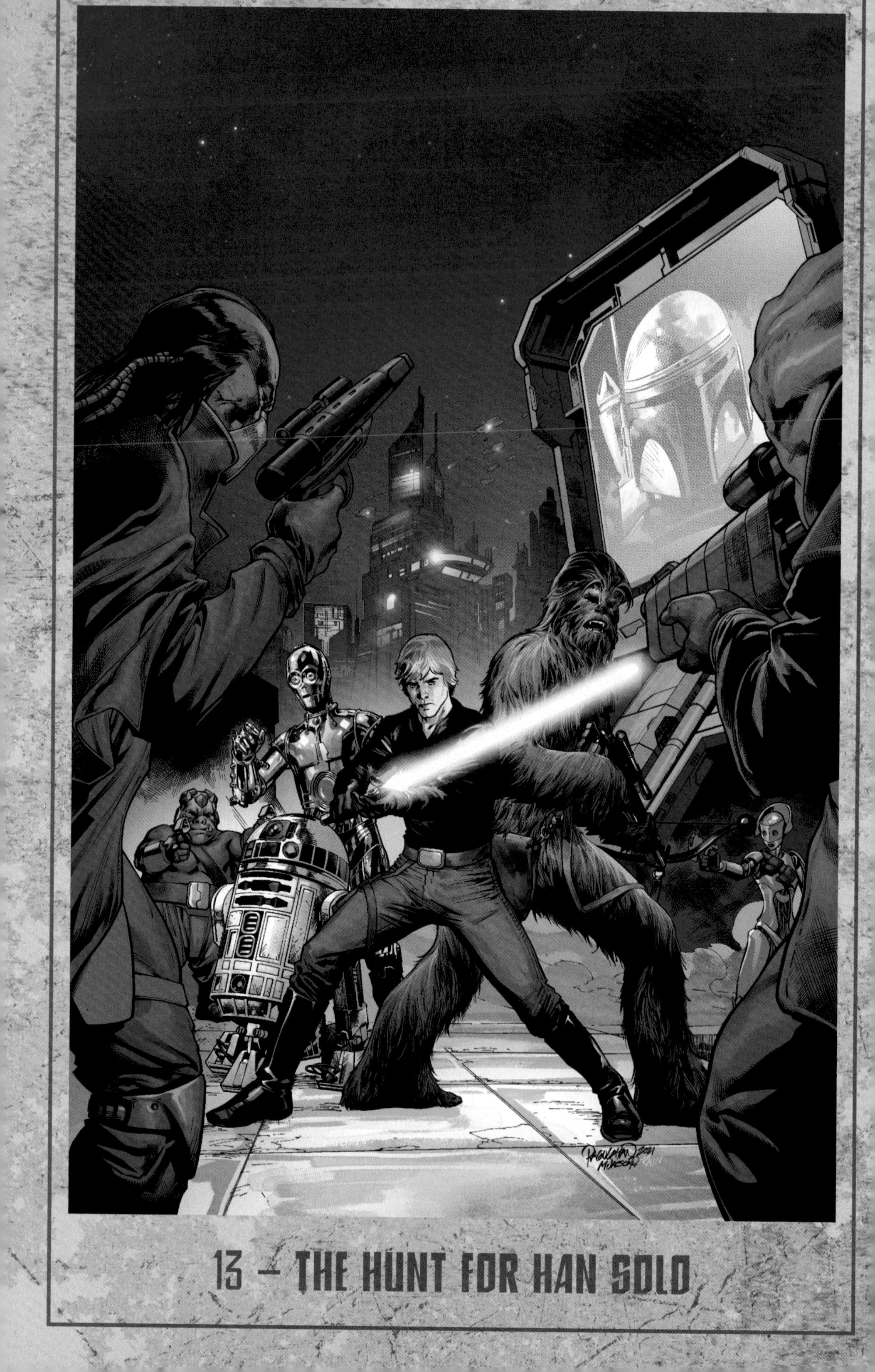

13 – THE HUNT FOR HAN SOLO

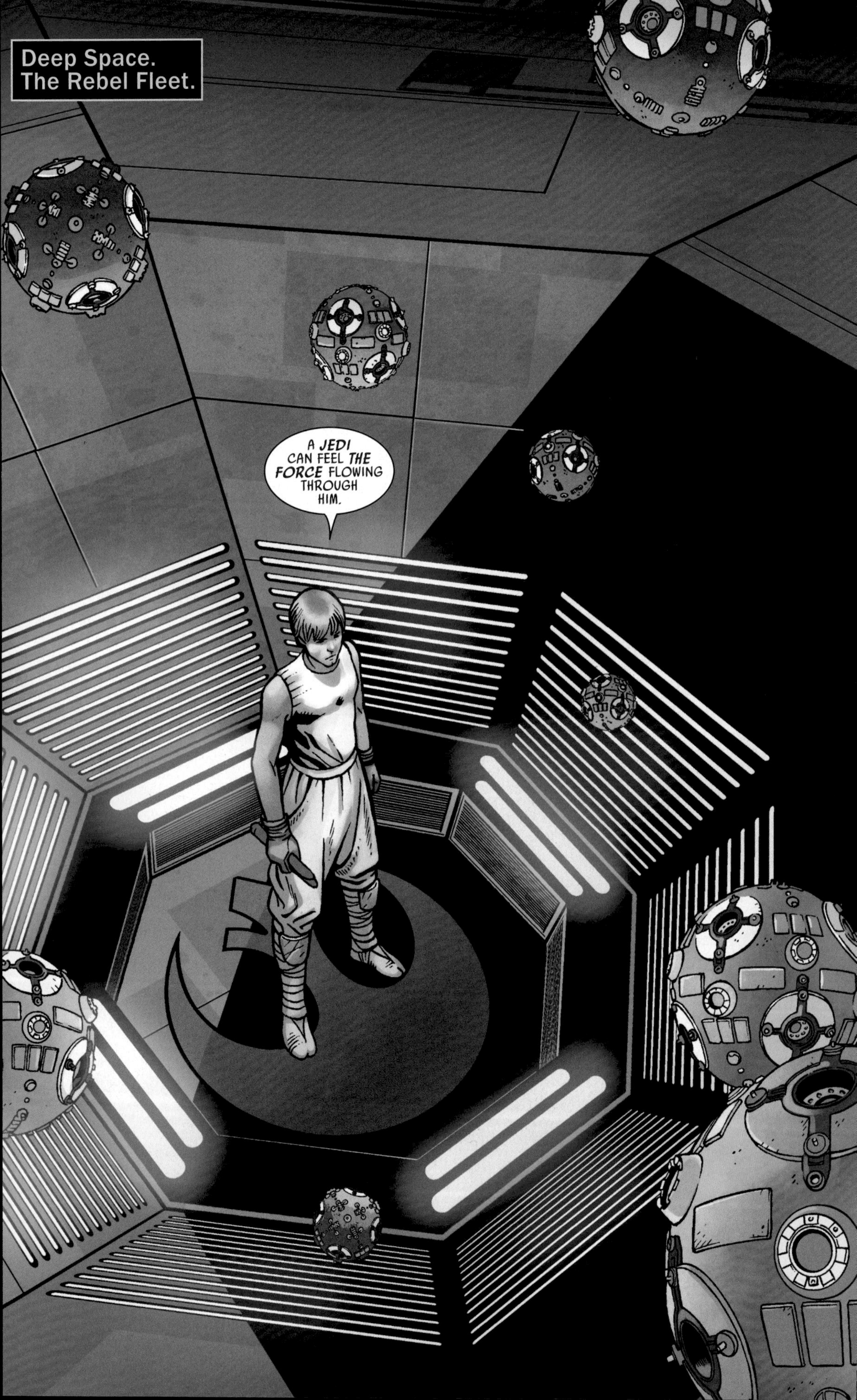
Deep Space.
The Rebel Fleet.
A JEDI CAN FEEL THE FORCE FLOWING THROUGH HIM.

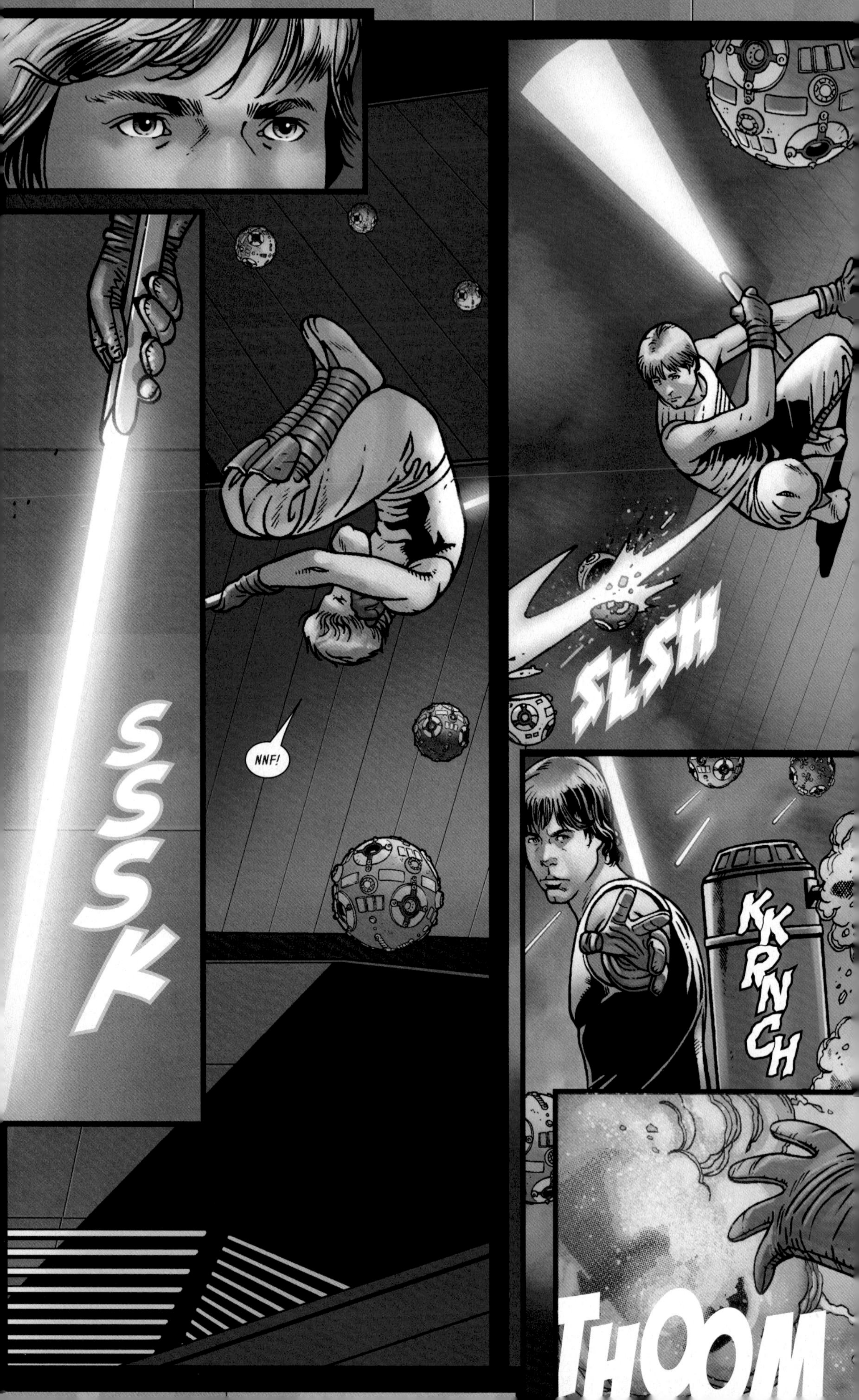
SSSK
NNF!
SLSH
KKRNCH
THOOM

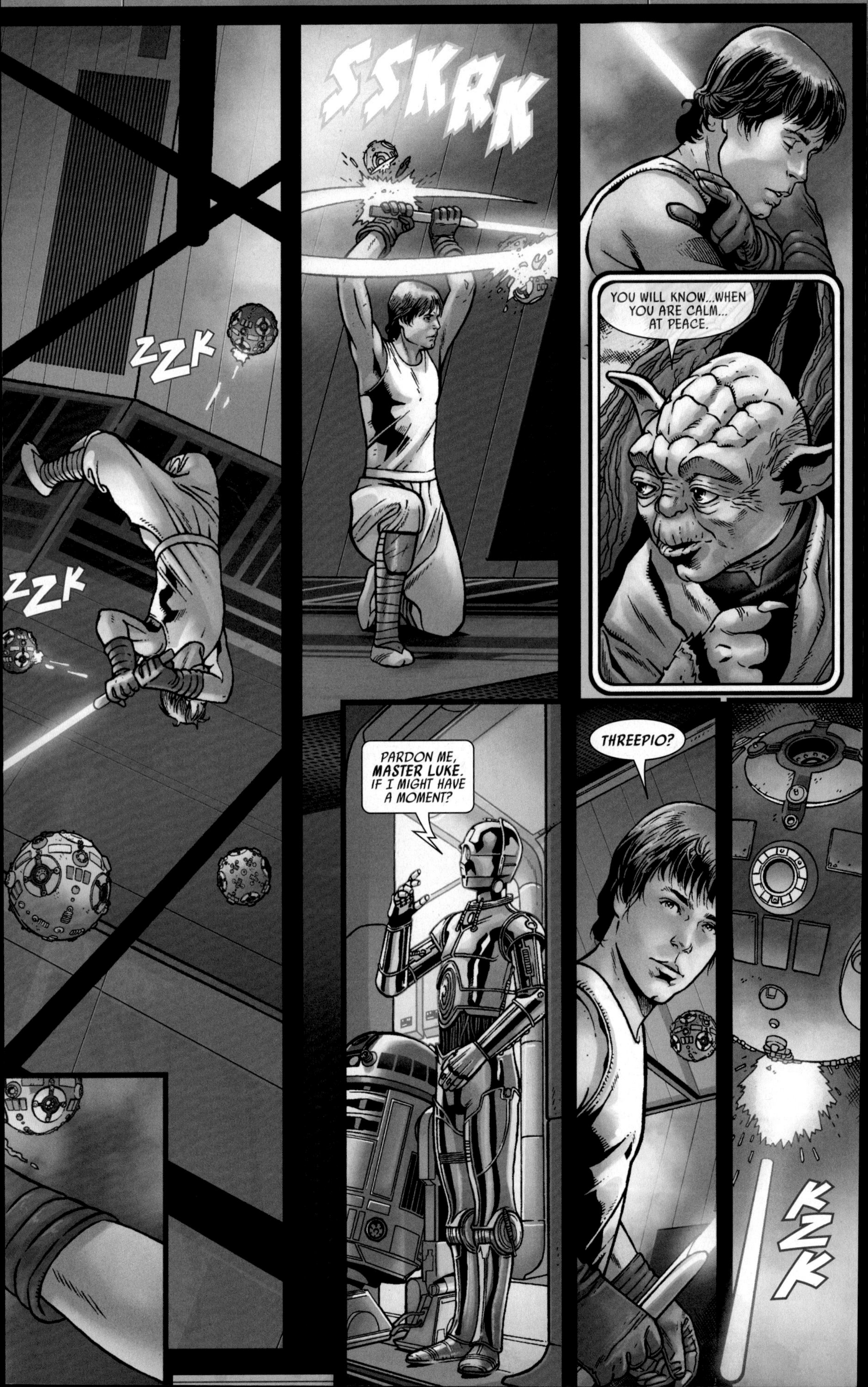
ZZK
ZZK
SSKRK
YOU WILL KNOW...WHEN YOU ARE CALM... AT PEACE.
PARDON ME, MASTER LUKE. IF I MIGHT HAVE A MOMENT?
THREEPIO?
KZK

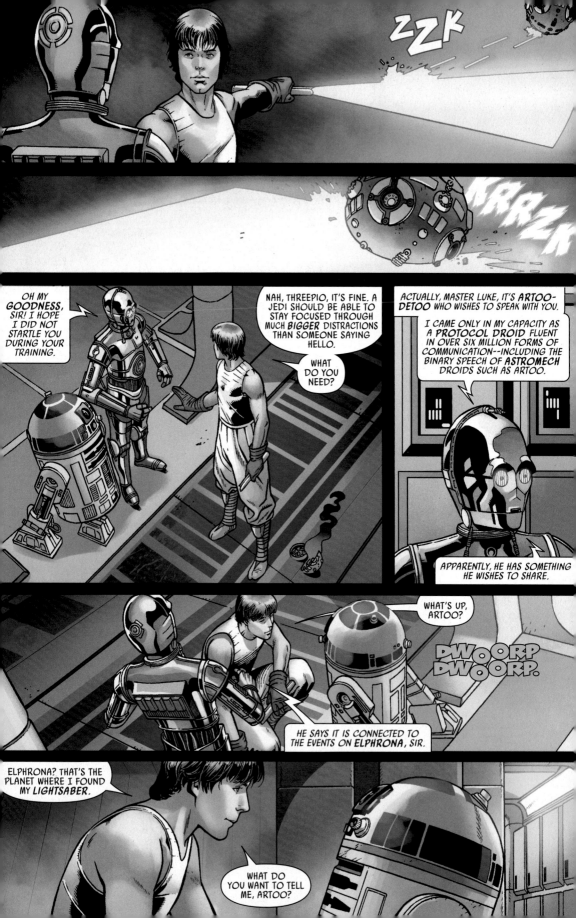

ZZK

KRRZK

OH MY GOODNESS, SIR! I HOPE I DID NOT STARTLE YOU DURING YOUR TRAINING.

NAH, THREEPIO, IT'S FINE. A JEDI SHOULD BE ABLE TO STAY FOCUSED THROUGH MUCH *BIGGER* DISTRACTIONS THAN SOMEONE SAYING HELLO.

WHAT DO YOU NEED?

ACTUALLY, MASTER LUKE, IT'S *ARTOO-DETOO* WHO WISHES TO SPEAK WITH YOU.

I CAME ONLY IN MY CAPACITY AS A *PROTOCOL DROID* FLUENT IN OVER SIX MILLION FORMS OF COMMUNICATION--INCLUDING THE BINARY SPEECH OF *ASTROMECH* DROIDS SUCH AS ARTOO.

APPARENTLY, HE HAS SOMETHING HE WISHES TO SHARE.

WHAT'S UP, ARTOO?

DWOORP DWOORP.

HE SAYS IT IS CONNECTED TO THE EVENTS ON *ELPHRONA*, SIR.

ELPHRONA? THAT'S THE PLANET WHERE I FOUND MY *LIGHTSABER*.

WHAT DO YOU WANT TO TELL ME, ARTOO?

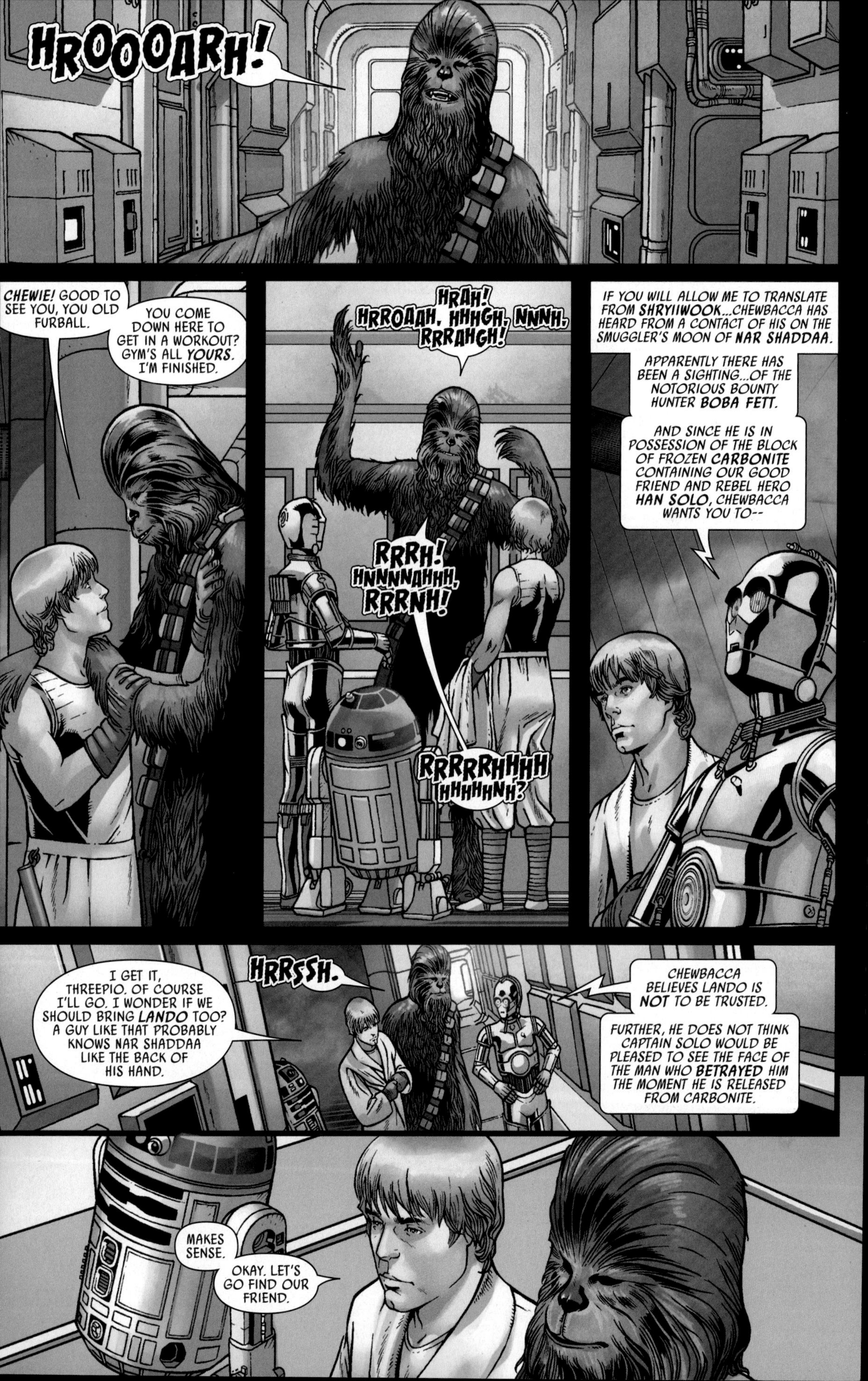
HROOOARH!
CHEWIE! GOOD TO SEE YOU, YOU OLD FURBALL.
YOU COME DOWN HERE TO GET IN A WORKOUT? GYM'S ALL YOURS. I'M FINISHED.
HRAH! HRROAAH, HHHGH, NNNH, RRRAHGH!
RRRH! HNNNNAHHH, RRRNH!
RRRRRHHHH HHHHHNH?
IF YOU WILL ALLOW ME TO TRANSLATE FROM SHRYIIWOOK...CHEWBACCA HAS HEARD FROM A CONTACT OF HIS ON THE SMUGGLER'S MOON OF NAR SHADDAA.
APPARENTLY THERE HAS BEEN A SIGHTING...OF THE NOTORIOUS BOUNTY HUNTER BOBA FETT.
AND SINCE HE IS IN POSSESSION OF THE BLOCK OF FROZEN CARBONITE CONTAINING OUR GOOD FRIEND AND REBEL HERO HAN SOLO, CHEWBACCA WANTS YOU TO--
I GET IT, THREEPIO. OF COURSE I'LL GO. I WONDER IF WE SHOULD BRING LANDO TOO? A GUY LIKE THAT PROBABLY KNOWS NAR SHADDAA LIKE THE BACK OF HIS HAND.
HRRSSH.
CHEWBACCA BELIEVES LANDO IS NOT TO BE TRUSTED.
FURTHER, HE DOES NOT THINK CAPTAIN SOLO WOULD BE PLEASED TO SEE THE FACE OF THE MAN WHO BETRAYED HIM THE MOMENT HE IS RELEASED FROM CARBONITE.
MAKES SENSE.
OKAY. LET'S GO FIND OUR FRIEND.

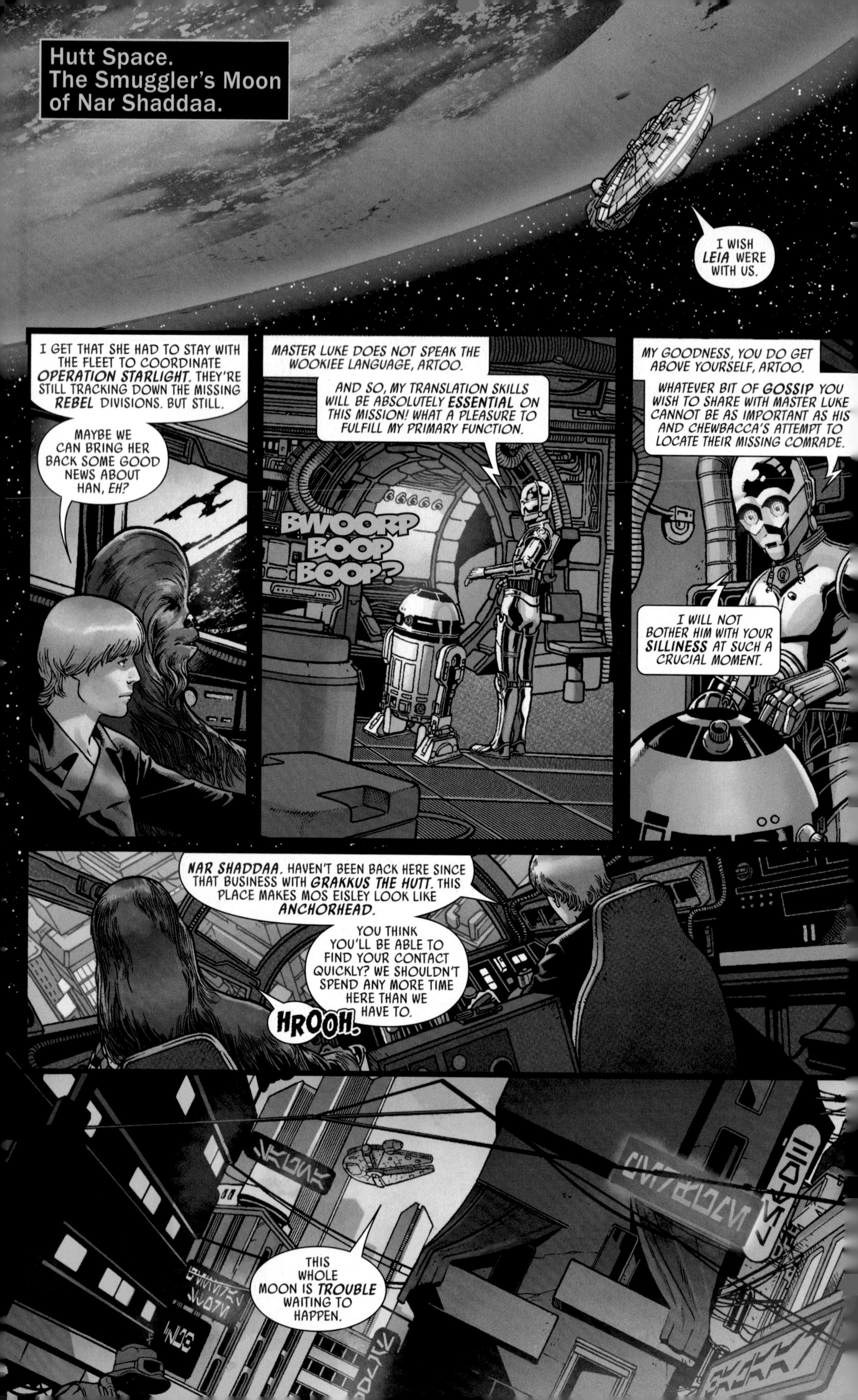
Hutt Space.
The Smuggler's Moon of Nar Shaddaa.
I WISH LEIA WERE WITH US.
I GET THAT SHE HAD TO STAY WITH THE FLEET TO COORDINATE OPERATION STARLIGHT. THEY'RE STILL TRACKING DOWN THE MISSING REBEL DIVISIONS. BUT STILL.
MAYBE WE CAN BRING HER BACK SOME GOOD NEWS ABOUT HAN, EH?
MASTER LUKE DOES NOT SPEAK THE WOOKIEE LANGUAGE, ARTOO.
AND SO, MY TRANSLATION SKILLS WILL BE ABSOLUTELY ESSENTIAL ON THIS MISSION! WHAT A PLEASURE TO FULFILL MY PRIMARY FUNCTION.
BWOORP BOOP BOOP?
MY GOODNESS, YOU DO GET ABOVE YOURSELF, ARTOO.
WHATEVER BIT OF GOSSIP YOU WISH TO SHARE WITH MASTER LUKE CANNOT BE AS IMPORTANT AS HIS AND CHEWBACCA'S ATTEMPT TO LOCATE THEIR MISSING COMRADE.
I WILL NOT BOTHER HIM WITH YOUR SILLINESS AT SUCH A CRUCIAL MOMENT.
NAR SHADDAA. HAVEN'T BEEN BACK HERE SINCE THAT BUSINESS WITH GRAKKUS THE HUTT. THIS PLACE MAKES MOS EISLEY LOOK LIKE ANCHORHEAD.
YOU THINK YOU'LL BE ABLE TO FIND YOUR CONTACT QUICKLY? WE SHOULDN'T SPEND ANY MORE TIME HERE THAN WE HAVE TO.
HROOH.
THIS WHOLE MOON IS TROUBLE WAITING TO HAPPEN.

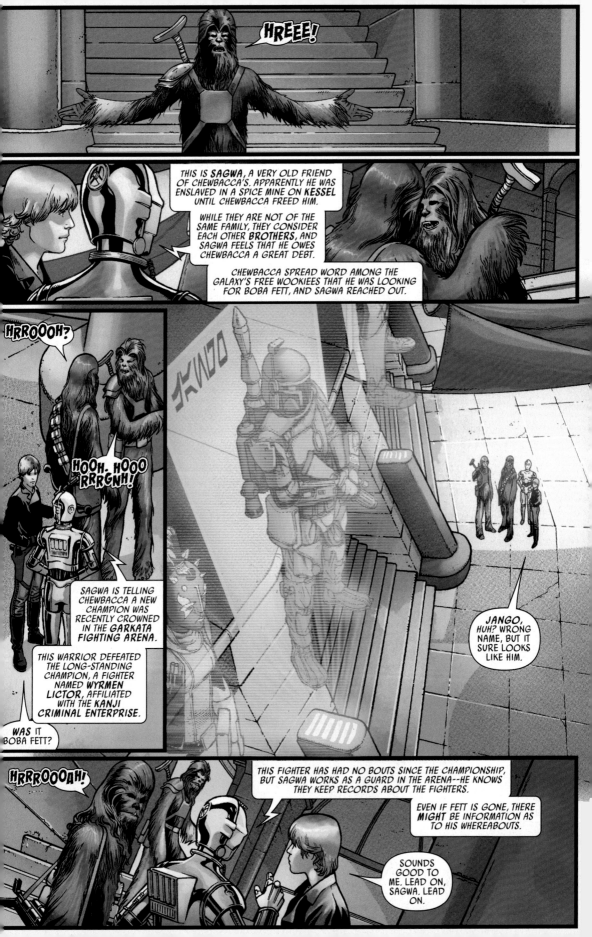

HREEE!

THIS IS **SAGWA**, A VERY OLD FRIEND OF CHEWBACCA'S. APPARENTLY HE WAS ENSLAVED IN A SPICE MINE ON **KESSEL** UNTIL CHEWBACCA FREED HIM.

WHILE THEY ARE NOT OF THE SAME FAMILY, THEY CONSIDER EACH OTHER **BROTHERS**, AND SAGWA FEELS THAT HE OWES CHEWBACCA A GREAT DEBT.

CHEWBACCA SPREAD WORD AMONG THE GALAXY'S FREE WOOKIEES THAT HE WAS LOOKING FOR BOBA FETT, AND SAGWA REACHED OUT.

HRROOOH?

HOOH. HOOOO RRRGNH!

SAGWA IS TELLING CHEWBACCA A NEW CHAMPION WAS RECENTLY CROWNED IN THE **GARKATA** FIGHTING ARENA.

THIS WARRIOR DEFEATED THE LONG-STANDING CHAMPION, A FIGHTER NAMED **WYRMEN LICTOR**, AFFILIATED WITH THE **KANJI** CRIMINAL ENTERPRISE.

WAS IT BOBA FETT?

JANGO, HUH? WRONG NAME, BUT IT SURE LOOKS LIKE HIM.

HRRROOOAH!

THIS FIGHTER HAS HAD NO BOUTS SINCE THE CHAMPIONSHIP, BUT SAGWA WORKS AS A GUARD IN THE ARENA--HE KNOWS THEY KEEP RECORDS ABOUT THE FIGHTERS.

EVEN IF FETT IS GONE, THERE **MIGHT** BE INFORMATION AS TO HIS WHEREABOUTS.

SOUNDS GOOD TO ME. LEAD ON, SAGWA. LEAD ON.

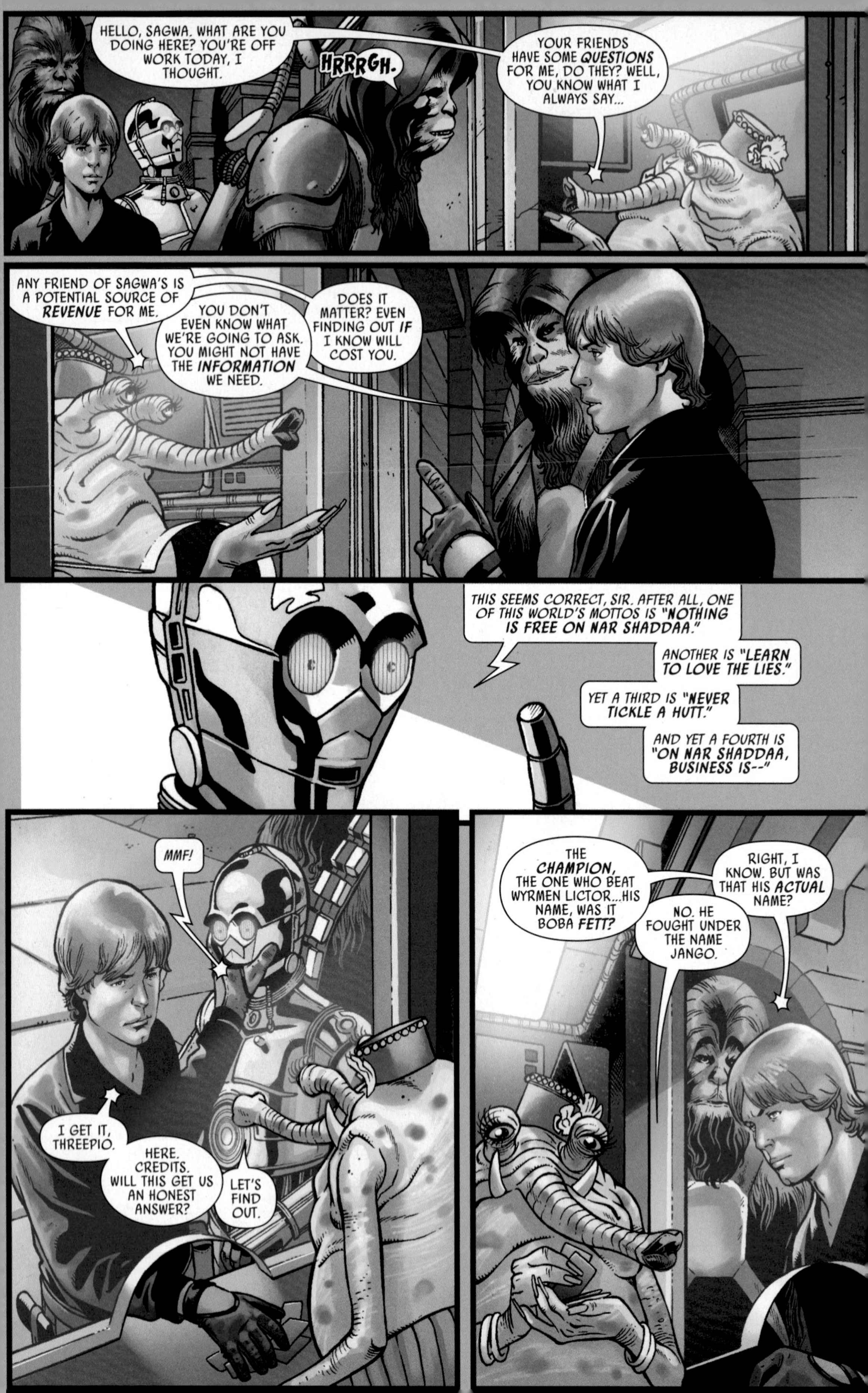
HELLO, SAGWA. WHAT ARE YOU DOING HERE? YOU'RE OFF WORK TODAY, I THOUGHT.
HRRRGH.
YOUR FRIENDS HAVE SOME QUESTIONS FOR ME, DO THEY? WELL, YOU KNOW WHAT I ALWAYS SAY...
ANY FRIEND OF SAGWA'S IS A POTENTIAL SOURCE OF REVENUE FOR ME.
YOU DON'T EVEN KNOW WHAT WE'RE GOING TO ASK. YOU MIGHT NOT HAVE THE INFORMATION WE NEED.
DOES IT MATTER? EVEN FINDING OUT IF I KNOW WILL COST YOU.
THIS SEEMS CORRECT, SIR. AFTER ALL, ONE OF THIS WORLD'S MOTTOS IS "NOTHING IS FREE ON NAR SHADDAA."
ANOTHER IS "LEARN TO LOVE THE LIES."
YET A THIRD IS "NEVER TICKLE A HUTT."
AND YET A FOURTH IS "ON NAR SHADDAA, BUSINESS IS--"
MMF!
I GET IT, THREEPIO.
HERE. CREDITS. WILL THIS GET US AN HONEST ANSWER?
LET'S FIND OUT.
THE CHAMPION, THE ONE WHO BEAT WYRMEN LICTOR...HIS NAME, WAS IT BOBA FETT?
NO. HE FOUGHT UNDER THE NAME JANGO.
RIGHT, I KNOW. BUT WAS THAT HIS ACTUAL NAME?

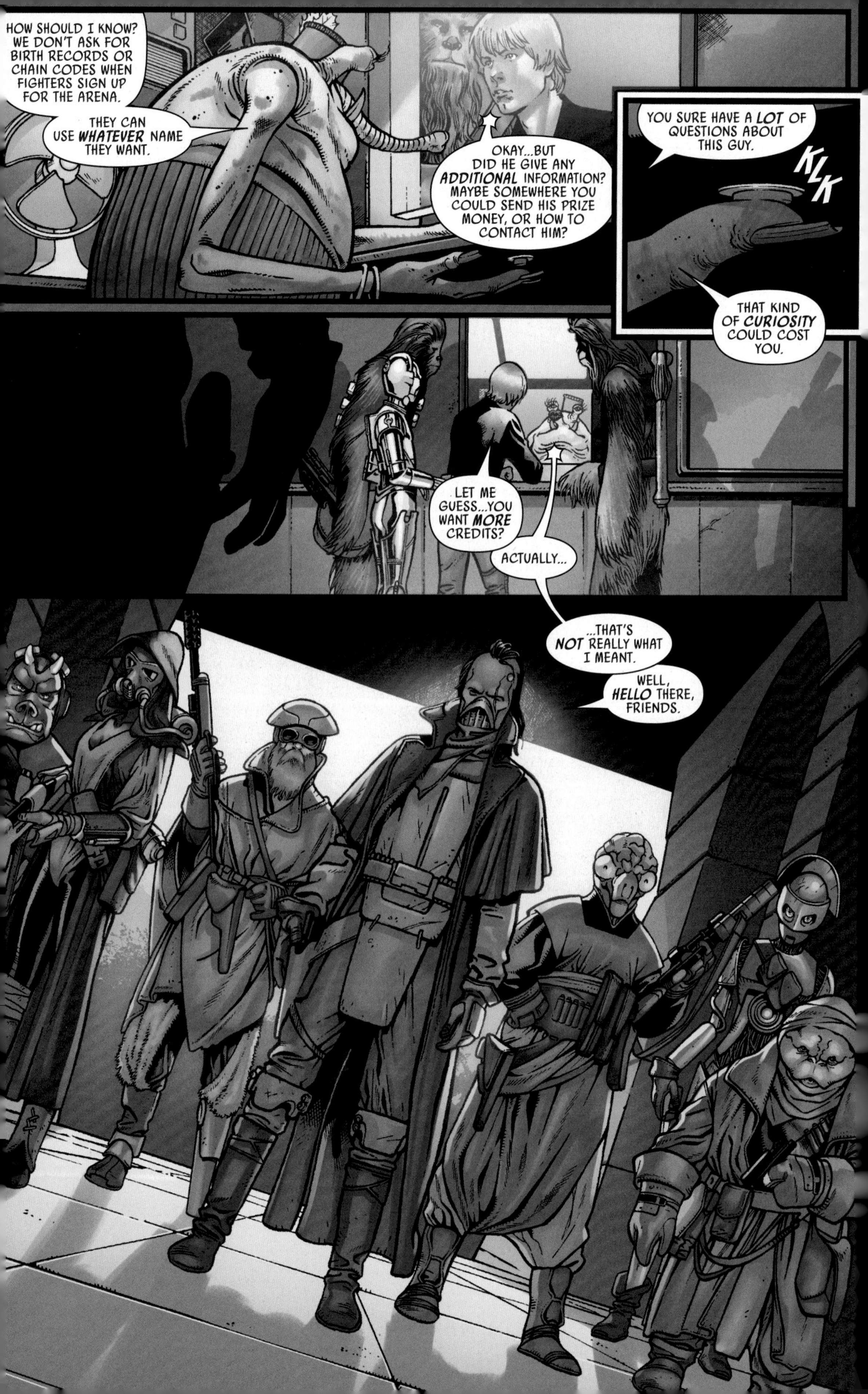
HOW SHOULD I KNOW? WE DON'T ASK FOR BIRTH RECORDS OR CHAIN CODES WHEN FIGHTERS SIGN UP FOR THE ARENA.
THEY CAN USE WHATEVER NAME THEY WANT.
OKAY...BUT DID HE GIVE ANY ADDITIONAL INFORMATION? MAYBE SOMEWHERE YOU COULD SEND HIS PRIZE MONEY, OR HOW TO CONTACT HIM?
YOU SURE HAVE A LOT OF QUESTIONS ABOUT THIS GUY.
KLK
THAT KIND OF CURIOSITY COULD COST YOU.
LET ME GUESS...YOU WANT MORE CREDITS?
ACTUALLY...
...THAT'S NOT REALLY WHAT I MEANT.
WELL, HELLO THERE, FRIENDS.

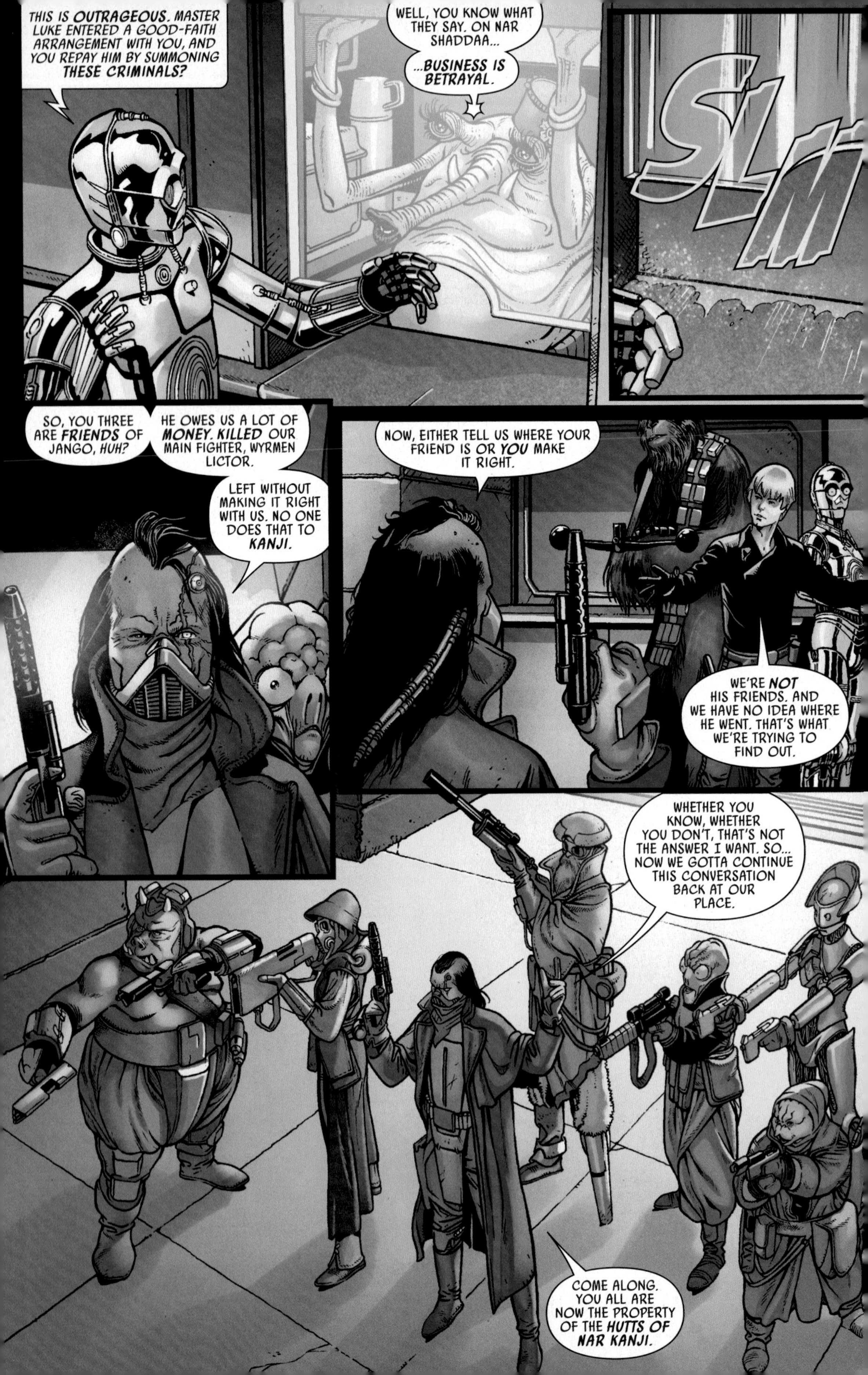
THIS IS OUTRAGEOUS. MASTER LUKE ENTERED A GOOD-FAITH ARRANGEMENT WITH YOU, AND YOU REPAY HIM BY SUMMONING THESE CRIMINALS?
WELL, YOU KNOW WHAT THEY SAY. ON NAR SHADDAA...
...BUSINESS IS BETRAYAL.
SLM
SO, YOU THREE ARE FRIENDS OF JANGO, HUH?
HE OWES US A LOT OF MONEY. KILLED OUR MAIN FIGHTER, WYRMEN LICTOR.
LEFT WITHOUT MAKING IT RIGHT WITH US. NO ONE DOES THAT TO KANJI.
NOW, EITHER TELL US WHERE YOUR FRIEND IS OR YOU MAKE IT RIGHT.
WE'RE NOT HIS FRIENDS. AND WE HAVE NO IDEA WHERE HE WENT. THAT'S WHAT WE'RE TRYING TO FIND OUT.
WHETHER YOU KNOW, WHETHER YOU DON'T, THAT'S NOT THE ANSWER I WANT. SO... NOW WE GOTTA CONTINUE THIS CONVERSATION BACK AT OUR PLACE.
COME ALONG. YOU ALL ARE NOW THE PROPERTY OF THE HUTTS OF NAR KANJI.

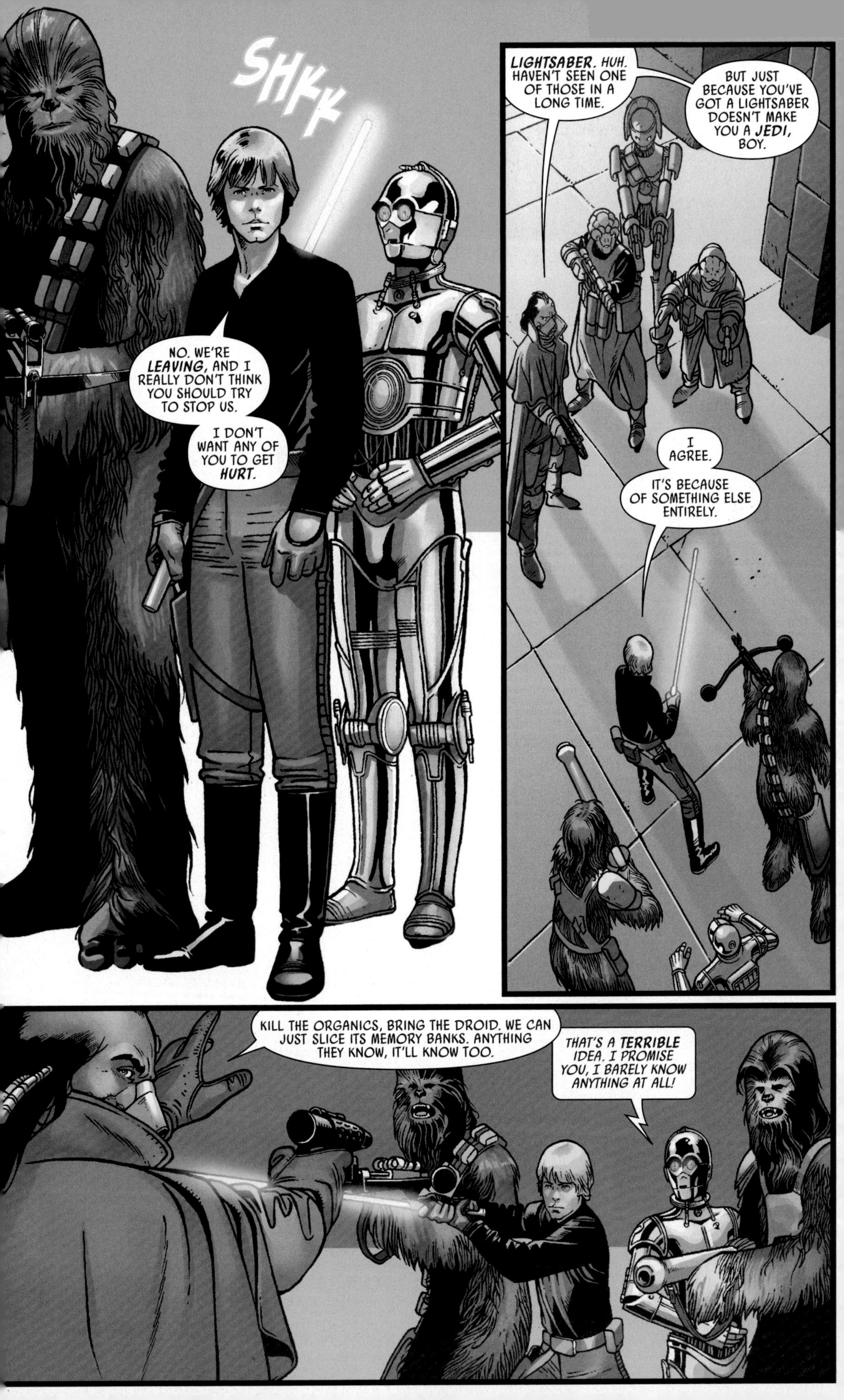
SHKK
NO. WE'RE LEAVING, AND I REALLY DON'T THINK YOU SHOULD TRY TO STOP US.
I DON'T WANT ANY OF YOU TO GET HURT.
LIGHTSABER. HUH. HAVEN'T SEEN ONE OF THOSE IN A LONG TIME.
BUT JUST BECAUSE YOU'VE GOT A LIGHTSABER DOESN'T MAKE YOU A JEDI, BOY.
I AGREE.
IT'S BECAUSE OF SOMETHING ELSE ENTIRELY.
KILL THE ORGANICS, BRING THE DROID. WE CAN JUST SLICE ITS MEMORY BANKS. ANYTHING THEY KNOW, IT'LL KNOW TOO.
THAT'S A TERRIBLE IDEA. I PROMISE YOU, I BARELY KNOW ANYTHING AT ALL!

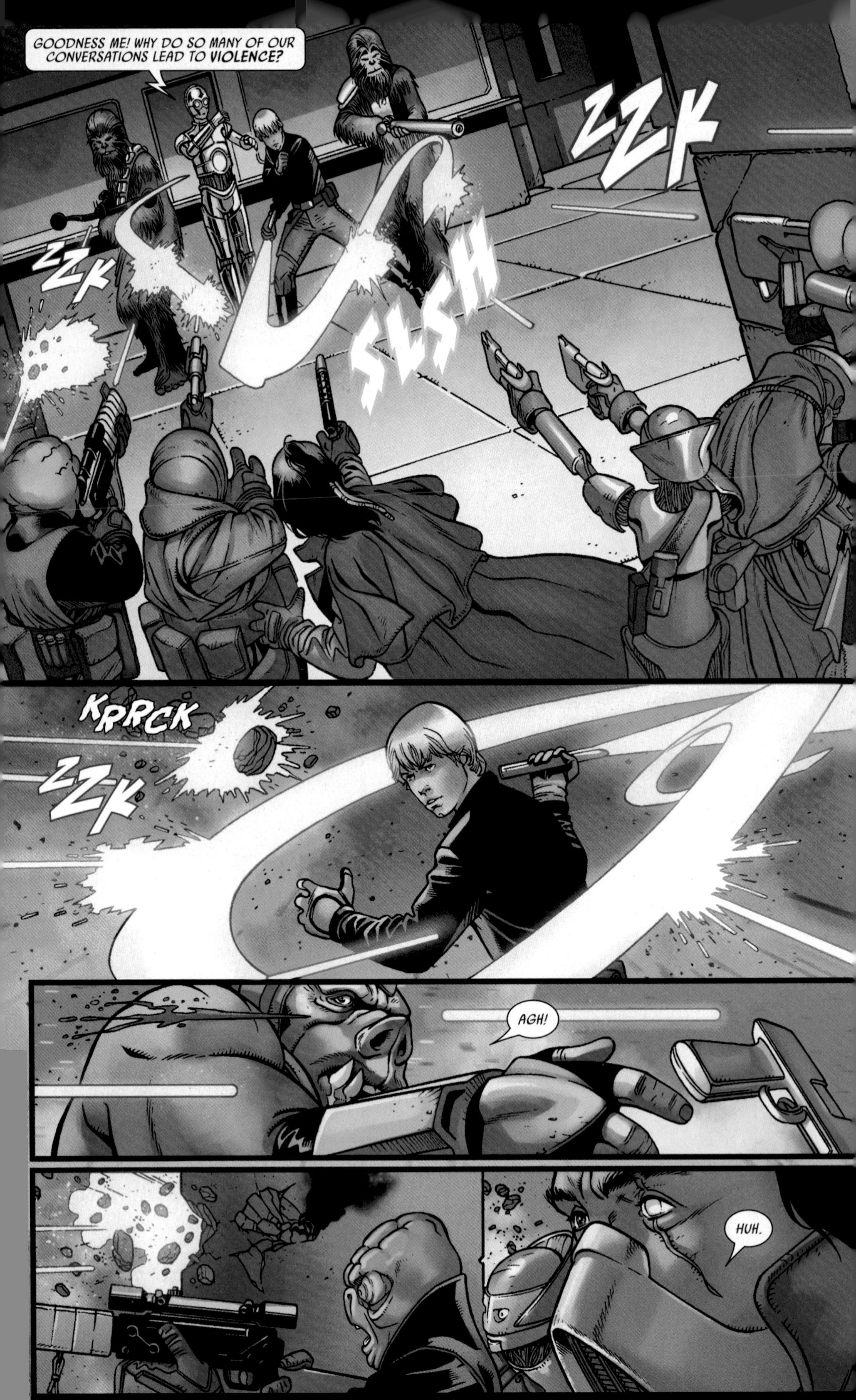
GOODNESS ME! WHY DO SO MANY OF OUR CONVERSATIONS LEAD TO VIOLENCE?
ZZK
ZZK
SLSH
KRRCK
ZZK
AGH!
HUH.

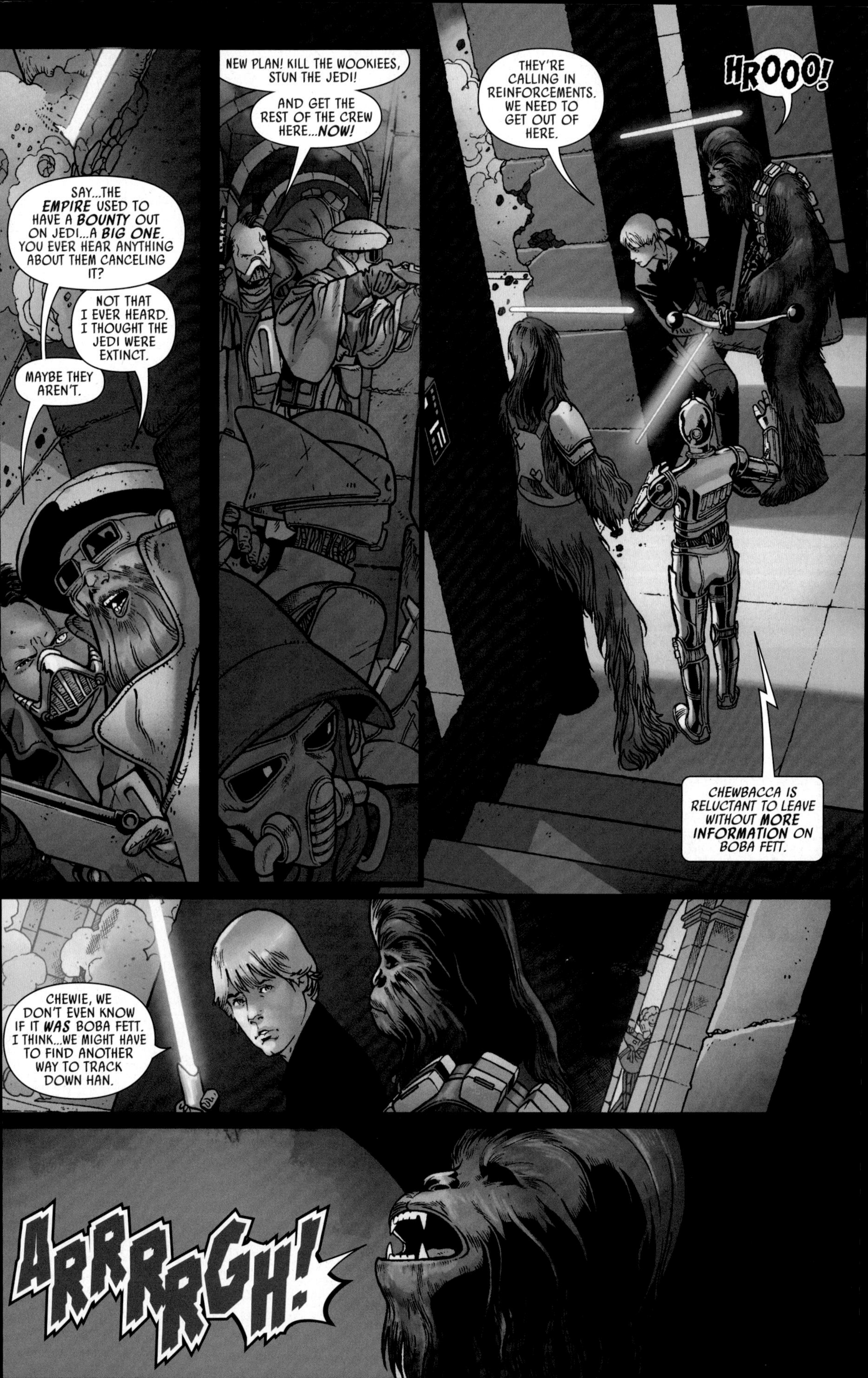

SAY...THE EMPIRE USED TO HAVE A BOUNTY OUT ON JEDI...A BIG ONE. YOU EVER HEAR ANYTHING ABOUT THEM CANCELING IT?
NOT THAT I EVER HEARD. I THOUGHT THE JEDI WERE EXTINCT.
MAYBE THEY AREN'T.
NEW PLAN! KILL THE WOOKIEES, STUN THE JEDI!
AND GET THE REST OF THE CREW HERE...NOW!
THEY'RE CALLING IN REINFORCEMENTS. WE NEED TO GET OUT OF HERE.
HROOO!
CHEWBACCA IS RELUCTANT TO LEAVE WITHOUT MORE INFORMATION ON BOBA FETT.
CHEWIE, WE DON'T EVEN KNOW IF IT WAS BOBA FETT. I THINK...WE MIGHT HAVE TO FIND ANOTHER WAY TO TRACK DOWN HAN.
ARRRRGH!

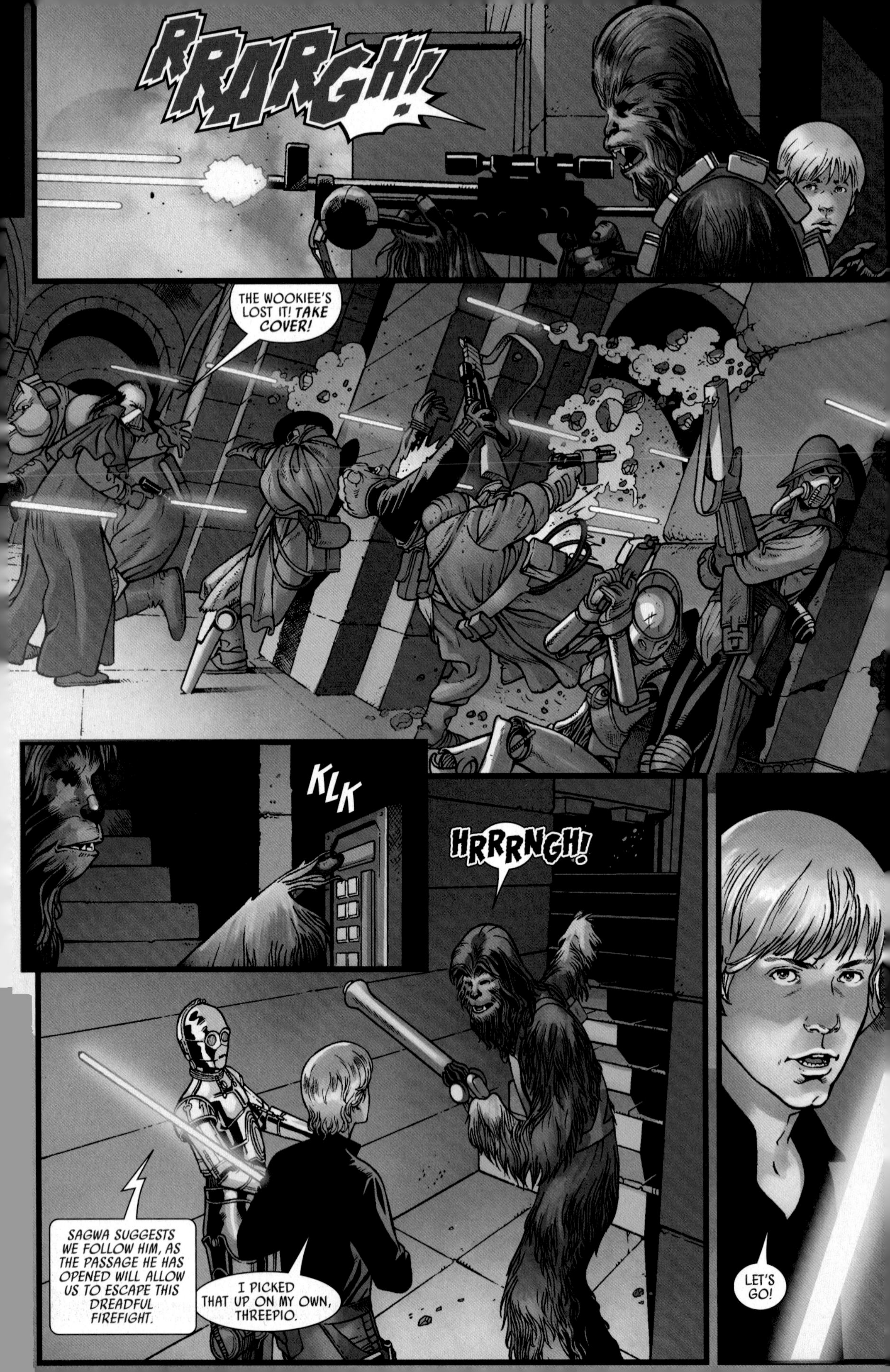
RRARGH!
THE WOOKIEE'S LOST IT! TAKE COVER!
KLK
HRRRNGH!
SAGWA SUGGESTS WE FOLLOW HIM, AS THE PASSAGE HE HAS OPENED WILL ALLOW US TO ESCAPE THIS DREADFUL FIREFIGHT.
I PICKED THAT UP ON MY OWN, THREEPIO.
LET'S GO!

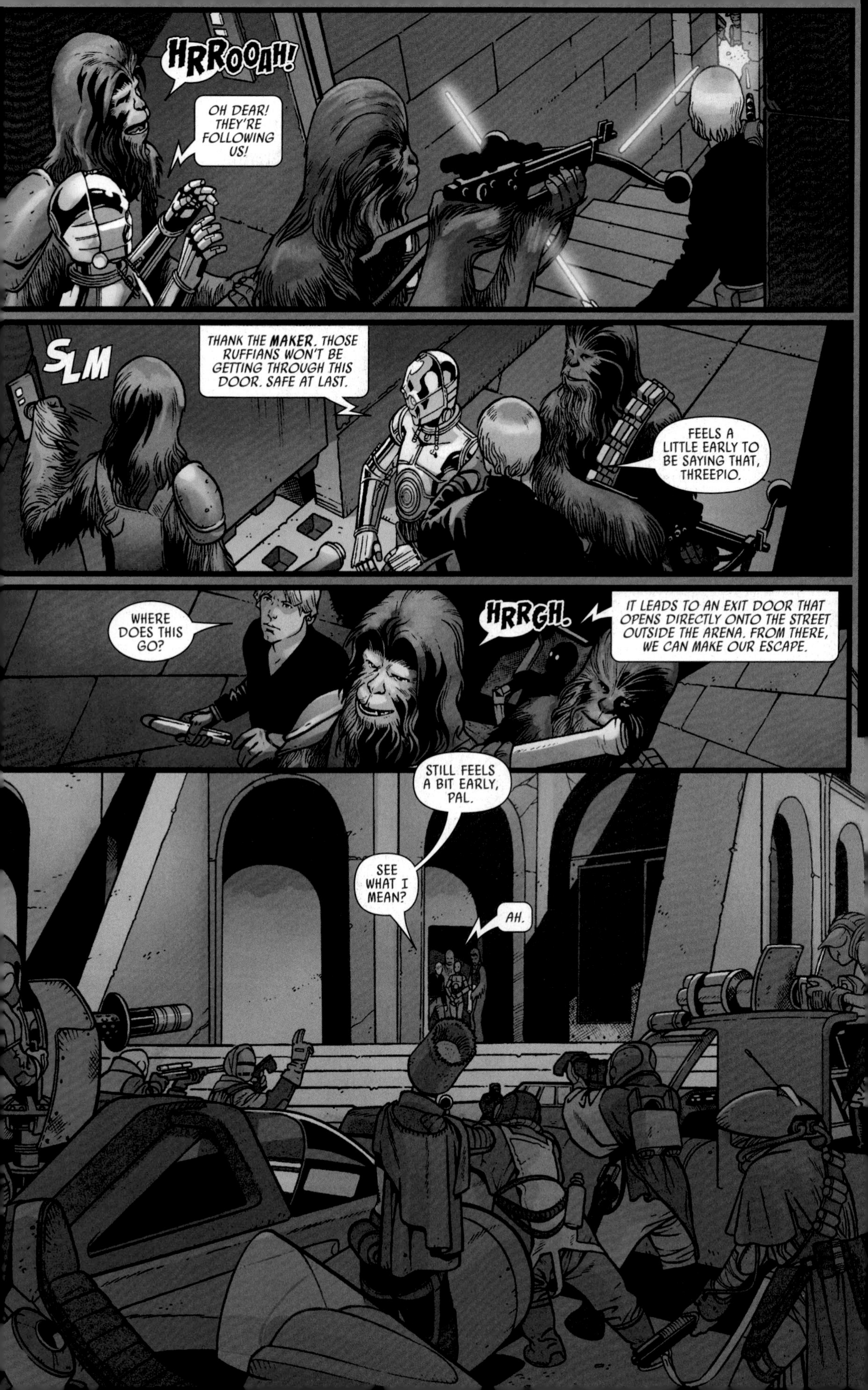
HRROOAH!
OH DEAR! THEY'RE FOLLOWING US!
SLM
THANK THE MAKER. THOSE RUFFIANS WON'T BE GETTING THROUGH THIS DOOR. SAFE AT LAST.
FEELS A LITTLE EARLY TO BE SAYING THAT, THREEPIO.
WHERE DOES THIS GO?
HRRGH.
IT LEADS TO AN EXIT DOOR THAT OPENS DIRECTLY ONTO THE STREET OUTSIDE THE ARENA. FROM THERE, WE CAN MAKE OUR ESCAPE.
SEE WHAT I MEAN?
STILL FEELS A BIT EARLY, PAL.
AH.

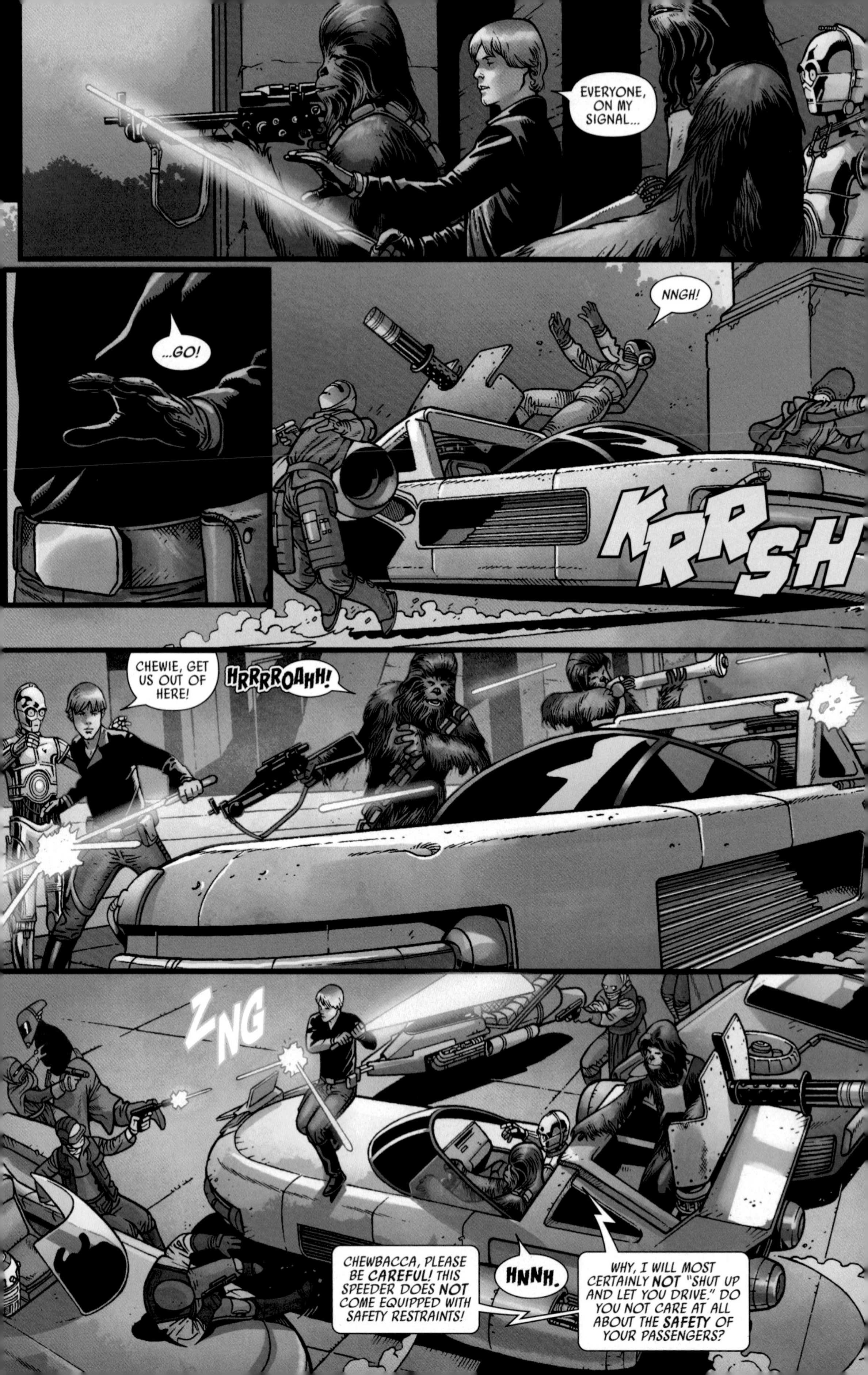
EVERYONE, ON MY SIGNAL...
...GO!
NNGH!
KRRSH
CHEWIE, GET US OUT OF HERE!
HRRRROAHH!
ZNG
CHEWBACCA, PLEASE BE CAREFUL! THIS SPEEDER DOES NOT COME EQUIPPED WITH SAFETY RESTRAINTS!
HNNH.
WHY, I WILL MOST CERTAINLY NOT "SHUT UP AND LET YOU DRIVE." DO YOU NOT CARE AT ALL ABOUT THE SAFETY OF YOUR PASSENGERS?

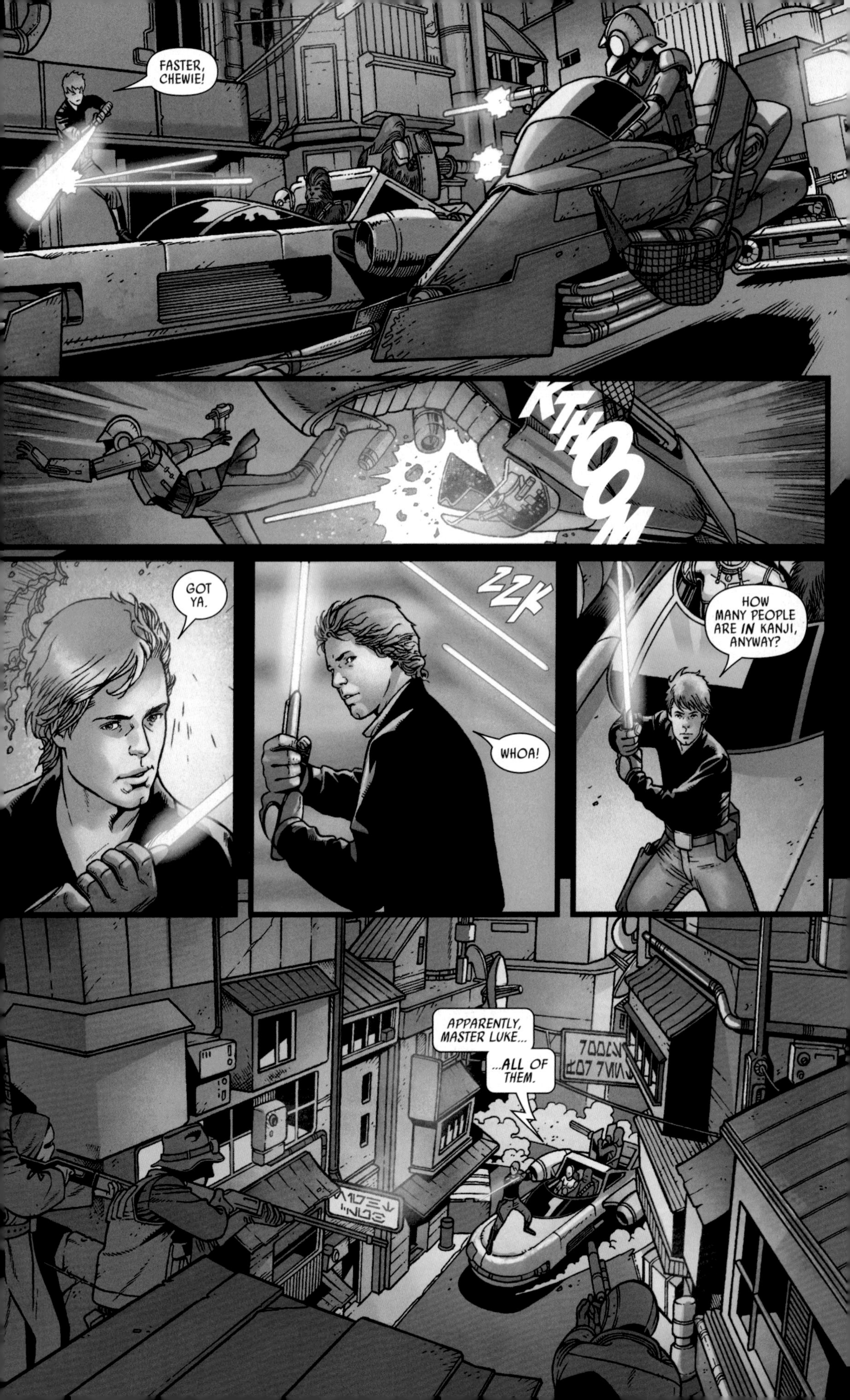
FASTER, CHEWIE!
KTHOOM
GOT YA.
ZZK
WHOA!
HOW MANY PEOPLE ARE IN KANJI, ANYWAY?
APPARENTLY, MASTER LUKE...
...ALL OF THEM.

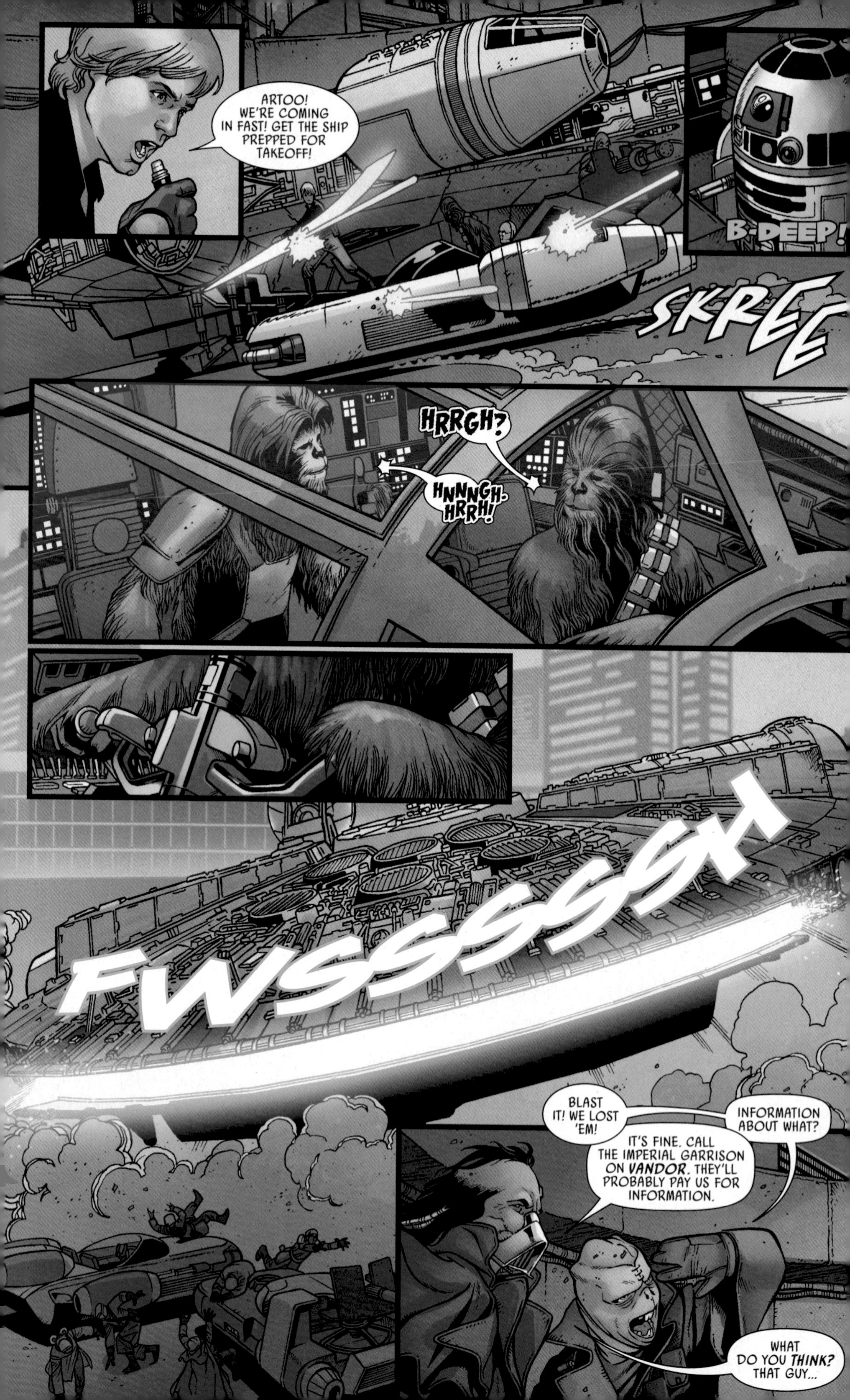
ARTOO! WE'RE COMING IN FAST! GET THE SHIP PREPPED FOR TAKEOFF!
B-DEEP!
SKREE
HRRGH?
HNNNGH. HRRH!
FWSSSSSH
BLAST IT! WE LOST 'EM!
IT'S FINE. CALL THE IMPERIAL GARRISON ON VANDOR. THEY'LL PROBABLY PAY US FOR INFORMATION.
INFORMATION ABOUT WHAT?
WHAT DO YOU THINK? THAT GUY...

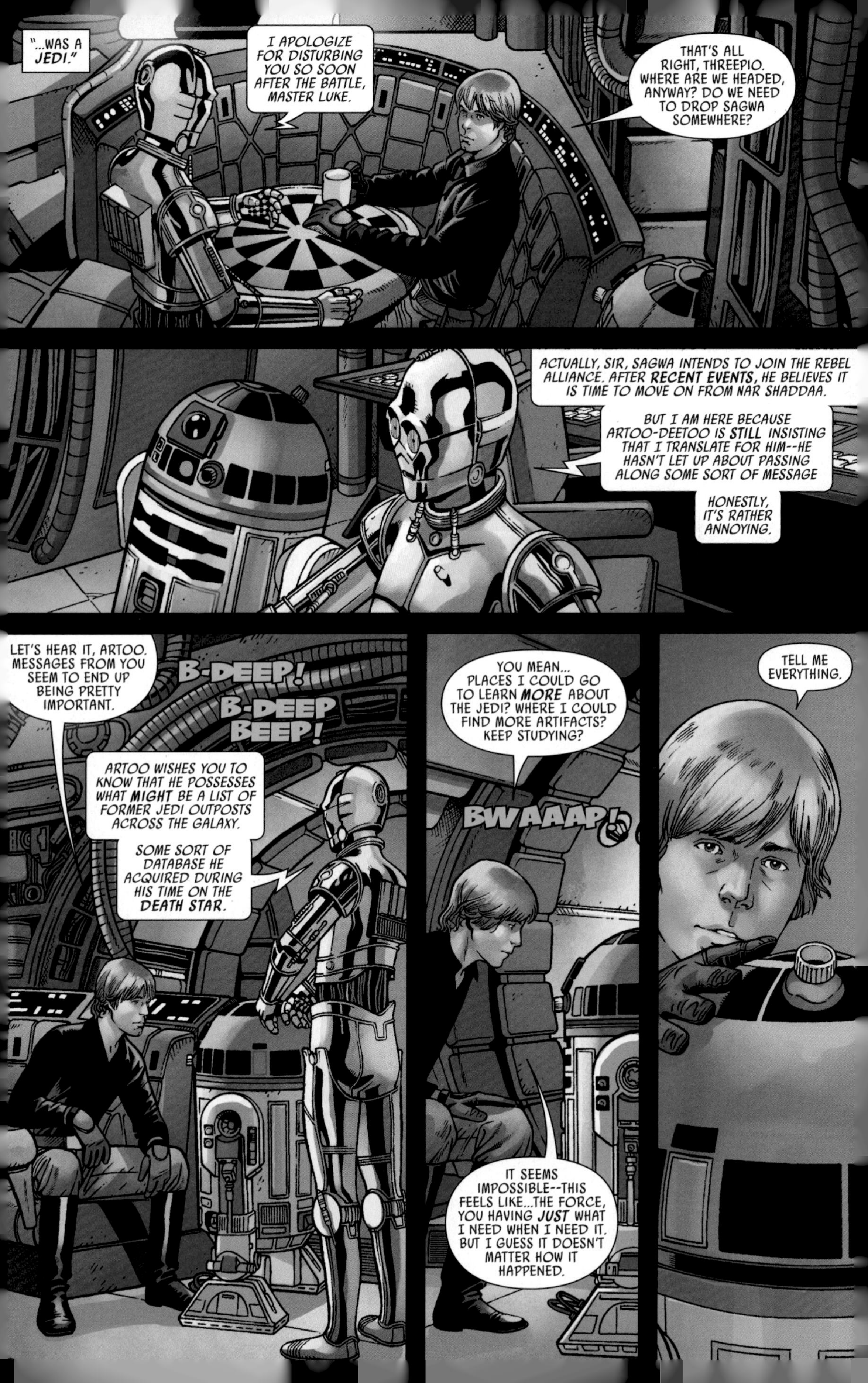

"...WAS A JEDI."
I APOLOGIZE FOR DISTURBING YOU SO SOON AFTER THE BATTLE, MASTER LUKE.
THAT'S ALL RIGHT, THREEPIO. WHERE ARE WE HEADED, ANYWAY? DO WE NEED TO DROP SAGWA SOMEWHERE?
ACTUALLY, SIR, SAGWA INTENDS TO JOIN THE REBEL ALLIANCE. AFTER RECENT EVENTS, HE BELIEVES IT IS TIME TO MOVE ON FROM NAR SHADDAA.
BUT I AM HERE BECAUSE ARTOO-DEETOO IS STILL INSISTING THAT I TRANSLATE FOR HIM--HE HASN'T LET UP ABOUT PASSING ALONG SOME SORT OF MESSAGE
HONESTLY, IT'S RATHER ANNOYING.
LET'S HEAR IT, ARTOO. MESSAGES FROM YOU SEEM TO END UP BEING PRETTY IMPORTANT.
B-DEEP!
B-DEEP BEEP!
ARTOO WISHES YOU TO KNOW THAT HE POSSESSES WHAT MIGHT BE A LIST OF FORMER JEDI OUTPOSTS ACROSS THE GALAXY.
SOME SORT OF DATABASE HE ACQUIRED DURING HIS TIME ON THE DEATH STAR.
YOU MEAN... PLACES I COULD GO TO LEARN MORE ABOUT THE JEDI? WHERE I COULD FIND MORE ARTIFACTS? KEEP STUDYING?
BWAAAP!
IT SEEMS IMPOSSIBLE--THIS FEELS LIKE...THE FORCE, YOU HAVING JUST WHAT I NEED WHEN I NEED IT. BUT I GUESS IT DOESN'T MATTER HOW IT HAPPENED.
TELL ME EVERYTHING.

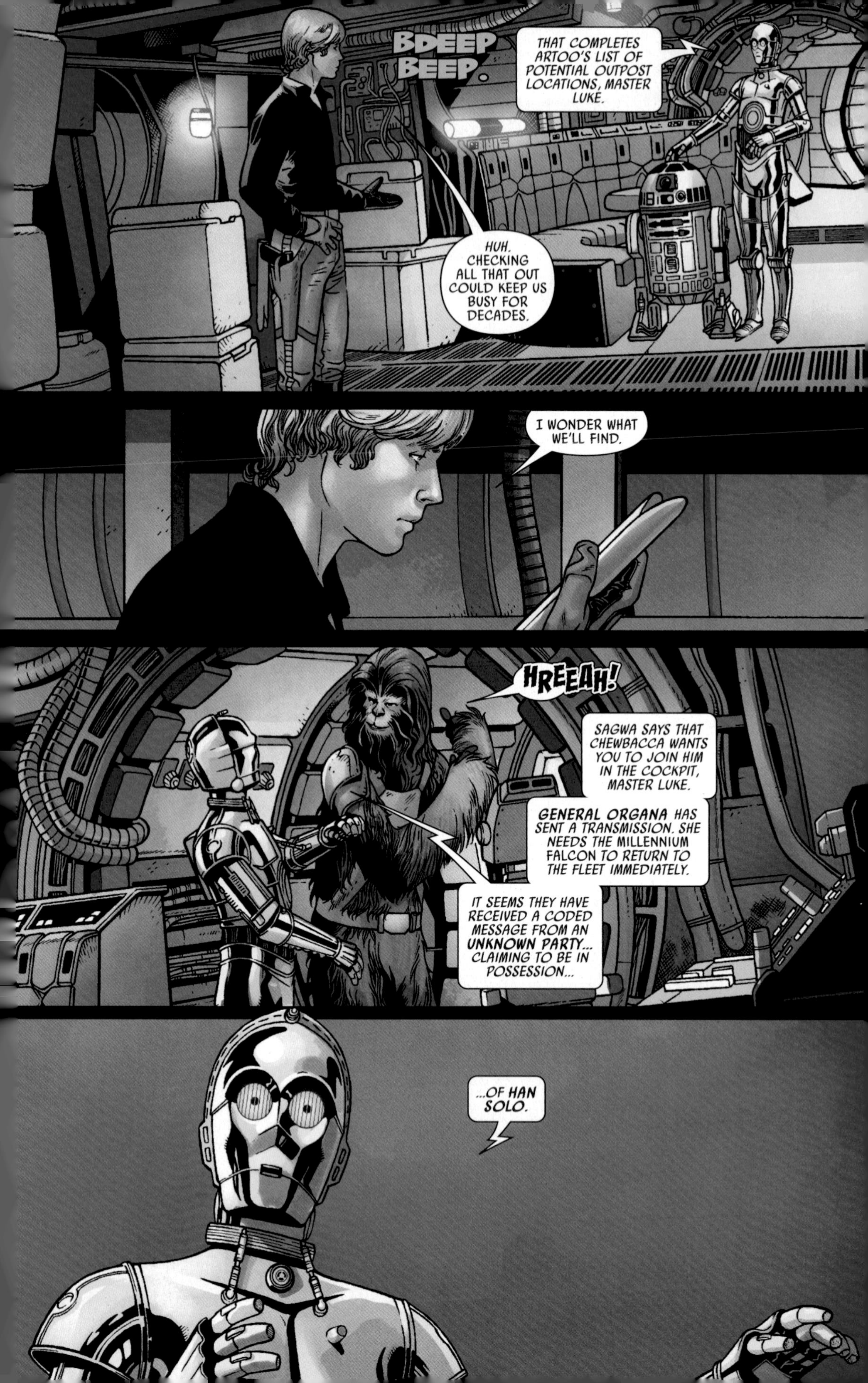
BDEEP BEEP
THAT COMPLETES ARTOO'S LIST OF POTENTIAL OUTPOST LOCATIONS, MASTER LUKE.
HUH. CHECKING ALL THAT OUT COULD KEEP US BUSY FOR DECADES.
I WONDER WHAT WE'LL FIND.
HREEAH!
SAGWA SAYS THAT CHEWBACCA WANTS YOU TO JOIN HIM IN THE COCKPIT, MASTER LUKE.
GENERAL ORGANA HAS SENT A TRANSMISSION. SHE NEEDS THE MILLENNIUM FALCON TO RETURN TO THE FLEET IMMEDIATELY.
IT SEEMS THEY HAVE RECEIVED A CODED MESSAGE FROM AN UNKNOWN PARTY... CLAIMING TO BE IN POSSESSION...
...OF HAN SOLO.

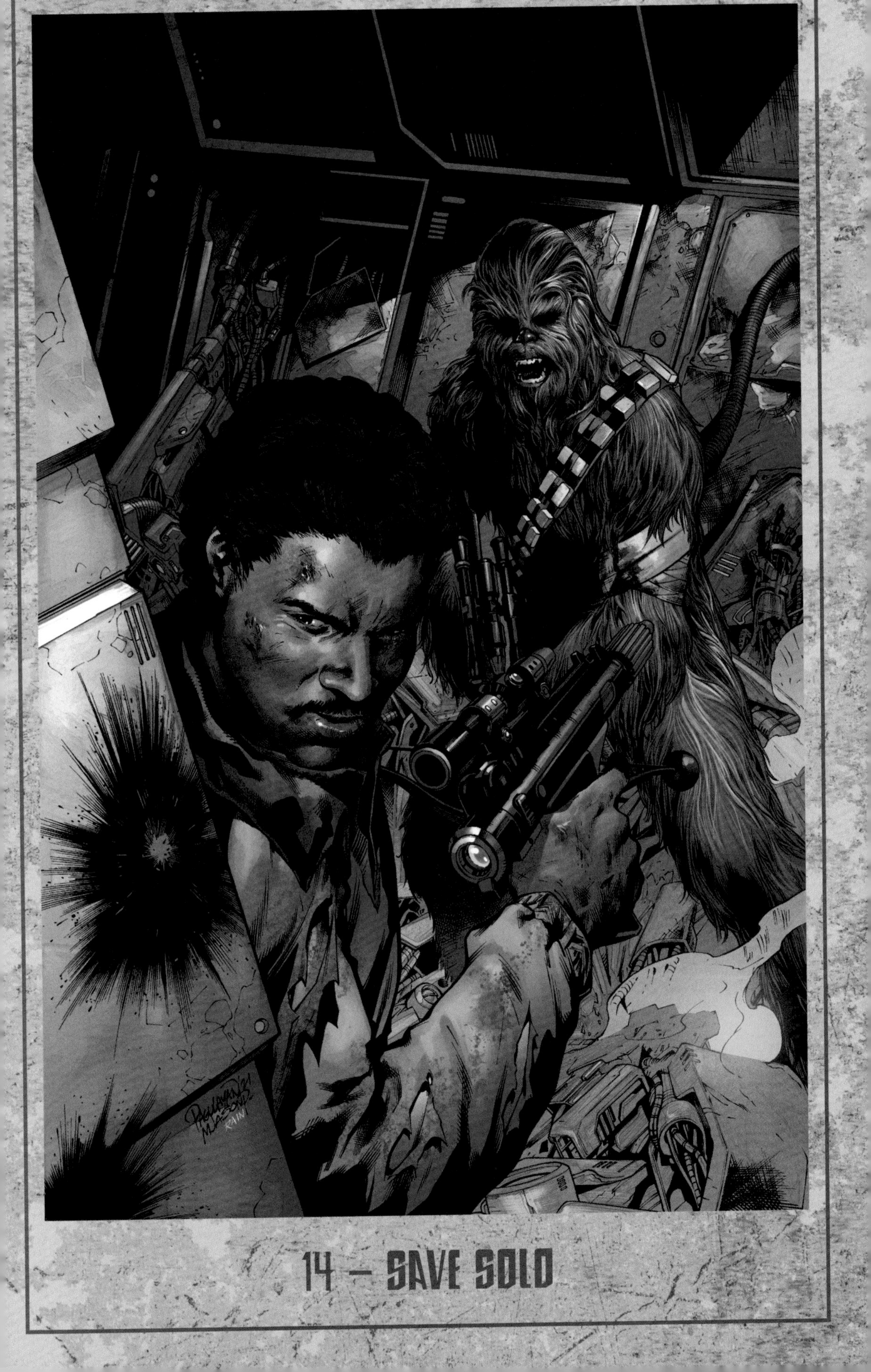

14 – SAVE SOLO

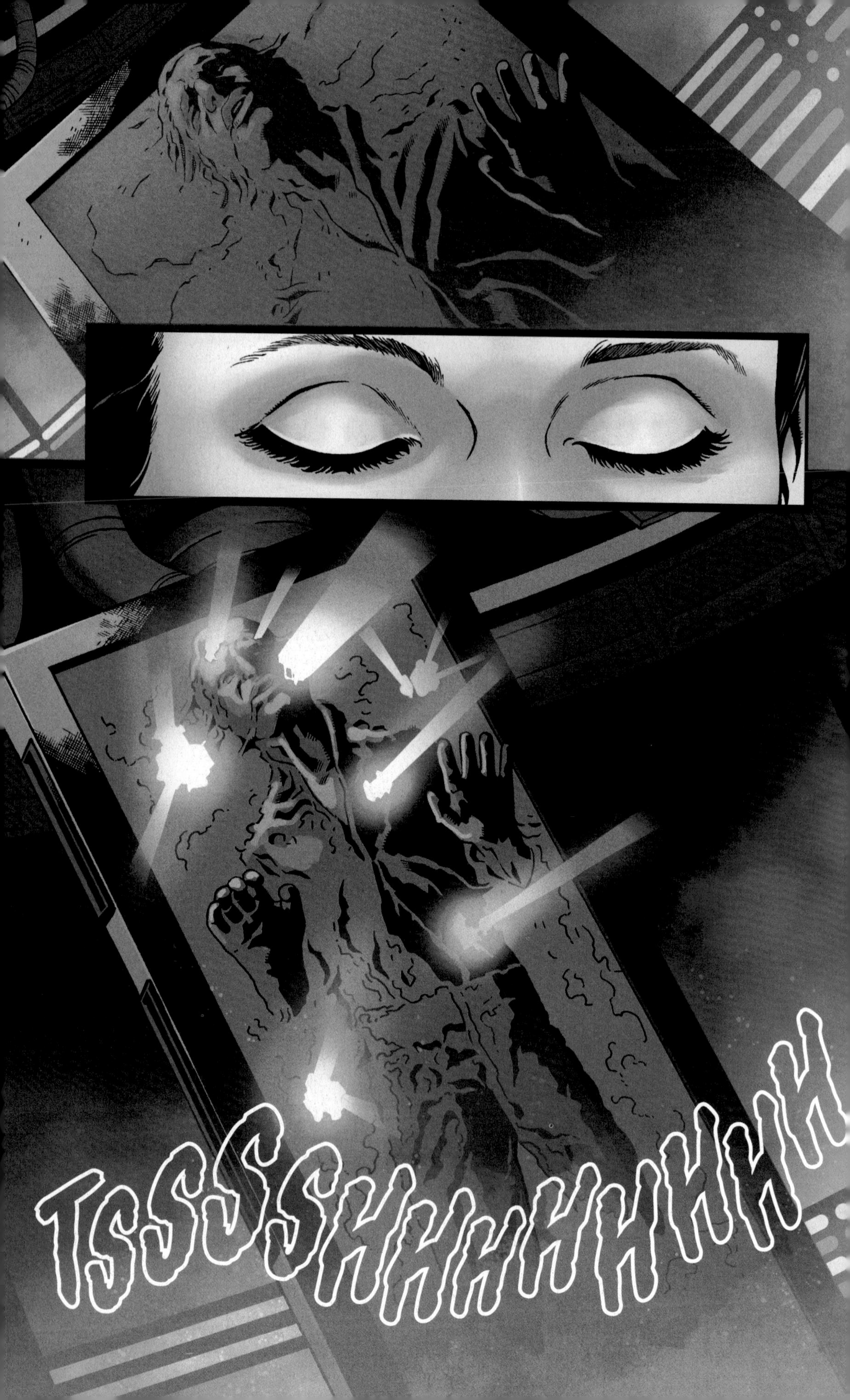
TSSSSHHHHHHHHH

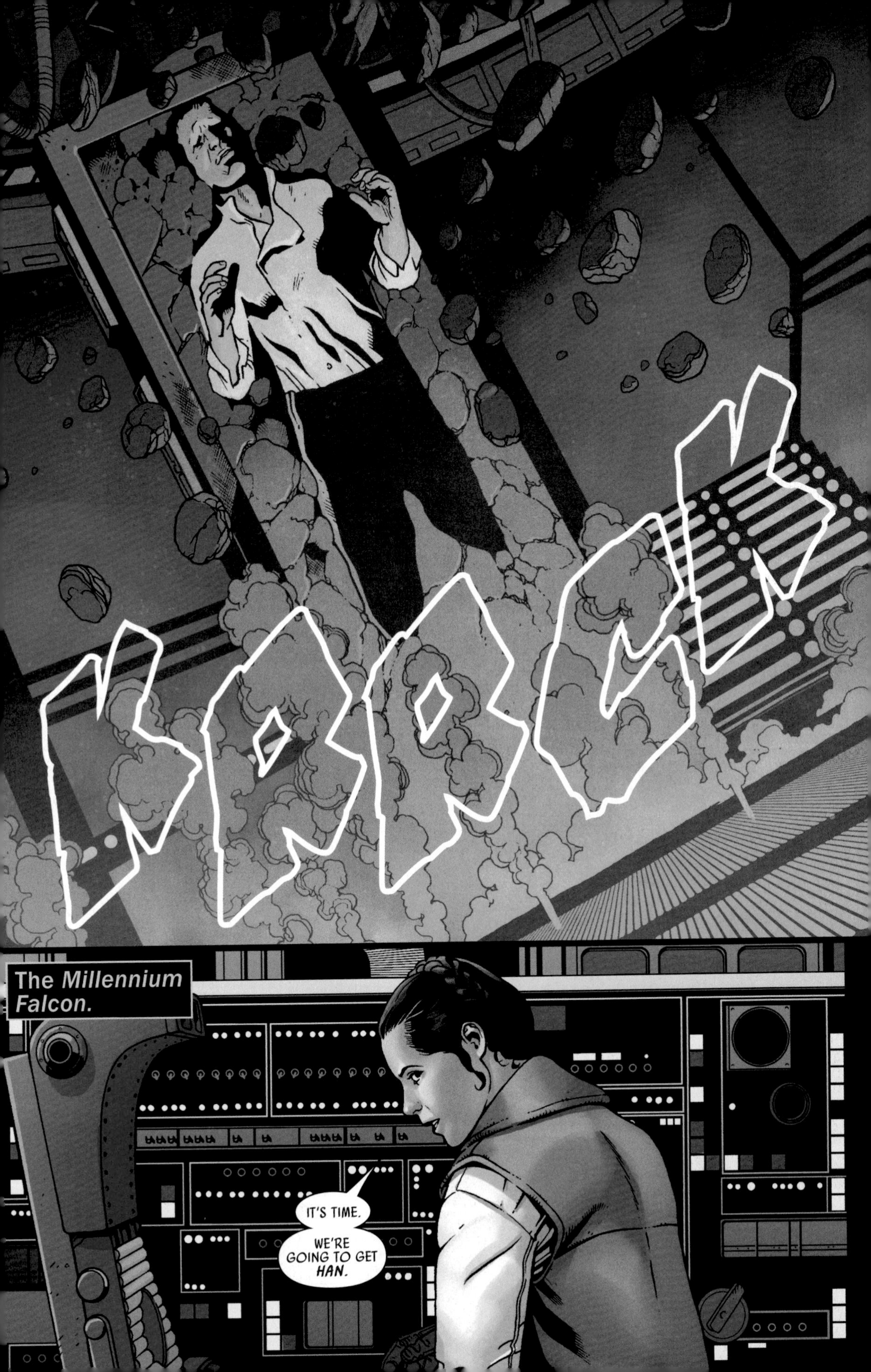
KRACK
The *Millennium Falcon.*
IT'S TIME.
WE'RE GOING TO GET *HAN.*

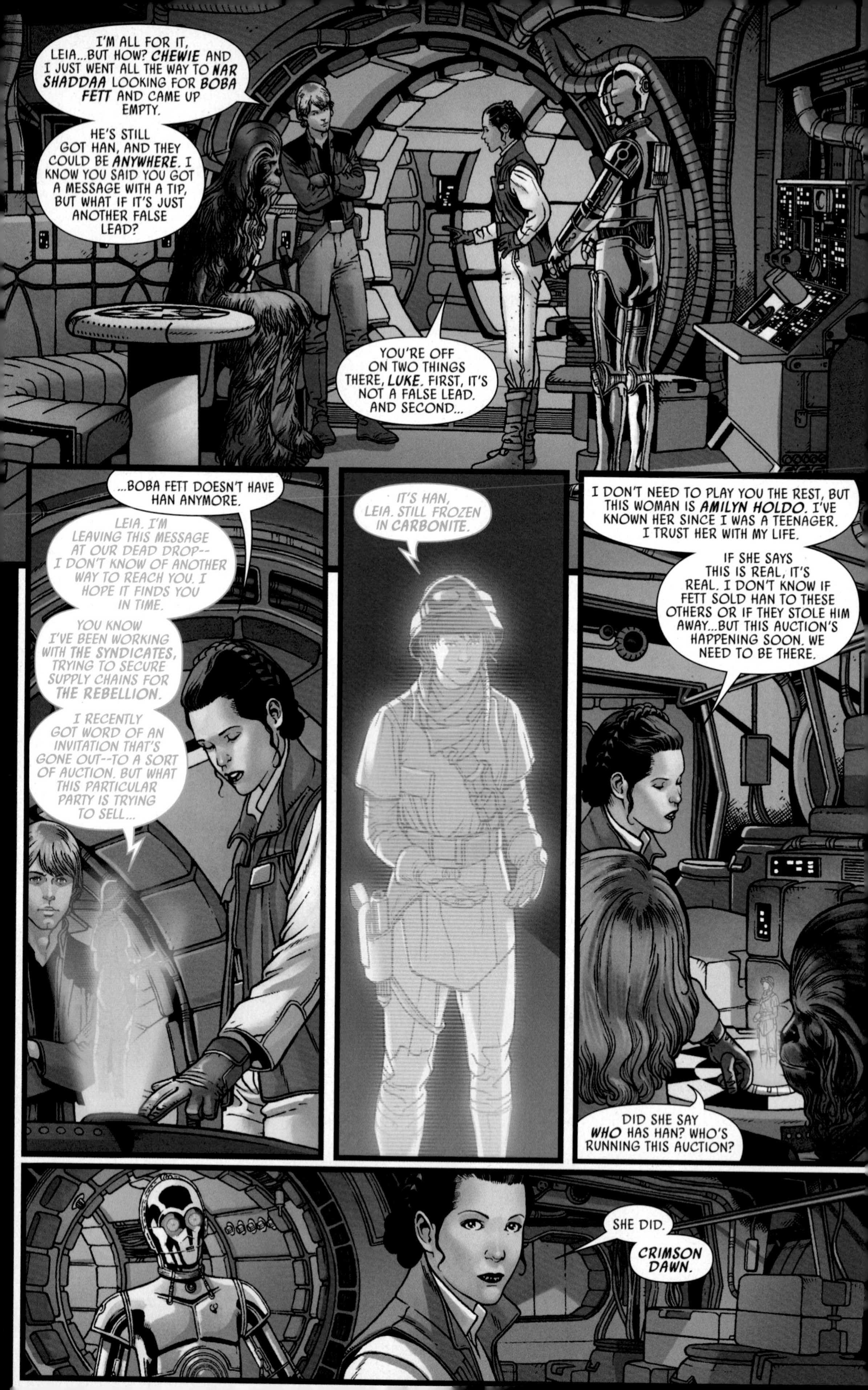
I'M ALL FOR IT, LEIA...BUT HOW? CHEWIE AND I JUST WENT ALL THE WAY TO NAR SHADDAA LOOKING FOR BOBA FETT AND CAME UP EMPTY.
HE'S STILL GOT HAN, AND THEY COULD BE ANYWHERE. I KNOW YOU SAID YOU GOT A MESSAGE WITH A TIP, BUT WHAT IF IT'S JUST ANOTHER FALSE LEAD?
YOU'RE OFF ON TWO THINGS THERE, LUKE. FIRST, IT'S NOT A FALSE LEAD. AND SECOND...
...BOBA FETT DOESN'T HAVE HAN ANYMORE.
LEIA. I'M LEAVING THIS MESSAGE AT OUR DEAD DROP-- I DON'T KNOW OF ANOTHER WAY TO REACH YOU. I HOPE IT FINDS YOU IN TIME.
YOU KNOW I'VE BEEN WORKING WITH THE SYNDICATES, TRYING TO SECURE SUPPLY CHAINS FOR THE REBELLION.
I RECENTLY GOT WORD OF AN INVITATION THAT'S GONE OUT--TO A SORT OF AUCTION. BUT WHAT THIS PARTICULAR PARTY IS TRYING TO SELL...
IT'S HAN, LEIA. STILL FROZEN IN CARBONITE.
I DON'T NEED TO PLAY YOU THE REST, BUT THIS WOMAN IS AMILYN HOLDO. I'VE KNOWN HER SINCE I WAS A TEENAGER. I TRUST HER WITH MY LIFE.
IF SHE SAYS THIS IS REAL, IT'S REAL. I DON'T KNOW IF FETT SOLD HAN TO THESE OTHERS OR IF THEY STOLE HIM AWAY...BUT THIS AUCTION'S HAPPENING SOON. WE NEED TO BE THERE.
DID SHE SAY WHO HAS HAN? WHO'S RUNNING THIS AUCTION?
SHE DID.
CRIMSON DAWN.

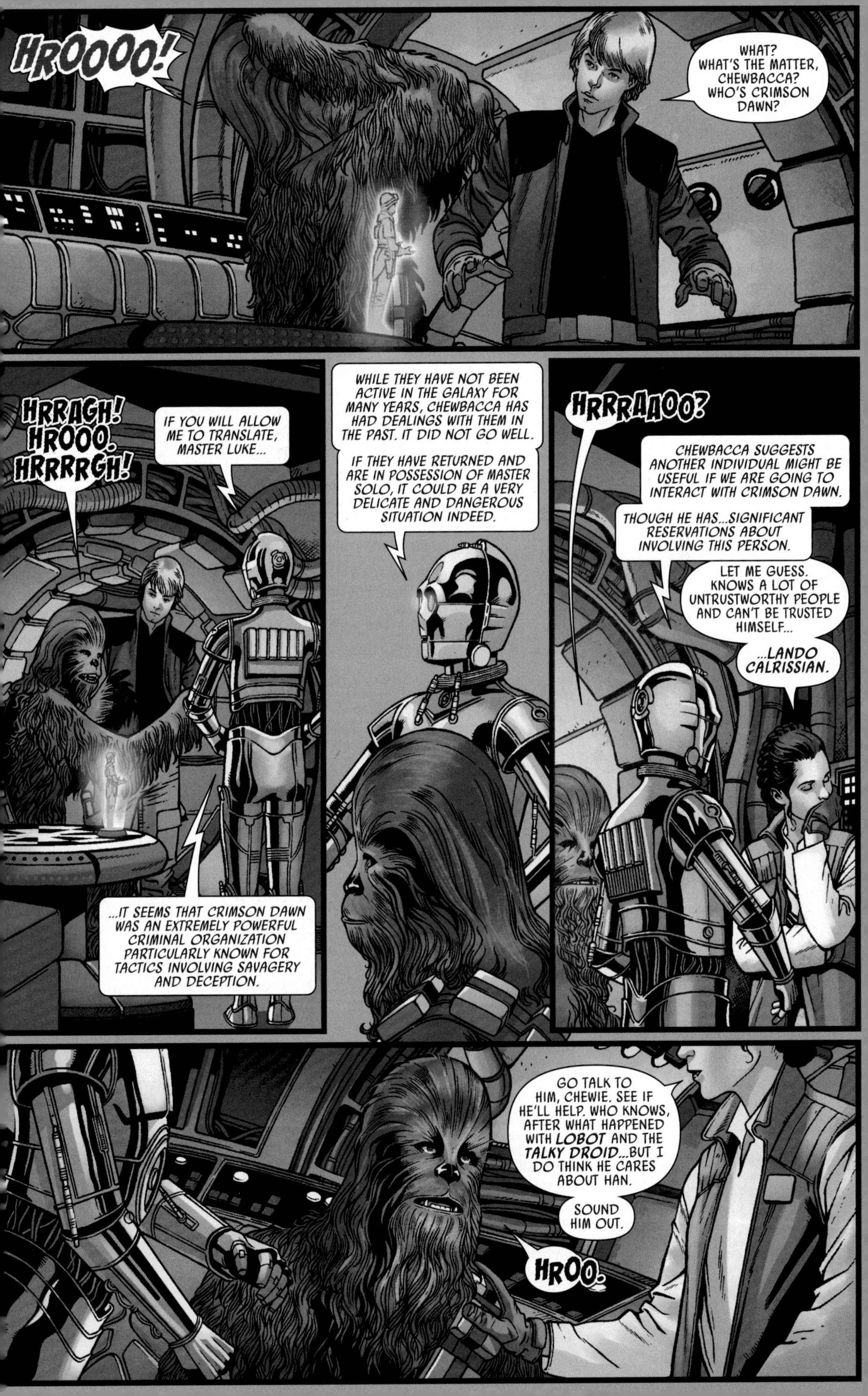
HROOOO!
WHAT? WHAT'S THE MATTER, CHEWBACCA? WHO'S CRIMSON DAWN?
HRRAGH! HROOO. HRRRRGH!
IF YOU WILL ALLOW ME TO TRANSLATE, MASTER LUKE...
...IT SEEMS THAT CRIMSON DAWN WAS AN EXTREMELY POWERFUL CRIMINAL ORGANIZATION PARTICULARLY KNOWN FOR TACTICS INVOLVING SAVAGERY AND DECEPTION.
WHILE THEY HAVE NOT BEEN ACTIVE IN THE GALAXY FOR MANY YEARS, CHEWBACCA HAS HAD DEALINGS WITH THEM IN THE PAST. IT DID NOT GO WELL.
IF THEY HAVE RETURNED AND ARE IN POSSESSION OF MASTER SOLO, IT COULD BE A VERY DELICATE AND DANGEROUS SITUATION INDEED.
HRRRAAOO?
CHEWBACCA SUGGESTS ANOTHER INDIVIDUAL MIGHT BE USEFUL IF WE ARE GOING TO INTERACT WITH CRIMSON DAWN.
THOUGH HE HAS...SIGNIFICANT RESERVATIONS ABOUT INVOLVING THIS PERSON.
LET ME GUESS. KNOWS A LOT OF UNTRUSTWORTHY PEOPLE AND CAN'T BE TRUSTED HIMSELF...
...LANDO CALRISSIAN.
GO TALK TO HIM, CHEWIE. SEE IF HE'LL HELP. WHO KNOWS, AFTER WHAT HAPPENED WITH LOBOT AND THE TALKY DROID...BUT I DO THINK HE CARES ABOUT HAN.
SOUND HIM OUT.
HROO.

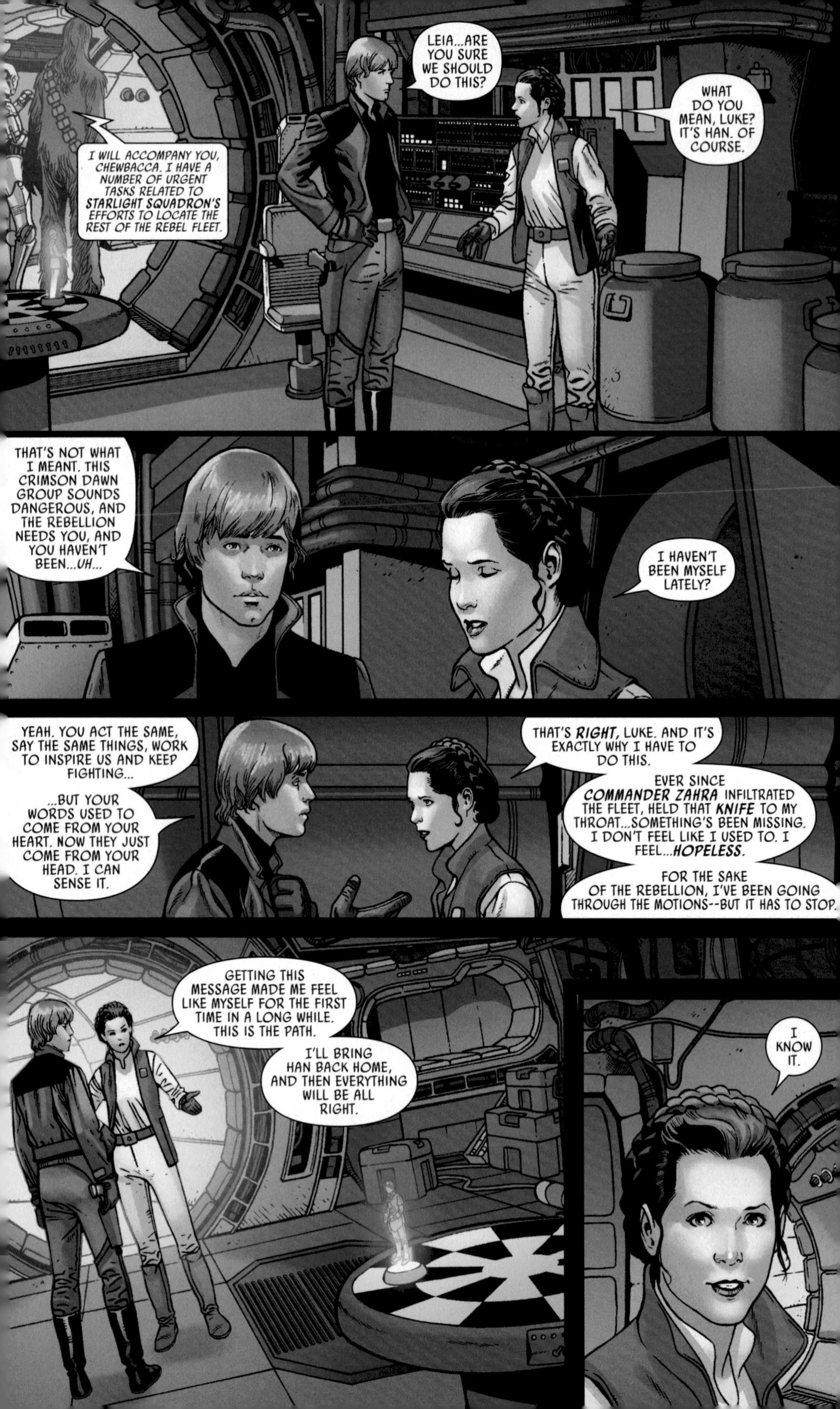
LEIA...ARE YOU SURE WE SHOULD DO THIS?
I WILL ACCOMPANY YOU, CHEWBACCA. I HAVE A NUMBER OF URGENT TASKS RELATED TO STARLIGHT SQUADRON'S EFFORTS TO LOCATE THE REST OF THE REBEL FLEET.
WHAT DO YOU MEAN, LUKE? IT'S HAN, OF COURSE.
THAT'S NOT WHAT I MEANT. THIS CRIMSON DAWN GROUP SOUNDS DANGEROUS, AND THE REBELLION NEEDS YOU, AND YOU HAVEN'T BEEN...UH...
I HAVEN'T BEEN MYSELF LATELY?
YEAH. YOU ACT THE SAME, SAY THE SAME THINGS, WORK TO INSPIRE US AND KEEP FIGHTING...
...BUT YOUR WORDS USED TO COME FROM YOUR HEART. NOW THEY JUST COME FROM YOUR HEAD. I CAN SENSE IT.
THAT'S RIGHT, LUKE. AND IT'S EXACTLY WHY I HAVE TO DO THIS.
EVER SINCE COMMANDER ZAHRA INFILTRATED THE FLEET, HELD THAT KNIFE TO MY THROAT...SOMETHING'S BEEN MISSING. I DON'T FEEL LIKE I USED TO. I FEEL...HOPELESS.
FOR THE SAKE OF THE REBELLION, I'VE BEEN GOING THROUGH THE MOTIONS--BUT IT HAS TO STOP.
GETTING THIS MESSAGE MADE ME FEEL LIKE MYSELF FOR THE FIRST TIME IN A LONG WHILE. THIS IS THE PATH.
I'LL BRING HAN BACK HOME, AND THEN EVERYTHING WILL BE ALL RIGHT.
I KNOW IT.

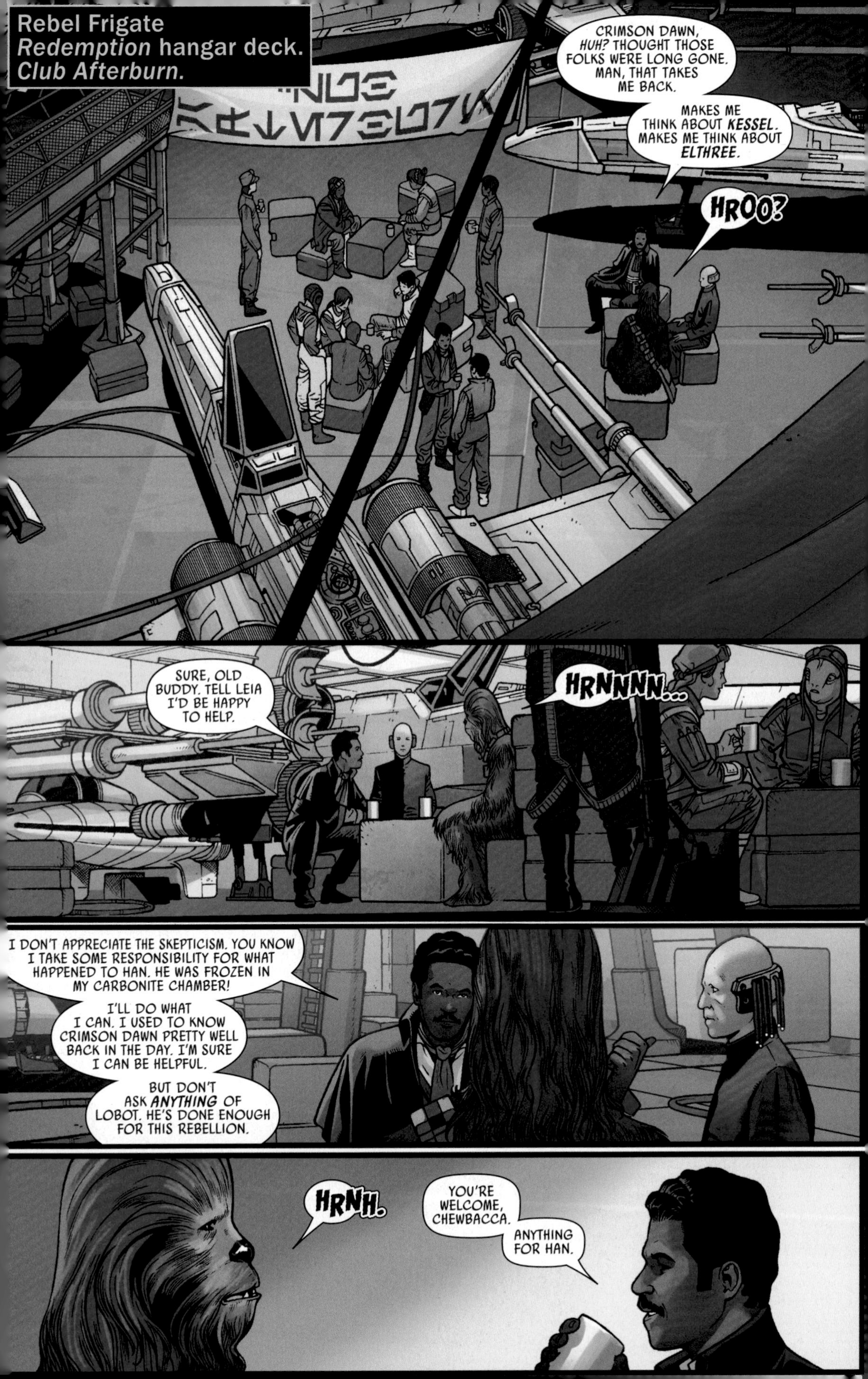
Rebel Frigate *Redemption* hangar deck. *Club Afterburn.*
CRIMSON DAWN, *HUH?* THOUGHT THOSE FOLKS WERE LONG GONE. MAN, THAT TAKES ME BACK.
MAKES ME THINK ABOUT ***KESSEL***. MAKES ME THINK ABOUT ***ELTHREE***.
HROO?
SURE, OLD BUDDY. TELL LEIA I'D BE HAPPY TO HELP.
HRNNNN...
I DON'T APPRECIATE THE SKEPTICISM. YOU KNOW I TAKE SOME RESPONSIBILITY FOR WHAT HAPPENED TO HAN. HE WAS FROZEN IN MY CARBONITE CHAMBER!
I'LL DO WHAT I CAN. I USED TO KNOW CRIMSON DAWN PRETTY WELL BACK IN THE DAY. I'M SURE I CAN BE HELPFUL.
BUT DON'T ASK ***ANYTHING*** OF LOBOT. HE'S DONE ENOUGH FOR THIS REBELLION.
HRNH.
YOU'RE WELCOME, CHEWBACCA.
ANYTHING FOR HAN.

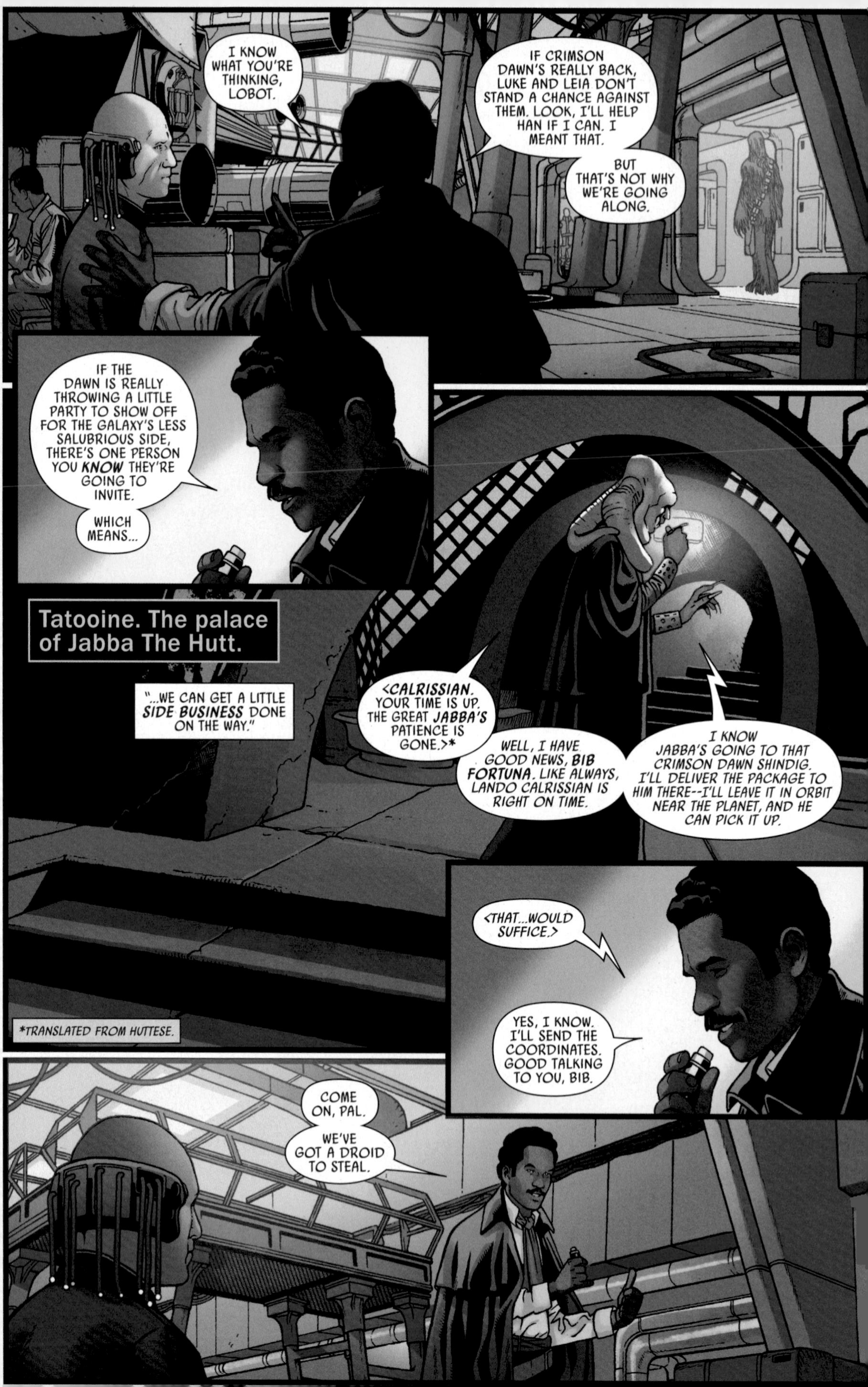
I KNOW WHAT YOU'RE THINKING, LOBOT.
IF CRIMSON DAWN'S REALLY BACK, LUKE AND LEIA DON'T STAND A CHANCE AGAINST THEM. LOOK, I'LL HELP HAN IF I CAN. I MEANT THAT.
BUT THAT'S NOT WHY WE'RE GOING ALONG.
IF THE DAWN IS REALLY THROWING A LITTLE PARTY TO SHOW OFF FOR THE GALAXY'S LESS SALUBRIOUS SIDE, THERE'S ONE PERSON YOU KNOW THEY'RE GOING TO INVITE.
WHICH MEANS...
Tatooine. The palace of Jabba The Hutt.
"...WE CAN GET A LITTLE SIDE BUSINESS DONE ON THE WAY."
<CALRISSIAN. YOUR TIME IS UP. THE GREAT JABBA'S PATIENCE IS GONE.>*
WELL, I HAVE GOOD NEWS, BIB FORTUNA. LIKE ALWAYS, LANDO CALRISSIAN IS RIGHT ON TIME.
I KNOW JABBA'S GOING TO THAT CRIMSON DAWN SHINDIG. I'LL DELIVER THE PACKAGE TO HIM THERE--I'LL LEAVE IT IN ORBIT NEAR THE PLANET, AND HE CAN PICK IT UP.
<THAT...WOULD SUFFICE.>
YES, I KNOW. I'LL SEND THE COORDINATES. GOOD TALKING TO YOU, BIB.
*TRANSLATED FROM HUTTESE.
COME ON, PAL.
WE'VE GOT A DROID TO STEAL.

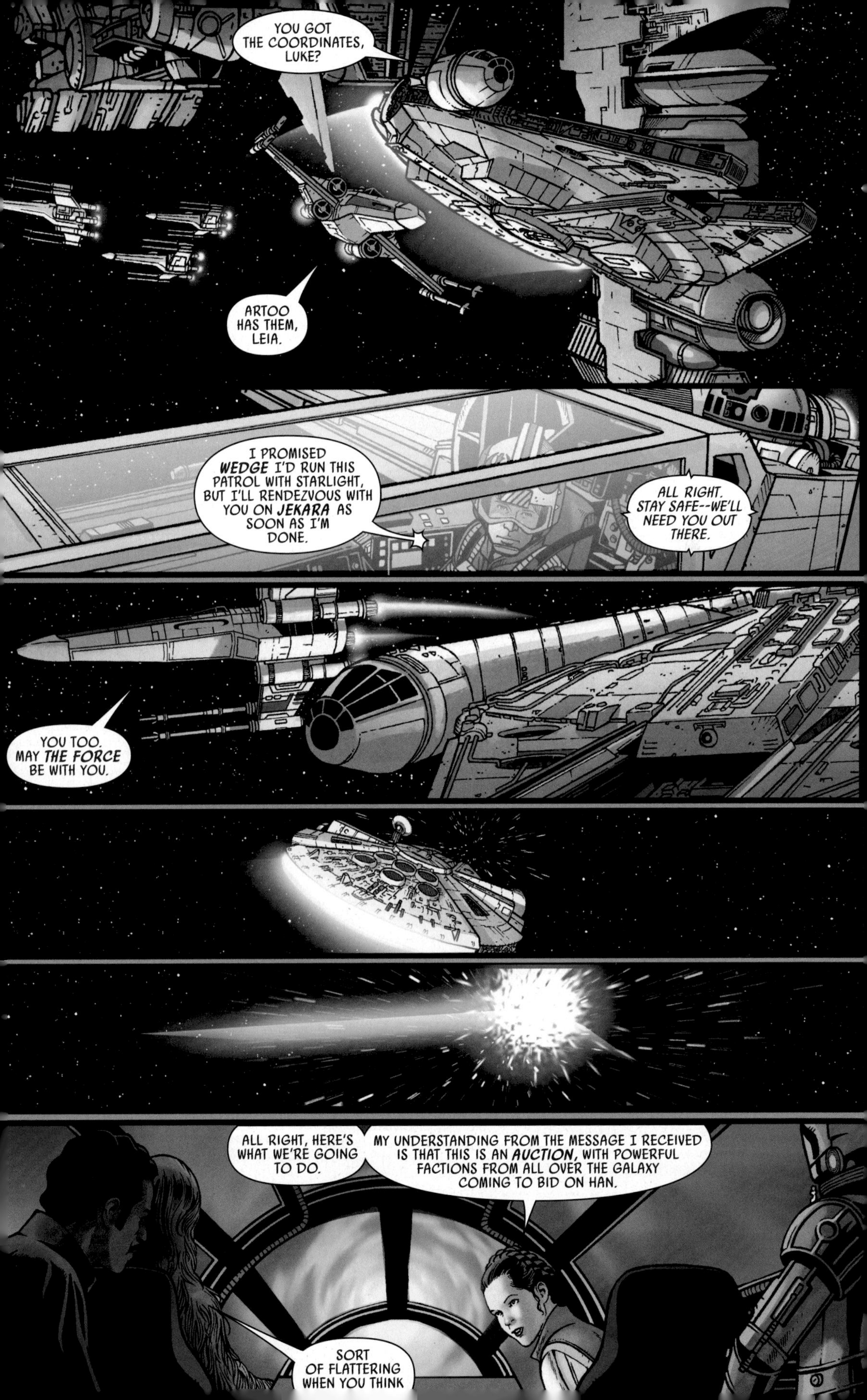
YOU GOT THE COORDINATES, LUKE?
ARTOO HAS THEM, LEIA.
I PROMISED WEDGE I'D RUN THIS PATROL WITH STARLIGHT, BUT I'LL RENDEZVOUS WITH YOU ON JEKARA AS SOON AS I'M DONE.
ALL RIGHT. STAY SAFE--WE'LL NEED YOU OUT THERE.
YOU TOO. MAY THE FORCE BE WITH YOU.
ALL RIGHT, HERE'S WHAT WE'RE GOING TO DO.
MY UNDERSTANDING FROM THE MESSAGE I RECEIVED IS THAT THIS IS AN AUCTION, WITH POWERFUL FACTIONS FROM ALL OVER THE GALAXY COMING TO BID ON HAN.
SORT OF FLATTERING WHEN YOU THINK

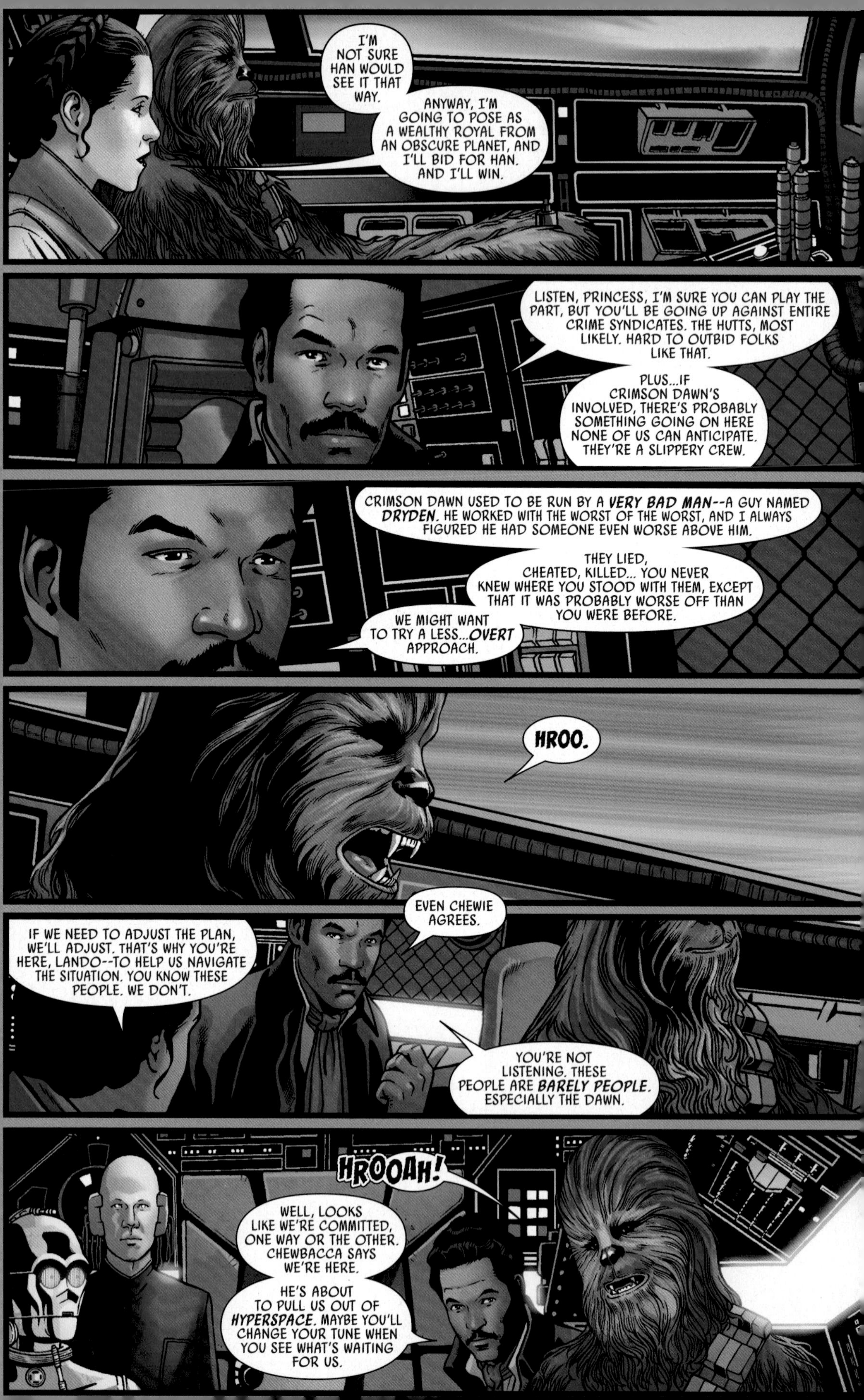
I'M NOT SURE HAN WOULD SEE IT THAT WAY.
ANYWAY, I'M GOING TO POSE AS A WEALTHY ROYAL FROM AN OBSCURE PLANET, AND I'LL BID FOR HAN. AND I'LL WIN.
LISTEN, PRINCESS, I'M SURE YOU CAN PLAY THE PART, BUT YOU'LL BE GOING UP AGAINST ENTIRE CRIME SYNDICATES. THE HUTTS, MOST LIKELY. HARD TO OUTBID FOLKS LIKE THAT.
PLUS...IF CRIMSON DAWN'S INVOLVED, THERE'S PROBABLY SOMETHING GOING ON HERE NONE OF US CAN ANTICIPATE. THEY'RE A SLIPPERY CREW.
CRIMSON DAWN USED TO BE RUN BY A VERY BAD MAN--A GUY NAMED DRYDEN. HE WORKED WITH THE WORST OF THE WORST, AND I ALWAYS FIGURED HE HAD SOMEONE EVEN WORSE ABOVE HIM.
THEY LIED, CHEATED, KILLED... YOU NEVER KNEW WHERE YOU STOOD WITH THEM, EXCEPT THAT IT WAS PROBABLY WORSE OFF THAN YOU WERE BEFORE.
WE MIGHT WANT TO TRY A LESS...OVERT APPROACH.
HROO.
IF WE NEED TO ADJUST THE PLAN, WE'LL ADJUST. THAT'S WHY YOU'RE HERE, LANDO--TO HELP US NAVIGATE THE SITUATION. YOU KNOW THESE PEOPLE. WE DON'T.
EVEN CHEWIE AGREES.
YOU'RE NOT LISTENING. THESE PEOPLE ARE BARELY PEOPLE. ESPECIALLY THE DAWN.
HROOAH!
WELL, LOOKS LIKE WE'RE COMMITTED, ONE WAY OR THE OTHER. CHEWBACCA SAYS WE'RE HERE.
HE'S ABOUT TO PULL US OUT OF HYPERSPACE. MAYBE YOU'LL CHANGE YOUR TUNE WHEN YOU SEE WHAT'S WAITING FOR US.

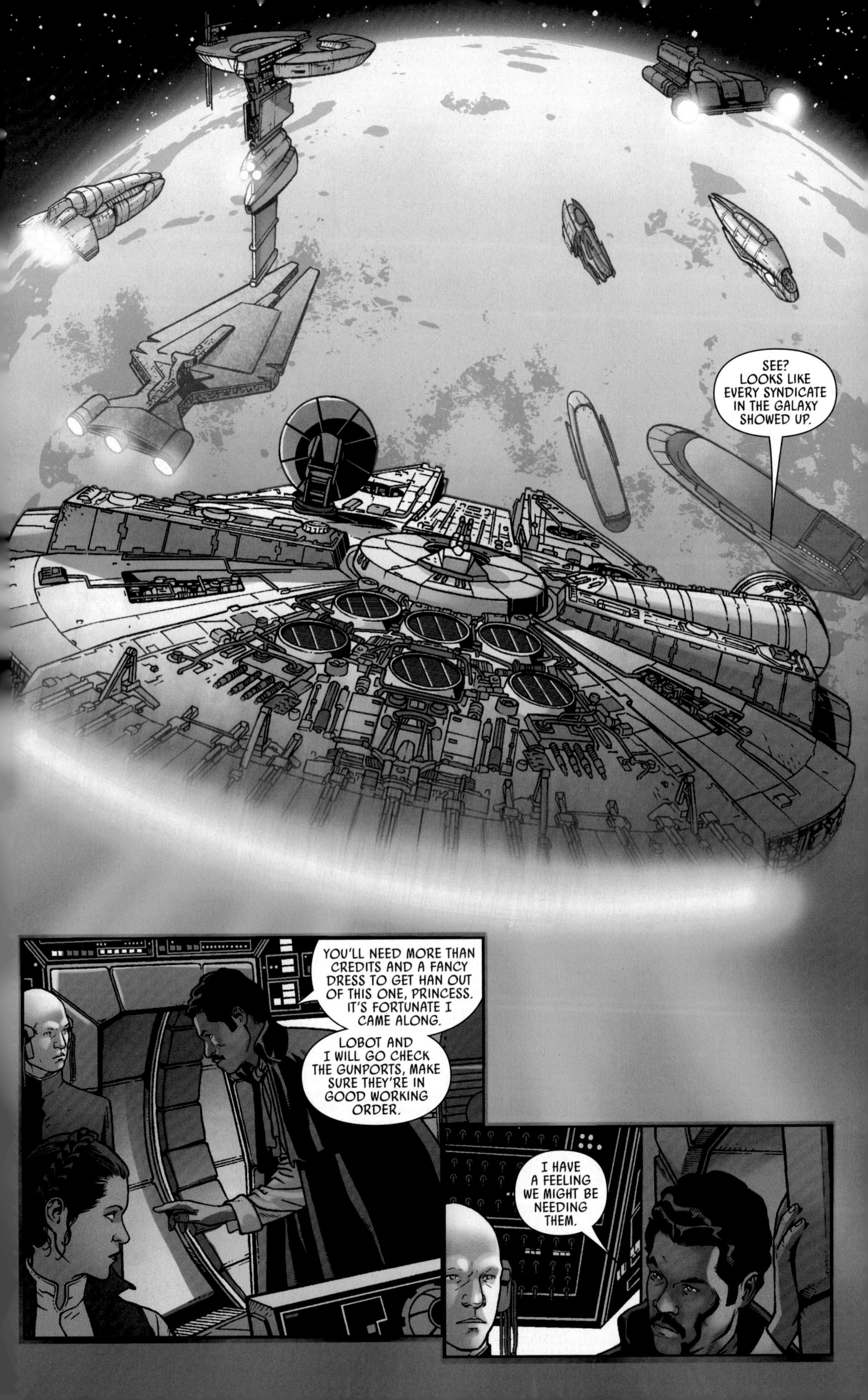
SEE? LOOKS LIKE EVERY SYNDICATE IN THE GALAXY SHOWED UP.
YOU'LL NEED MORE THAN CREDITS AND A FANCY DRESS TO GET HAN OUT OF THIS ONE, PRINCESS. IT'S FORTUNATE I CAME ALONG.
LOBOT AND I WILL GO CHECK THE GUNPORTS, MAKE SURE THEY'RE IN GOOD WORKING ORDER.
I HAVE A FEELING WE MIGHT BE NEEDING THEM.

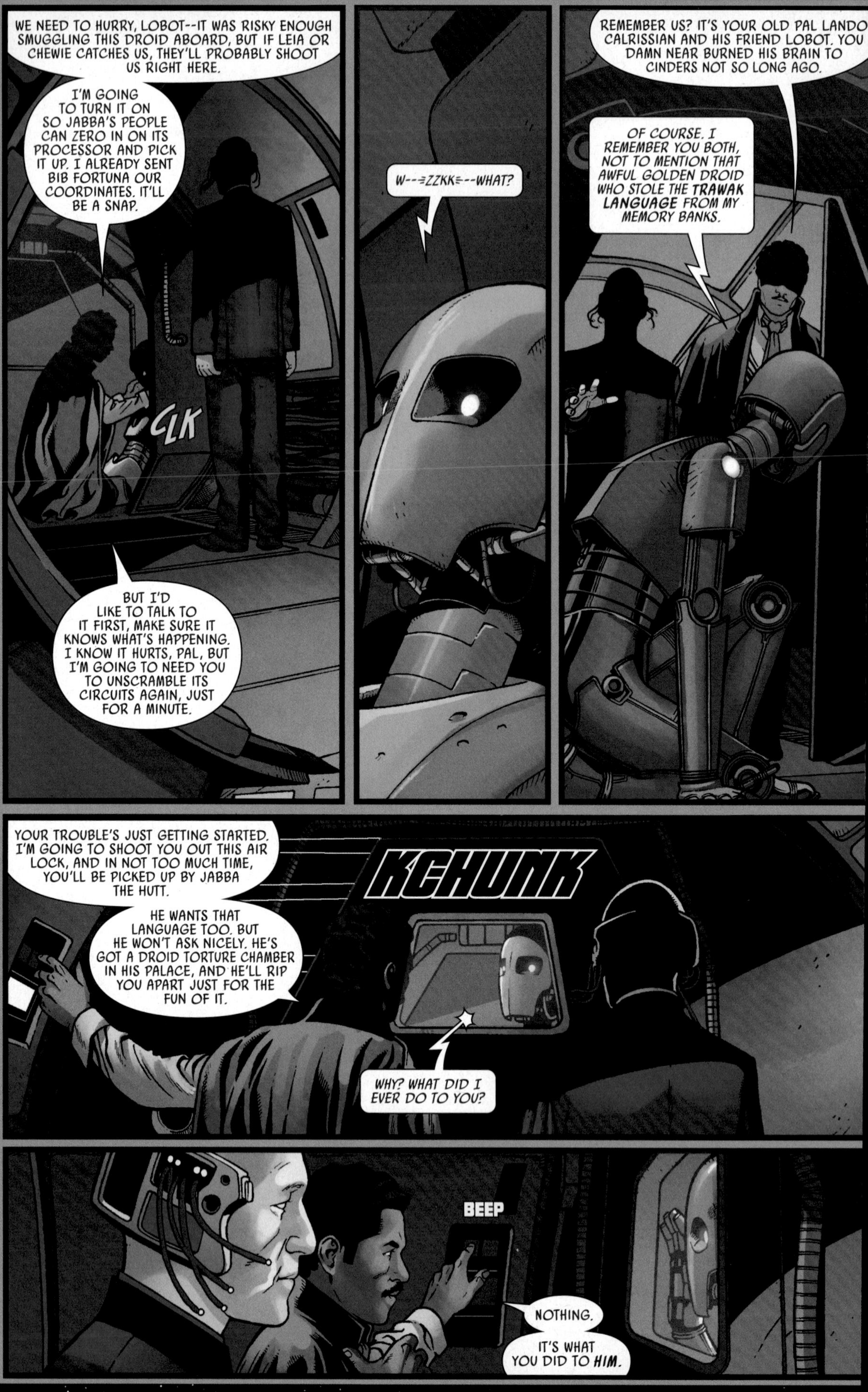

WE NEED TO HURRY, LOBOT--IT WAS RISKY ENOUGH SMUGGLING THIS DROID ABOARD, BUT IF LEIA OR CHEWIE CATCHES US, THEY'LL PROBABLY SHOOT US RIGHT HERE.
I'M GOING TO TURN IT ON SO JABBA'S PEOPLE CAN ZERO IN ON ITS PROCESSOR AND PICK IT UP. I ALREADY SENT BIB FORTUNA OUR COORDINATES. IT'LL BE A SNAP.
CLK
BUT I'D LIKE TO TALK TO IT FIRST, MAKE SURE IT KNOWS WHAT'S HAPPENING. I KNOW IT HURTS, PAL, BUT I'M GOING TO NEED YOU TO UNSCRAMBLE ITS CIRCUITS AGAIN, JUST FOR A MINUTE.
W--ZZKK--WHAT?
REMEMBER US? IT'S YOUR OLD PAL LANDO CALRISSIAN AND HIS FRIEND LOBOT. YOU DAMN NEAR BURNED HIS BRAIN TO CINDERS NOT SO LONG AGO.
OF COURSE. I REMEMBER YOU BOTH, NOT TO MENTION THAT AWFUL GOLDEN DROID WHO STOLE THE TRAWAK LANGUAGE FROM MY MEMORY BANKS.
YOUR TROUBLE'S JUST GETTING STARTED. I'M GOING TO SHOOT YOU OUT THIS AIR LOCK, AND IN NOT TOO MUCH TIME, YOU'LL BE PICKED UP BY JABBA THE HUTT.
KCHUNK
HE WANTS THAT LANGUAGE TOO. BUT HE WON'T ASK NICELY. HE'S GOT A DROID TORTURE CHAMBER IN HIS PALACE, AND HE'LL RIP YOU APART JUST FOR THE FUN OF IT.
WHY? WHAT DID I EVER DO TO YOU?
BEEP
NOTHING.
IT'S WHAT YOU DID TO HIM.

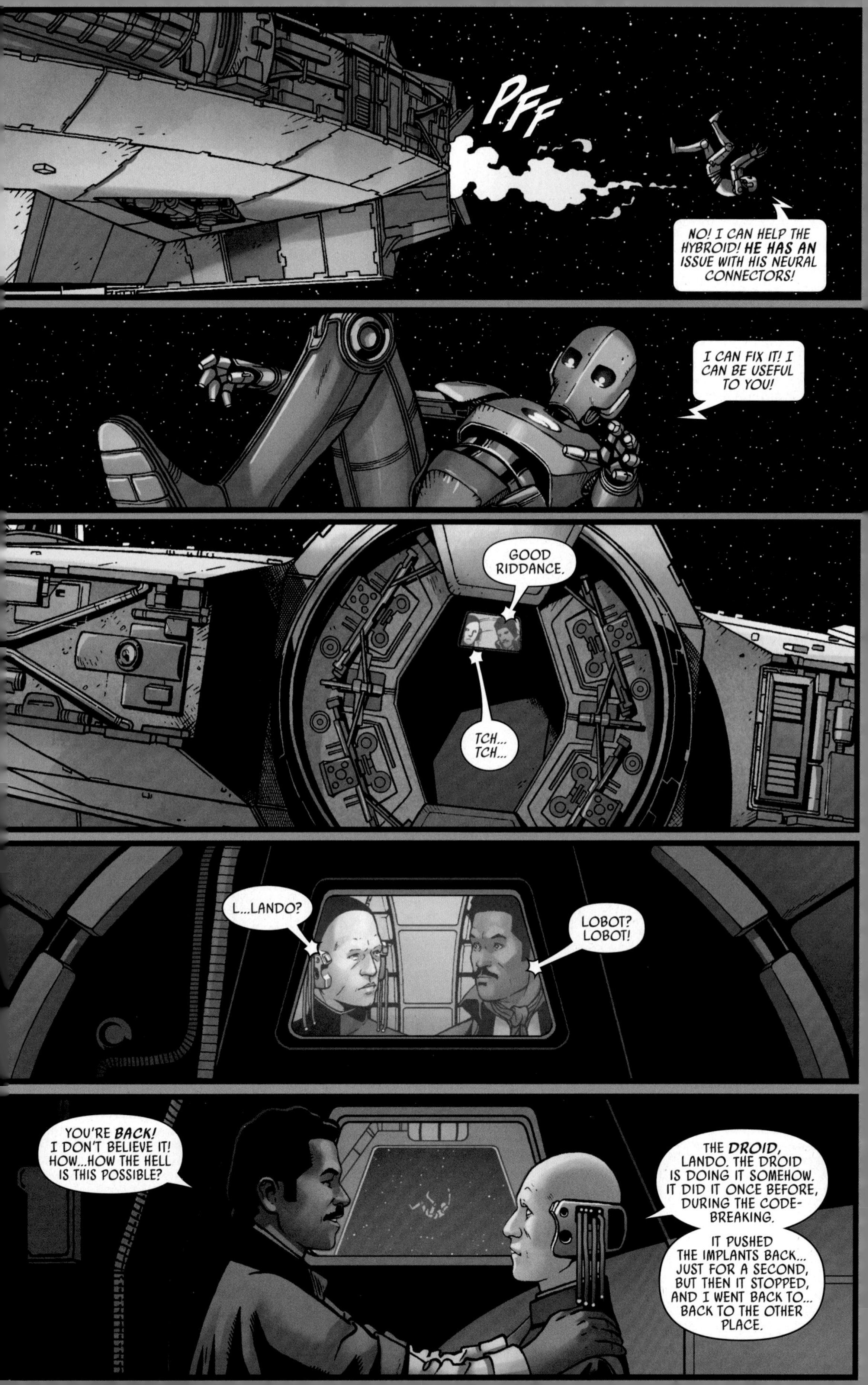
PFF
NO! I CAN HELP THE HYBROID! HE HAS AN ISSUE WITH HIS NEURAL CONNECTORS!
I CAN FIX IT! I CAN BE USEFUL TO YOU!
GOOD RIDDANCE.
TCH... TCH...
L...LANDO?
LOBOT? LOBOT!
YOU'RE BACK! I DON'T BELIEVE IT! HOW...HOW THE HELL IS THIS POSSIBLE?
THE DROID, LANDO. THE DROID IS DOING IT SOMEHOW. IT DID IT ONCE BEFORE, DURING THE CODE-BREAKING.
IT PUSHED THE IMPLANTS BACK... JUST FOR A SECOND, BUT THEN IT STOPPED, AND I WENT BACK TO... BACK TO THE OTHER PLACE.

OH NO.

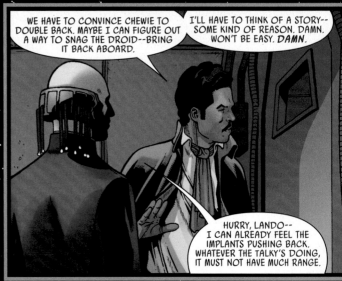

WE HAVE TO CONVINCE CHEWIE TO DOUBLE BACK. MAYBE I CAN FIGURE OUT A WAY TO SNAG THE DROID--BRING IT BACK ABOARD.

I'LL HAVE TO THINK OF A STORY-- SOME KIND OF REASON. DAMN. WON'T BE EASY. *DAMN.*

HURRY, LANDO-- I CAN ALREADY FEEL THE IMPLANTS PUSHING BACK. WHATEVER THE TALKY'S DOING, IT MUST NOT HAVE MUCH RANGE.

I CAN HELP. I CAN...ZZZHK!

WE'RE GOING TO MAKE THIS WORK. I KNOW IT. AND I GOTTA SAY, IT'S SO GOOD TO HAVE YOU BACK.

SHHGLLKGD10011100--

...LOBOT?

NO.

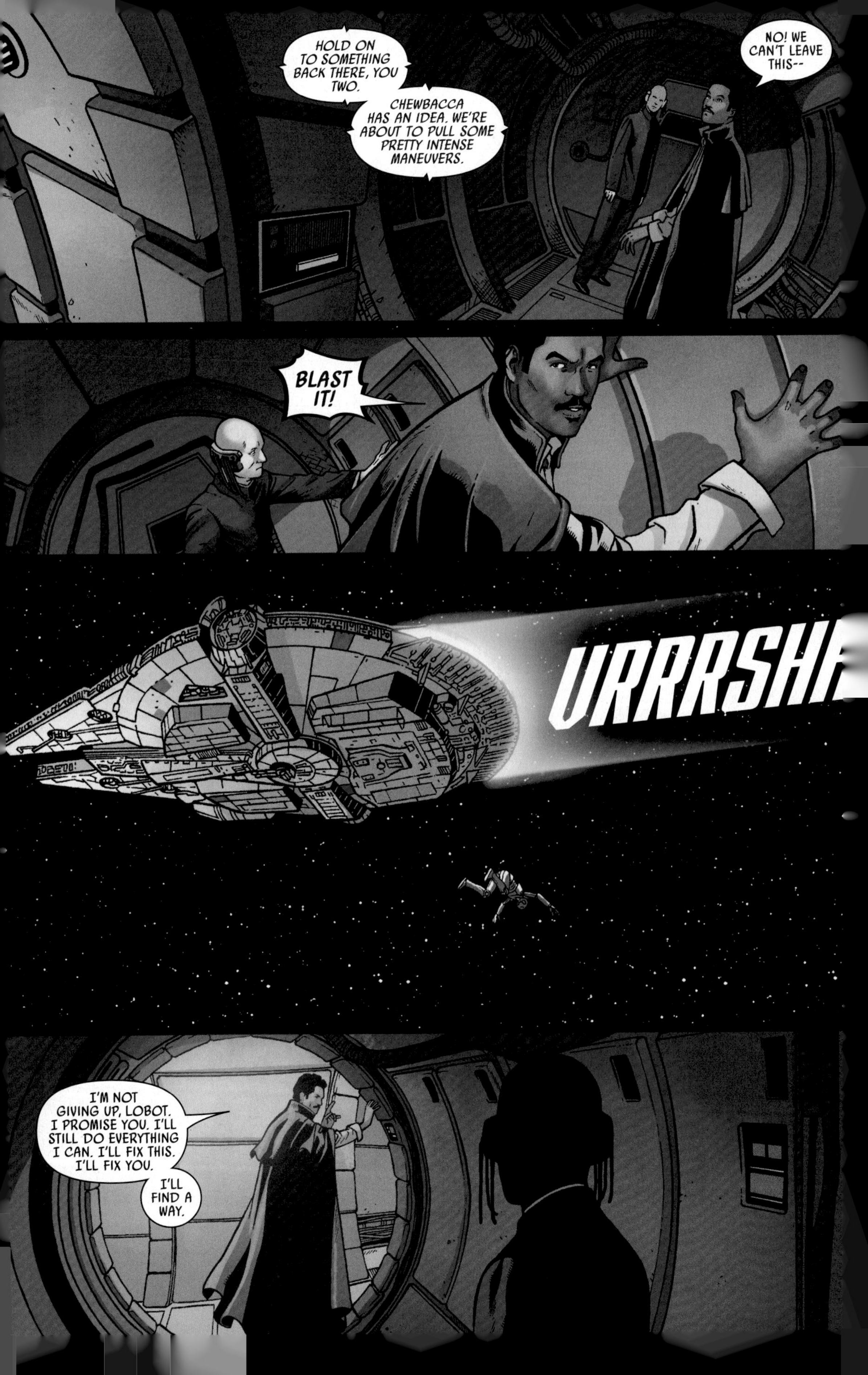
HOLD ON TO SOMETHING BACK THERE, YOU TWO.
CHEWBACCA HAS AN IDEA. WE'RE ABOUT TO PULL SOME PRETTY INTENSE MANEUVERS.
NO! WE CAN'T LEAVE THIS--
BLAST IT!
URRRSHH
I'M NOT GIVING UP, LOBOT. I PROMISE YOU. I'LL STILL DO EVERYTHING I CAN. I'LL FIX THIS. I'LL FIX YOU.
I'LL FIND A WAY.

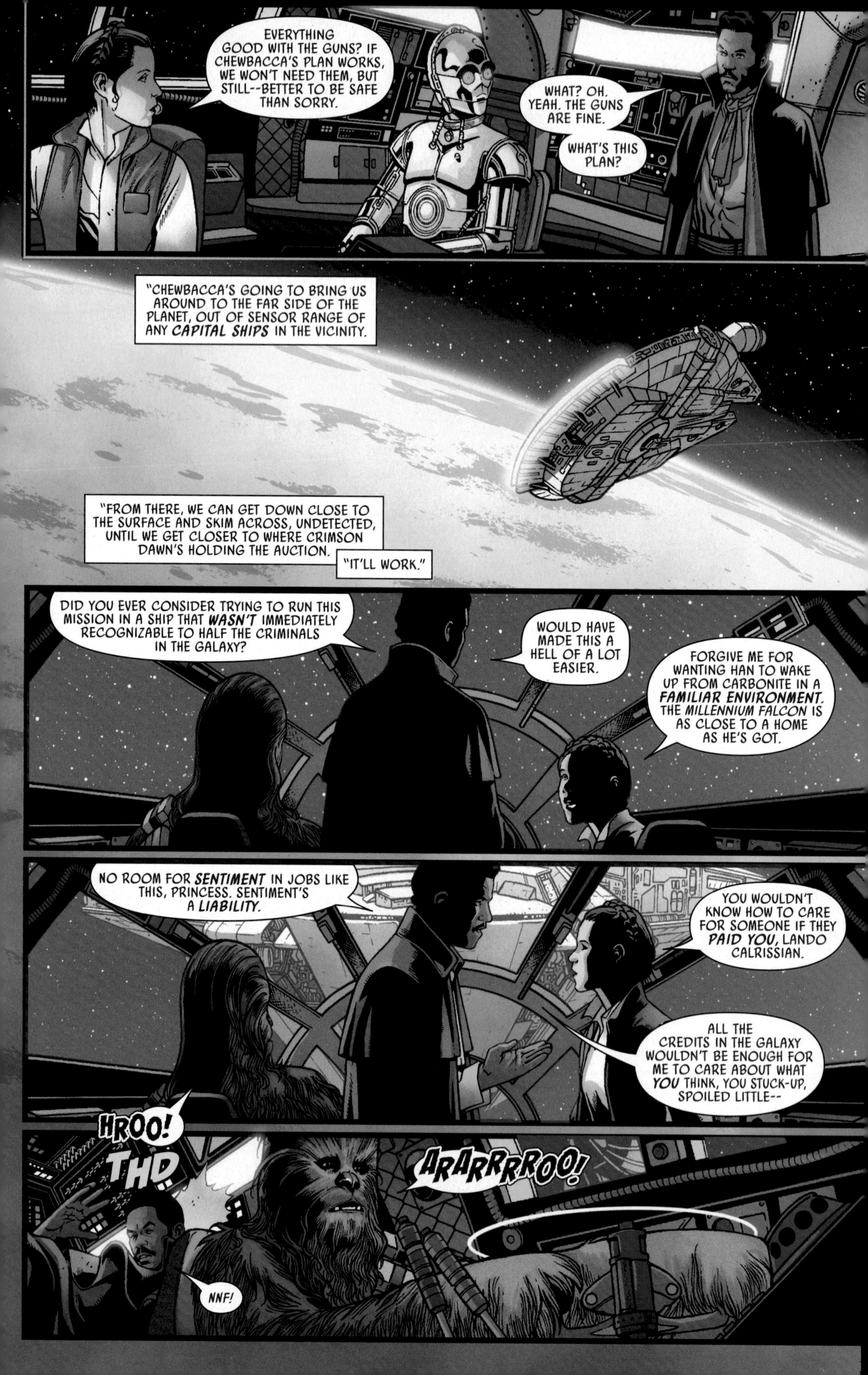
EVERYTHING GOOD WITH THE GUNS? IF CHEWBACCA'S PLAN WORKS, WE WON'T NEED THEM, BUT STILL--BETTER TO BE SAFE THAN SORRY.
WHAT? OH. YEAH. THE GUNS ARE FINE.
WHAT'S THIS PLAN?
"CHEWBACCA'S GOING TO BRING US AROUND TO THE FAR SIDE OF THE PLANET, OUT OF SENSOR RANGE OF ANY CAPITAL SHIPS IN THE VICINITY.
"FROM THERE, WE CAN GET DOWN CLOSE TO THE SURFACE AND SKIM ACROSS, UNDETECTED, UNTIL WE GET CLOSER TO WHERE CRIMSON DAWN'S HOLDING THE AUCTION.
"IT'LL WORK."
DID YOU EVER CONSIDER TRYING TO RUN THIS MISSION IN A SHIP THAT WASN'T IMMEDIATELY RECOGNIZABLE TO HALF THE CRIMINALS IN THE GALAXY?
WOULD HAVE MADE THIS A HELL OF A LOT EASIER.
FORGIVE ME FOR WANTING HAN TO WAKE UP FROM CARBONITE IN A FAMILIAR ENVIRONMENT. THE MILLENNIUM FALCON IS AS CLOSE TO A HOME AS HE'S GOT.
NO ROOM FOR SENTIMENT IN JOBS LIKE THIS, PRINCESS. SENTIMENT'S A LIABILITY.
YOU WOULDN'T KNOW HOW TO CARE FOR SOMEONE IF THEY PAID YOU, LANDO CALRISSIAN.
ALL THE CREDITS IN THE GALAXY WOULDN'T BE ENOUGH FOR ME TO CARE ABOUT WHAT YOU THINK, YOU STUCK-UP, SPOILED LITTLE--
HROO!
THD
ARARRRROO!
NNF!

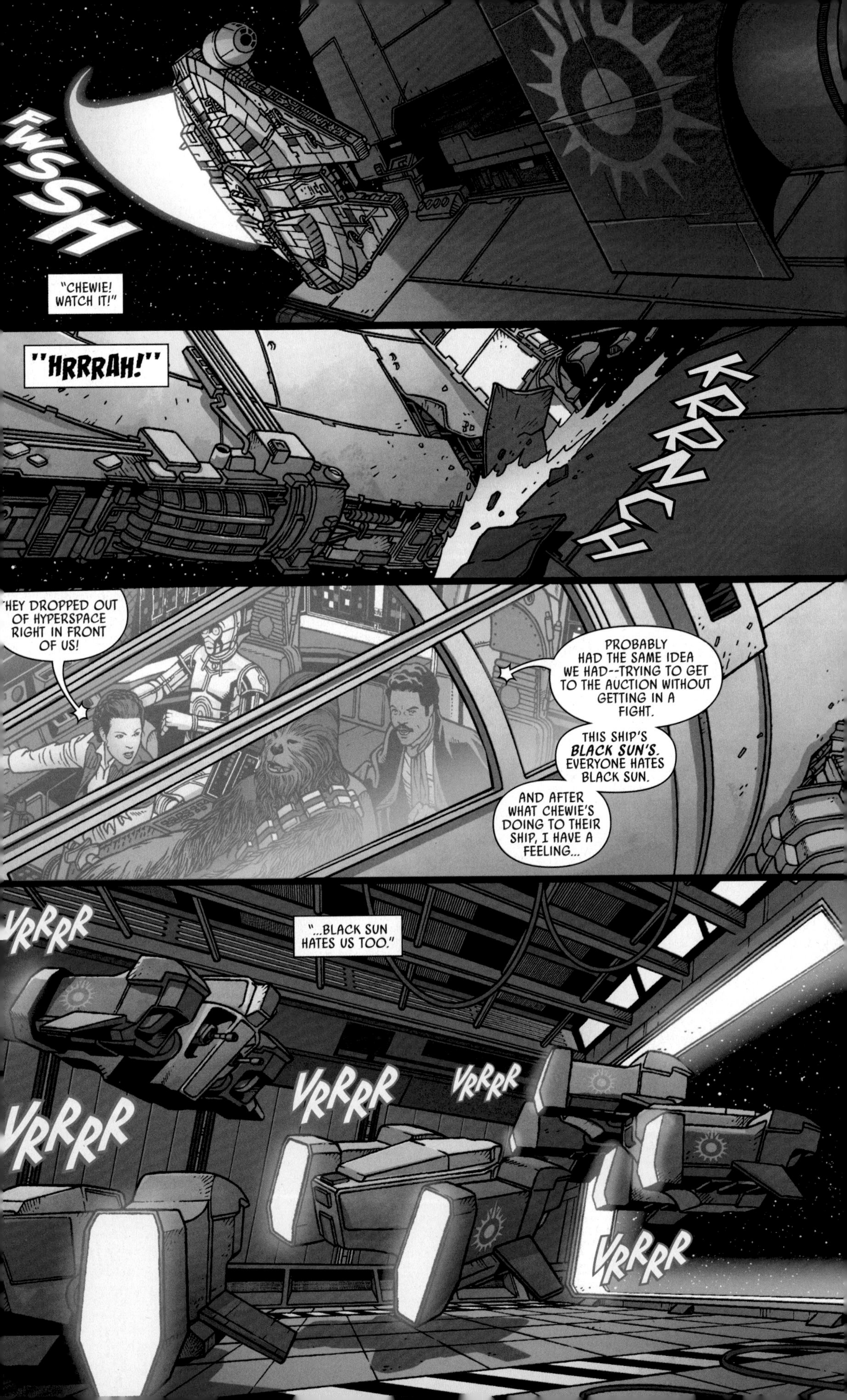
FWSSH
"CHEWIE! WATCH IT!"
"HRRRAH!"
KRRNCH
THEY DROPPED OUT OF HYPERSPACE RIGHT IN FRONT OF US!
PROBABLY HAD THE SAME IDEA WE HAD--TRYING TO GET TO THE AUCTION WITHOUT GETTING IN A FIGHT.
THIS SHIP'S BLACK SUN'S. EVERYONE HATES BLACK SUN.
AND AFTER WHAT CHEWIE'S DOING TO THEIR SHIP, I HAVE A FEELING...
VRRRR
"...BLACK SUN HATES US TOO."
VRRRR
VRRRR
VRRRR
VRRRR

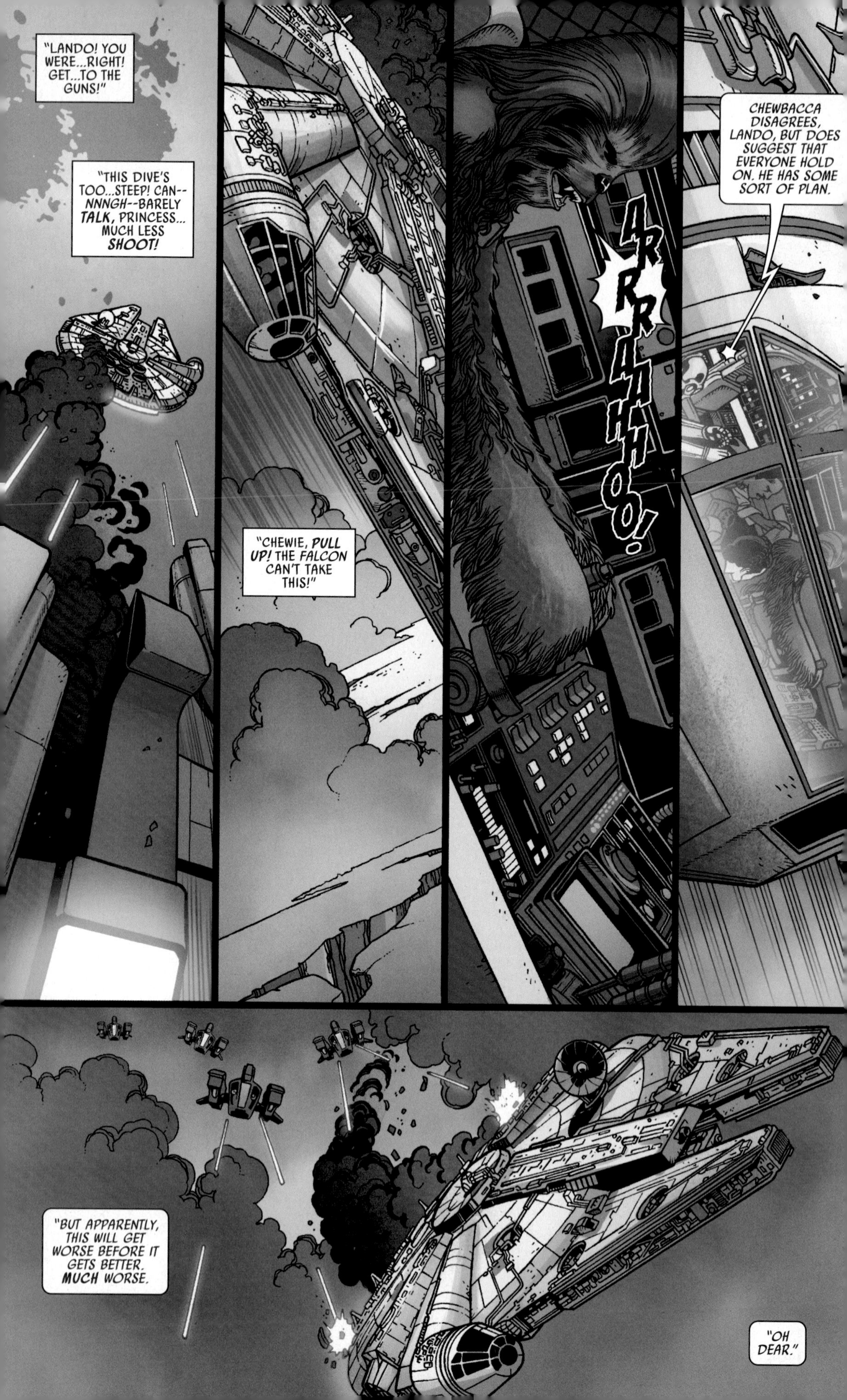
"LANDO! YOU WERE...RIGHT! GET...TO THE GUNS!"
"THIS DIVE'S TOO...STEEP! CAN--NNNGH--BARELY TALK, PRINCESS... MUCH LESS SHOOT!
"CHEWIE, PULL UP! THE FALCON CAN'T TAKE THIS!"
ARRRAAHHOO!
CHEWBACCA DISAGREES, LANDO, BUT DOES SUGGEST THAT EVERYONE HOLD ON. HE HAS SOME SORT OF PLAN.
"BUT APPARENTLY, THIS WILL GET WORSE BEFORE IT GETS BETTER. MUCH WORSE.
"OH DEAR."

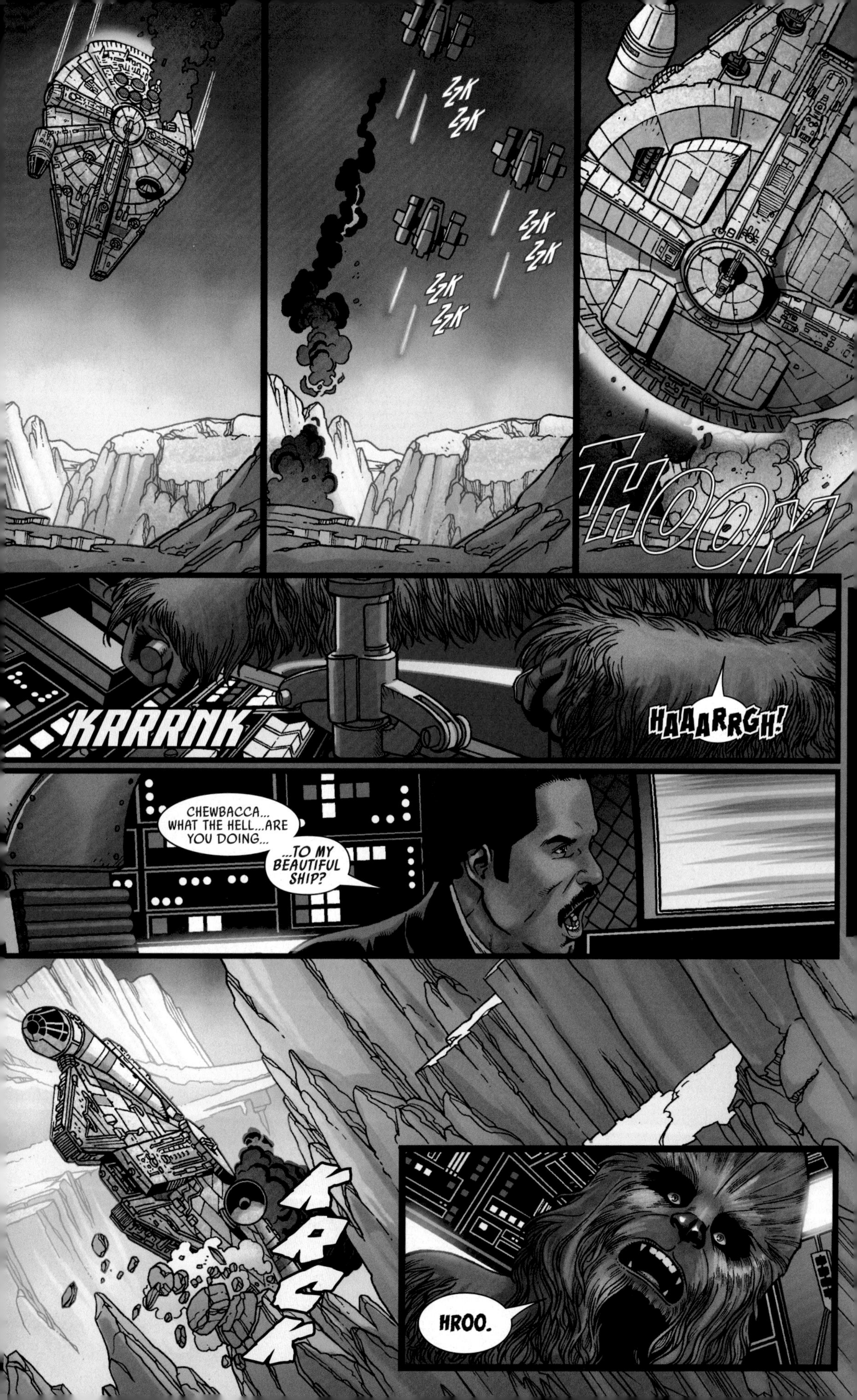
ZZK
ZZK
ZZK
ZZK
ZZK
ZZK
THOOM
KRRRNK
HAAARRGH!
CHEWBACCA... WHAT THE HELL...ARE YOU DOING...
...TO MY BEAUTIFUL SHIP?
KRACK
HROO.

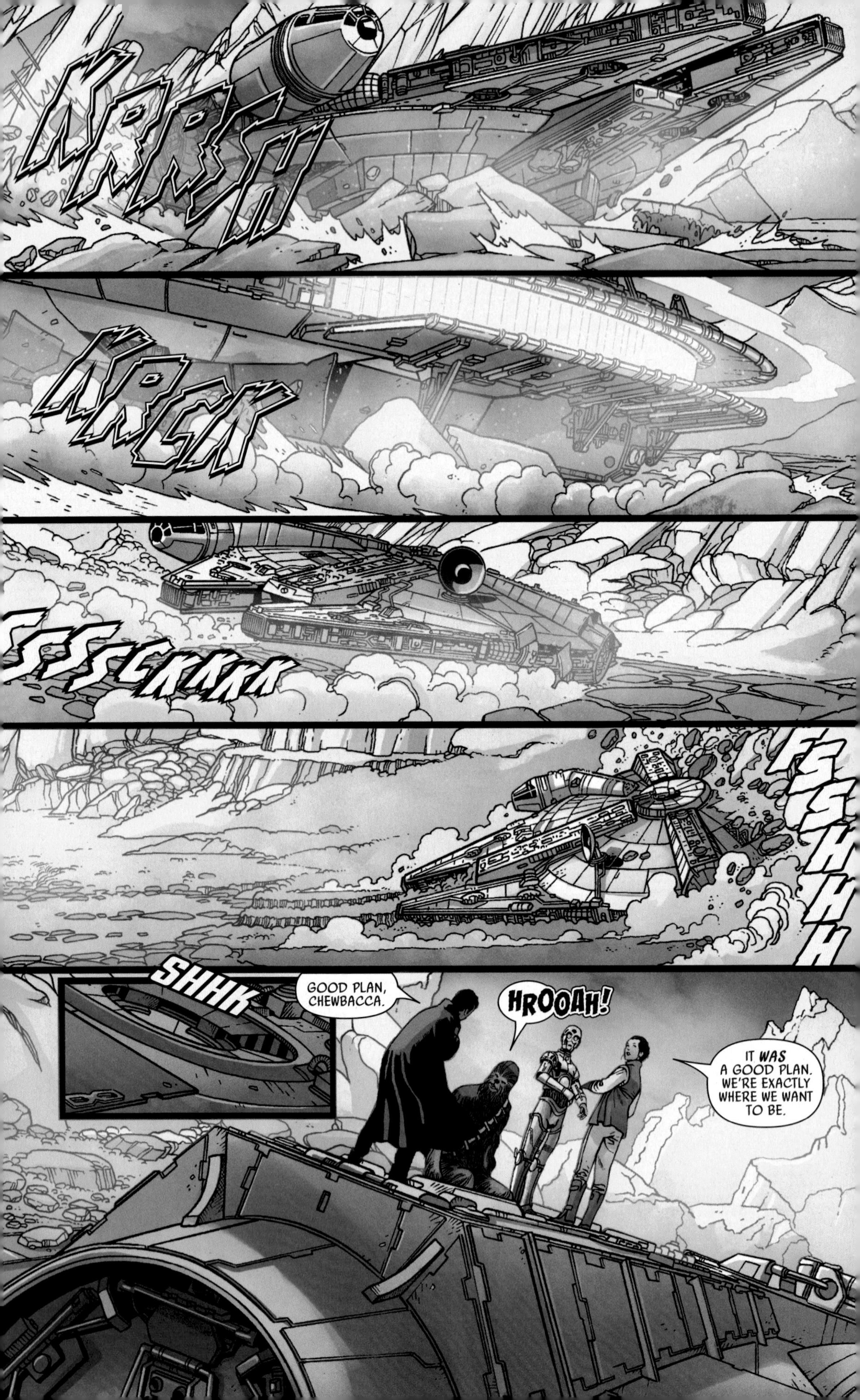
KRRSH
KRCK
SSSCKKKKK
FSSHHHH
SHHK
GOOD PLAN, CHEWBACCA.
HROOAH!
IT *WAS* A GOOD PLAN. WE'RE EXACTLY WHERE WE WANT TO BE.

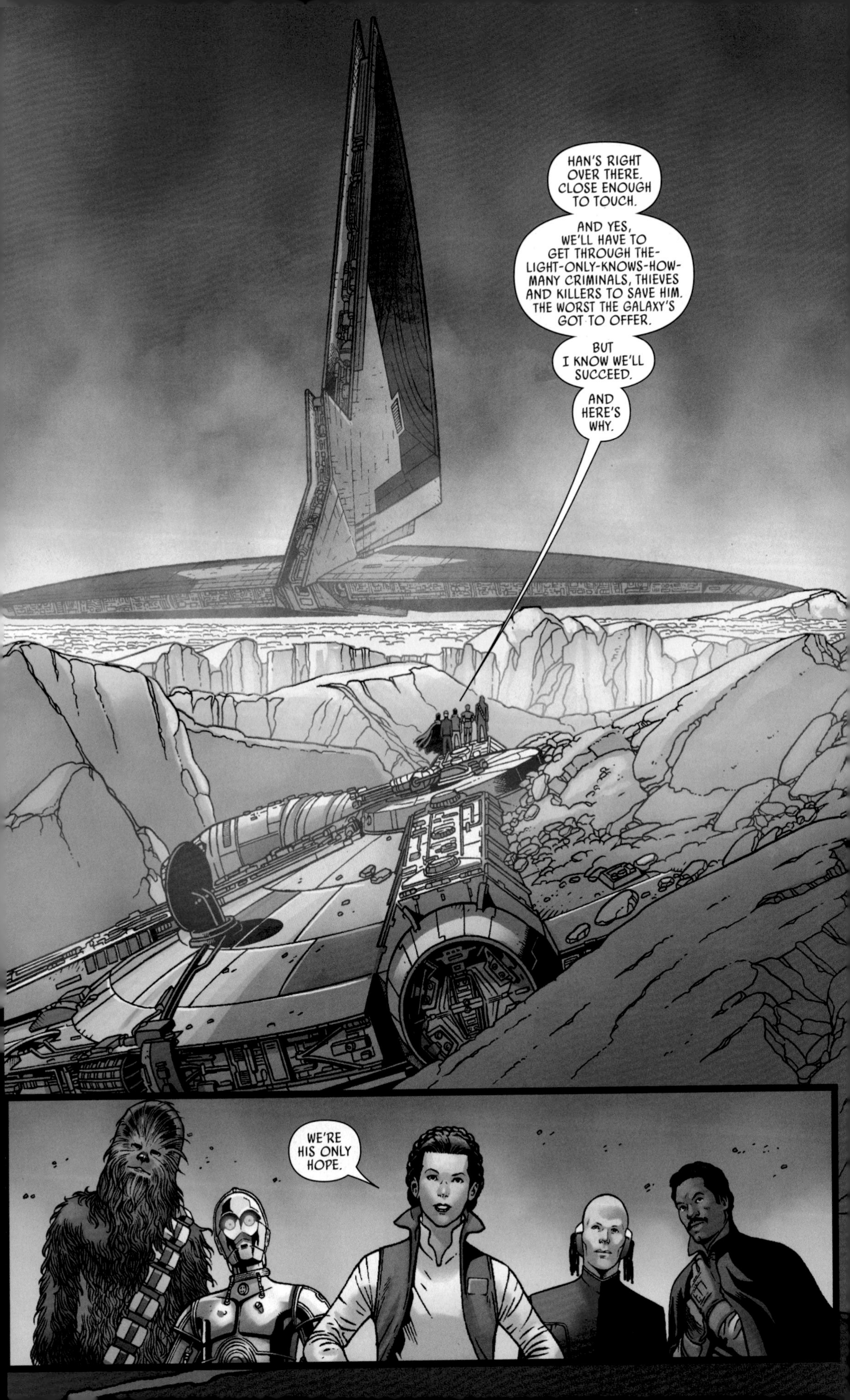
HAN'S RIGHT OVER THERE. CLOSE ENOUGH TO TOUCH.
AND YES, WE'LL HAVE TO GET THROUGH THE-LIGHT-ONLY-KNOWS-HOW-MANY CRIMINALS, THIEVES AND KILLERS TO SAVE HIM. THE WORST THE GALAXY'S GOT TO OFFER.
BUT I KNOW WE'LL SUCCEED.
AND HERE'S WHY.
WE'RE HIS ONLY HOPE.

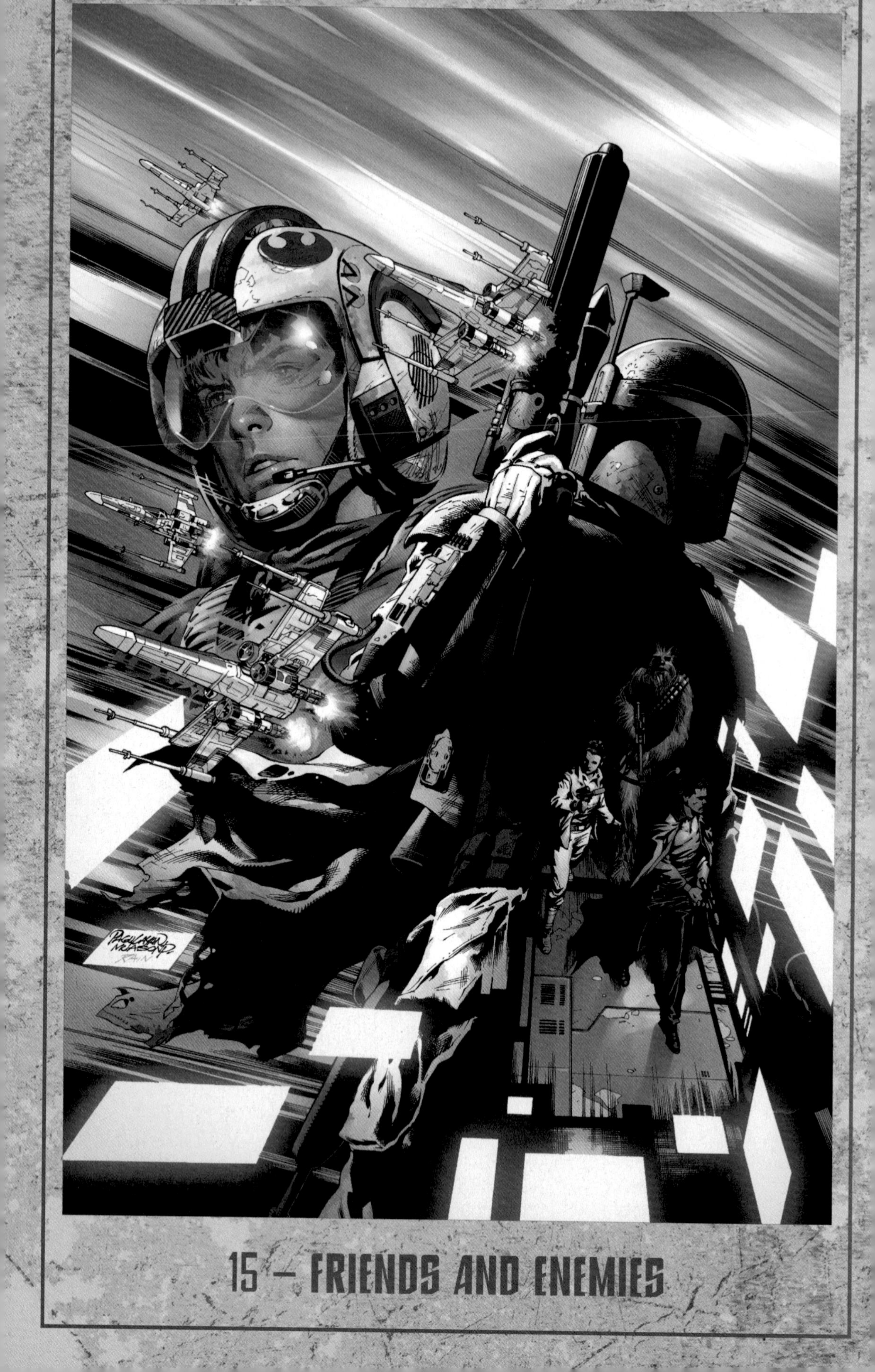

15 – FRIENDS AND ENEMIES

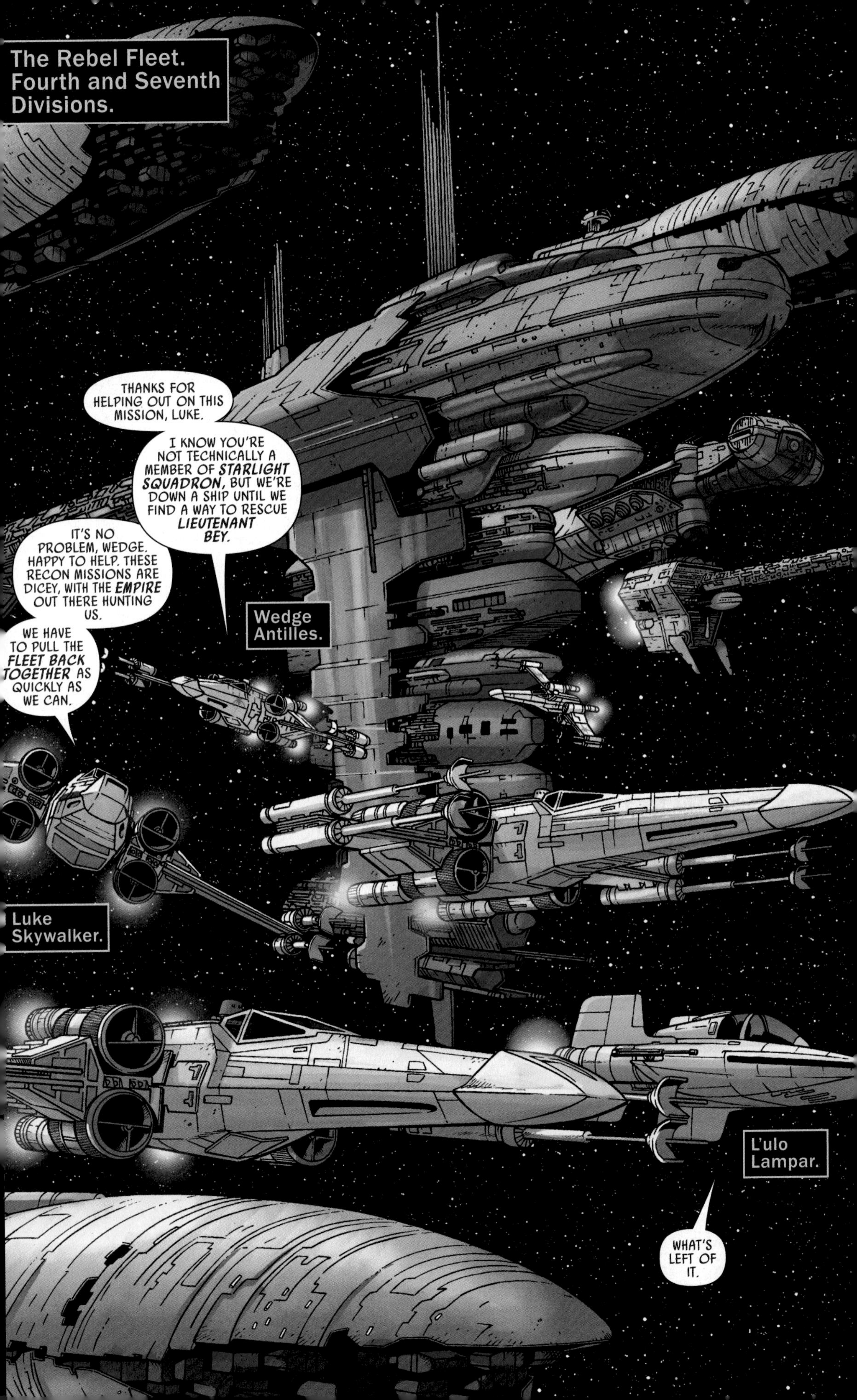
The Rebel Fleet. Fourth and Seventh Divisions.
THANKS FOR HELPING OUT ON THIS MISSION, LUKE.
I KNOW YOU'RE NOT TECHNICALLY A MEMBER OF STARLIGHT SQUADRON, BUT WE'RE DOWN A SHIP UNTIL WE FIND A WAY TO RESCUE LIEUTENANT BEY.
Wedge Antilles.
IT'S NO PROBLEM, WEDGE. HAPPY TO HELP. THESE RECON MISSIONS ARE DICEY, WITH THE EMPIRE OUT THERE HUNTING US.
WE HAVE TO PULL THE FLEET BACK TOGETHER AS QUICKLY AS WE CAN.
Luke Skywalker.
L'ulo Lampar.
WHAT'S LEFT OF IT.

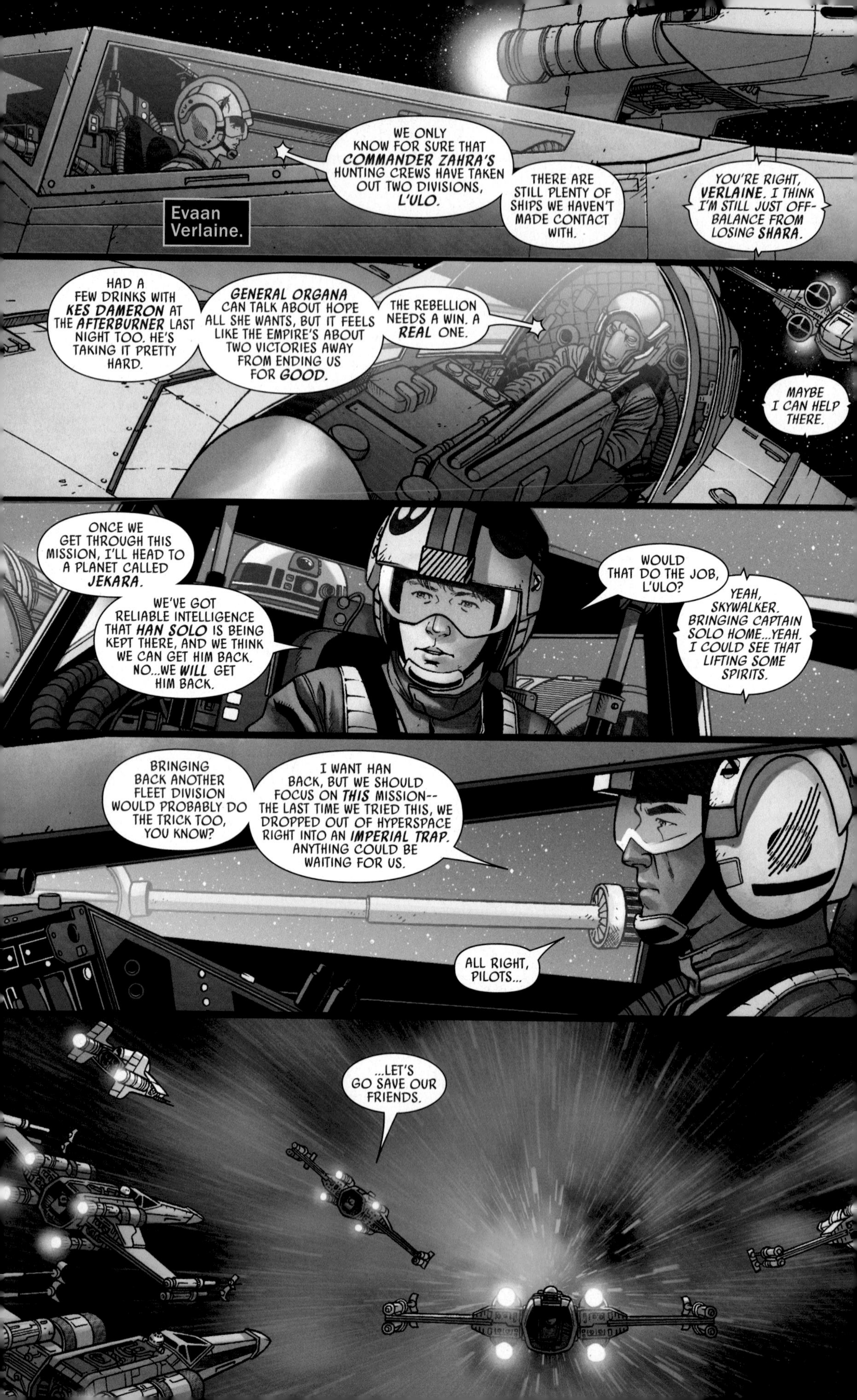

Evaan Verlaine.
WE ONLY KNOW FOR SURE THAT COMMANDER ZAHRA'S HUNTING CREWS HAVE TAKEN OUT TWO DIVISIONS, L'ULO.
THERE ARE STILL PLENTY OF SHIPS WE HAVEN'T MADE CONTACT WITH.
YOU'RE RIGHT, VERLAINE. I THINK I'M STILL JUST OFF-BALANCE FROM LOSING SHARA.
HAD A FEW DRINKS WITH KES DAMERON AT THE AFTERBURNER LAST NIGHT TOO. HE'S TAKING IT PRETTY HARD.
GENERAL ORGANA CAN TALK ABOUT HOPE ALL SHE WANTS, BUT IT FEELS LIKE THE EMPIRE'S ABOUT TWO VICTORIES AWAY FROM ENDING US FOR GOOD.
THE REBELLION NEEDS A WIN. A REAL ONE.
MAYBE I CAN HELP THERE.
ONCE WE GET THROUGH THIS MISSION, I'LL HEAD TO A PLANET CALLED JEKARA.
WE'VE GOT RELIABLE INTELLIGENCE THAT HAN SOLO IS BEING KEPT THERE, AND WE THINK WE CAN GET HIM BACK. NO...WE WILL GET HIM BACK.
WOULD THAT DO THE JOB, L'ULO?
YEAH, SKYWALKER. BRINGING CAPTAIN SOLO HOME...YEAH. I COULD SEE THAT LIFTING SOME SPIRITS.
BRINGING BACK ANOTHER FLEET DIVISION WOULD PROBABLY DO THE TRICK TOO, YOU KNOW?
I WANT HAN BACK, BUT WE SHOULD FOCUS ON THIS MISSION-- THE LAST TIME WE TRIED THIS, WE DROPPED OUT OF HYPERSPACE RIGHT INTO AN IMPERIAL TRAP. ANYTHING COULD BE WAITING FOR US.
ALL RIGHT, PILOTS...
...LET'S GO SAVE OUR FRIENDS.

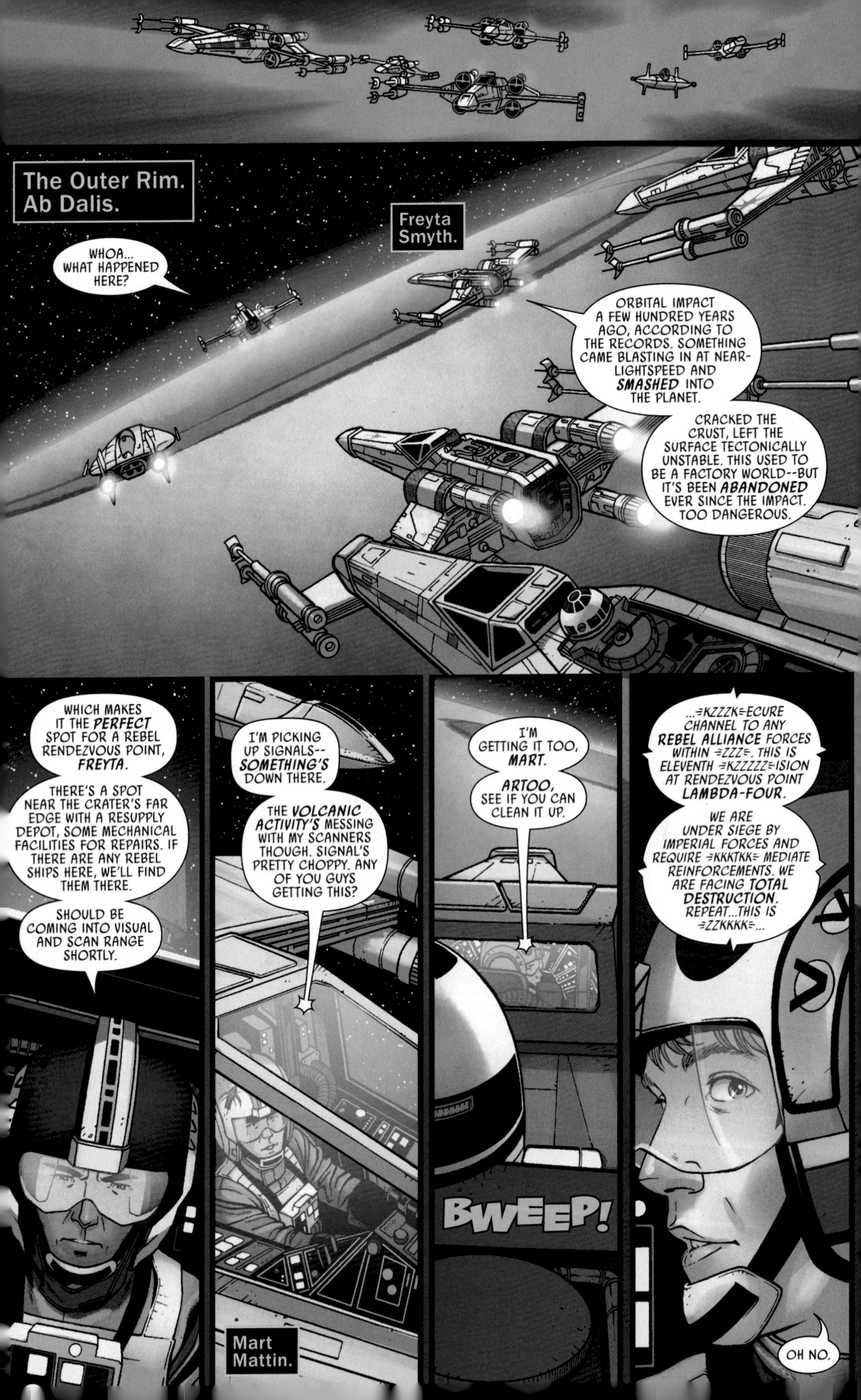
The Outer Rim.
Ab Dalis.
WHOA... WHAT HAPPENED HERE?
Freyta Smyth.
ORBITAL IMPACT A FEW HUNDRED YEARS AGO, ACCORDING TO THE RECORDS. SOMETHING CAME BLASTING IN AT NEAR-LIGHTSPEED AND SMASHED INTO THE PLANET.
CRACKED THE CRUST, LEFT THE SURFACE TECTONICALLY UNSTABLE. THIS USED TO BE A FACTORY WORLD--BUT IT'S BEEN ABANDONED EVER SINCE THE IMPACT. TOO DANGEROUS.
WHICH MAKES IT THE PERFECT SPOT FOR A REBEL RENDEZVOUS POINT, FREYTA.
THERE'S A SPOT NEAR THE CRATER'S FAR EDGE WITH A RESUPPLY DEPOT, SOME MECHANICAL FACILITIES FOR REPAIRS. IF THERE ARE ANY REBEL SHIPS HERE, WE'LL FIND THEM THERE.
SHOULD BE COMING INTO VISUAL AND SCAN RANGE SHORTLY.
I'M PICKING UP SIGNALS--SOMETHING'S DOWN THERE.
THE VOLCANIC ACTIVITY'S MESSING WITH MY SCANNERS THOUGH. SIGNAL'S PRETTY CHOPPY. ANY OF YOU GUYS GETTING THIS?
Mart Mattin.
I'M GETTING IT TOO, MART.
ARTOO, SEE IF YOU CAN CLEAN IT UP.
BWEEP!
...=KZZZK=ECURE CHANNEL TO ANY REBEL ALLIANCE FORCES WITHIN =ZZZ=. THIS IS ELEVENTH =KZZZZZ=ISION AT RENDEZVOUS POINT LAMBDA-FOUR.
WE ARE UNDER SIEGE BY IMPERIAL FORCES AND REQUIRE =KKKTKK= MEDIATE REINFORCEMENTS. WE ARE FACING TOTAL DESTRUCTION. REPEAT...THIS IS =ZZKKKK=...
OH NO.

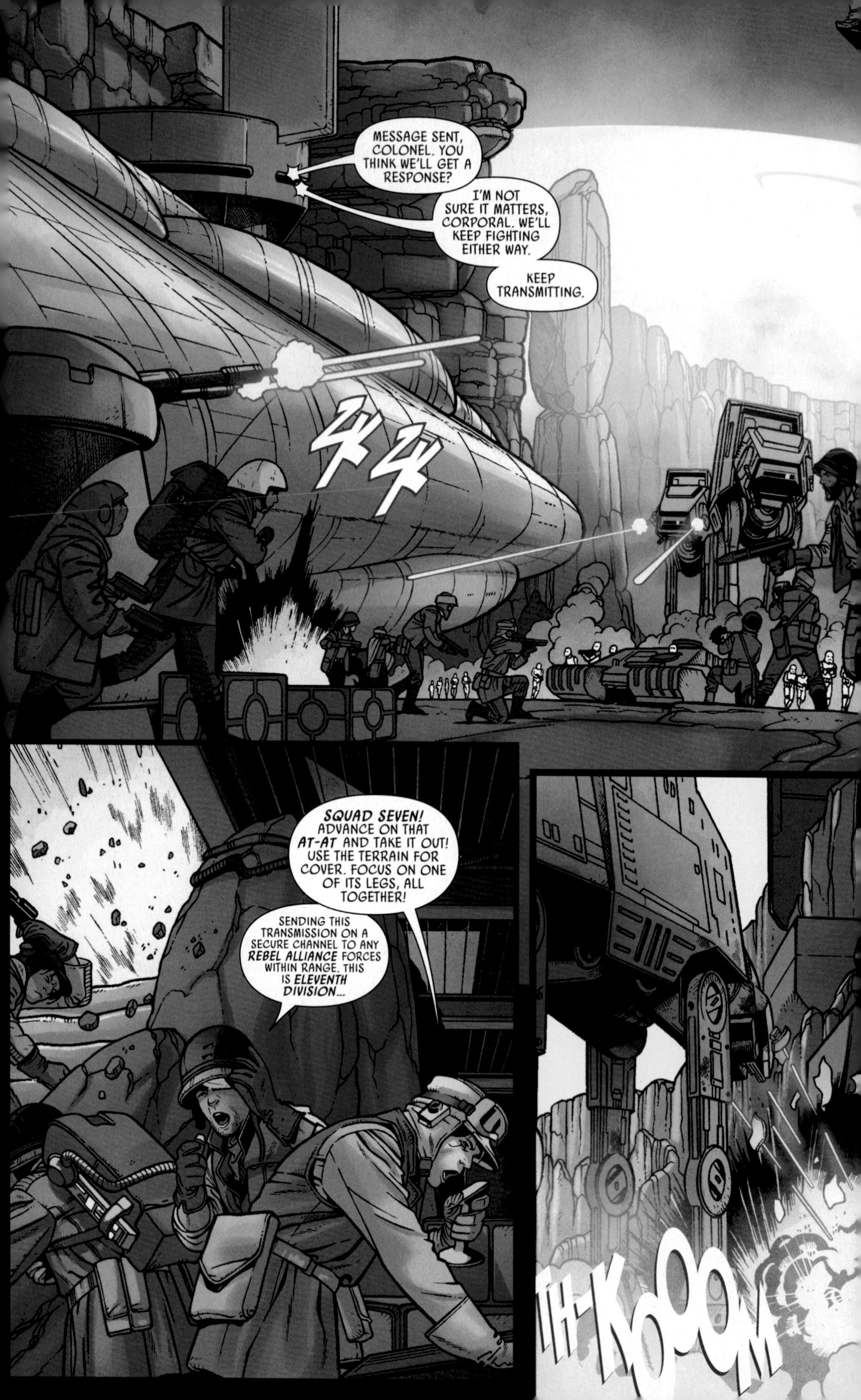

MESSAGE SENT, COLONEL. YOU THINK WE'LL GET A RESPONSE?
I'M NOT SURE IT MATTERS, CORPORAL. WE'LL KEEP FIGHTING EITHER WAY.
KEEP TRANSMITTING.
SQUAD SEVEN! ADVANCE ON THAT AT-AT AND TAKE IT OUT! USE THE TERRAIN FOR COVER. FOCUS ON ONE OF ITS LEGS, ALL TOGETHER!
SENDING THIS TRANSMISSION ON A SECURE CHANNEL TO ANY REBEL ALLIANCE FORCES WITHIN RANGE. THIS IS ELEVENTH DIVISION...
TH-KOOOOM

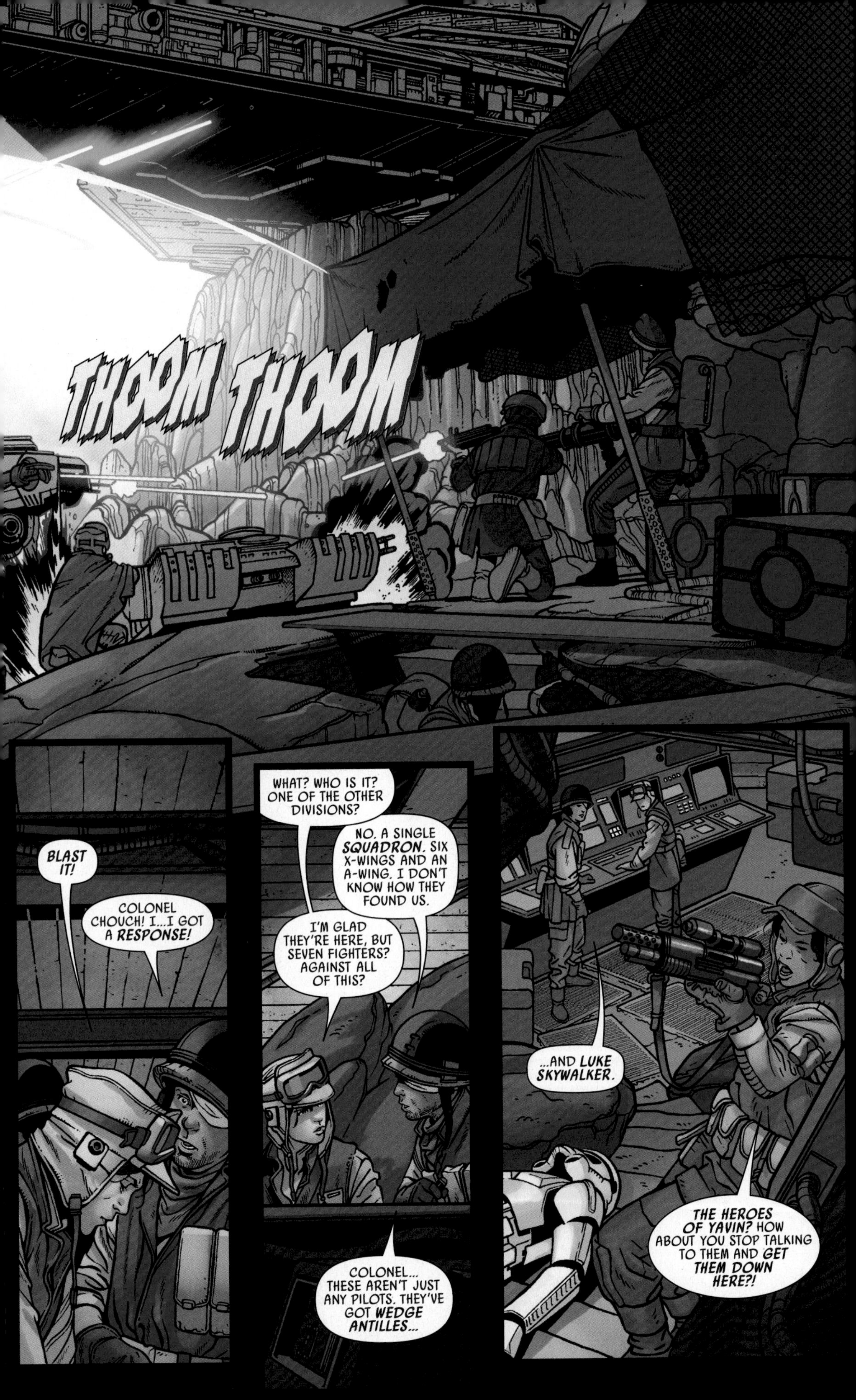
THOOM THOOM
BLAST IT!
COLONEL CHOUCH! I...I GOT A RESPONSE!
WHAT? WHO IS IT? ONE OF THE OTHER DIVISIONS?
NO. A SINGLE SQUADRON. SIX X-WINGS AND AN A-WING. I DON'T KNOW HOW THEY FOUND US.
I'M GLAD THEY'RE HERE, BUT SEVEN FIGHTERS? AGAINST ALL OF THIS?
COLONEL... THESE AREN'T JUST ANY PILOTS. THEY'VE GOT WEDGE ANTILLES...
...AND LUKE SKYWALKER.
THE HEROES OF YAVIN? HOW ABOUT YOU STOP TALKING TO THEM AND GET THEM DOWN HERE?!

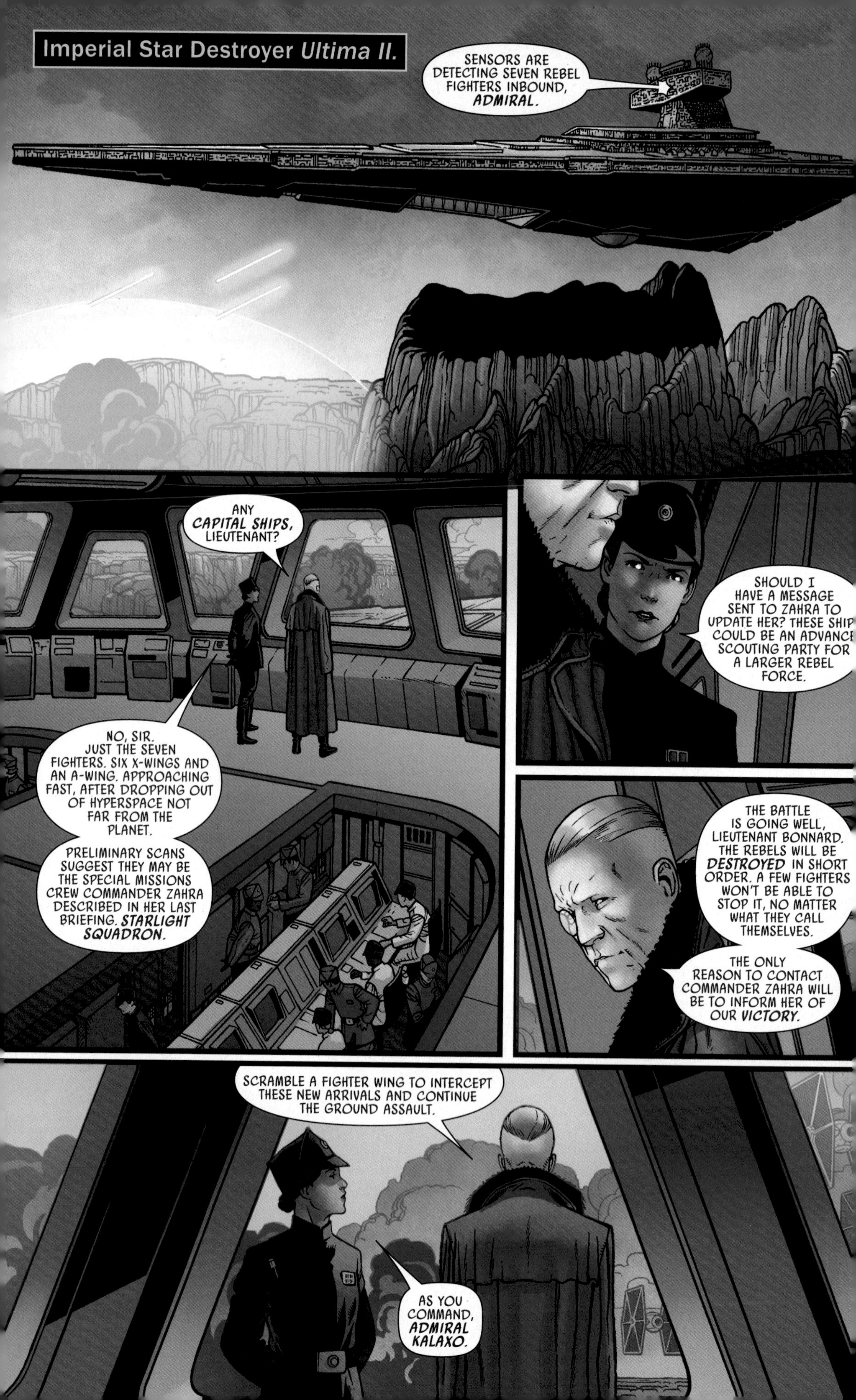
Imperial Star Destroyer *Ultima II.*
SENSORS ARE DETECTING SEVEN REBEL FIGHTERS INBOUND, ADMIRAL.
ANY CAPITAL SHIPS, LIEUTENANT?
NO, SIR. JUST THE SEVEN FIGHTERS. SIX X-WINGS AND AN A-WING. APPROACHING FAST, AFTER DROPPING OUT OF HYPERSPACE NOT FAR FROM THE PLANET.
PRELIMINARY SCANS SUGGEST THEY MAY BE THE SPECIAL MISSIONS CREW COMMANDER ZAHRA DESCRIBED IN HER LAST BRIEFING. STARLIGHT SQUADRON.
SHOULD I HAVE A MESSAGE SENT TO ZAHRA TO UPDATE HER? THESE SHIP COULD BE AN ADVANC SCOUTING PARTY FOR A LARGER REBEL FORCE.
THE BATTLE IS GOING WELL, LIEUTENANT BONNARD. THE REBELS WILL BE DESTROYED IN SHORT ORDER. A FEW FIGHTERS WON'T BE ABLE TO STOP IT, NO MATTER WHAT THEY CALL THEMSELVES.
THE ONLY REASON TO CONTACT COMMANDER ZAHRA WILL BE TO INFORM HER OF OUR VICTORY.
SCRAMBLE A FIGHTER WING TO INTERCEPT THESE NEW ARRIVALS AND CONTINUE THE GROUND ASSAULT.
AS YOU COMMAND, ADMIRAL KALAXO.

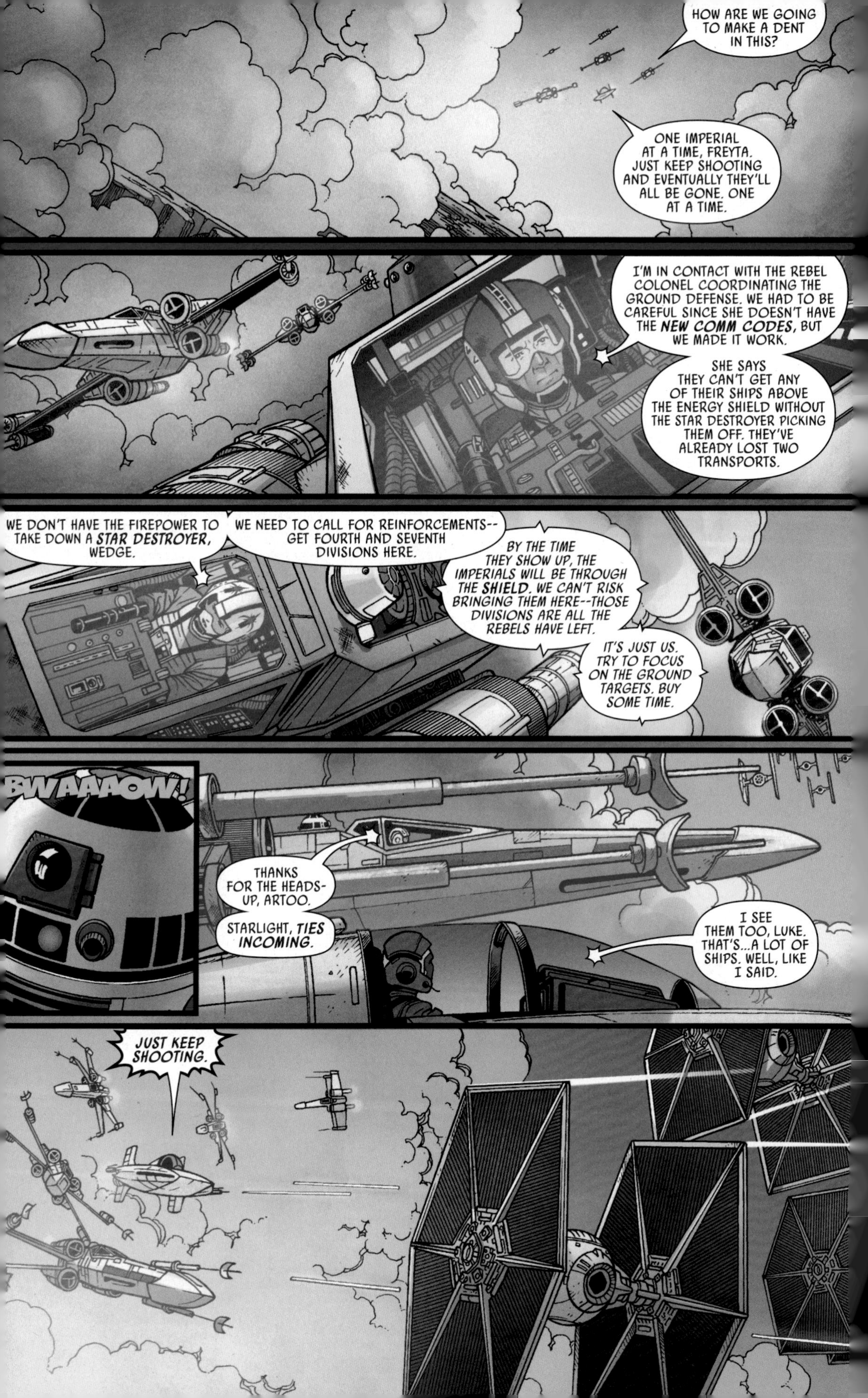
HOW ARE WE GOING TO MAKE A DENT IN THIS?
ONE IMPERIAL AT A TIME, FREYTA. JUST KEEP SHOOTING AND EVENTUALLY THEY'LL ALL BE GONE. ONE AT A TIME.
I'M IN CONTACT WITH THE REBEL COLONEL COORDINATING THE GROUND DEFENSE. WE HAD TO BE CAREFUL SINCE SHE DOESN'T HAVE THE NEW COMM CODES, BUT WE MADE IT WORK.
SHE SAYS THEY CAN'T GET ANY OF THEIR SHIPS ABOVE THE ENERGY SHIELD WITHOUT THE STAR DESTROYER PICKING THEM OFF. THEY'VE ALREADY LOST TWO TRANSPORTS.
WE DON'T HAVE THE FIREPOWER TO TAKE DOWN A STAR DESTROYER, WEDGE.
WE NEED TO CALL FOR REINFORCEMENTS-- GET FOURTH AND SEVENTH DIVISIONS HERE.
BY THE TIME THEY SHOW UP, THE IMPERIALS WILL BE THROUGH THE SHIELD. WE CAN'T RISK BRINGING THEM HERE--THOSE DIVISIONS ARE ALL THE REBELS HAVE LEFT.
IT'S JUST US. TRY TO FOCUS ON THE GROUND TARGETS. BUY SOME TIME.
BWAAAOW!
THANKS FOR THE HEADS-UP, ARTOO.
STARLIGHT, TIES INCOMING.
I SEE THEM TOO, LUKE. THAT'S...A LOT OF SHIPS. WELL, LIKE I SAID.
JUST KEEP SHOOTING.

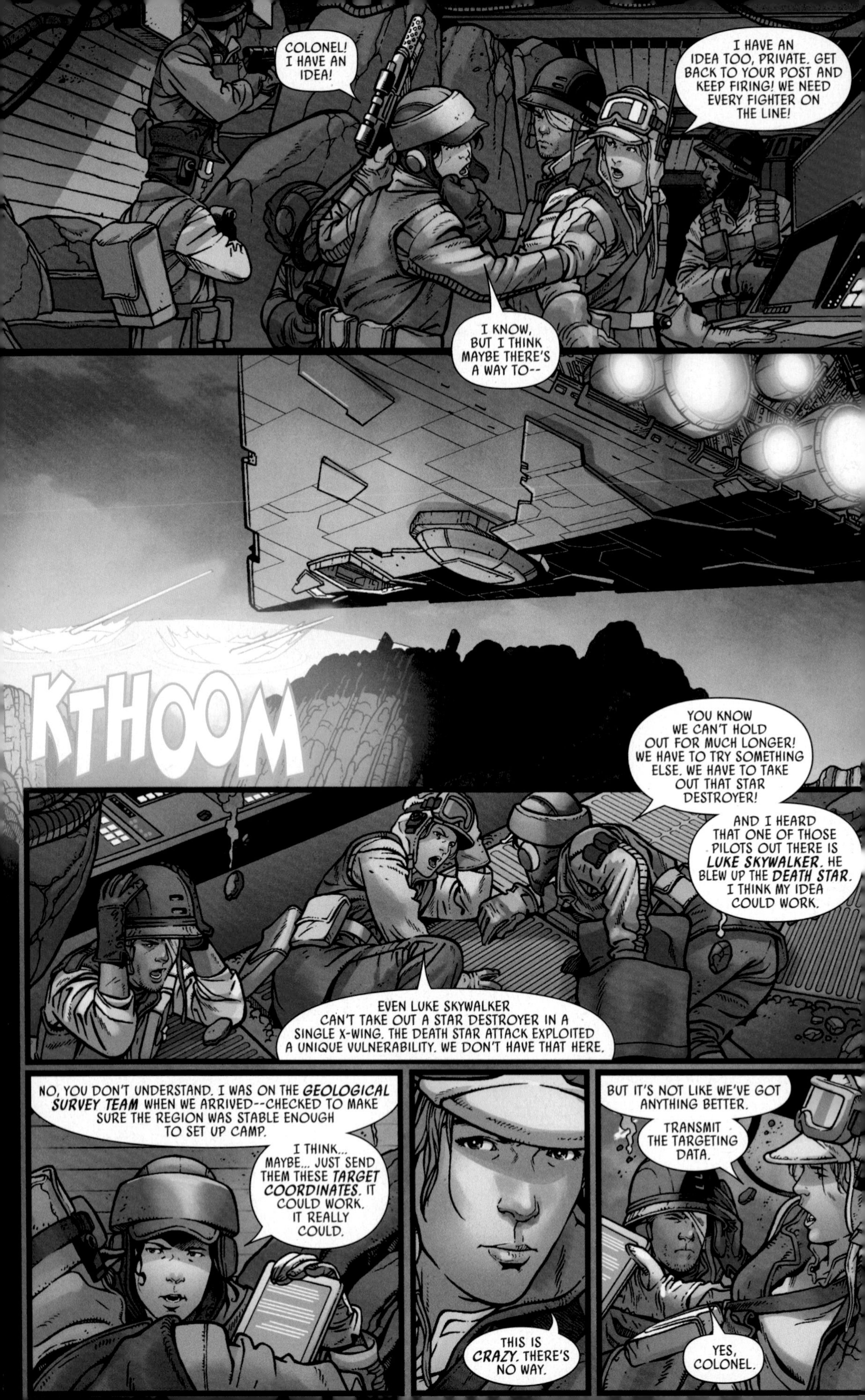
COLONEL! I HAVE AN IDEA!
I HAVE AN IDEA TOO, PRIVATE. GET BACK TO YOUR POST AND KEEP FIRING! WE NEED EVERY FIGHTER ON THE LINE!
I KNOW, BUT I THINK MAYBE THERE'S A WAY TO--
KTHOOM
YOU KNOW WE CAN'T HOLD OUT FOR MUCH LONGER! WE HAVE TO TRY SOMETHING ELSE. WE HAVE TO TAKE OUT THAT STAR DESTROYER!
AND I HEARD THAT ONE OF THOSE PILOTS OUT THERE IS LUKE SKYWALKER. HE BLEW UP THE DEATH STAR. I THINK MY IDEA COULD WORK.
EVEN LUKE SKYWALKER CAN'T TAKE OUT A STAR DESTROYER IN A SINGLE X-WING. THE DEATH STAR ATTACK EXPLOITED A UNIQUE VULNERABILITY. WE DON'T HAVE THAT HERE.
NO, YOU DON'T UNDERSTAND. I WAS ON THE GEOLOGICAL SURVEY TEAM WHEN WE ARRIVED--CHECKED TO MAKE SURE THE REGION WAS STABLE ENOUGH TO SET UP CAMP.
I THINK... MAYBE... JUST SEND THEM THESE TARGET COORDINATES. IT COULD WORK. IT REALLY COULD.
THIS IS CRAZY. THERE'S NO WAY.
BUT IT'S NOT LIKE WE'VE GOT ANYTHING BETTER.
TRANSMIT THE TARGETING DATA.
YES, COLONEL.

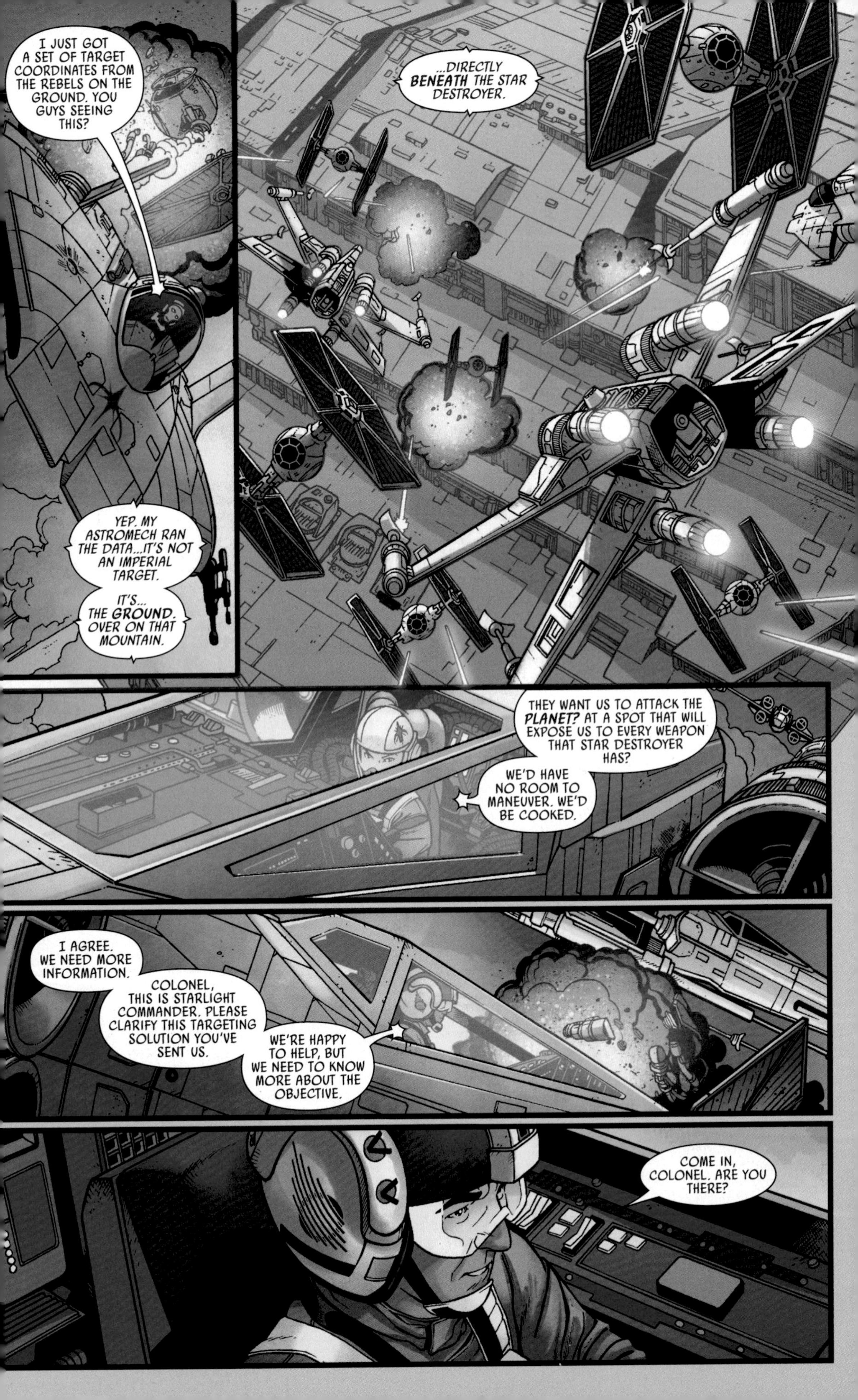
I JUST GOT A SET OF TARGET COORDINATES FROM THE REBELS ON THE GROUND. YOU GUYS SEEING THIS?
...DIRECTLY BENEATH THE STAR DESTROYER.
YEP. MY ASTROMECH RAN THE DATA...IT'S NOT AN IMPERIAL TARGET.
IT'S... THE GROUND. OVER ON THAT MOUNTAIN.
THEY WANT US TO ATTACK THE PLANET? AT A SPOT THAT WILL EXPOSE US TO EVERY WEAPON THAT STAR DESTROYER HAS?
WE'D HAVE NO ROOM TO MANEUVER. WE'D BE COOKED.
I AGREE. WE NEED MORE INFORMATION.
COLONEL, THIS IS STARLIGHT COMMANDER. PLEASE CLARIFY THIS TARGETING SOLUTION YOU'VE SENT US.
WE'RE HAPPY TO HELP, BUT WE NEED TO KNOW MORE ABOUT THE OBJECTIVE.
COME IN, COLONEL. ARE YOU THERE?

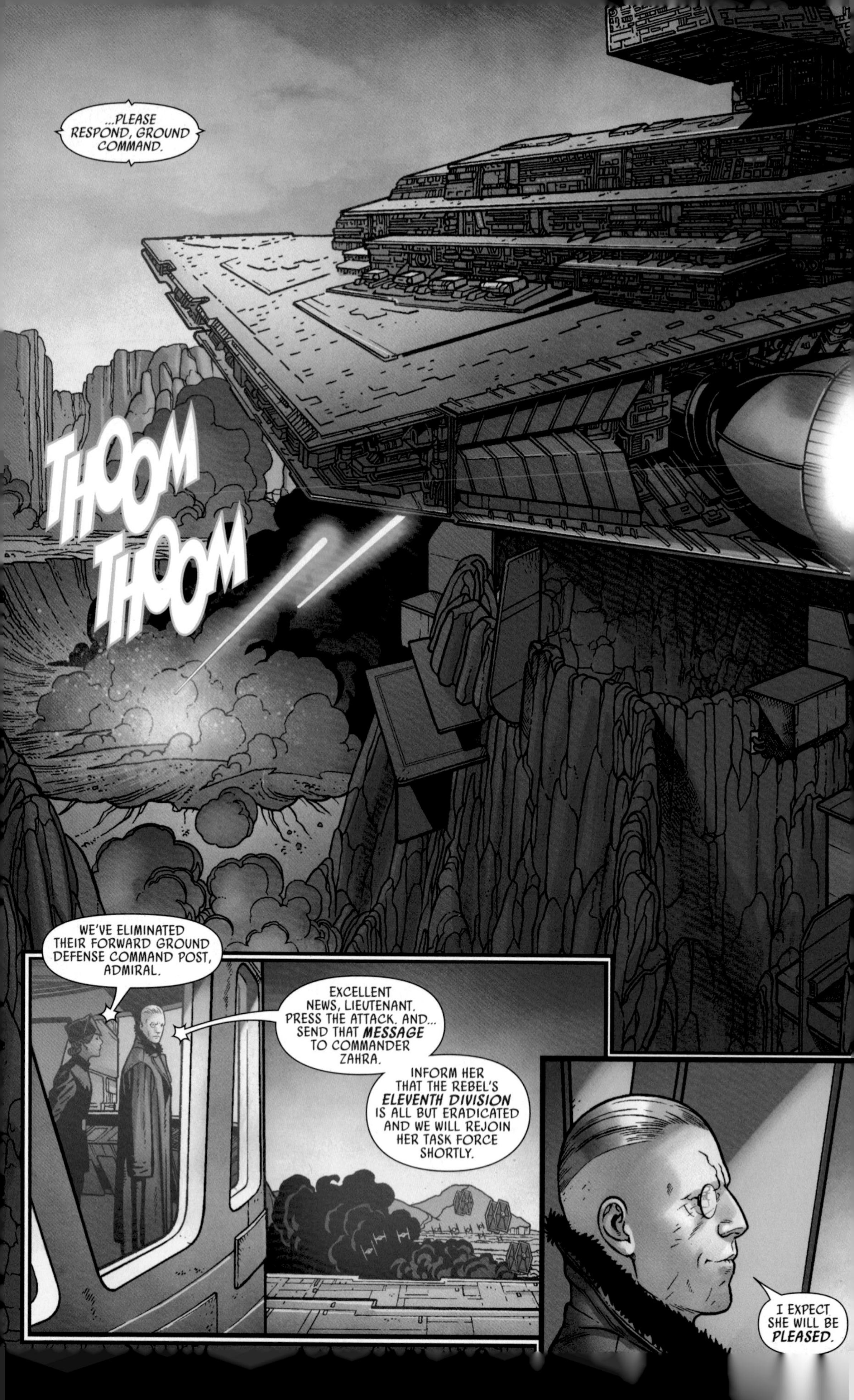

...PLEASE RESPOND, GROUND COMMAND.
THOOM
THOOM
WE'VE ELIMINATED THEIR FORWARD GROUND DEFENSE COMMAND POST, ADMIRAL.
EXCELLENT NEWS, LIEUTENANT. PRESS THE ATTACK. AND... SEND THAT MESSAGE TO COMMANDER ZAHRA.
INFORM HER THAT THE REBEL'S ELEVENTH DIVISION IS ALL BUT ERADICATED AND WE WILL REJOIN HER TASK FORCE SHORTLY.
I EXPECT SHE WILL BE PLEASED.

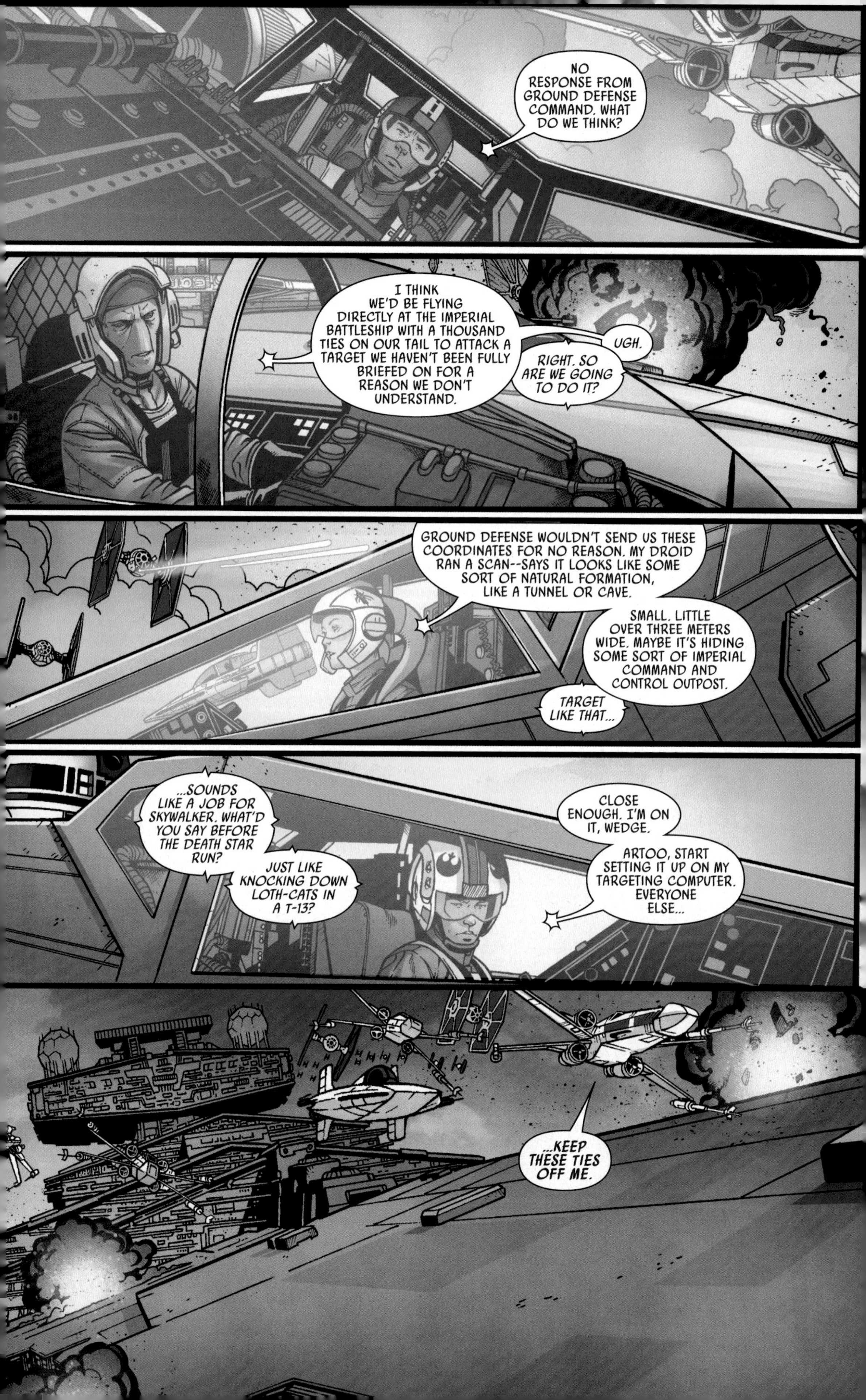
NO RESPONSE FROM GROUND DEFENSE COMMAND. WHAT DO WE THINK?
I THINK WE'D BE FLYING DIRECTLY AT THE IMPERIAL BATTLESHIP WITH A THOUSAND TIES ON OUR TAIL TO ATTACK A TARGET WE HAVEN'T BEEN FULLY BRIEFED ON FOR A REASON WE DON'T UNDERSTAND.
UGH.
RIGHT. SO ARE WE GOING TO DO IT?
GROUND DEFENSE WOULDN'T SEND US THESE COORDINATES FOR NO REASON. MY DROID RAN A SCAN--SAYS IT LOOKS LIKE SOME SORT OF NATURAL FORMATION, LIKE A TUNNEL OR CAVE.
SMALL. LITTLE OVER THREE METERS WIDE. MAYBE IT'S HIDING SOME SORT OF IMPERIAL COMMAND AND CONTROL OUTPOST.
TARGET LIKE THAT...
...SOUNDS LIKE A JOB FOR SKYWALKER. WHAT'D YOU SAY BEFORE THE DEATH STAR RUN?
JUST LIKE KNOCKING DOWN LOTH-CATS IN A T-13?
CLOSE ENOUGH. I'M ON IT, WEDGE.
ARTOO, START SETTING IT UP ON MY TARGETING COMPUTER. EVERYONE ELSE...
...KEEP THESE TIES OFF ME.

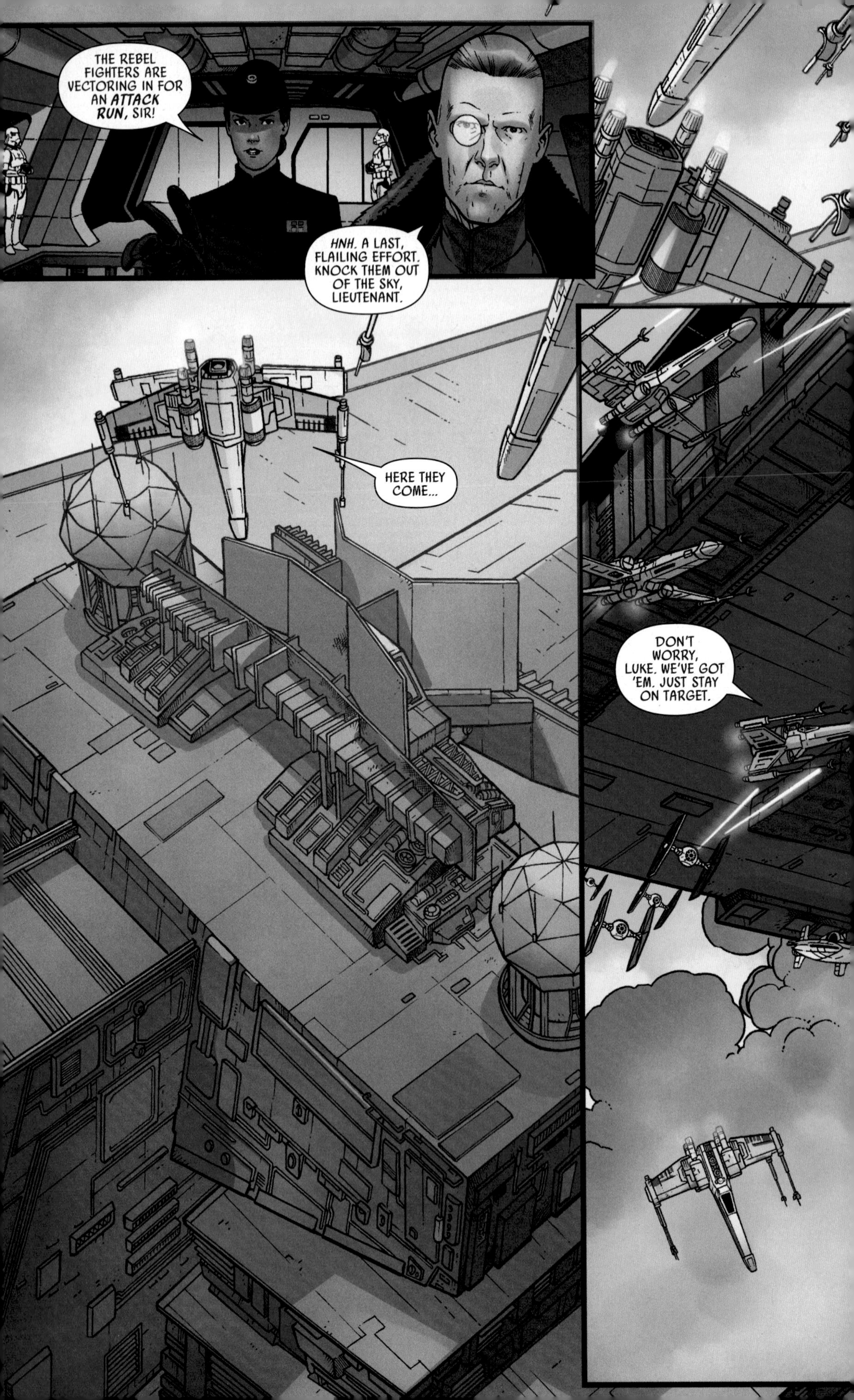
THE REBEL FIGHTERS ARE VECTORING IN FOR AN ATTACK RUN, SIR!
HNH. A LAST, FLAILING EFFORT. KNOCK THEM OUT OF THE SKY, LIEUTENANT.
HERE THEY COME...
DON'T WORRY, LUKE. WE'VE GOT 'EM. JUST STAY ON TARGET.

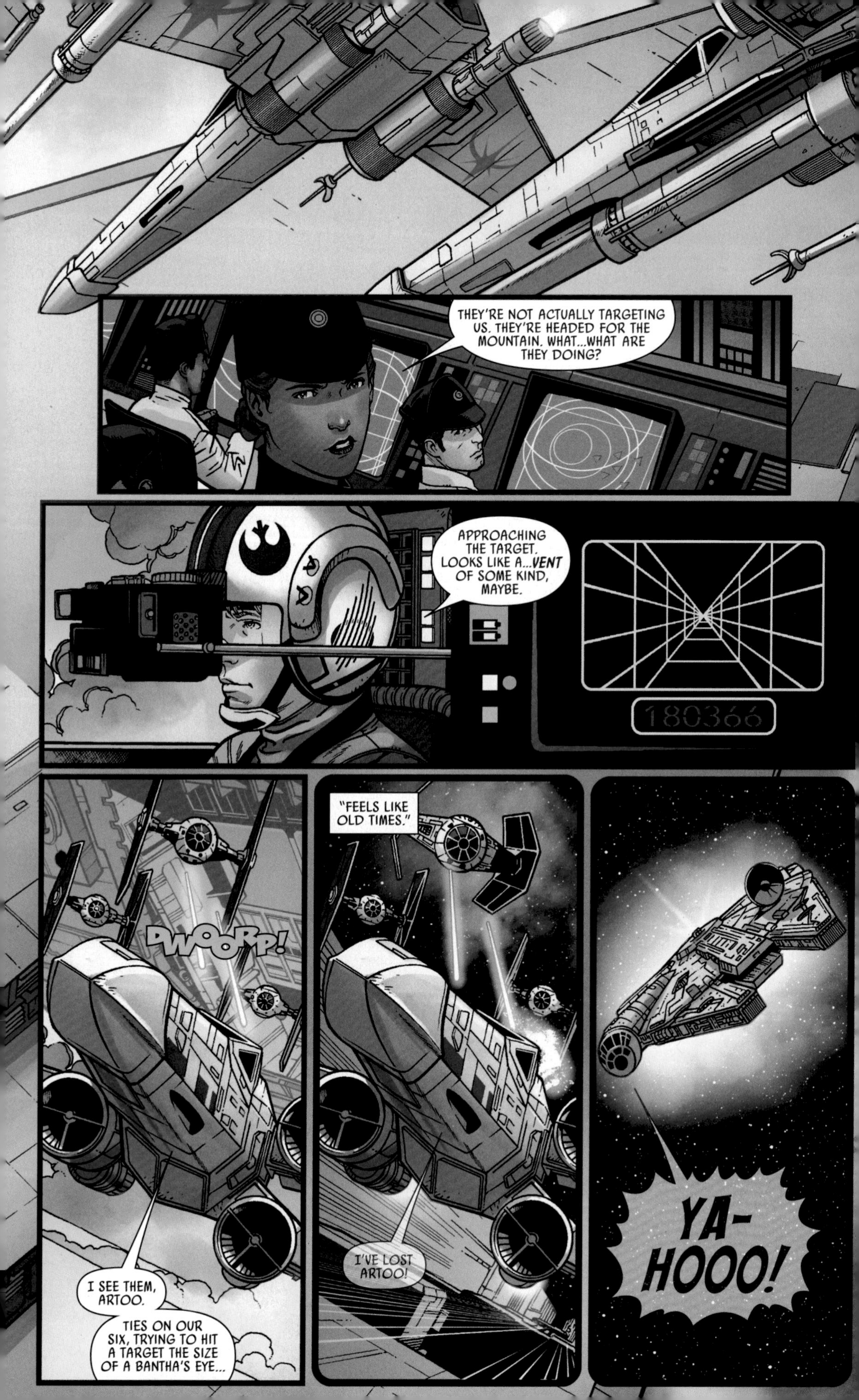
THEY'RE NOT ACTUALLY TARGETING US. THEY'RE HEADED FOR THE MOUNTAIN. WHAT...WHAT ARE THEY DOING?
APPROACHING THE TARGET. LOOKS LIKE A...VENT OF SOME KIND, MAYBE.
180366
DWOORP!
I SEE THEM, ARTOO.
TIES ON OUR SIX, TRYING TO HIT A TARGET THE SIZE OF A BANTHA'S EYE...
"FEELS LIKE OLD TIMES."
I'VE LOST ARTOO!
YA-HOOO!

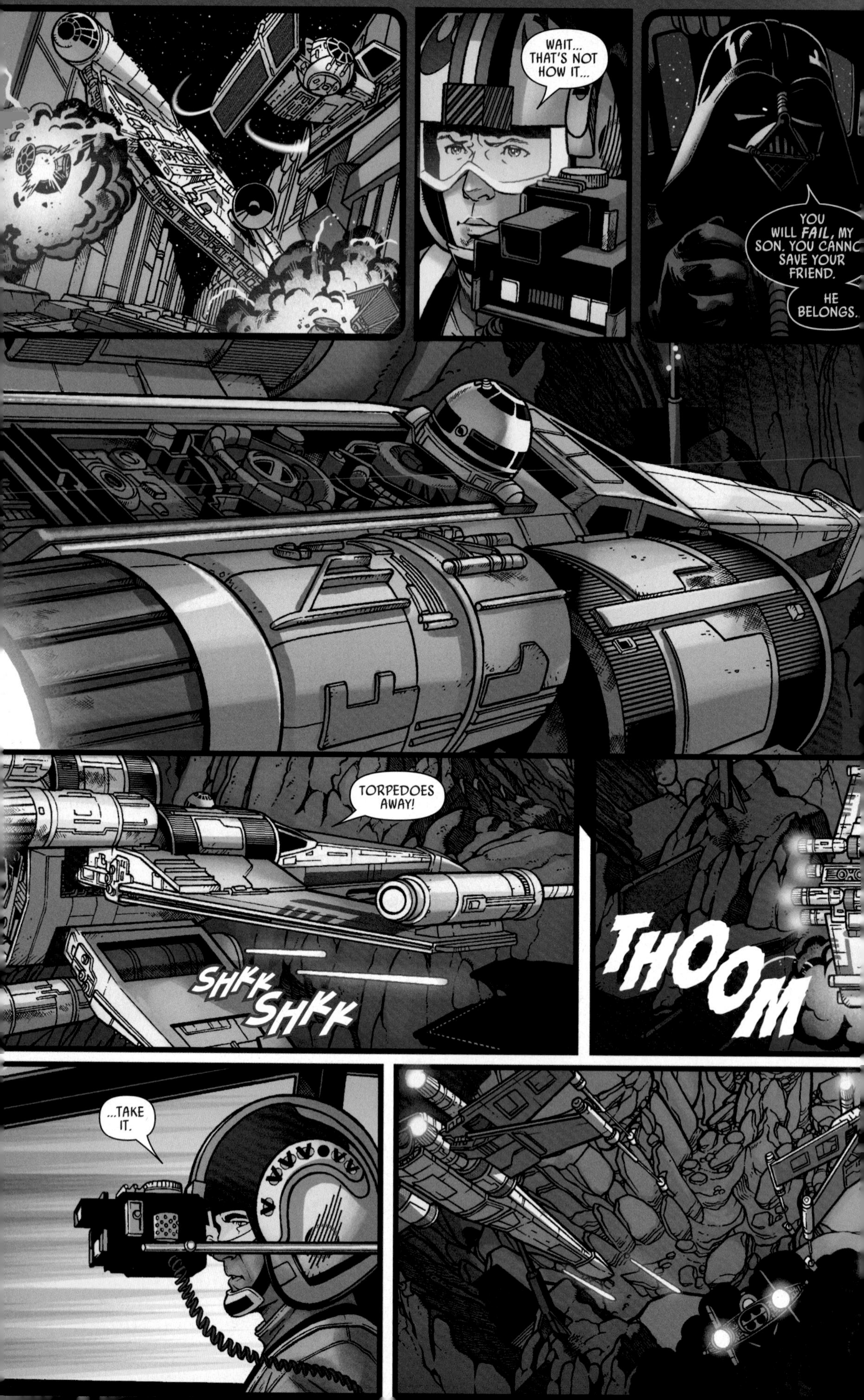
WAIT... THAT'S NOT HOW IT...
YOU WILL FAIL, MY SON. YOU CANNC SAVE YOUR FRIEND.
HE BELONGS...
TORPEDOES AWAY!
SHKK SHKK
THOOM
...TAKE IT.

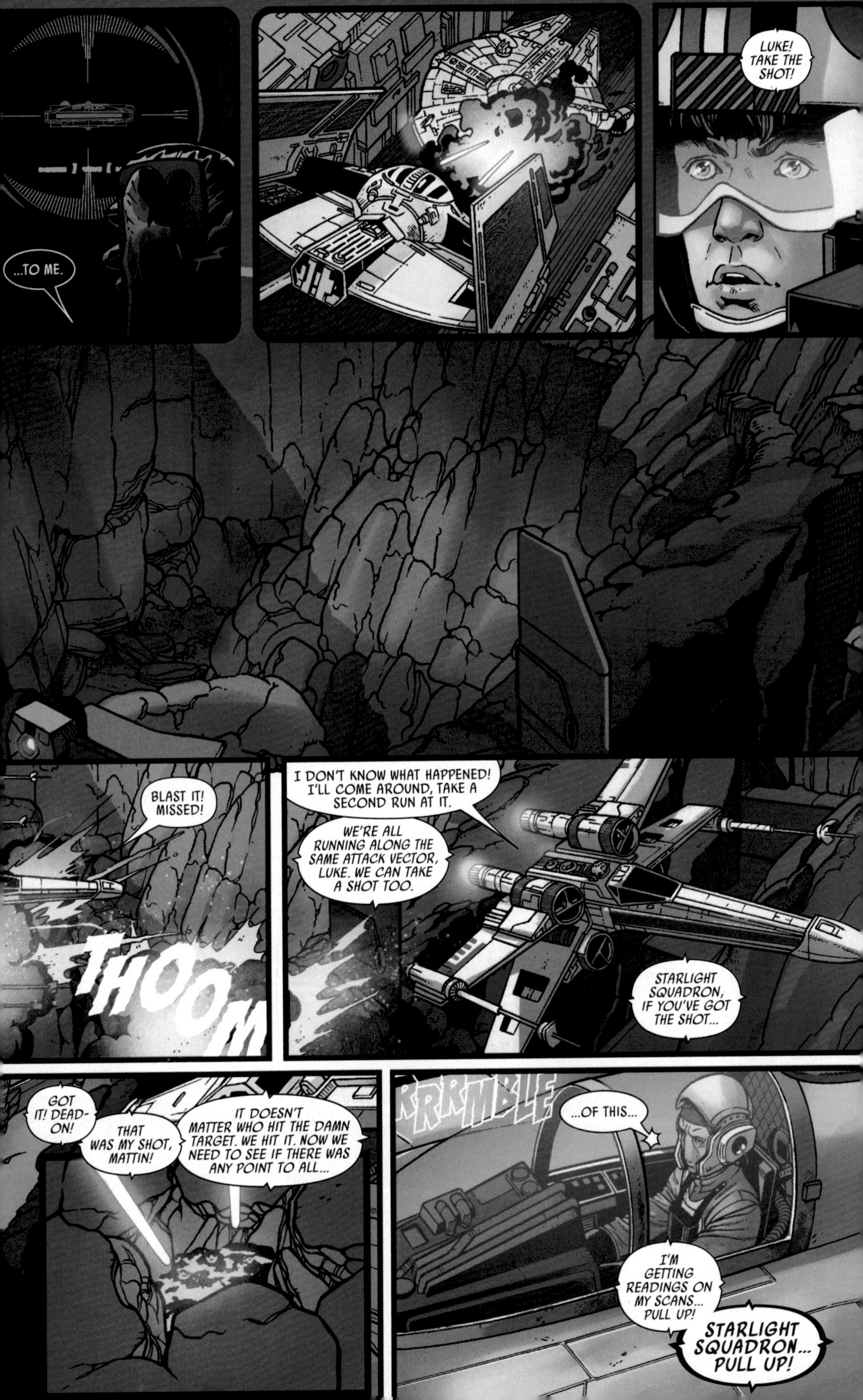

...TO ME.
LUKE! TAKE THE SHOT!
BLAST IT! MISSED!
THOOOM
I DON'T KNOW WHAT HAPPENED! I'LL COME AROUND, TAKE A SECOND RUN AT IT.
WE'RE ALL RUNNING ALONG THE SAME ATTACK VECTOR, LUKE. WE CAN TAKE A SHOT TOO.
STARLIGHT SQUADRON, IF YOU'VE GOT THE SHOT...
GOT IT! DEAD-ON!
THAT WAS MY SHOT, MATTIN!
IT DOESN'T MATTER WHO HIT THE DAMN TARGET. WE HIT IT. NOW WE NEED TO SEE IF THERE WAS ANY POINT TO ALL...
RRRMBLE
...OF THIS...
I'M GETTING READINGS ON MY SCANS... PULL UP!
STARLIGHT SQUADRON... PULL UP!

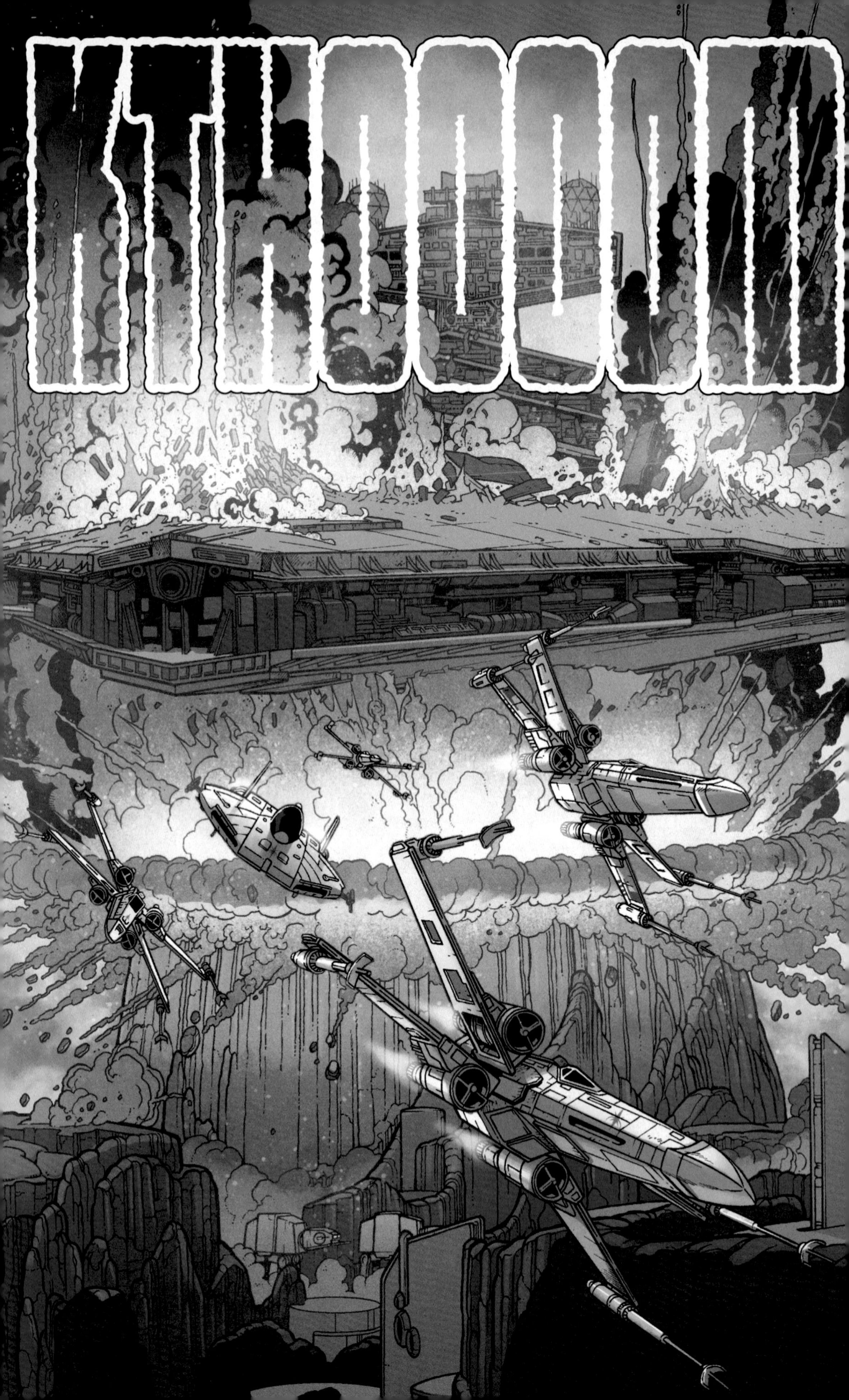
KTHOOOM

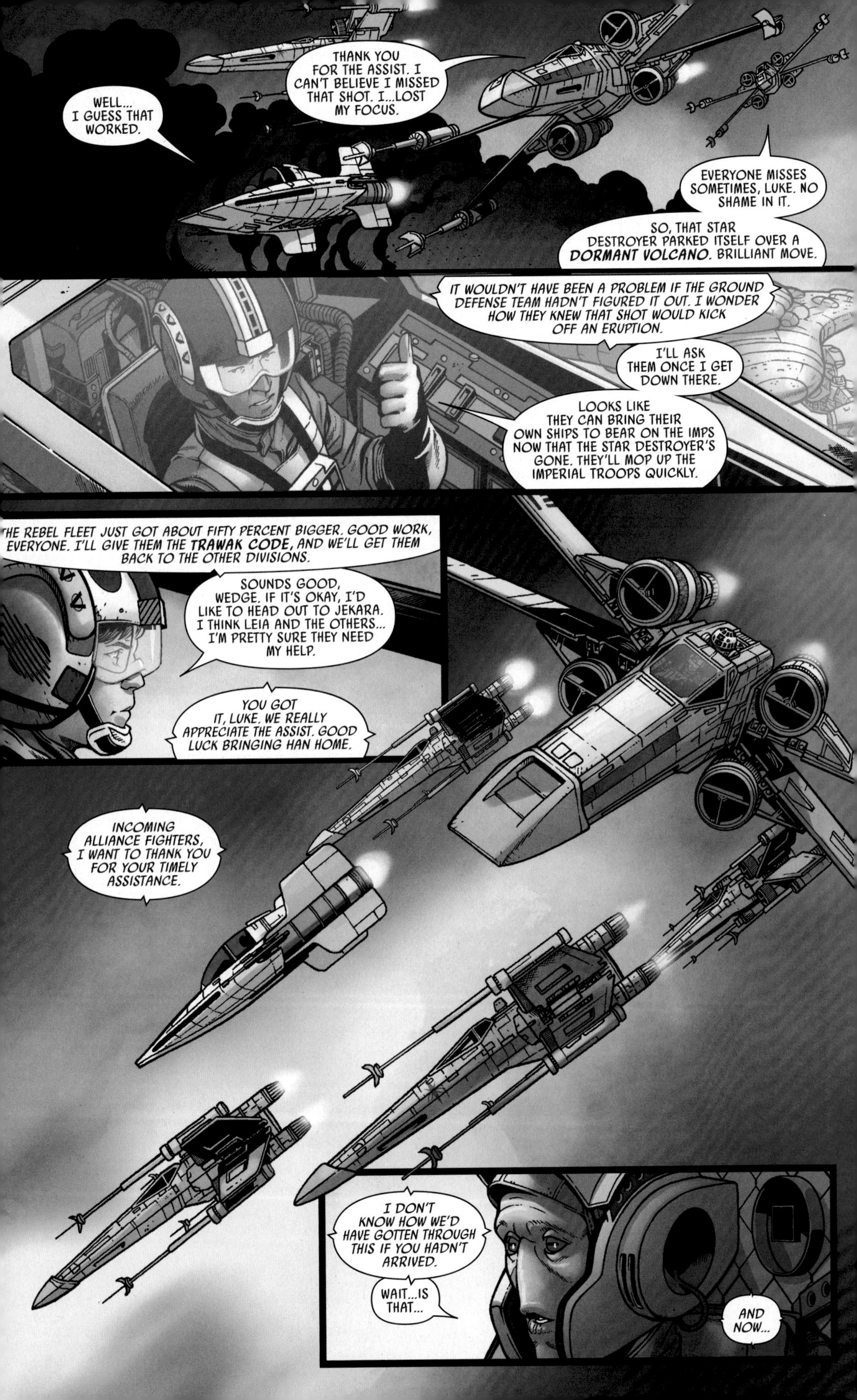
WELL... I GUESS THAT WORKED.
THANK YOU FOR THE ASSIST. I CAN'T BELIEVE I MISSED THAT SHOT. I...LOST MY FOCUS.
EVERYONE MISSES SOMETIMES, LUKE. NO SHAME IN IT.
SO, THAT STAR DESTROYER PARKED ITSELF OVER A DORMANT VOLCANO. BRILLIANT MOVE.
IT WOULDN'T HAVE BEEN A PROBLEM IF THE GROUND DEFENSE TEAM HADN'T FIGURED IT OUT. I WONDER HOW THEY KNEW THAT SHOT WOULD KICK OFF AN ERUPTION.
I'LL ASK THEM ONCE I GET DOWN THERE.
LOOKS LIKE THEY CAN BRING THEIR OWN SHIPS TO BEAR ON THE IMPS NOW THAT THE STAR DESTROYER'S GONE. THEY'LL MOP UP THE IMPERIAL TROOPS QUICKLY.
THE REBEL FLEET JUST GOT ABOUT FIFTY PERCENT BIGGER. GOOD WORK, EVERYONE. I'LL GIVE THEM THE TRAWAK CODE, AND WE'LL GET THEM BACK TO THE OTHER DIVISIONS.
SOUNDS GOOD, WEDGE. IF IT'S OKAY, I'D LIKE TO HEAD OUT TO JEKARA. I THINK LEIA AND THE OTHERS... I'M PRETTY SURE THEY NEED MY HELP.
YOU GOT IT, LUKE. WE REALLY APPRECIATE THE ASSIST. GOOD LUCK BRINGING HAN HOME.
INCOMING ALLIANCE FIGHTERS, I WANT TO THANK YOU FOR YOUR TIMELY ASSISTANCE.
I DON'T KNOW HOW WE'D HAVE GOTTEN THROUGH THIS IF YOU HADN'T ARRIVED.
WAIT...IS THAT...
AND NOW...

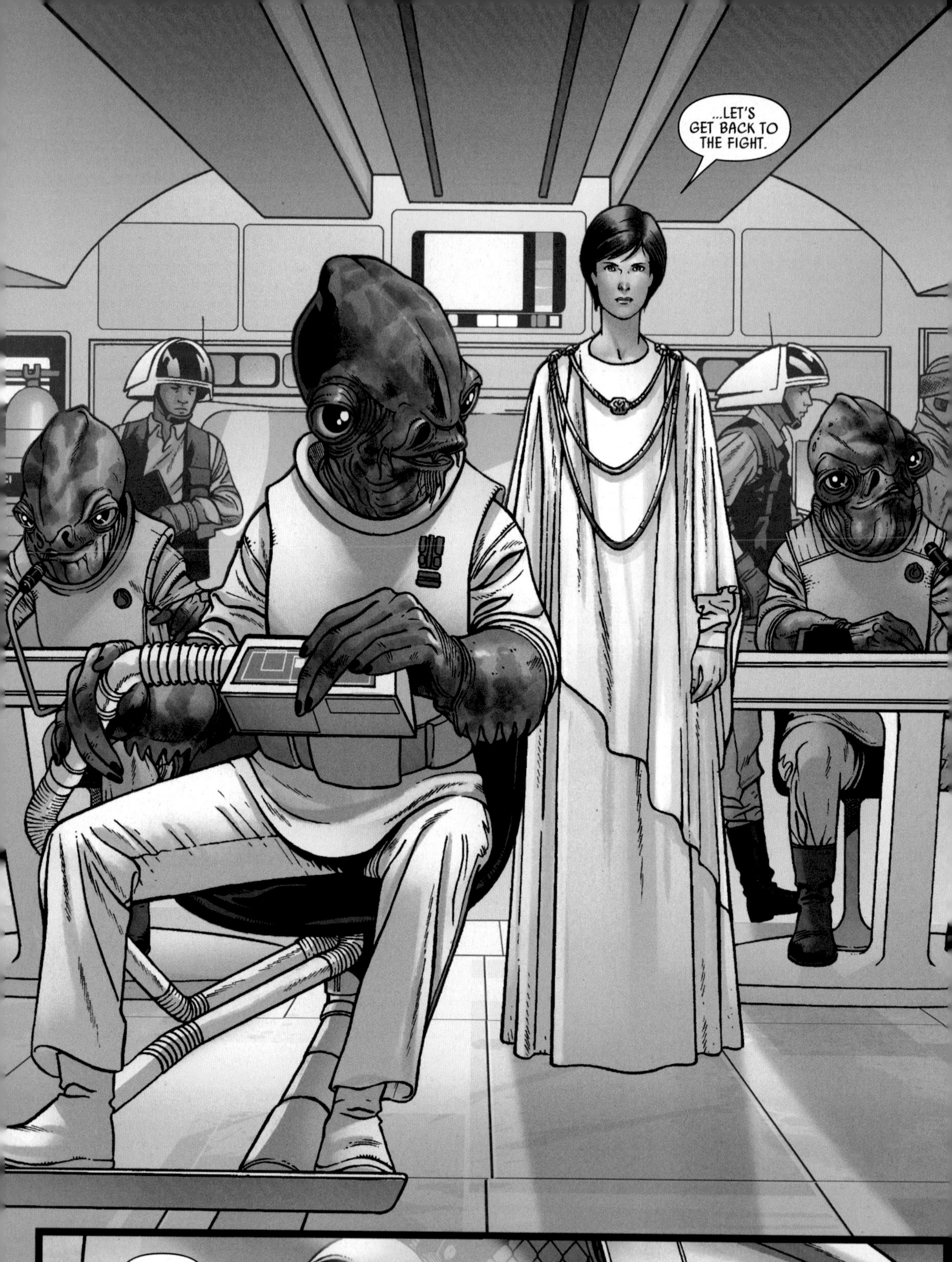
...LET'S
GET BACK TO
THE FIGHT.

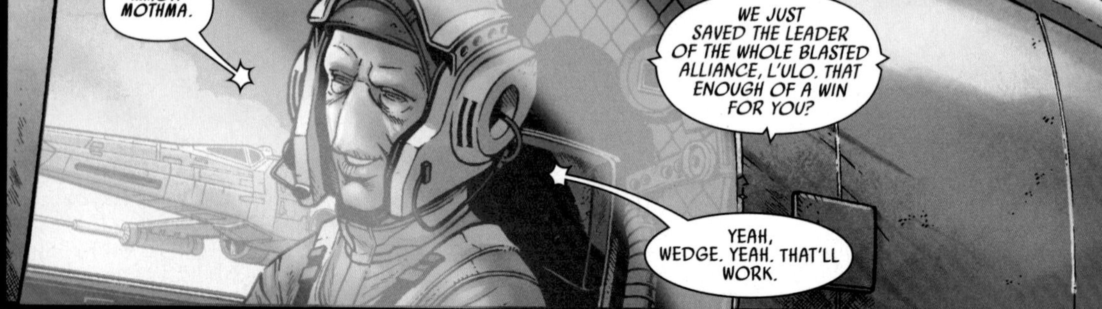
...MON
MOTHMA.
WE JUST
SAVED THE LEADER
OF THE WHOLE BLASTED
ALLIANCE, L'ULO. THAT
ENOUGH OF A WIN
FOR YOU?
YEAH,
WEDGE. YEAH. THAT'LL
WORK.

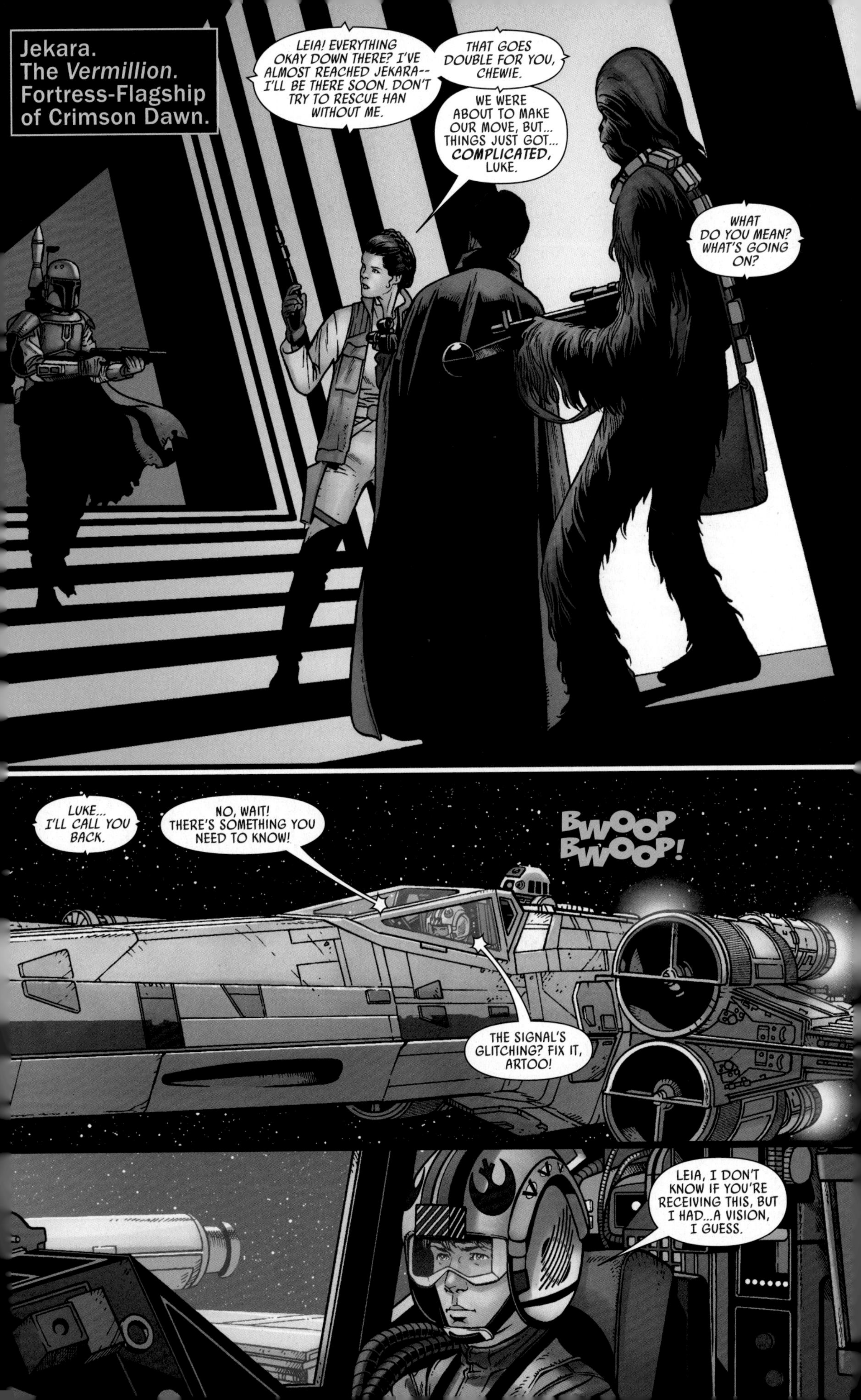
Jekara.
The *Vermillion.*
Fortress-Flagship of Crimson Dawn.
LEIA! EVERYTHING OKAY DOWN THERE? I'VE ALMOST REACHED JEKARA-- I'LL BE THERE SOON. DON'T TRY TO RESCUE HAN WITHOUT ME.
THAT GOES DOUBLE FOR YOU, CHEWIE.
WE WERE ABOUT TO MAKE OUR MOVE, BUT... THINGS JUST GOT... **COMPLICATED,** LUKE.
WHAT DO YOU MEAN? WHAT'S GOING ON?
LUKE... I'LL CALL YOU BACK.
NO, WAIT! THERE'S SOMETHING YOU NEED TO KNOW!
BWOOP BWOOP!
THE SIGNAL'S GLITCHING? FIX IT, ARTOO!
LEIA, I DON'T KNOW IF YOU'RE RECEIVING THIS, BUT I HAD...A VISION, I GUESS.

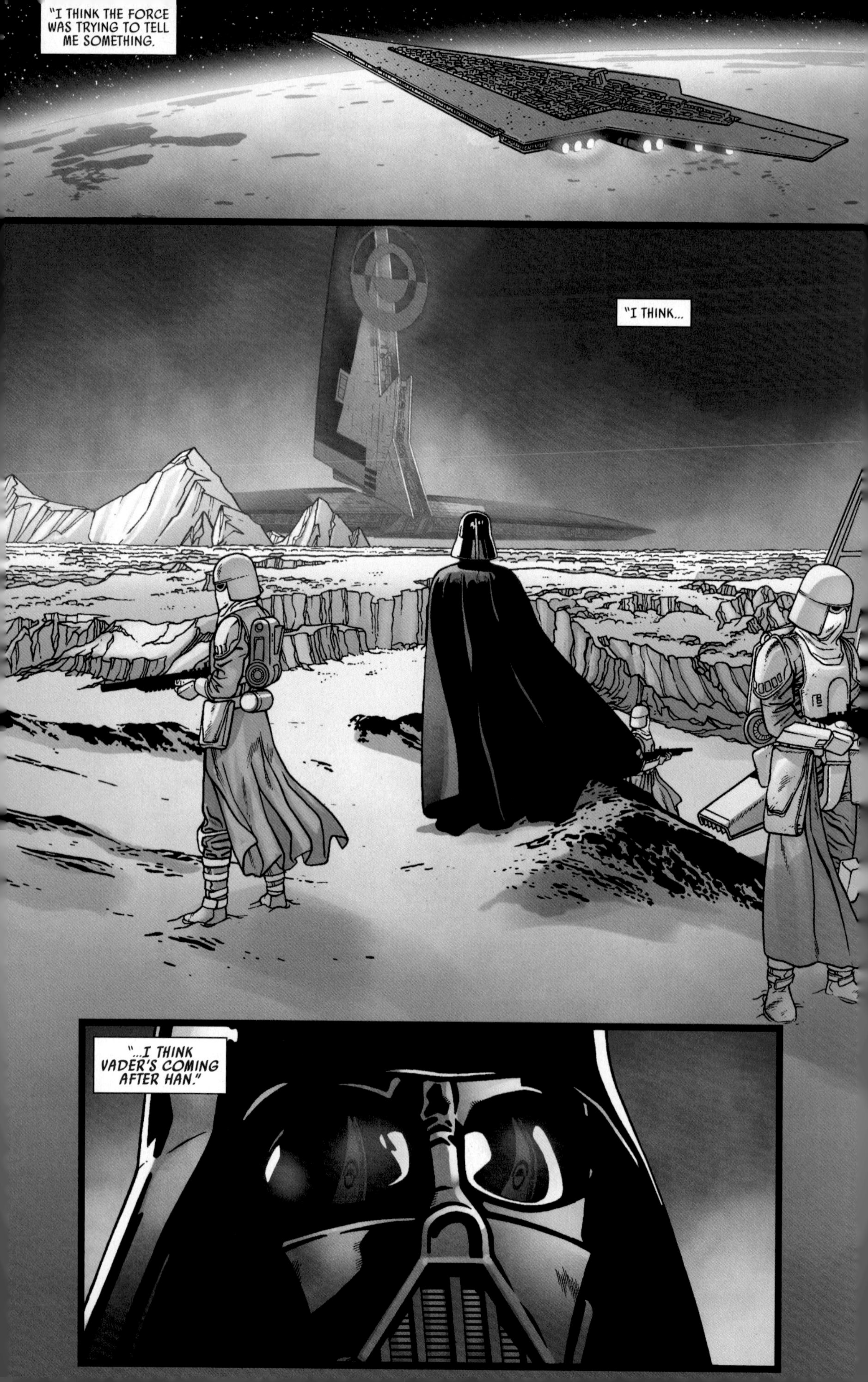
"I THINK THE FORCE WAS TRYING TO TELL ME SOMETHING.
"I THINK...
"...I THINK VADER'S COMING AFTER HAN."

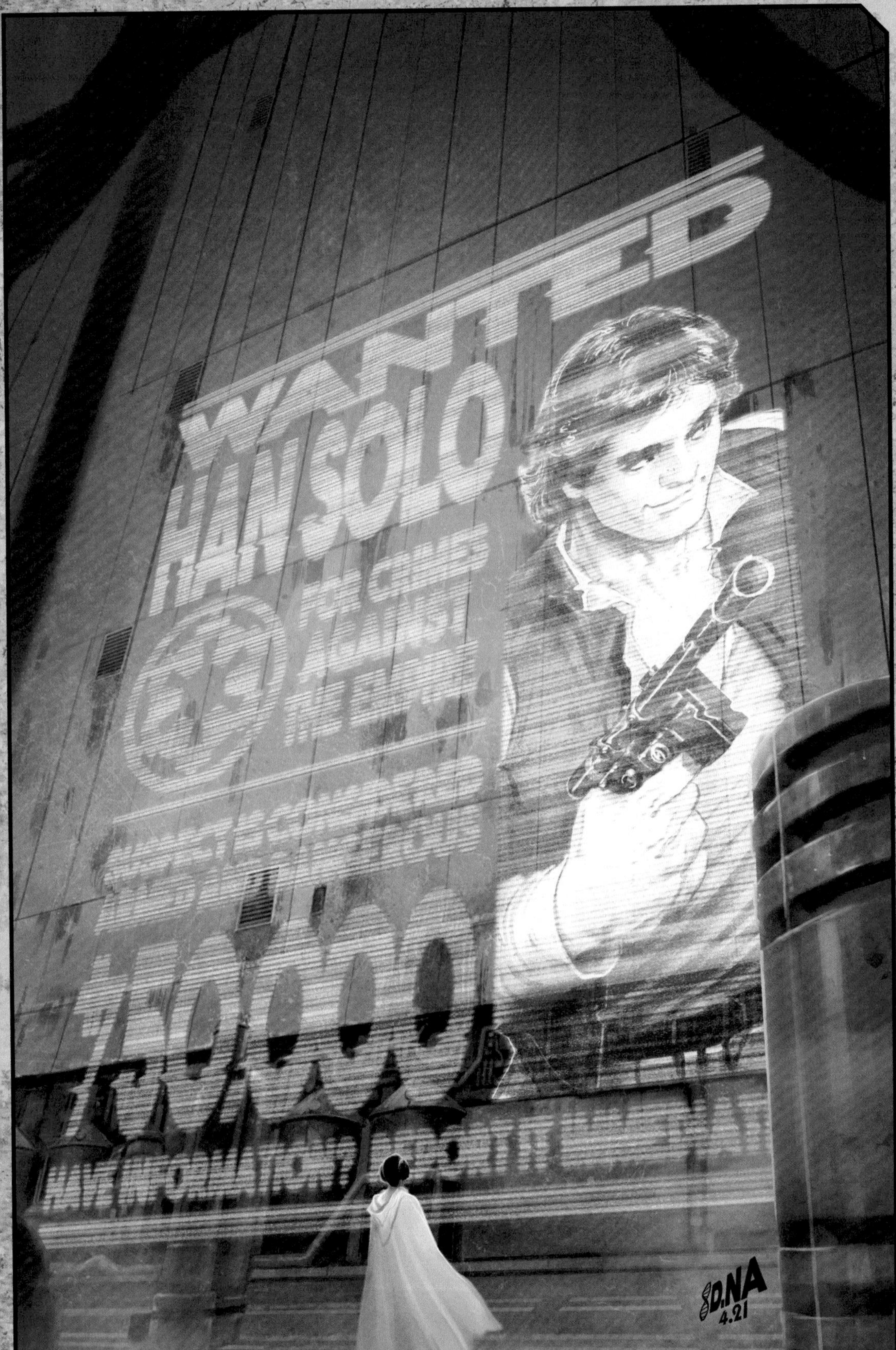
WANTED
HAN SOLO
FOR CRIMES AGAINST
D.NA 4.21

#16 Variant by
DAVID NAKAYAMA

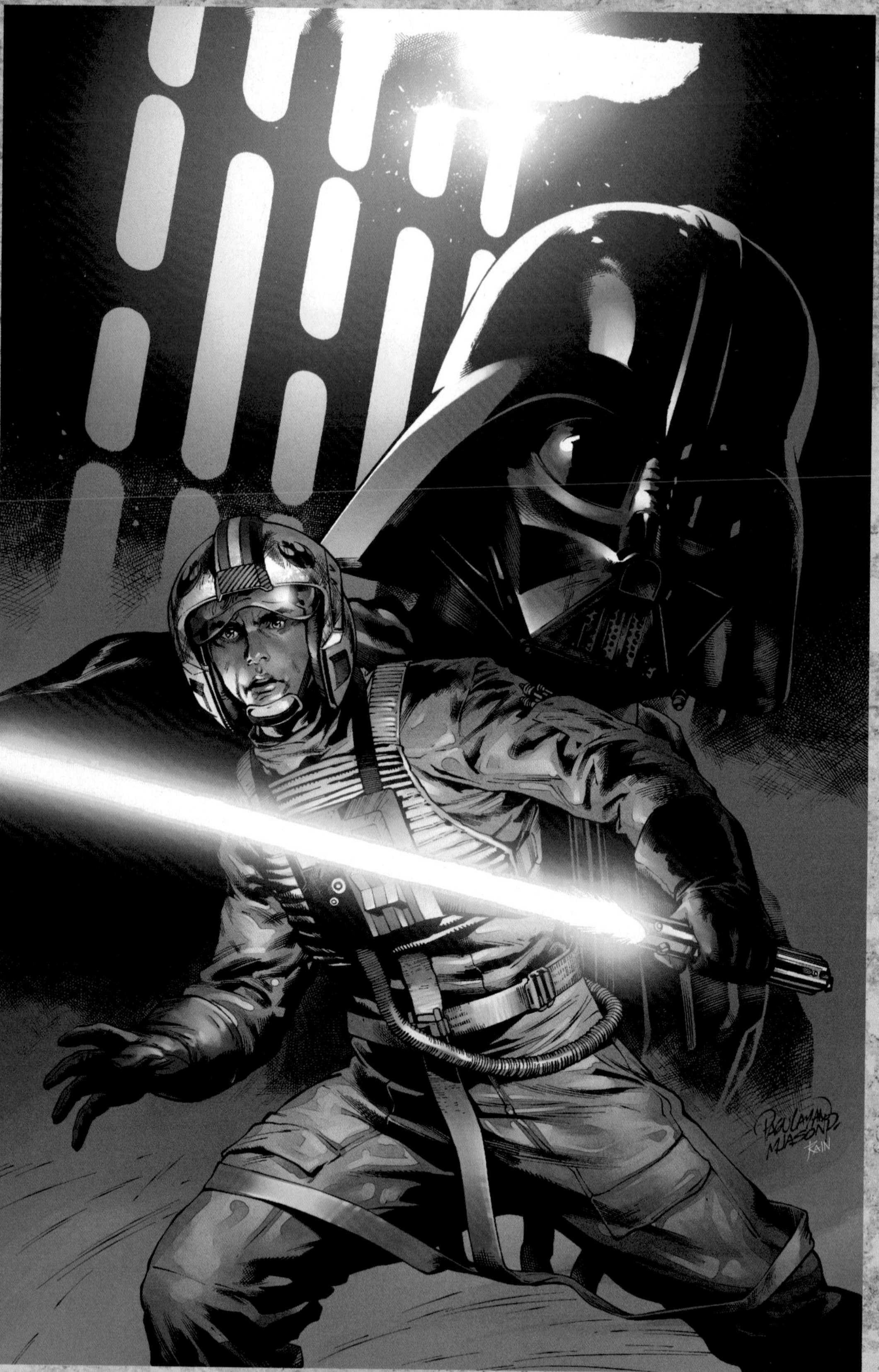

16 — MISSING IN ACTION

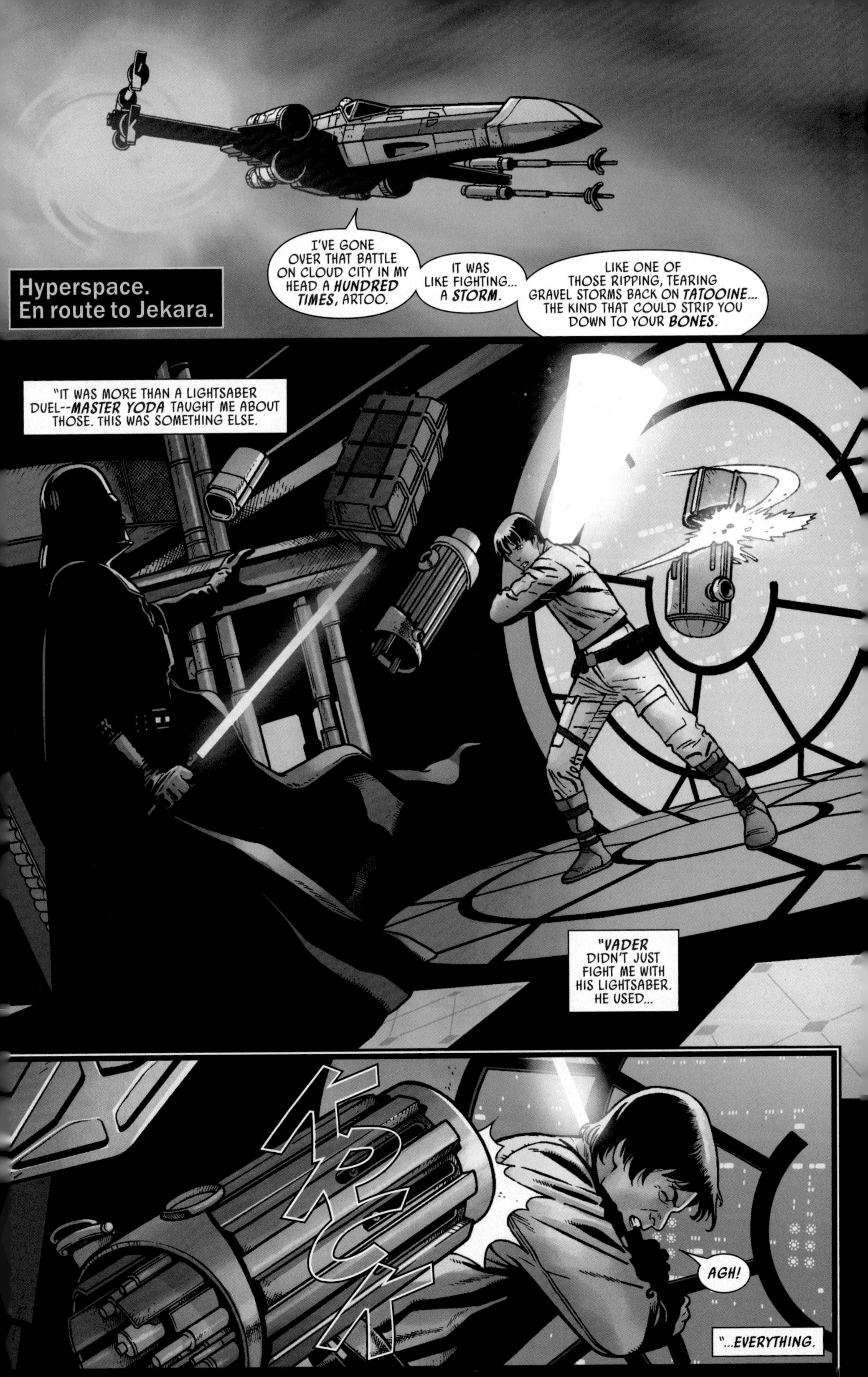
Hyperspace. En route to Jekara.
I'VE GONE OVER THAT BATTLE ON CLOUD CITY IN MY HEAD A HUNDRED TIMES, ARTOO.
IT WAS LIKE FIGHTING... A STORM.
LIKE ONE OF THOSE RIPPING, TEARING GRAVEL STORMS BACK ON TATOOINE... THE KIND THAT COULD STRIP YOU DOWN TO YOUR BONES.
"IT WAS MORE THAN A LIGHTSABER DUEL--MASTER YODA TAUGHT ME ABOUT THOSE. THIS WAS SOMETHING ELSE.
"VADER DIDN'T JUST FIGHT ME WITH HIS LIGHTSABER. HE USED...
KRACK
AGH!
"...EVERYTHING.

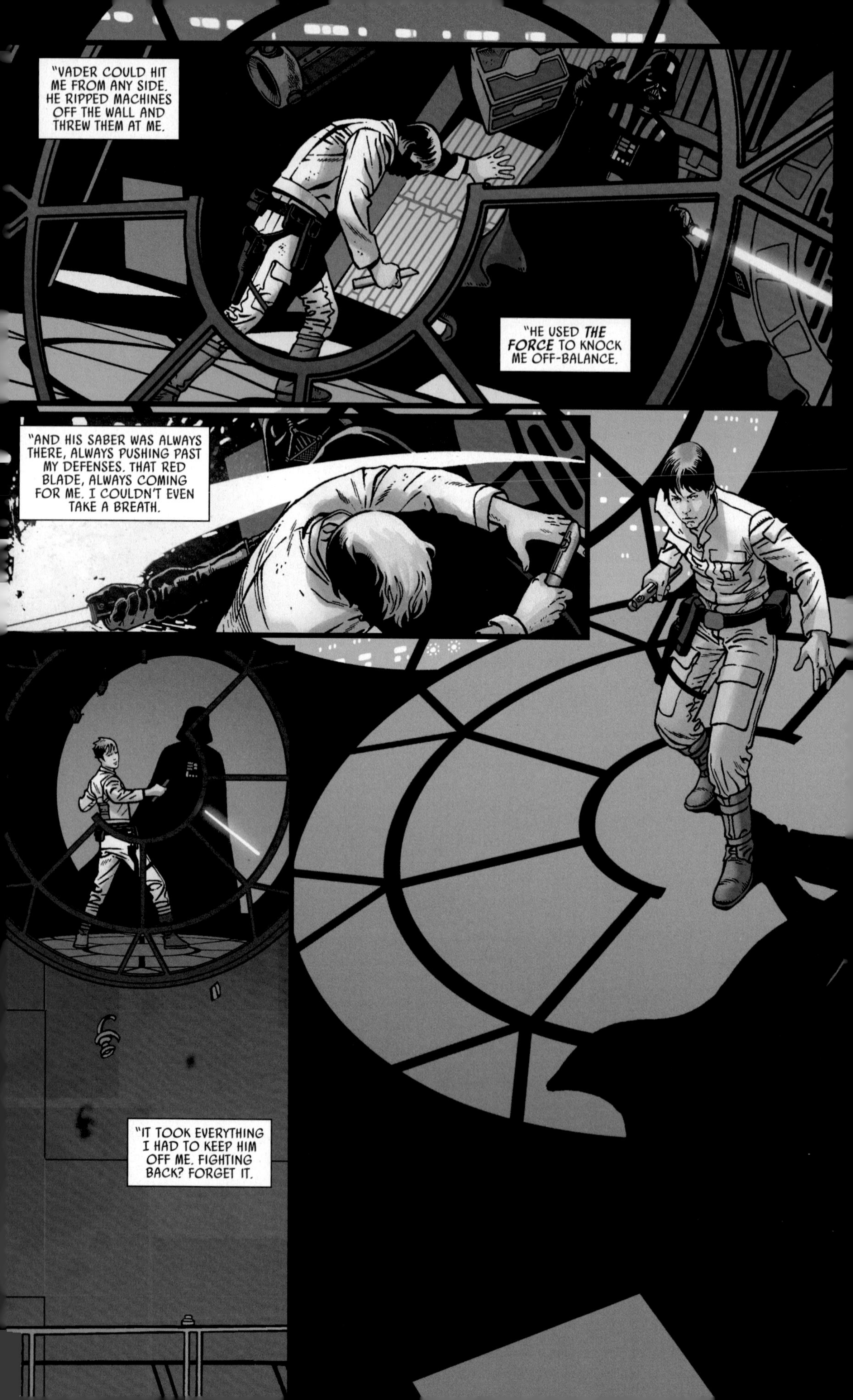
"VADER COULD HIT ME FROM ANY SIDE. HE RIPPED MACHINES OFF THE WALL AND THREW THEM AT ME.
"HE USED THE FORCE TO KNOCK ME OFF-BALANCE.
"AND HIS SABER WAS ALWAYS THERE, ALWAYS PUSHING PAST MY DEFENSES. THAT RED BLADE, ALWAYS COMING FOR ME. I COULDN'T EVEN TAKE A BREATH.
"IT TOOK EVERYTHING I HAD TO KEEP HIM OFF ME. FIGHTING BACK? FORGET IT.

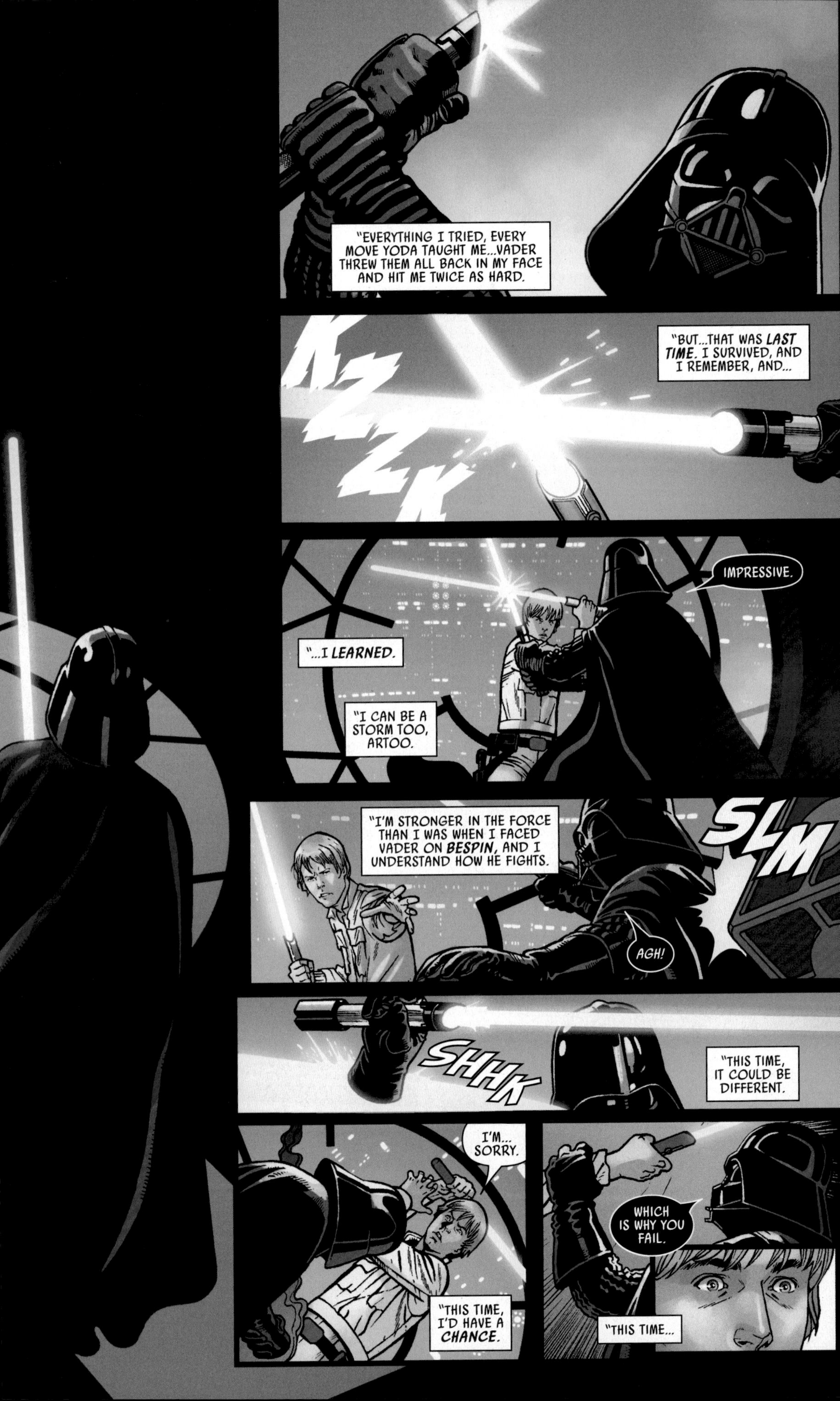

"EVERYTHING I TRIED, EVERY MOVE YODA TAUGHT ME...VADER THREW THEM ALL BACK IN MY FACE AND HIT ME TWICE AS HARD.
KZZK
"BUT...THAT WAS LAST TIME. I SURVIVED, AND I REMEMBER, AND...
IMPRESSIVE.
"...I LEARNED.
"I CAN BE A STORM TOO, ARTOO.
"I'M STRONGER IN THE FORCE THAN I WAS WHEN I FACED VADER ON BESPIN, AND I UNDERSTAND HOW HE FIGHTS.
SLM
AGH!
SHHK
"THIS TIME, IT COULD BE DIFFERENT.
I'M... SORRY.
"THIS TIME, I'D HAVE A CHANCE.
WHICH IS WHY YOU FAIL.
"THIS TIME...

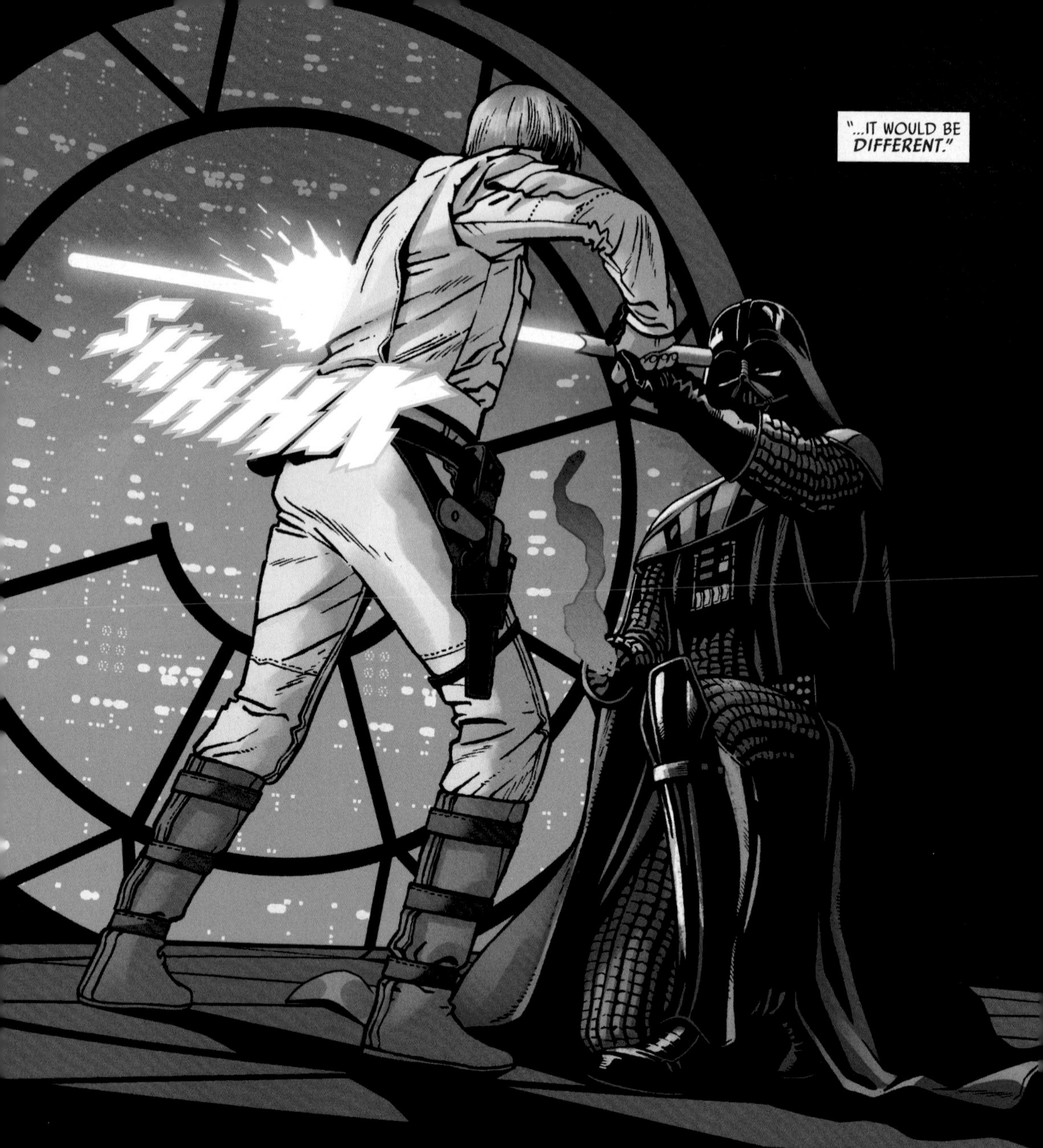
"...IT WOULD BE DIFFERENT."
SHHHK

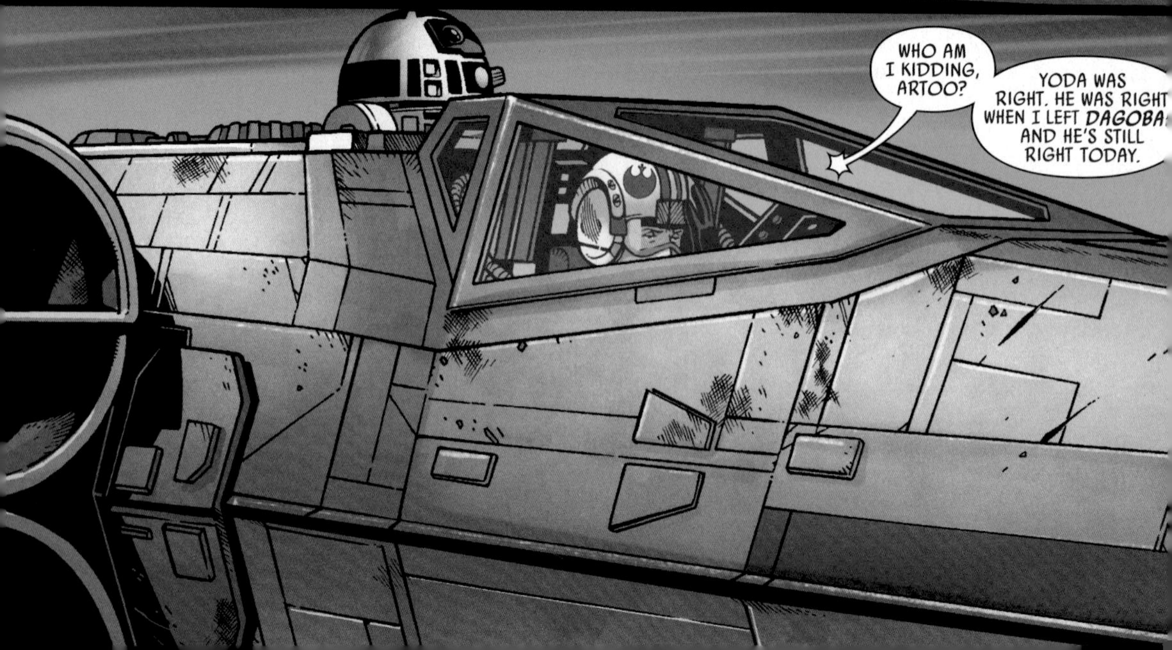
WHO AM I KIDDING, ARTOO?
YODA WAS RIGHT. HE WAS RIGHT WHEN I LEFT DAGOBA AND HE'S STILL RIGHT TODAY.

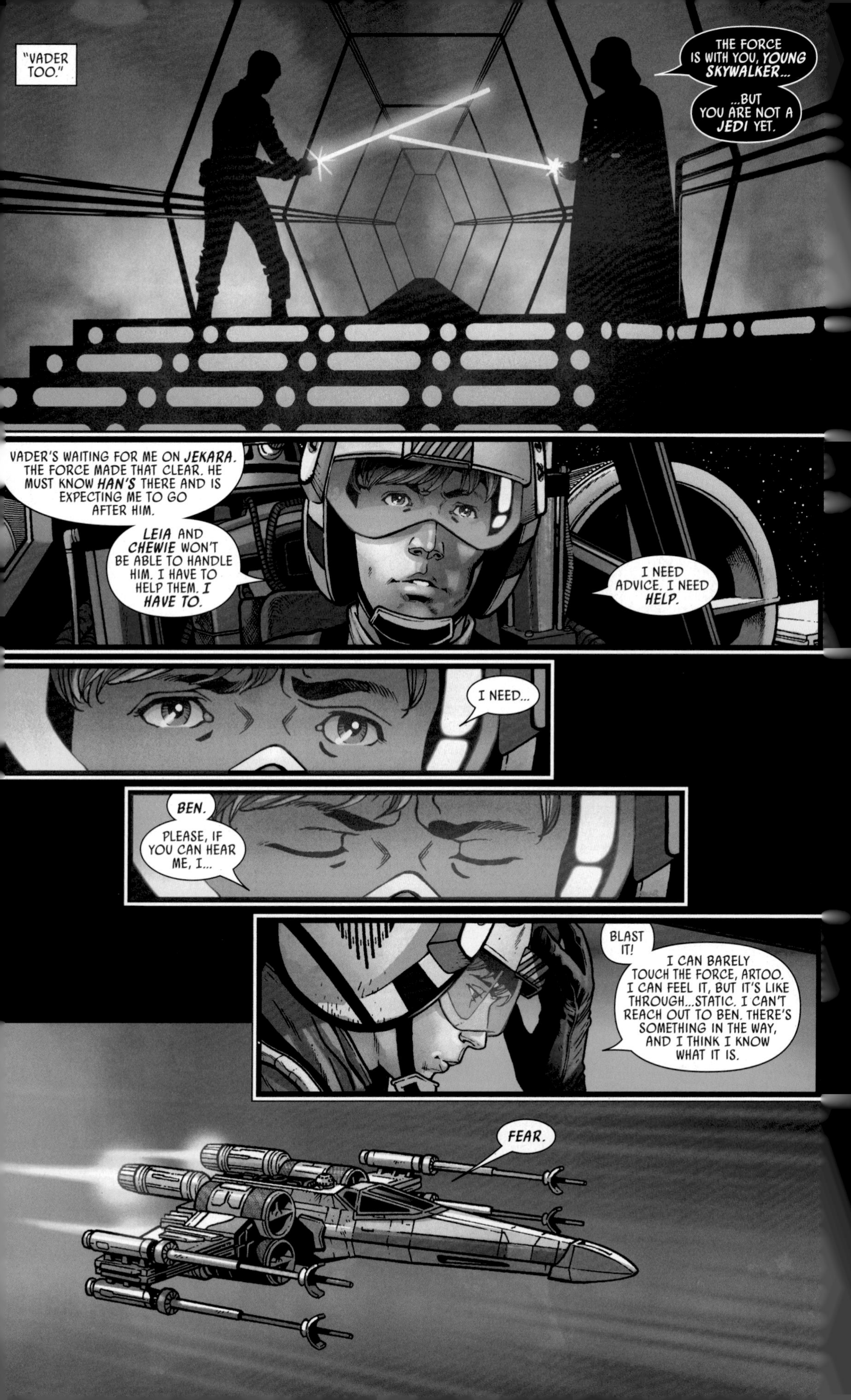
"VADER TOO."
THE FORCE IS WITH YOU, *YOUNG SKYWALKER*...
...BUT YOU ARE NOT A *JEDI* YET.
VADER'S WAITING FOR ME ON *JEKARA*. THE FORCE MADE THAT CLEAR. HE MUST KNOW *HAN'S* THERE AND IS EXPECTING ME TO GO AFTER HIM.
LEIA AND *CHEWIE* WON'T BE ABLE TO HANDLE HIM. I HAVE TO HELP THEM. *I HAVE TO.*
I NEED ADVICE. I NEED *HELP.*
I NEED...
BEN.
PLEASE, IF YOU CAN HEAR ME, I...
BLAST IT!
I CAN BARELY TOUCH THE FORCE, ARTOO. I CAN FEEL IT, BUT IT'S LIKE THROUGH...STATIC. I CAN'T REACH OUT TO BEN. THERE'S SOMETHING IN THE WAY, AND I THINK I KNOW WHAT IT IS.
FEAR.

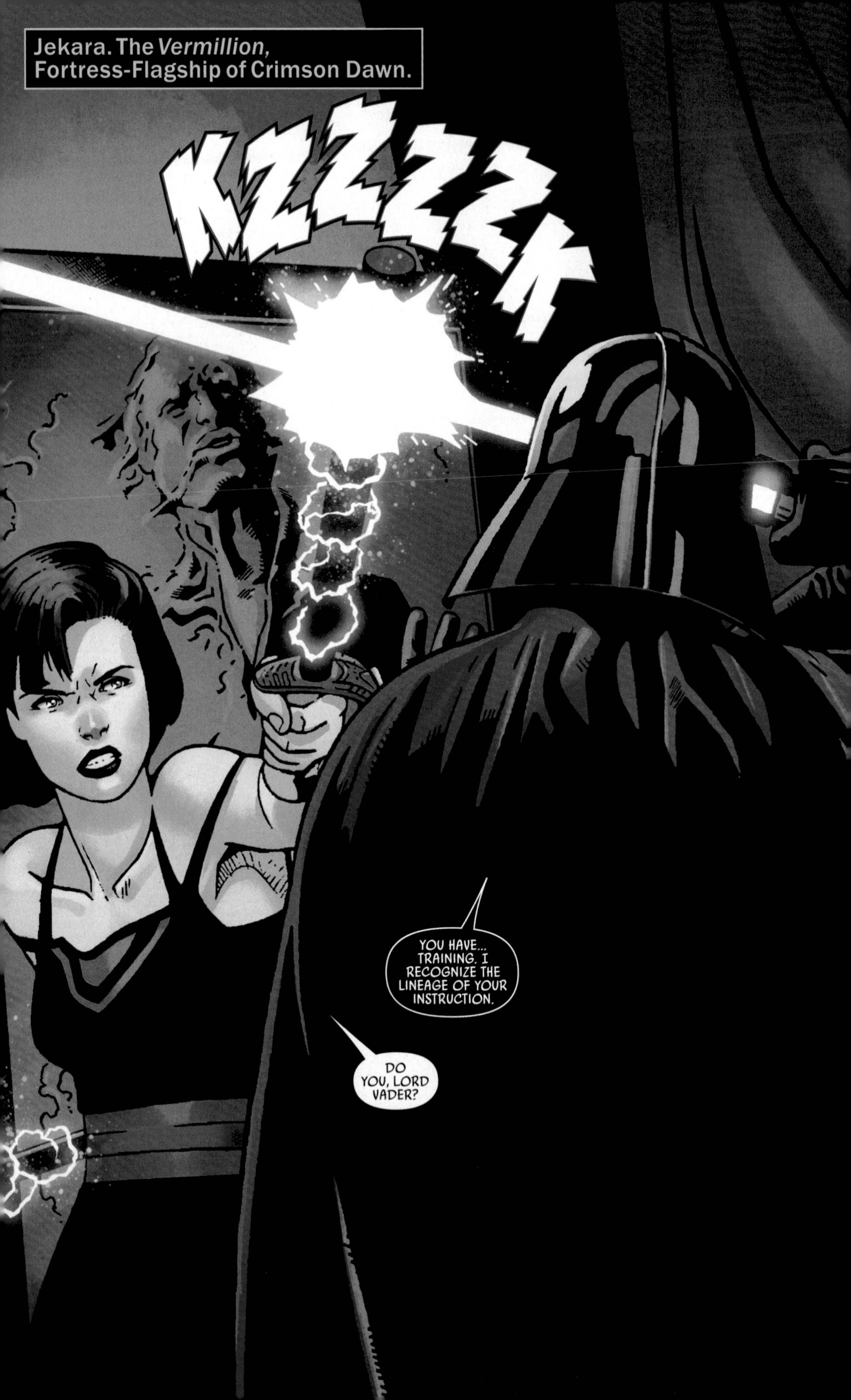
Jekara. The *Vermillion*,
Fortress-Flagship of Crimson Dawn.
KZZZZK
YOU HAVE... TRAINING. I RECOGNIZE THE LINEAGE OF YOUR INSTRUCTION.
DO YOU, LORD VADER?

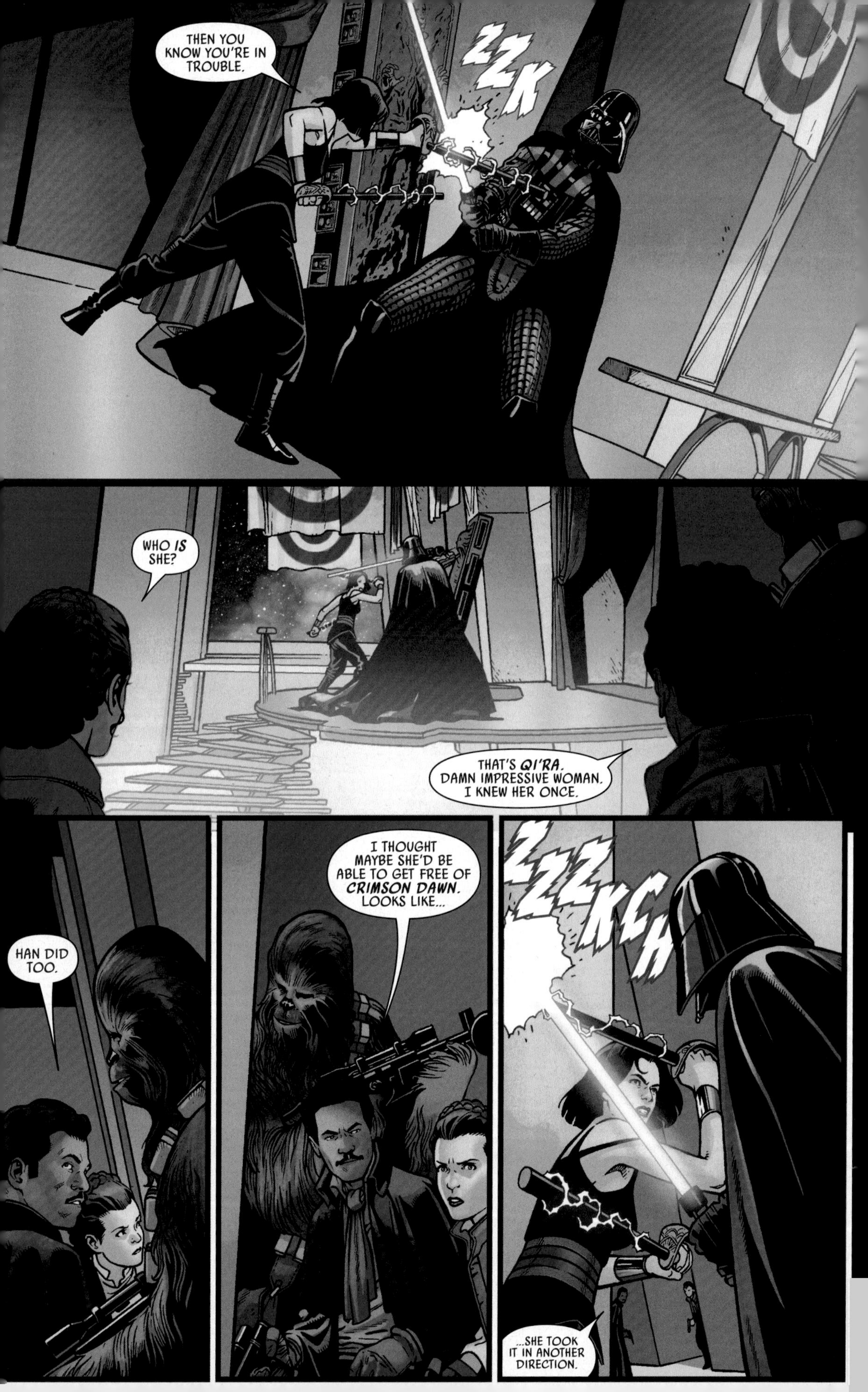

THEN YOU KNOW YOU'RE IN TROUBLE.
ZZK
WHO *IS* SHE?
THAT'S *QI'RA*. DAMN IMPRESSIVE WOMAN. I KNEW HER ONCE.
HAN DID TOO.
I THOUGHT MAYBE SHE'D BE ABLE TO GET FREE OF *CRIMSON DAWN*. LOOKS LIKE...
ZZZKCH
...SHE TOOK IT IN ANOTHER DIRECTION.

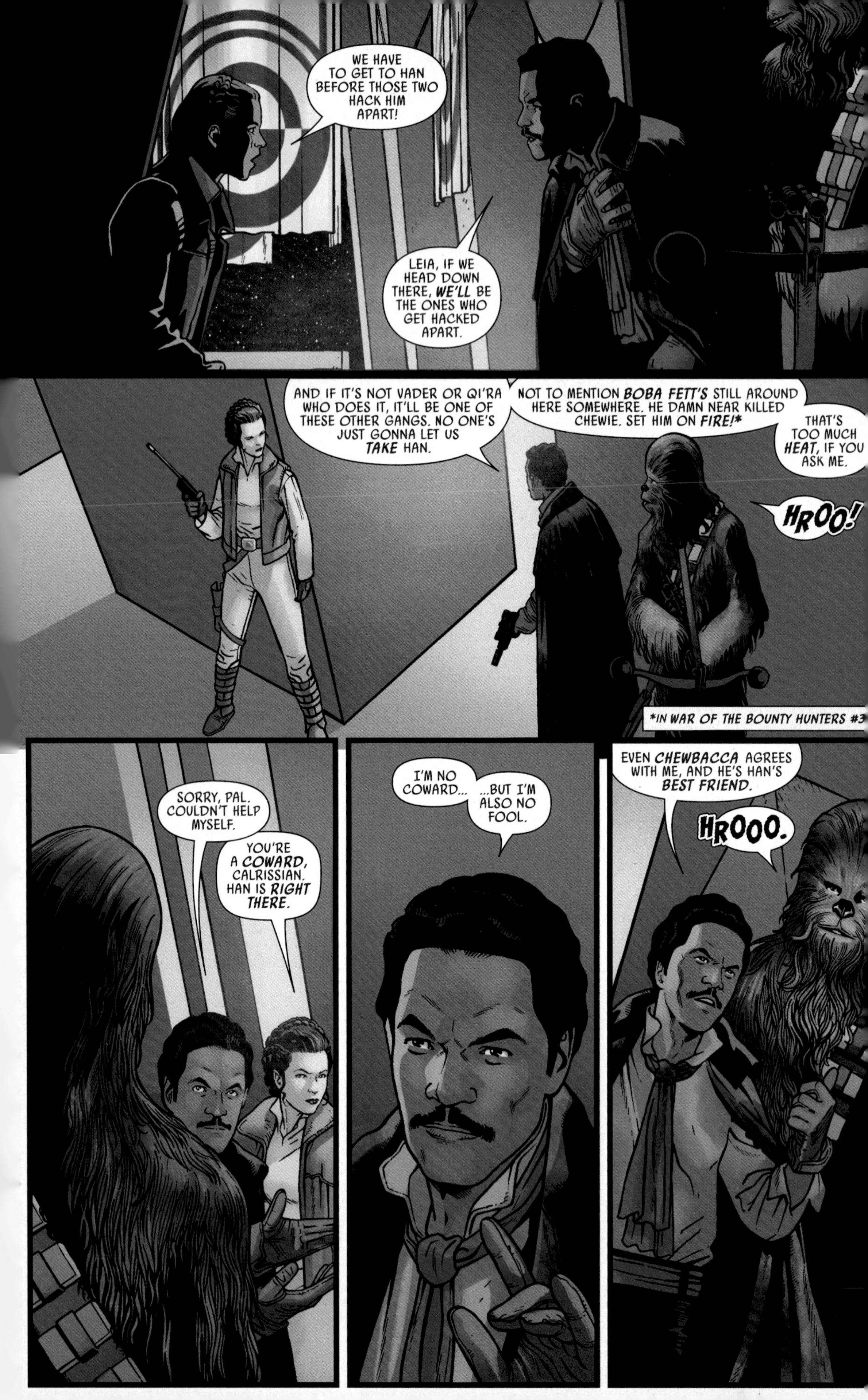

WE HAVE TO GET TO HAN BEFORE THOSE TWO HACK HIM APART!
LEIA, IF WE HEAD DOWN THERE, *WE'LL* BE THE ONES WHO GET HACKED APART.
AND IF IT'S NOT VADER OR QI'RA WHO DOES IT, IT'LL BE ONE OF THESE OTHER GANGS. NO ONE'S JUST GONNA LET US *TAKE* HAN.
NOT TO MENTION *BOBA FETT'S* STILL AROUND HERE SOMEWHERE. HE DAMN NEAR KILLED CHEWIE. SET HIM ON *FIRE!**
THAT'S TOO MUCH *HEAT,* IF YOU ASK ME.
HROO!
*IN WAR OF THE BOUNTY HUNTERS #3
SORRY, PAL. COULDN'T HELP MYSELF.
YOU'RE A *COWARD,* CALRISSIAN. HAN IS *RIGHT THERE.*
I'M NO COWARD...
...BUT I'M ALSO NO FOOL.
EVEN *CHEWBACCA* AGREES WITH ME, AND HE'S HAN'S *BEST FRIEND.*
HROOO.

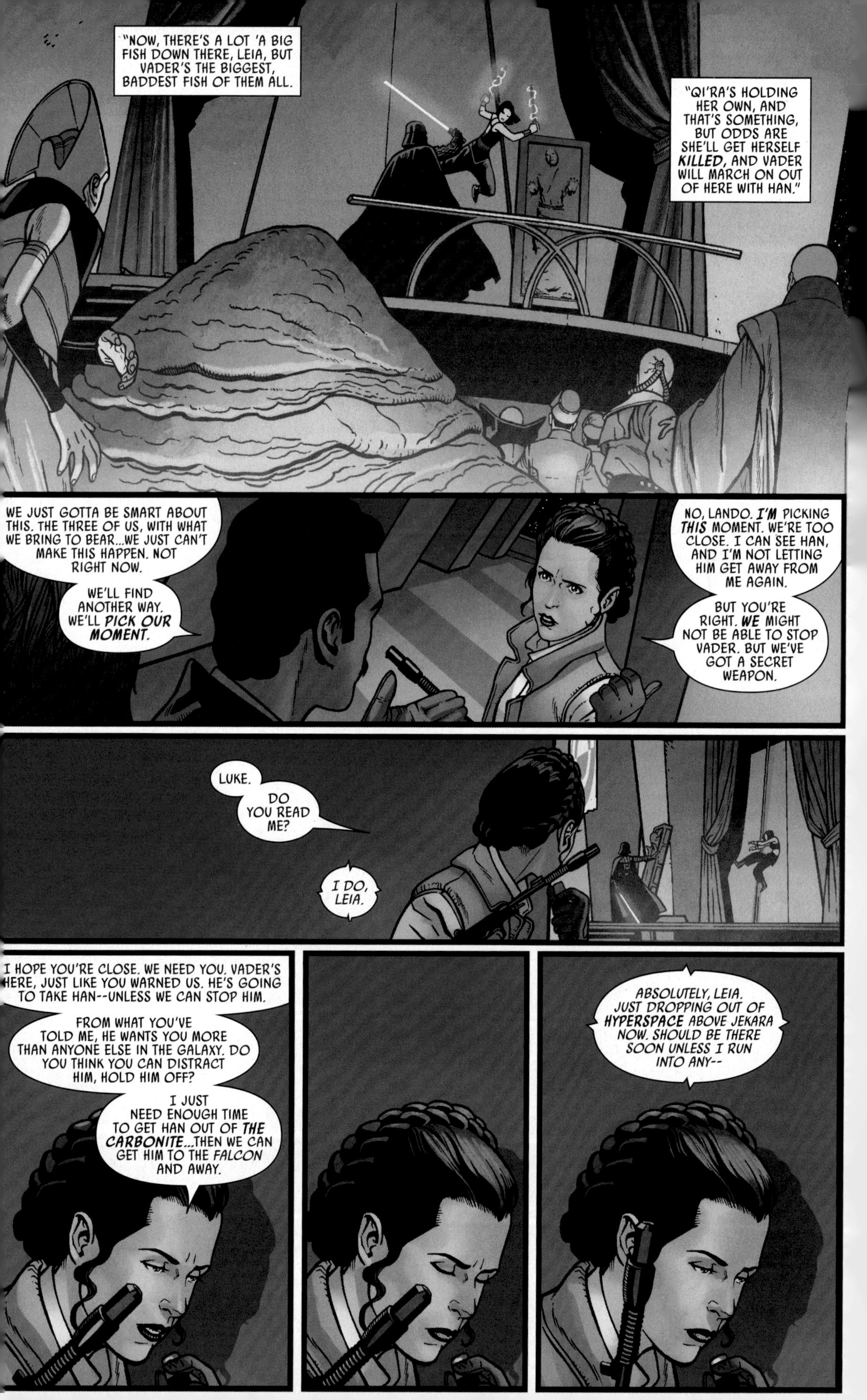
"NOW, THERE'S A LOT 'A BIG FISH DOWN THERE, LEIA, BUT VADER'S THE BIGGEST, BADDEST FISH OF THEM ALL.
"QI'RA'S HOLDING HER OWN, AND THAT'S SOMETHING, BUT ODDS ARE SHE'LL GET HERSELF KILLED, AND VADER WILL MARCH ON OUT OF HERE WITH HAN."
WE JUST GOTTA BE SMART ABOUT THIS. THE THREE OF US, WITH WHAT WE BRING TO BEAR...WE JUST CAN'T MAKE THIS HAPPEN. NOT RIGHT NOW.
WE'LL FIND ANOTHER WAY. WE'LL PICK OUR MOMENT.
NO, LANDO. I'M PICKING THIS MOMENT. WE'RE TOO CLOSE. I CAN SEE HAN, AND I'M NOT LETTING HIM GET AWAY FROM ME AGAIN.
BUT YOU'RE RIGHT. WE MIGHT NOT BE ABLE TO STOP VADER. BUT WE'VE GOT A SECRET WEAPON.
LUKE.
DO YOU READ ME?
I DO, LEIA.
I HOPE YOU'RE CLOSE. WE NEED YOU. VADER'S HERE, JUST LIKE YOU WARNED US. HE'S GOING TO TAKE HAN--UNLESS WE CAN STOP HIM.
FROM WHAT YOU'VE TOLD ME, HE WANTS YOU MORE THAN ANYONE ELSE IN THE GALAXY. DO YOU THINK YOU CAN DISTRACT HIM, HOLD HIM OFF?
I JUST NEED ENOUGH TIME TO GET HAN OUT OF THE CARBONITE...THEN WE CAN GET HIM TO THE FALCON AND AWAY.
ABSOLUTELY, LEIA. JUST DROPPING OUT OF HYPERSPACE ABOVE JEKARA NOW. SHOULD BE THERE SOON UNLESS I RUN INTO ANY--

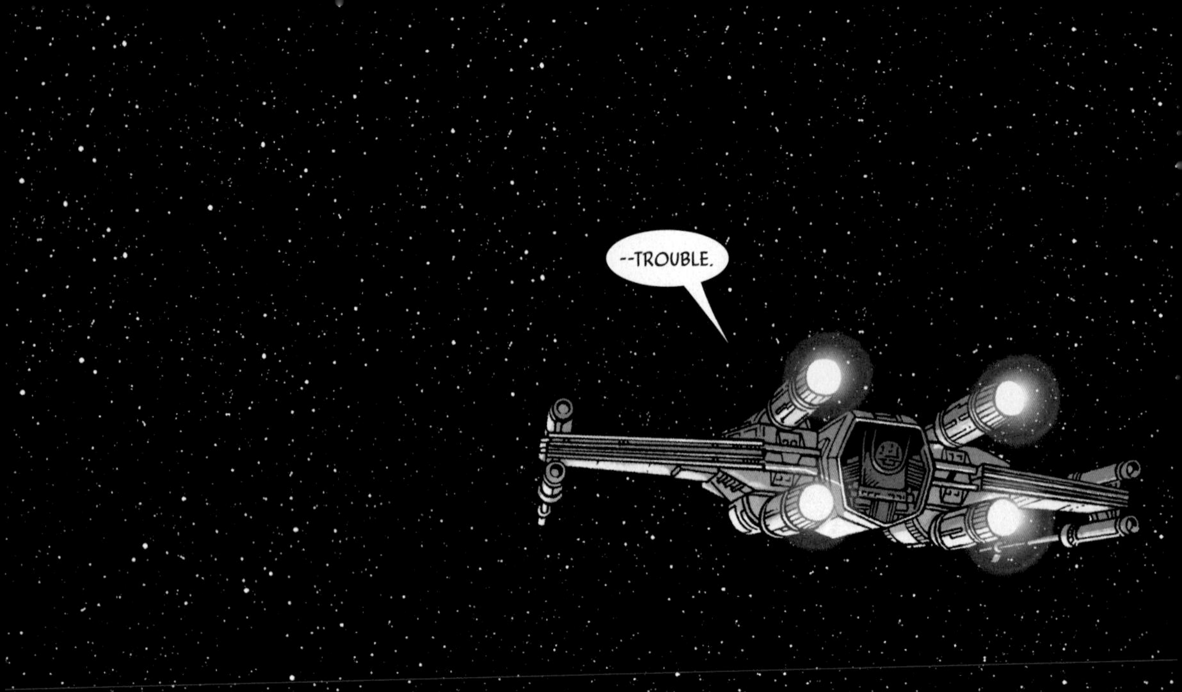
--TROUBLE.

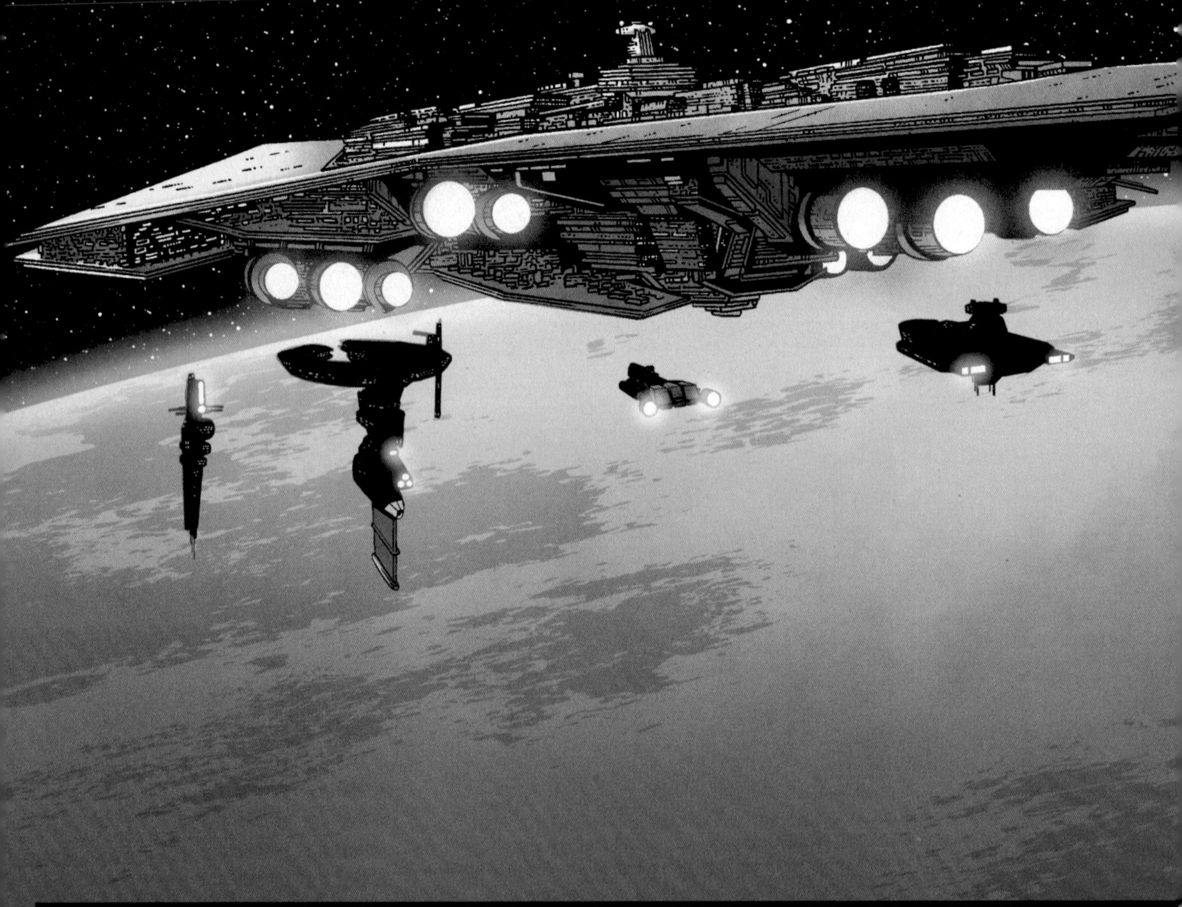

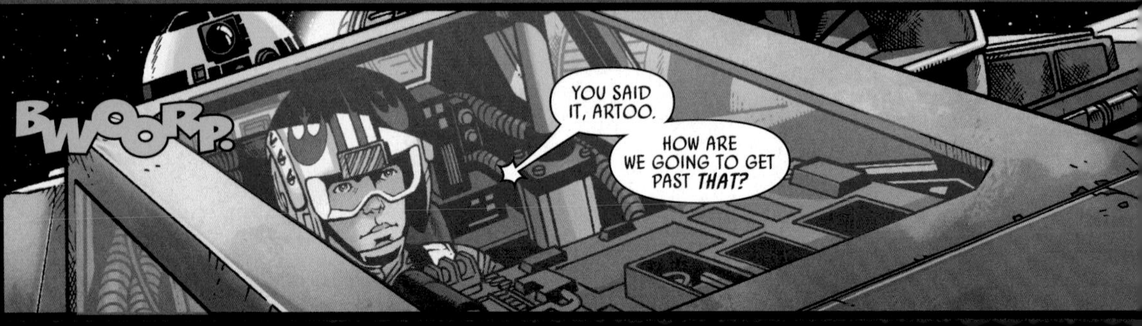
BWOORP.
YOU SAID IT, ARTOO.
HOW ARE WE GOING TO GET PAST THAT?

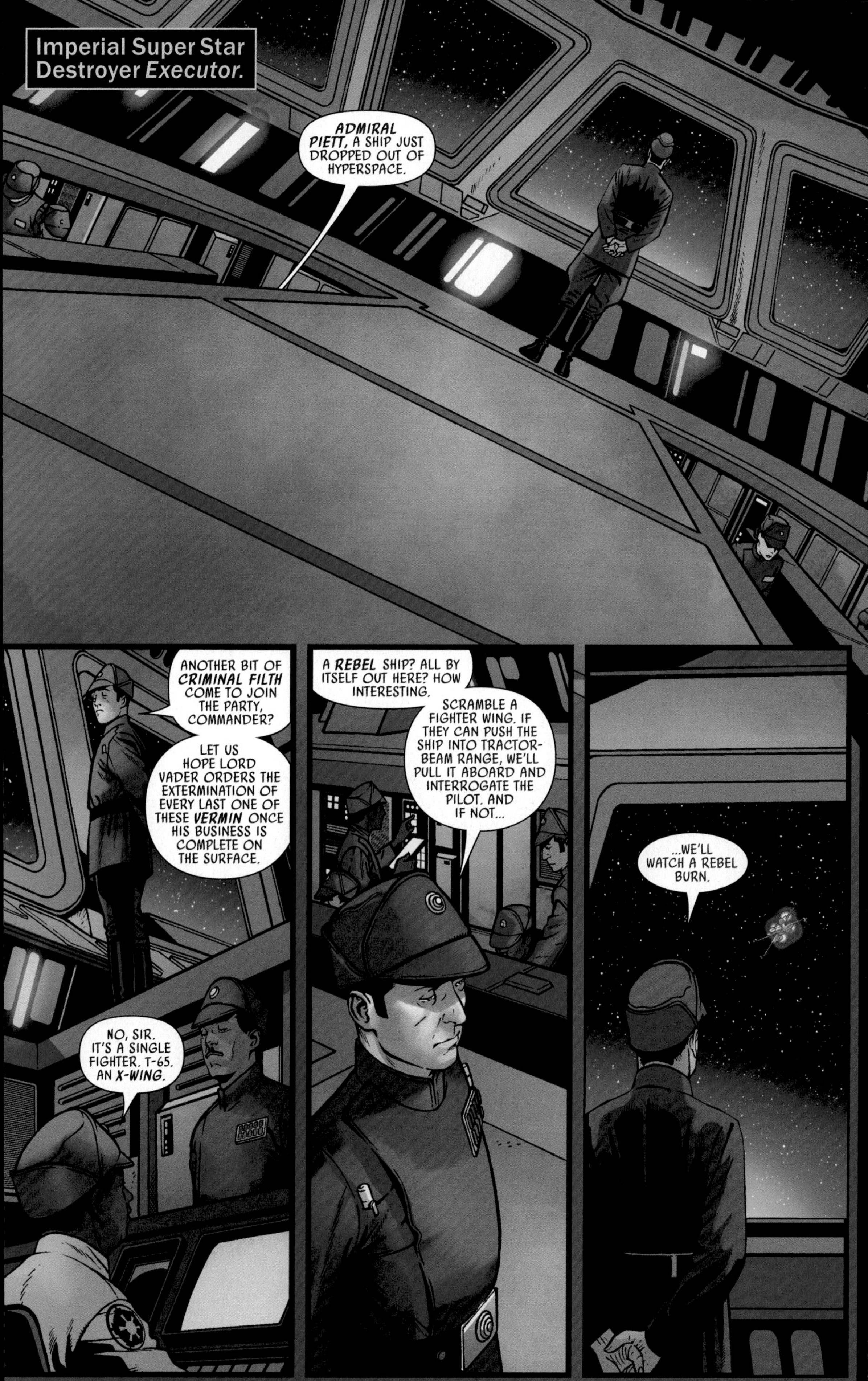
Imperial Super Star Destroyer Executor.
ADMIRAL PIETT, A SHIP JUST DROPPED OUT OF HYPERSPACE.
ANOTHER BIT OF CRIMINAL FILTH COME TO JOIN THE PARTY, COMMANDER?
LET US HOPE LORD VADER ORDERS THE EXTERMINATION OF EVERY LAST ONE OF THESE VERMIN ONCE HIS BUSINESS IS COMPLETE ON THE SURFACE.
NO, SIR. IT'S A SINGLE FIGHTER. T-65. AN X-WING.
A REBEL SHIP? ALL BY ITSELF OUT HERE? HOW INTERESTING.
SCRAMBLE A FIGHTER WING. IF THEY CAN PUSH THE SHIP INTO TRACTOR-BEAM RANGE, WE'LL PULL IT ABOARD AND INTERROGATE THE PILOT. AND IF NOT...
...WE'LL WATCH A REBEL BURN.

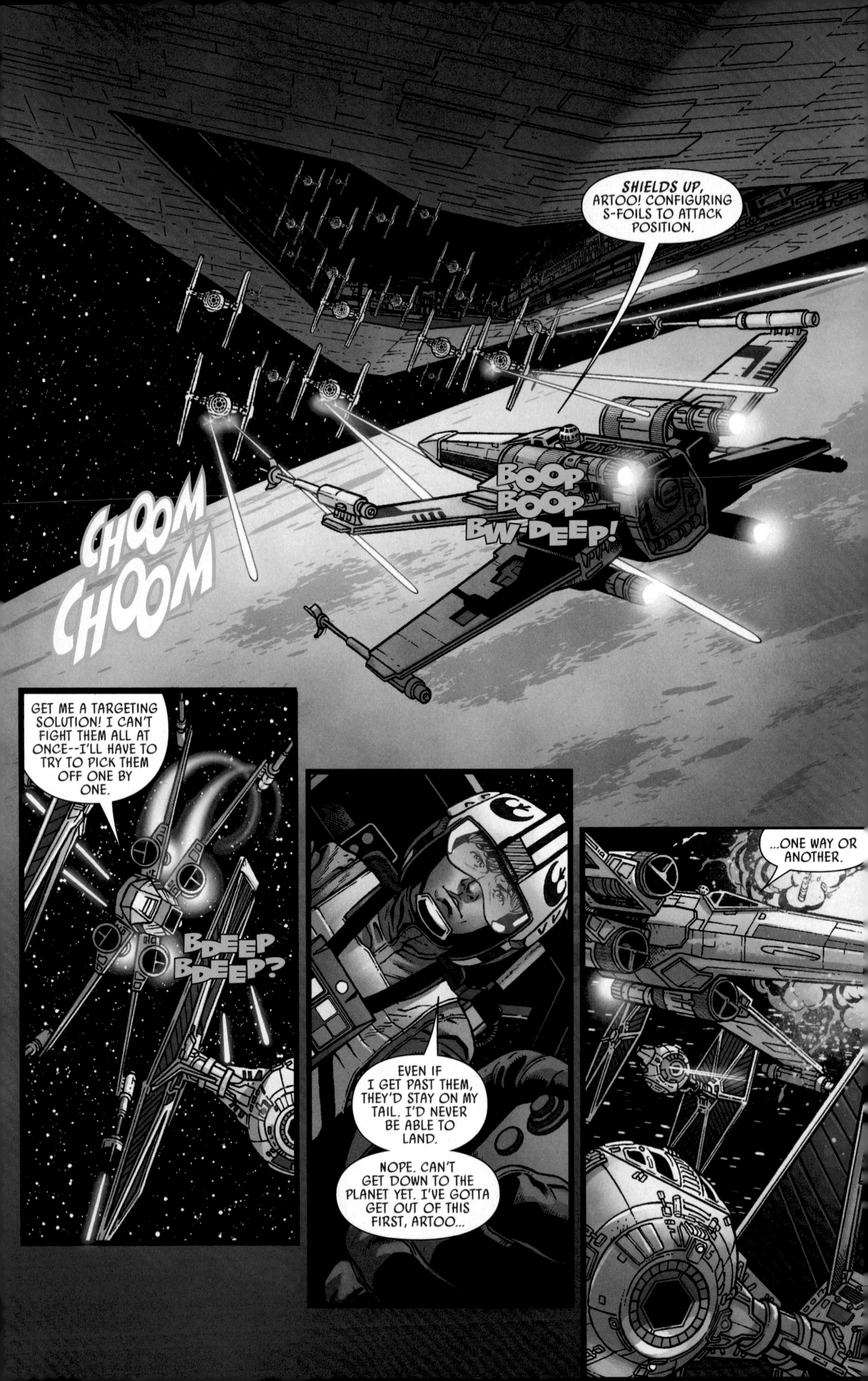
SHIELDS UP, ARTOO! CONFIGURING S-FOILS TO ATTACK POSITION.
BOOP BOOP BW-DEEP!
CHOOM CHOOM
GET ME A TARGETING SOLUTION! I CAN'T FIGHT THEM ALL AT ONCE--I'LL HAVE TO TRY TO PICK THEM OFF ONE BY ONE.
BDEEP BDEEP?
EVEN IF I GET PAST THEM, THEY'D STAY ON MY TAIL. I'D NEVER BE ABLE TO LAND.
NOPE. CAN'T GET DOWN TO THE PLANET YET. I'VE GOTTA GET OUT OF THIS FIRST, ARTOO...
...ONE WAY OR ANOTHER.

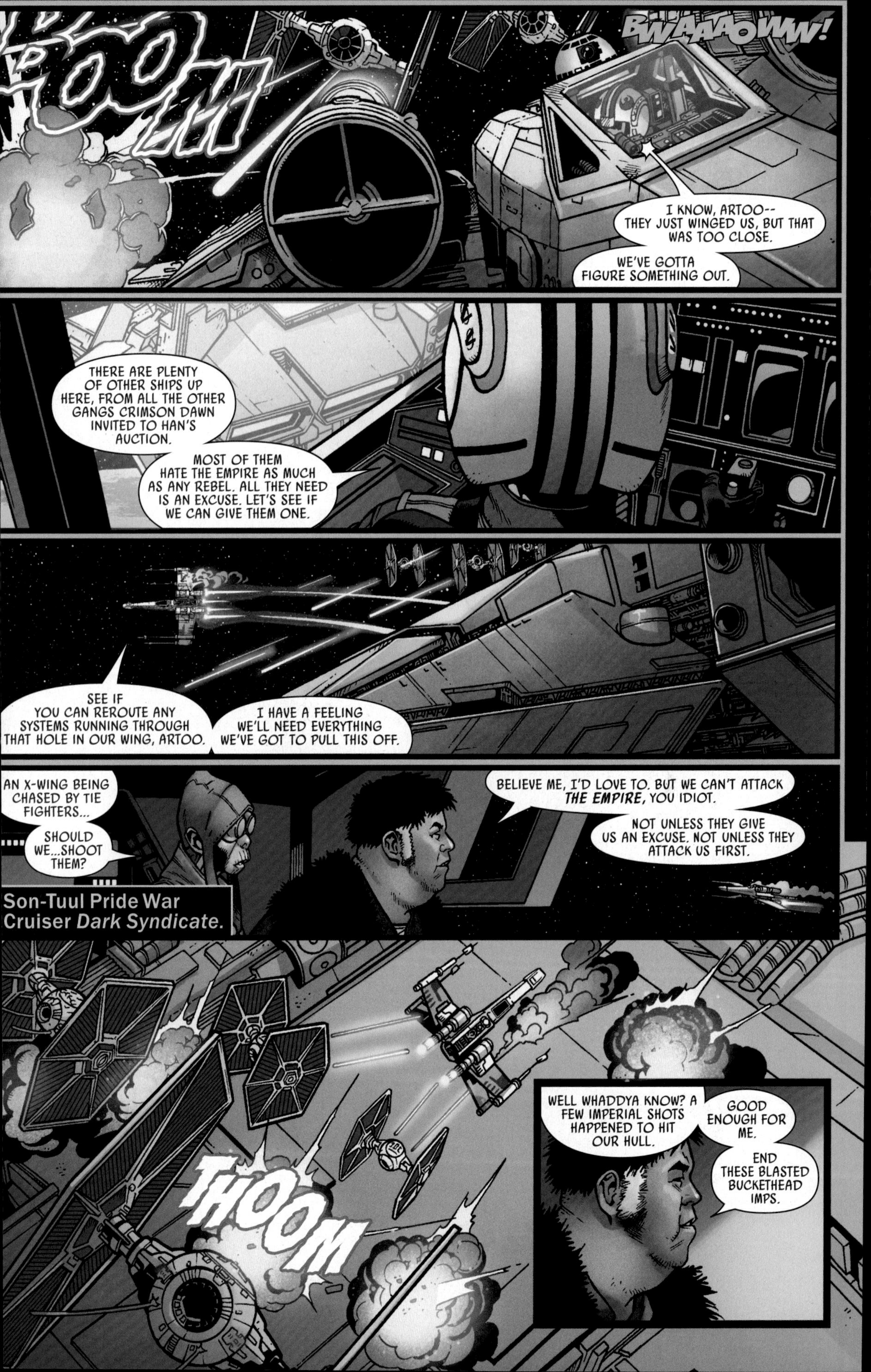
BWAAAOWW!
I KNOW, ARTOO-- THEY JUST WINGED US, BUT THAT WAS TOO CLOSE.
WE'VE GOTTA FIGURE SOMETHING OUT.
THERE ARE PLENTY OF OTHER SHIPS UP HERE, FROM ALL THE OTHER GANGS CRIMSON DAWN INVITED TO HAN'S AUCTION.
MOST OF THEM HATE THE EMPIRE AS MUCH AS ANY REBEL. ALL THEY NEED IS AN EXCUSE. LET'S SEE IF WE CAN GIVE THEM ONE.
SEE IF YOU CAN REROUTE ANY SYSTEMS RUNNING THROUGH THAT HOLE IN OUR WING, ARTOO.
I HAVE A FEELING WE'LL NEED EVERYTHING WE'VE GOT TO PULL THIS OFF.
Son-Tuul Pride War Cruiser *Dark Syndicate.*
AN X-WING BEING CHASED BY TIE FIGHTERS...
SHOULD WE...SHOOT THEM?
BELIEVE ME, I'D LOVE TO. BUT WE CAN'T ATTACK *THE EMPIRE,* YOU IDIOT.
NOT UNLESS THEY GIVE US AN EXCUSE. NOT UNLESS THEY ATTACK US FIRST.
THOOM
WELL WHADDYA KNOW? A FEW IMPERIAL SHOTS HAPPENED TO HIT OUR HULL.
GOOD ENOUGH FOR ME.
END THESE BLASTED BUCKETHEAD IMPS.

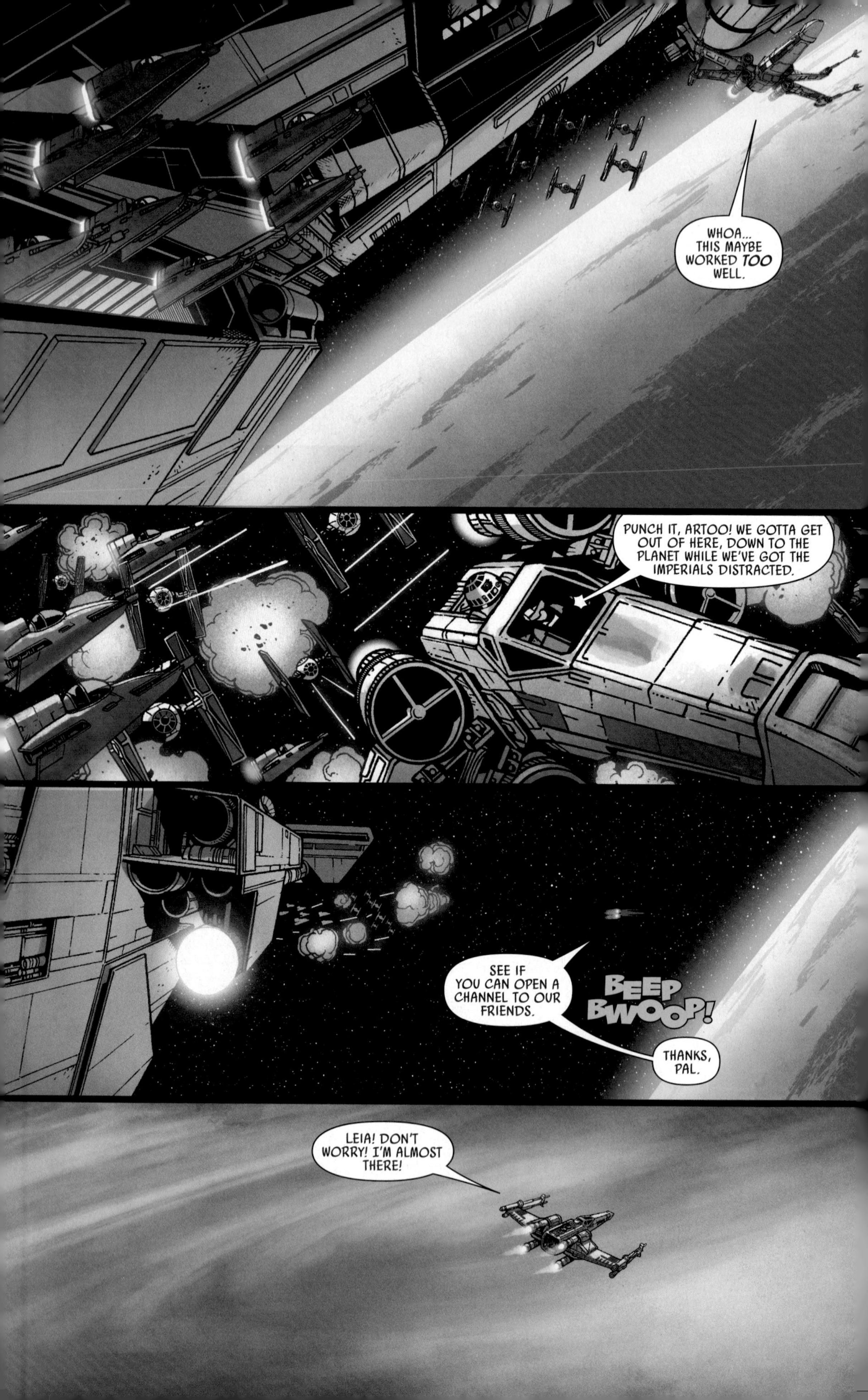
WHOA... THIS MAYBE WORKED TOO WELL.
PUNCH IT, ARTOO! WE GOTTA GET OUT OF HERE, DOWN TO THE PLANET WHILE WE'VE GOT THE IMPERIALS DISTRACTED.
SEE IF YOU CAN OPEN A CHANNEL TO OUR FRIENDS.
BEEP BWOOP!
THANKS, PAL.
LEIA! DON'T WORRY! I'M ALMOST THERE!

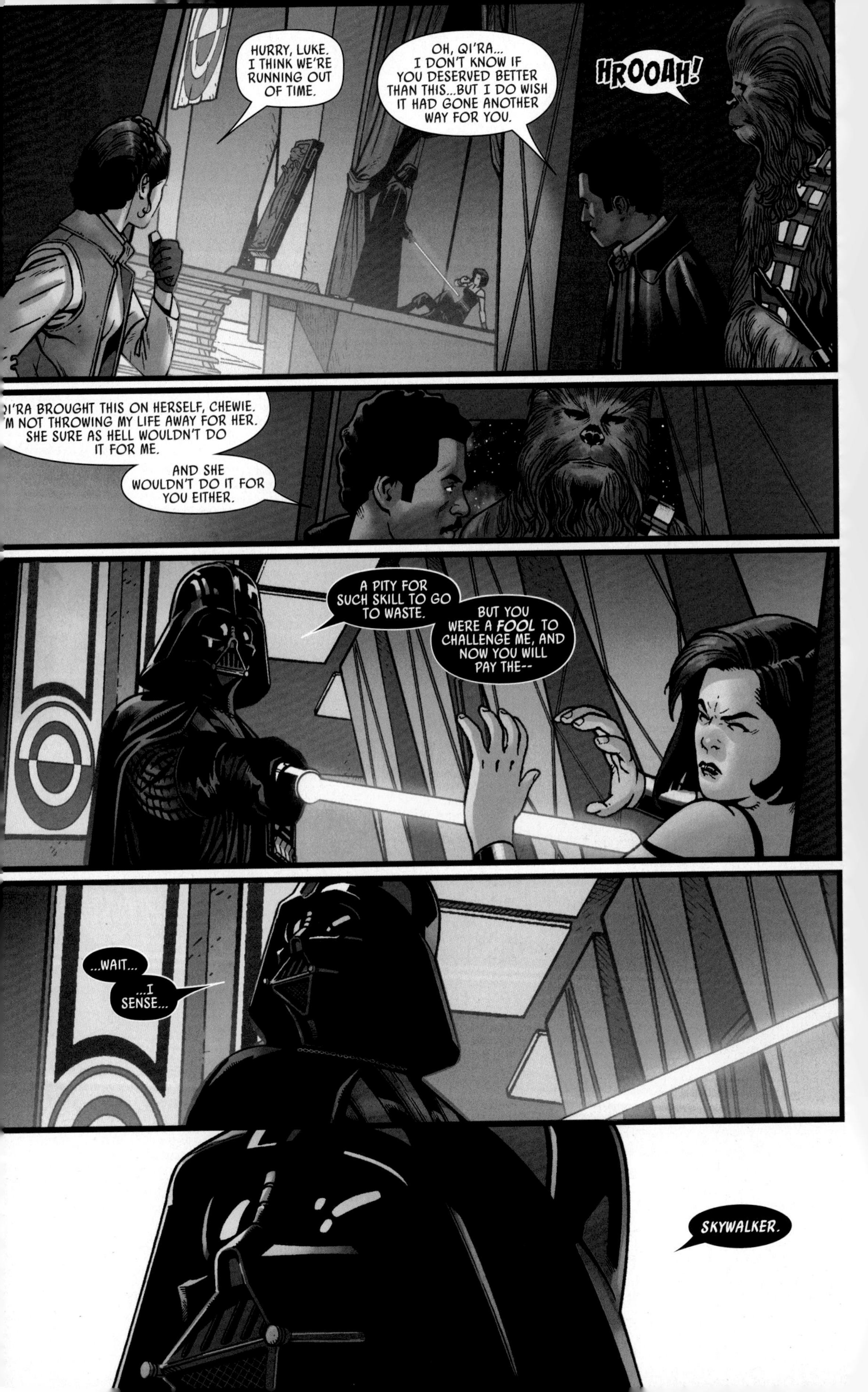
HURRY, LUKE. I THINK WE'RE RUNNING OUT OF TIME.
OH, QI'RA... I DON'T KNOW IF YOU DESERVED BETTER THAN THIS...BUT I DO WISH IT HAD GONE ANOTHER WAY FOR YOU.
HROOAH!
QI'RA BROUGHT THIS ON HERSELF, CHEWIE. I'M NOT THROWING MY LIFE AWAY FOR HER. SHE SURE AS HELL WOULDN'T DO IT FOR ME.
AND SHE WOULDN'T DO IT FOR YOU EITHER.
A PITY FOR SUCH SKILL TO GO TO WASTE.
BUT YOU WERE A *FOOL* TO CHALLENGE ME, AND NOW YOU WILL PAY THE--
...WAIT...
...I SENSE...
SKYWALKER.

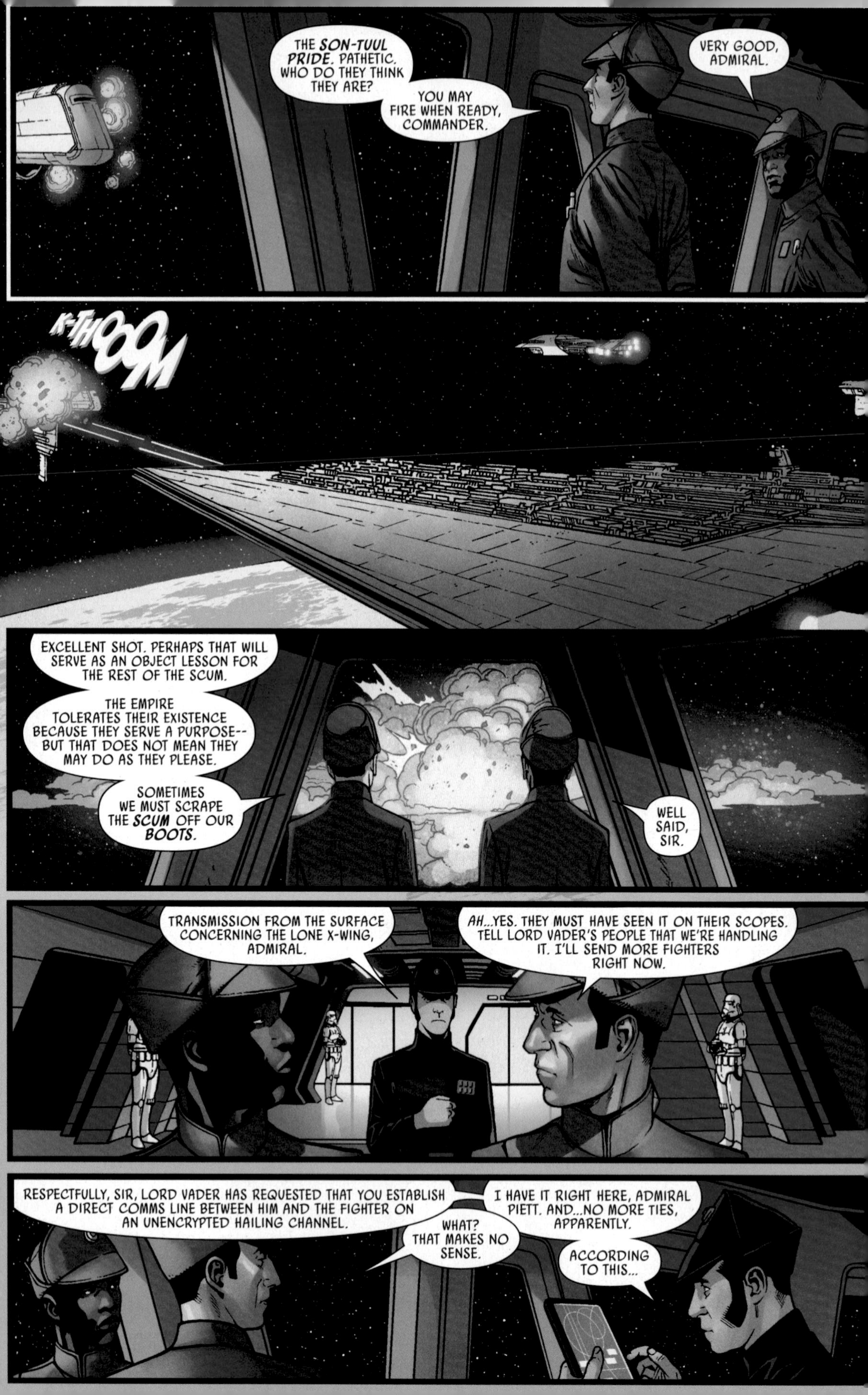
THE SON-TUUL PRIDE. PATHETIC. WHO DO THEY THINK THEY ARE?
YOU MAY FIRE WHEN READY, COMMANDER.
VERY GOOD, ADMIRAL.
K-THOOOM
EXCELLENT SHOT. PERHAPS THAT WILL SERVE AS AN OBJECT LESSON FOR THE REST OF THE SCUM.
THE EMPIRE TOLERATES THEIR EXISTENCE BECAUSE THEY SERVE A PURPOSE-- BUT THAT DOES NOT MEAN THEY MAY DO AS THEY PLEASE.
SOMETIMES WE MUST SCRAPE THE SCUM OFF OUR BOOTS.
WELL SAID, SIR.
TRANSMISSION FROM THE SURFACE CONCERNING THE LONE X-WING, ADMIRAL.
AH...YES. THEY MUST HAVE SEEN IT ON THEIR SCOPES. TELL LORD VADER'S PEOPLE THAT WE'RE HANDLING IT. I'LL SEND MORE FIGHTERS RIGHT NOW.
RESPECTFULLY, SIR, LORD VADER HAS REQUESTED THAT YOU ESTABLISH A DIRECT COMMS LINE BETWEEN HIM AND THE FIGHTER ON AN UNENCRYPTED HAILING CHANNEL.
WHAT? THAT MAKES NO SENSE.
I HAVE IT RIGHT HERE, ADMIRAL PIETT. AND...NO MORE TIES, APPARENTLY.
ACCORDING TO THIS...

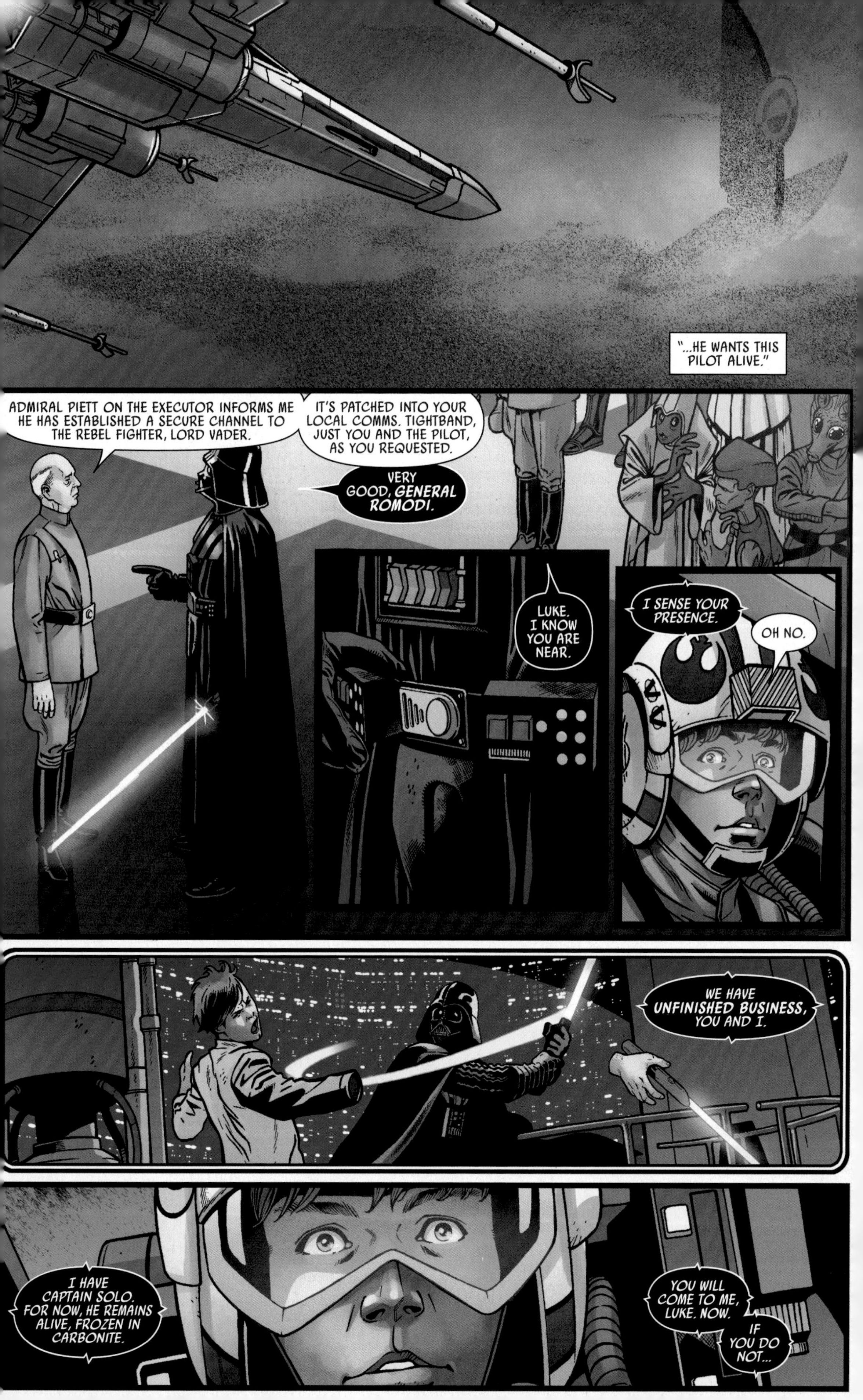
"...HE WANTS THIS PILOT ALIVE."
ADMIRAL PIETT ON THE EXECUTOR INFORMS ME HE HAS ESTABLISHED A SECURE CHANNEL TO THE REBEL FIGHTER, LORD VADER.
IT'S PATCHED INTO YOUR LOCAL COMMS. TIGHTBAND, JUST YOU AND THE PILOT, AS YOU REQUESTED.
VERY GOOD, GENERAL ROMODI.
LUKE. I KNOW YOU ARE NEAR.
I SENSE YOUR PRESENCE.
OH NO.
WE HAVE UNFINISHED BUSINESS, YOU AND I.
I HAVE CAPTAIN SOLO. FOR NOW, HE REMAINS ALIVE, FROZEN IN CARBONITE.
YOU WILL COME TO ME, LUKE. NOW.
IF YOU DO NOT...

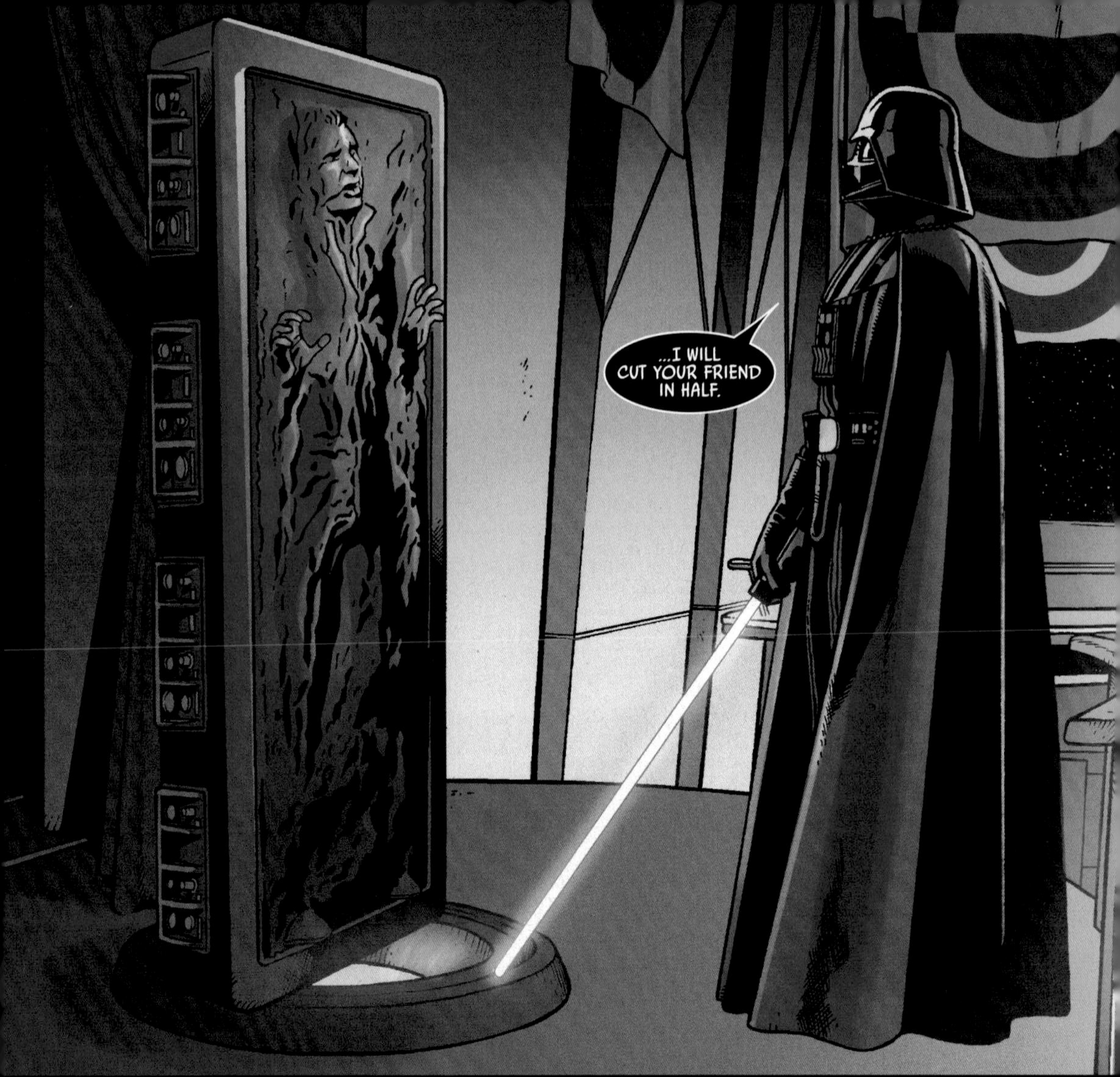
...I WILL CUT YOUR FRIEND IN HALF.
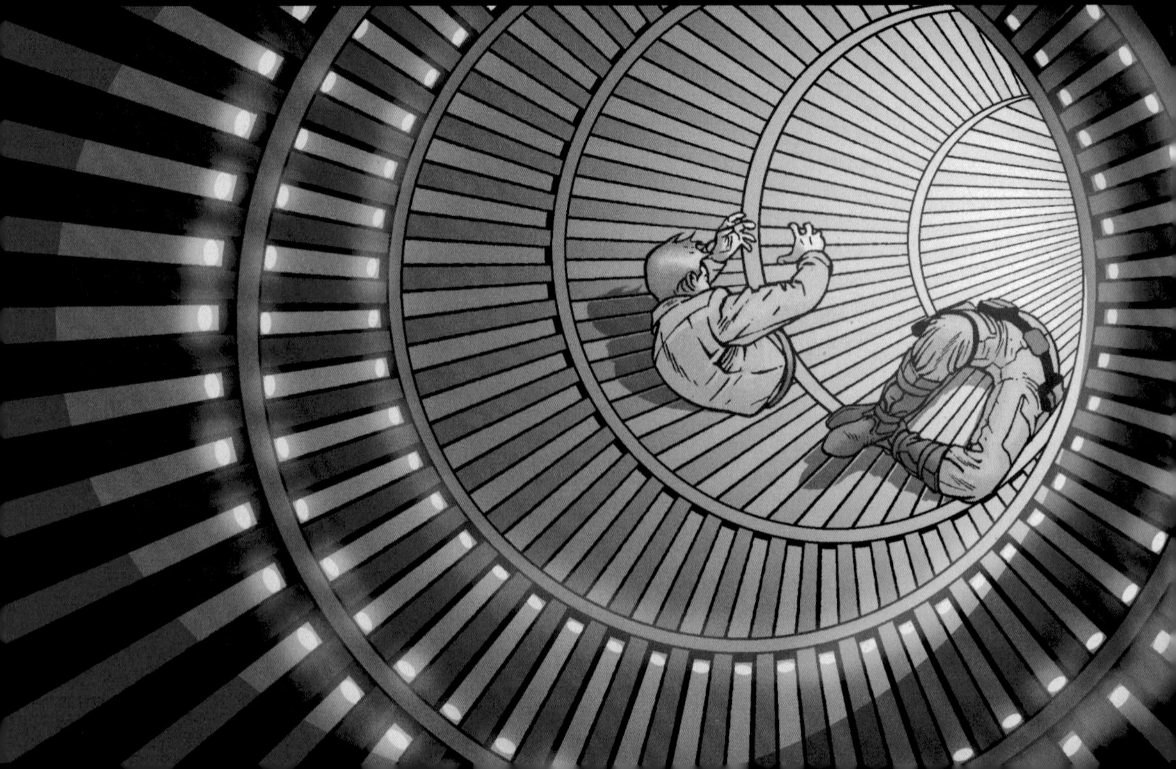

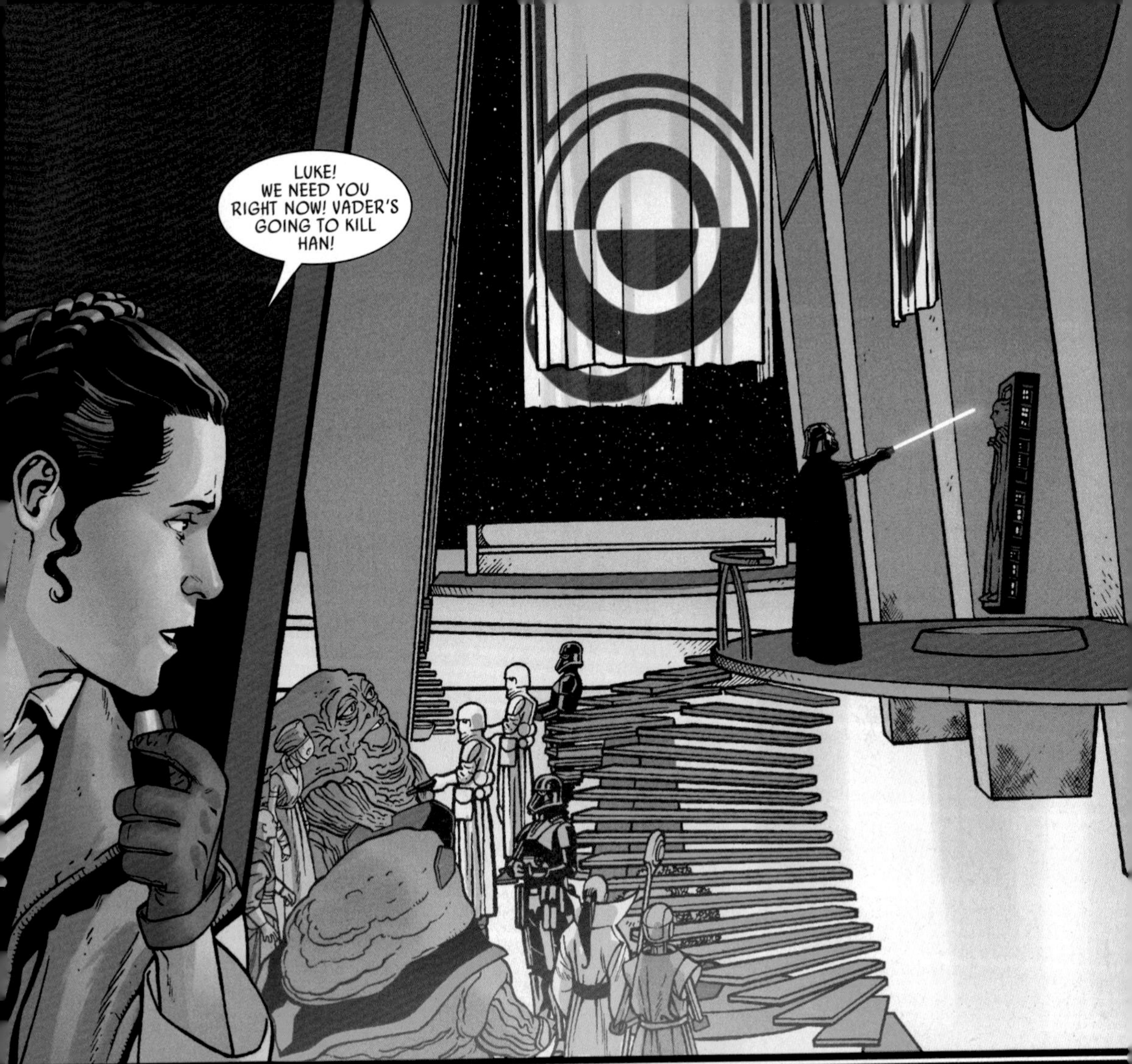
LUKE! WE NEED YOU RIGHT NOW! VADER'S GOING TO KILL HAN!

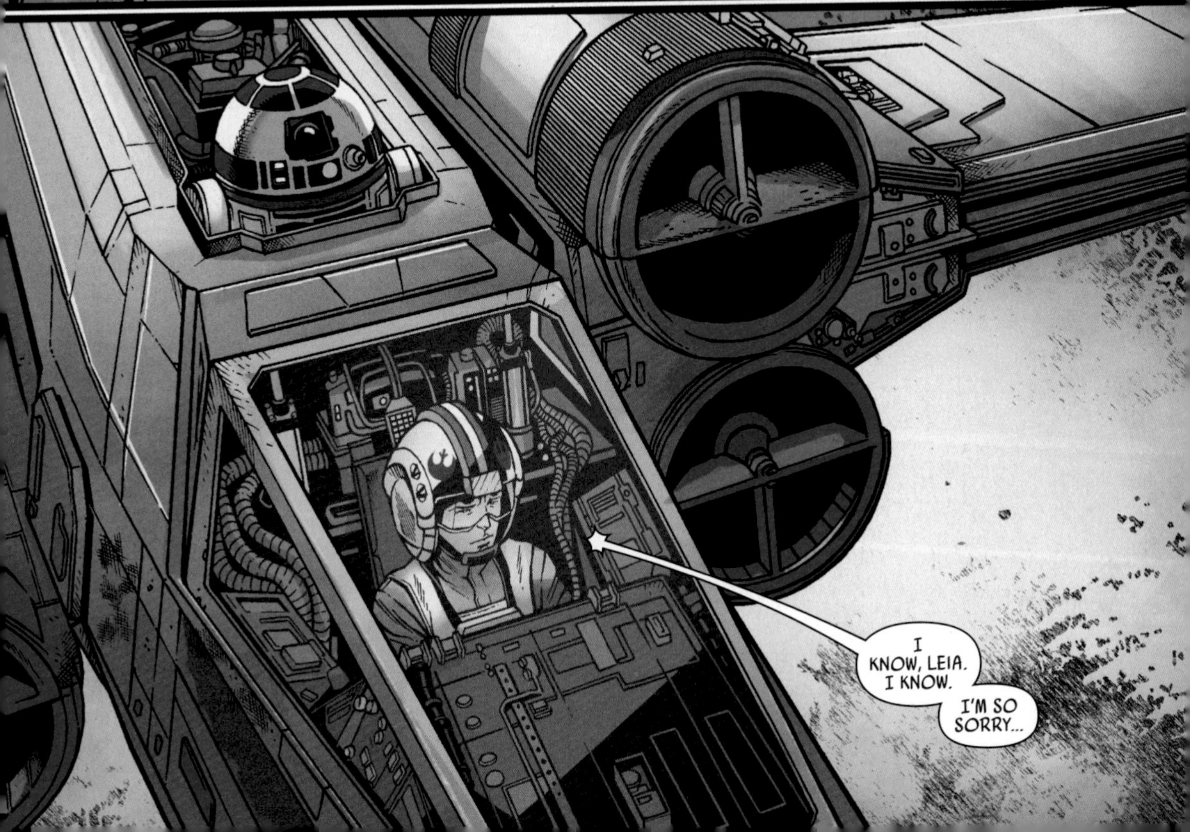
I KNOW, LEIA. I KNOW.
I'M SO SORRY...

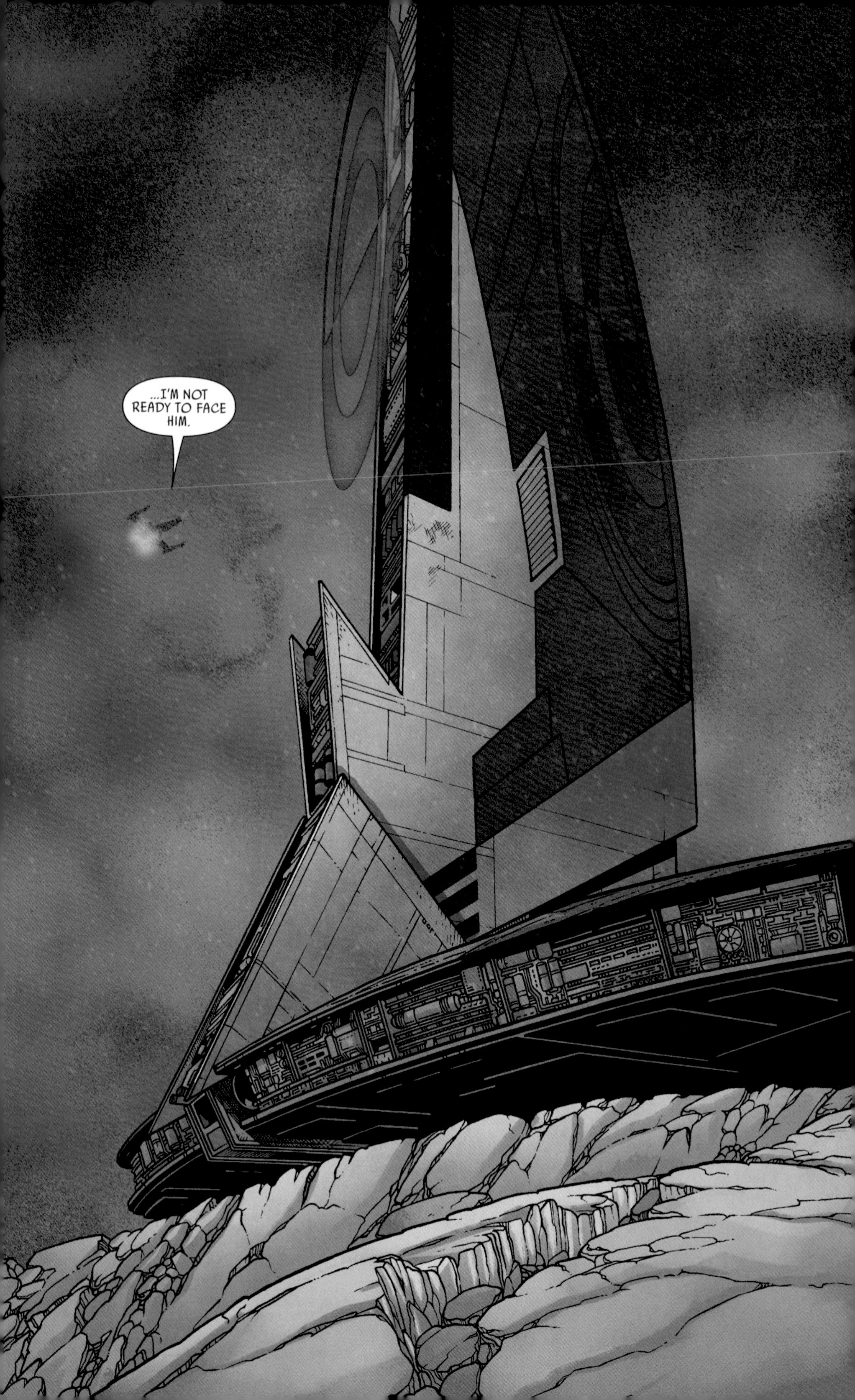
...I'M NOT READY TO FACE HIM.

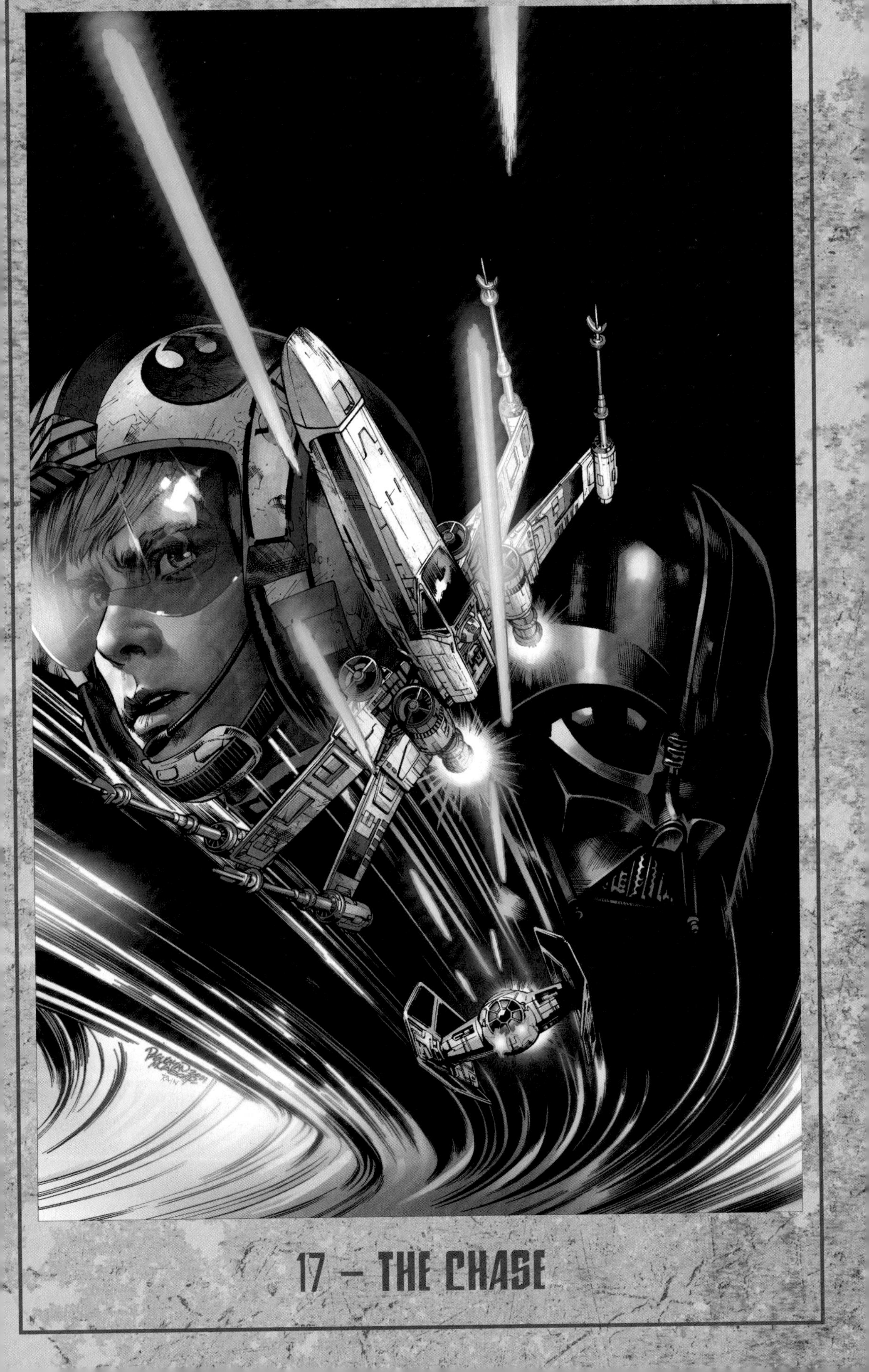

17 – THE CHASE

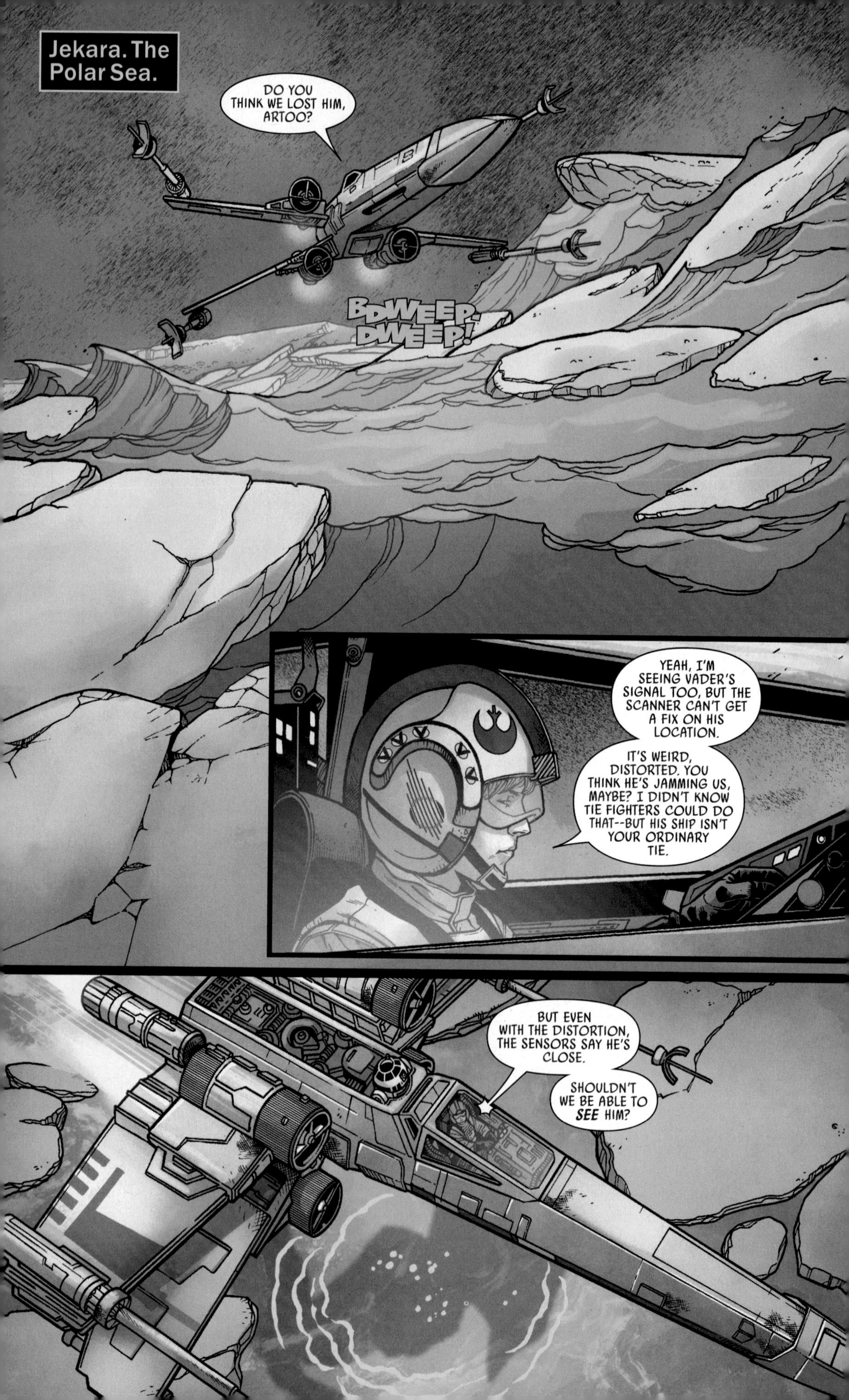
Jekara. The Polar Sea.
DO YOU THINK WE LOST HIM, ARTOO?
BDWEEP. DWEEP!
YEAH, I'M SEEING VADER'S SIGNAL TOO, BUT THE SCANNER CAN'T GET A FIX ON HIS LOCATION.
IT'S WEIRD, DISTORTED. YOU THINK HE'S JAMMING US, MAYBE? I DIDN'T KNOW TIE FIGHTERS COULD DO THAT--BUT HIS SHIP ISN'T YOUR ORDINARY TIE.
BUT EVEN WITH THE DISTORTION, THE SENSORS SAY HE'S CLOSE.
SHOULDN'T WE BE ABLE TO *SEE* HIM?

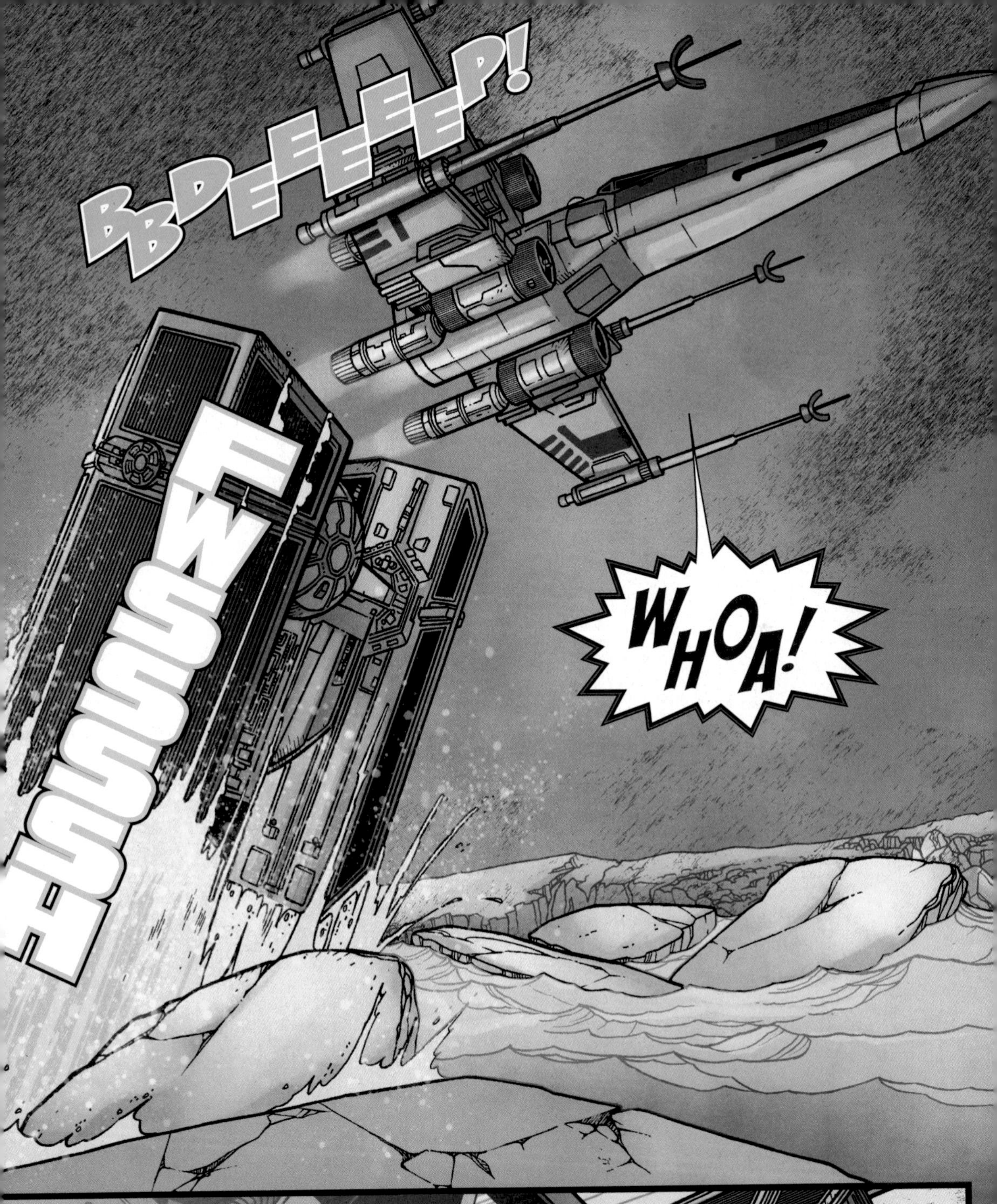
BBDEEEEEEP!
FWSSSH
WHOA!

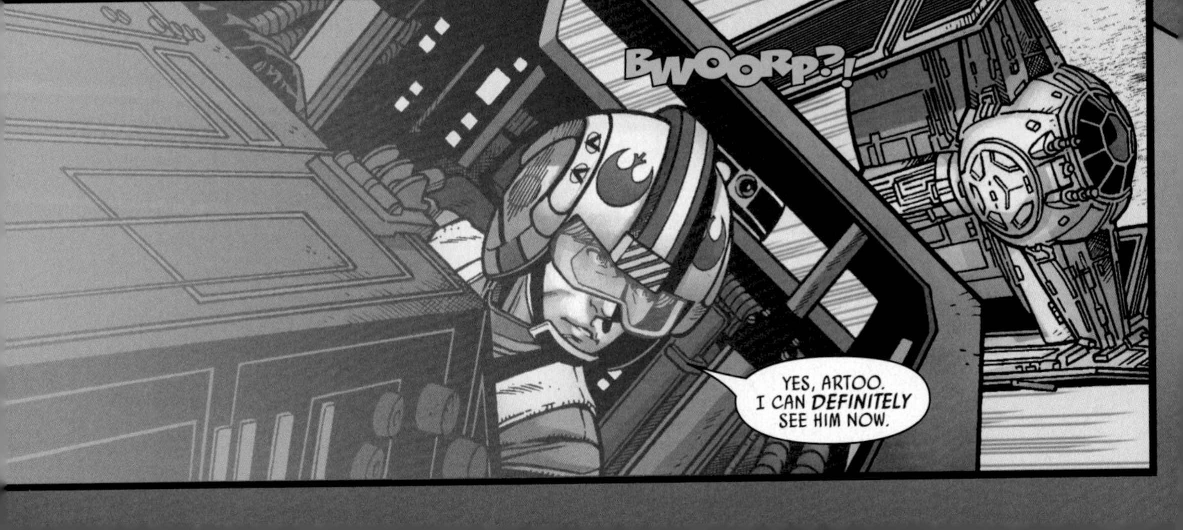
BWOORP?!
YES, ARTOO. I CAN *DEFINITELY* SEE HIM NOW.

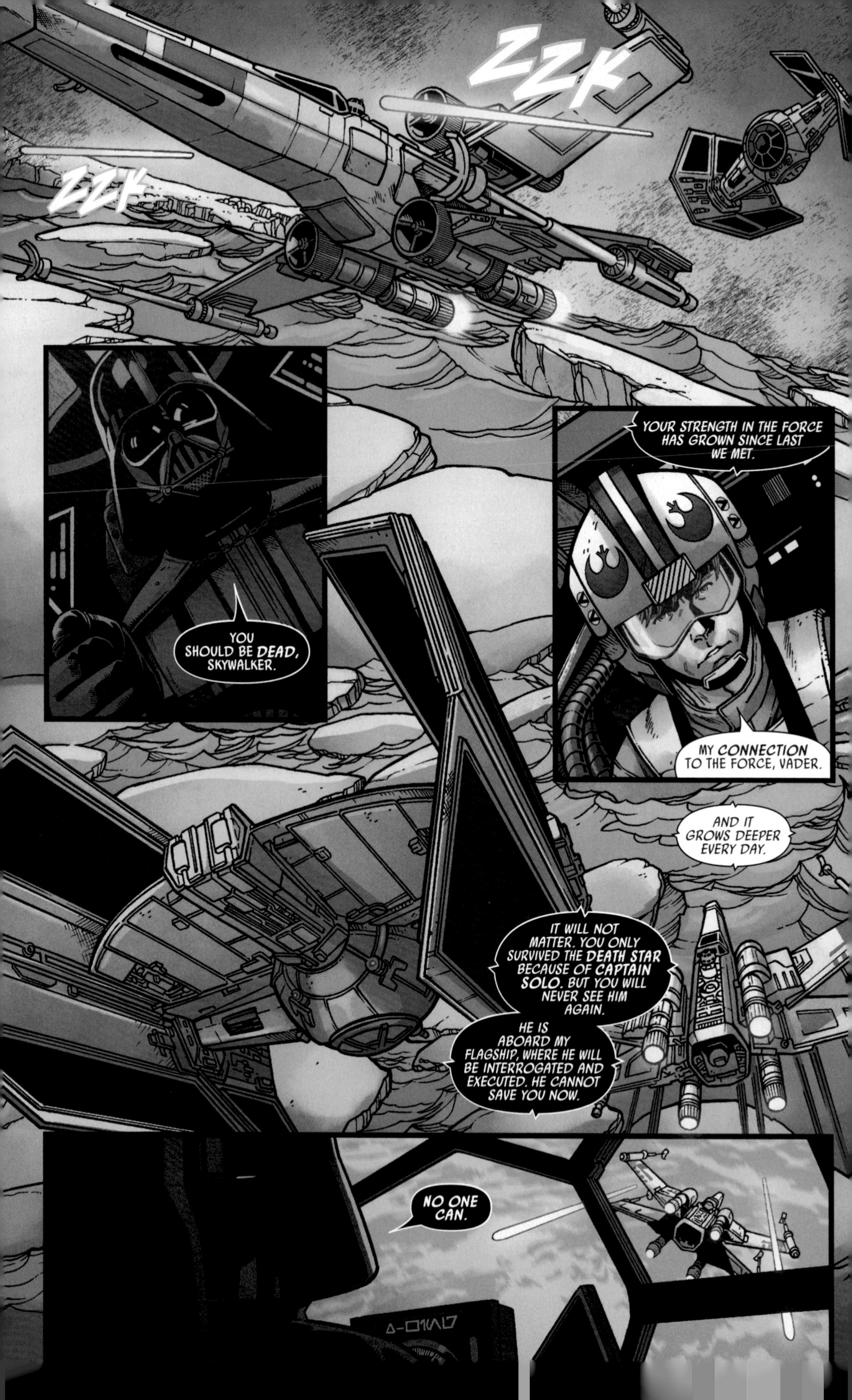
ZZK
ZZK
YOU SHOULD BE DEAD, SKYWALKER.
YOUR STRENGTH IN THE FORCE HAS GROWN SINCE LAST WE MET.
MY CONNECTION TO THE FORCE, VADER.
AND IT GROWS DEEPER EVERY DAY.
IT WILL NOT MATTER. YOU ONLY SURVIVED THE DEATH STAR BECAUSE OF CAPTAIN SOLO. BUT YOU WILL NEVER SEE HIM AGAIN.
HE IS ABOARD MY FLAGSHIP, WHERE HE WILL BE INTERROGATED AND EXECUTED. HE CANNOT SAVE YOU NOW.
NO ONE CAN.

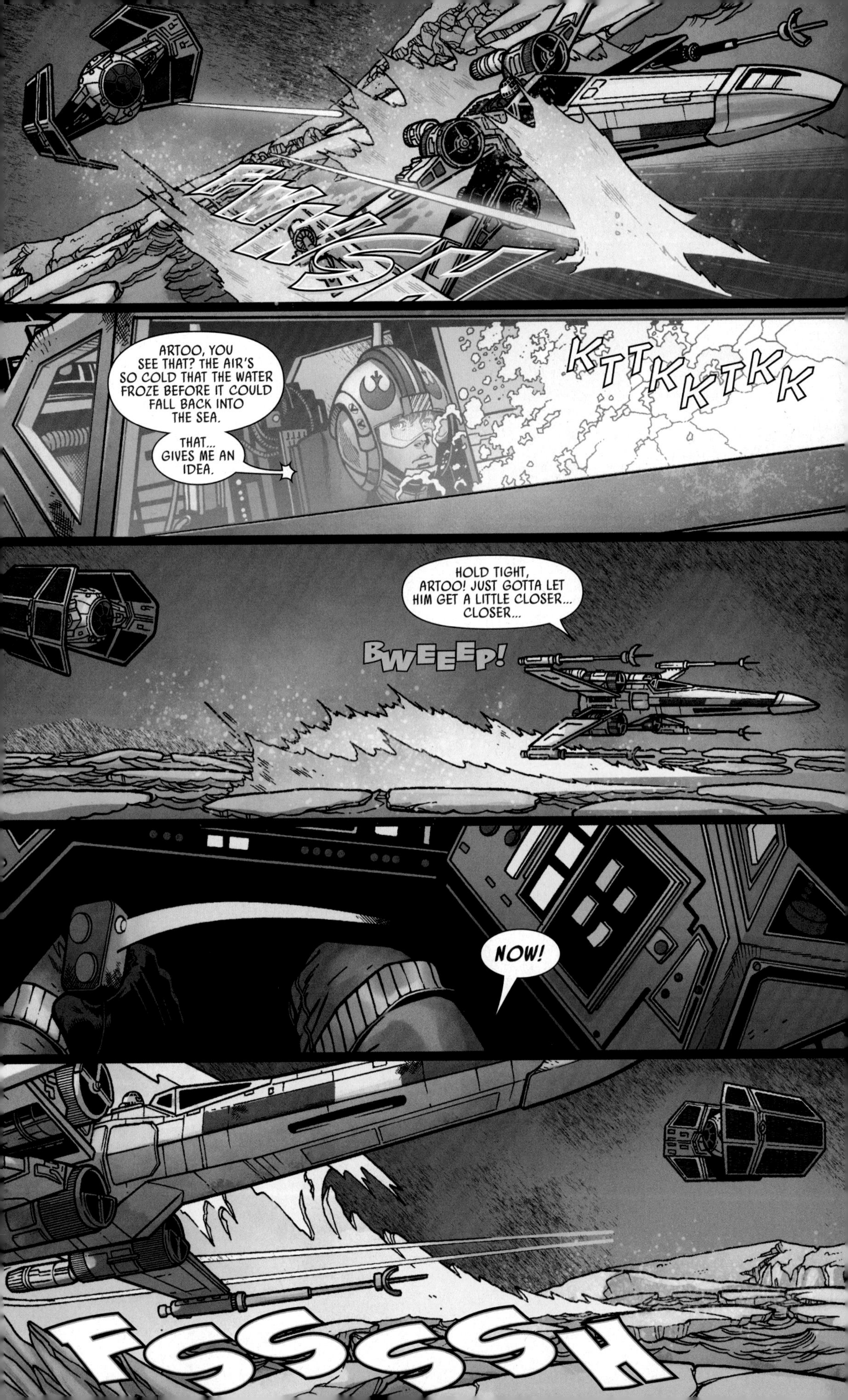
ARTOO, YOU SEE THAT? THE AIR'S SO COLD THAT THE WATER FROZE BEFORE IT COULD FALL BACK INTO THE SEA.
THAT... GIVES ME AN IDEA.
KTTKKKTKK
HOLD TIGHT, ARTOO! JUST GOTTA LET HIM GET A LITTLE CLOSER... CLOSER...
BWEEEP!
NOW!
FSSSSH

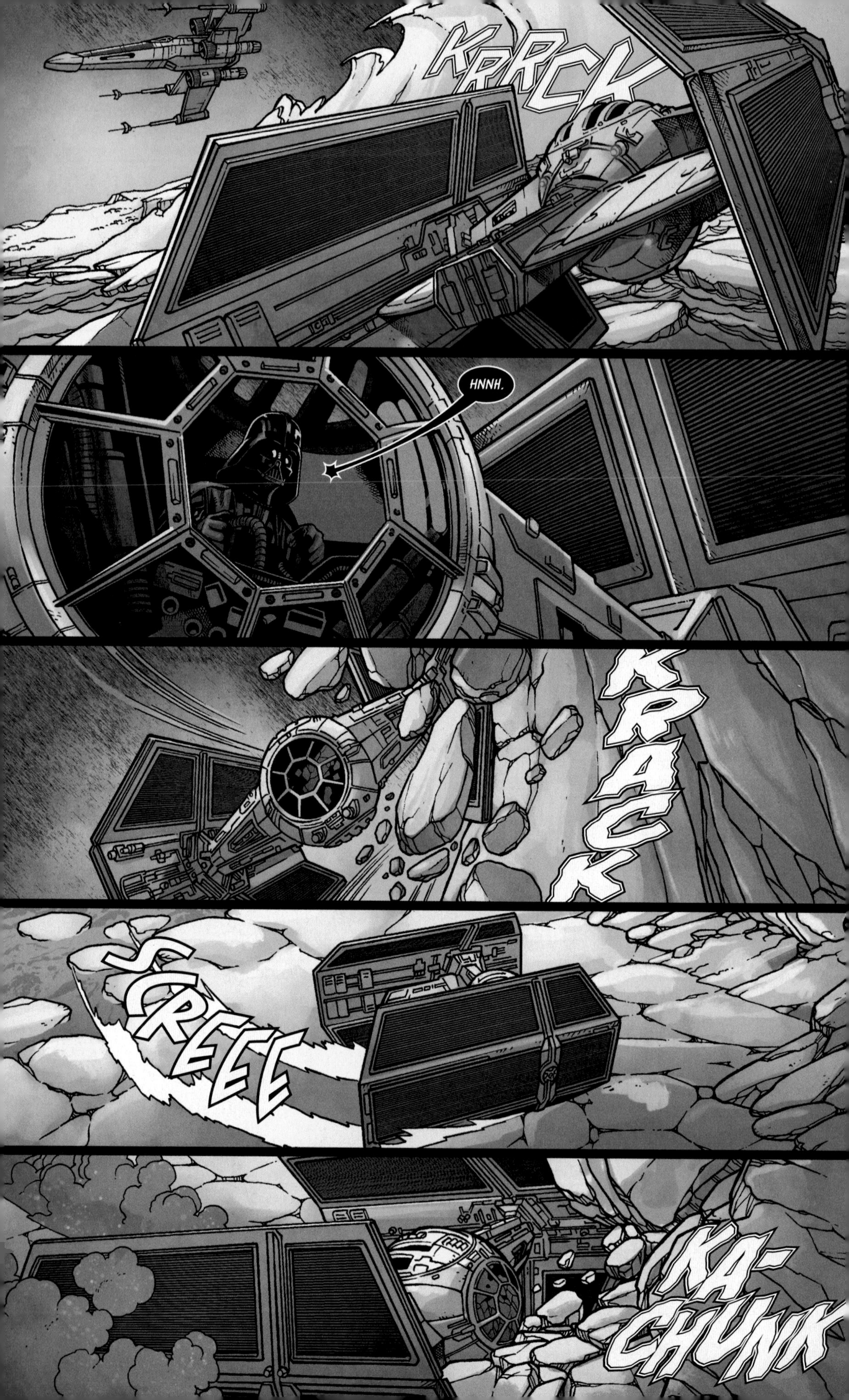
KRRCK
HNNH.
KRACK
SCREEE
KA-
CHUNK

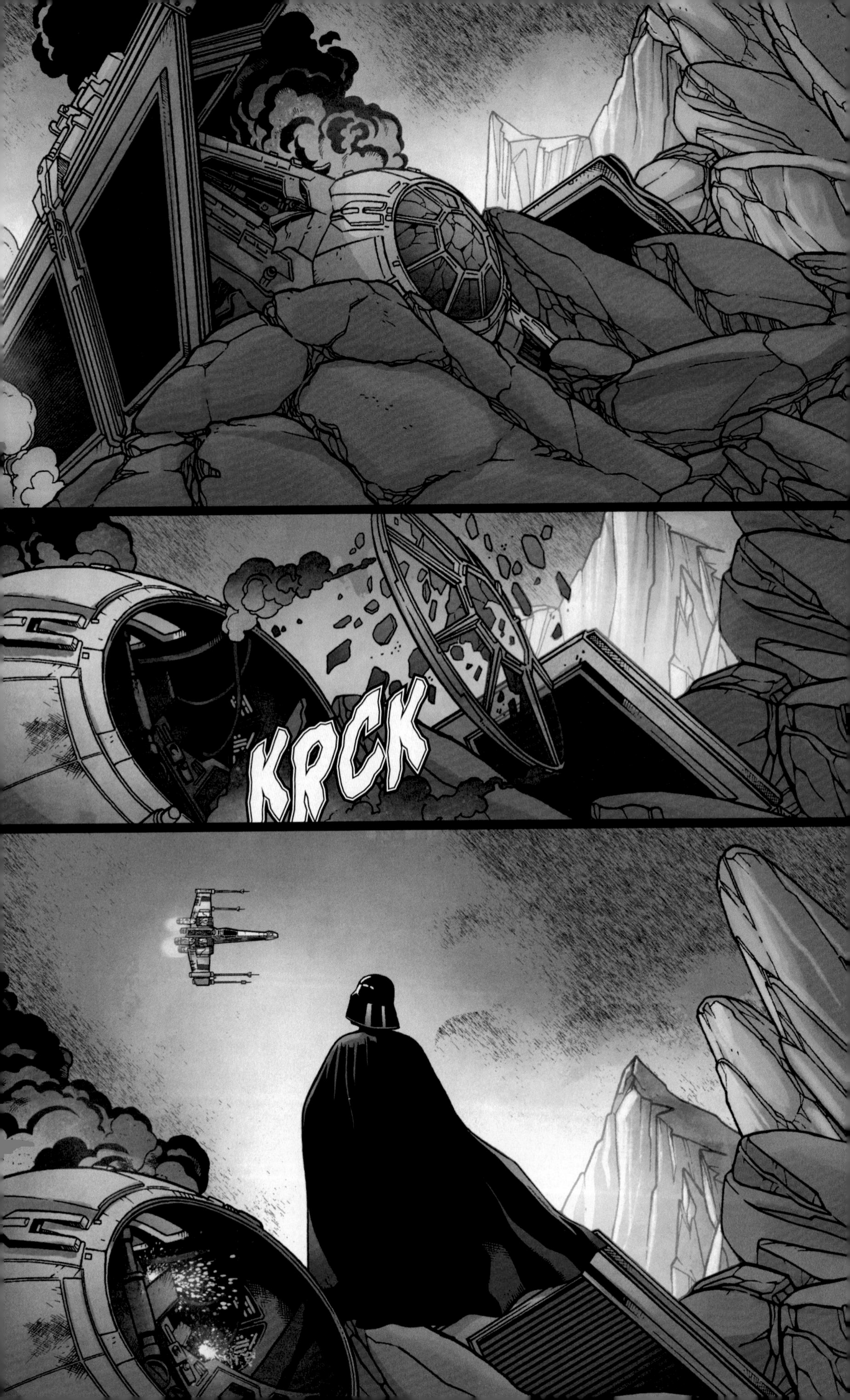
KRCK

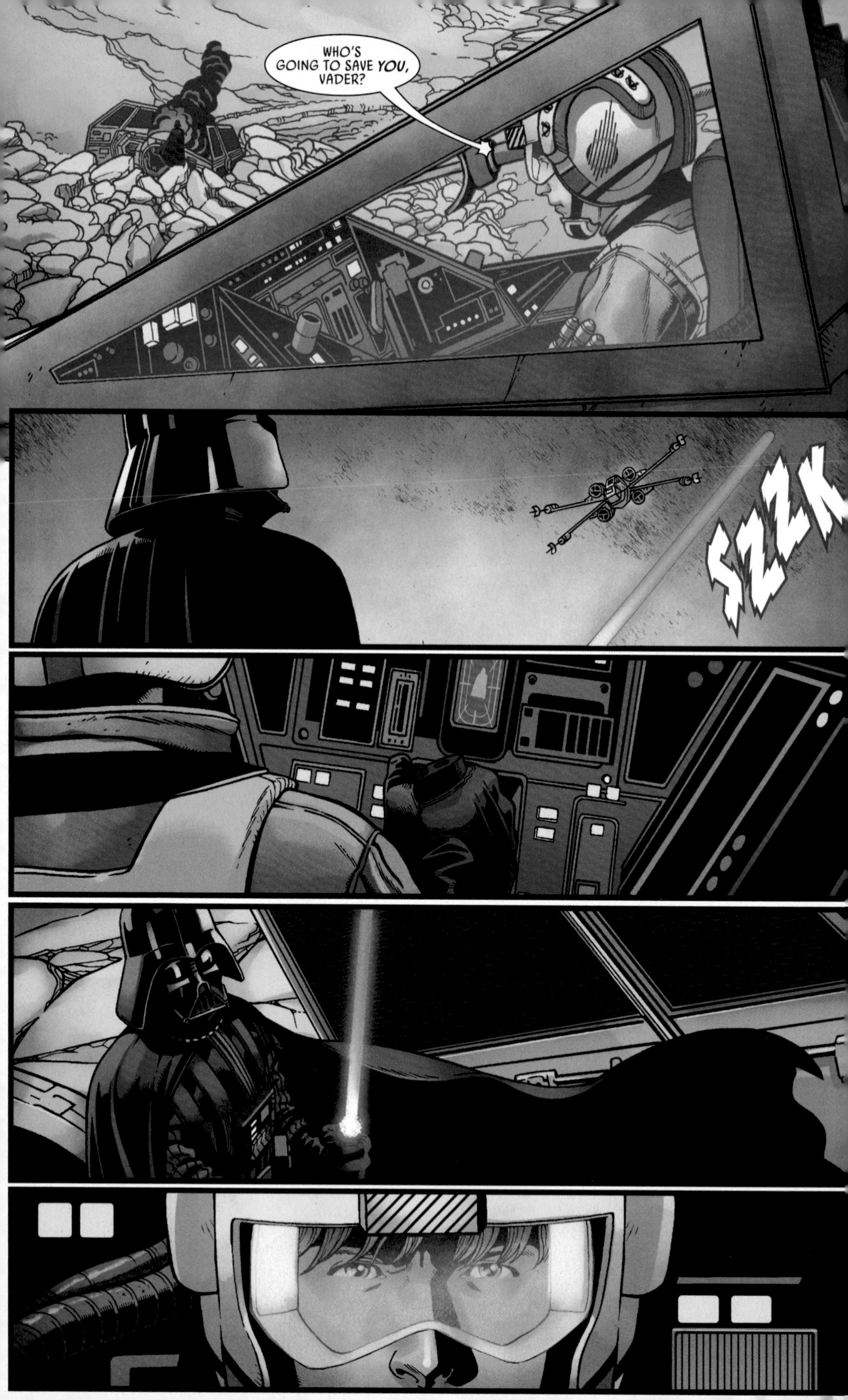
WHO'S GOING TO SAVE YOU, VADER?
SZZK

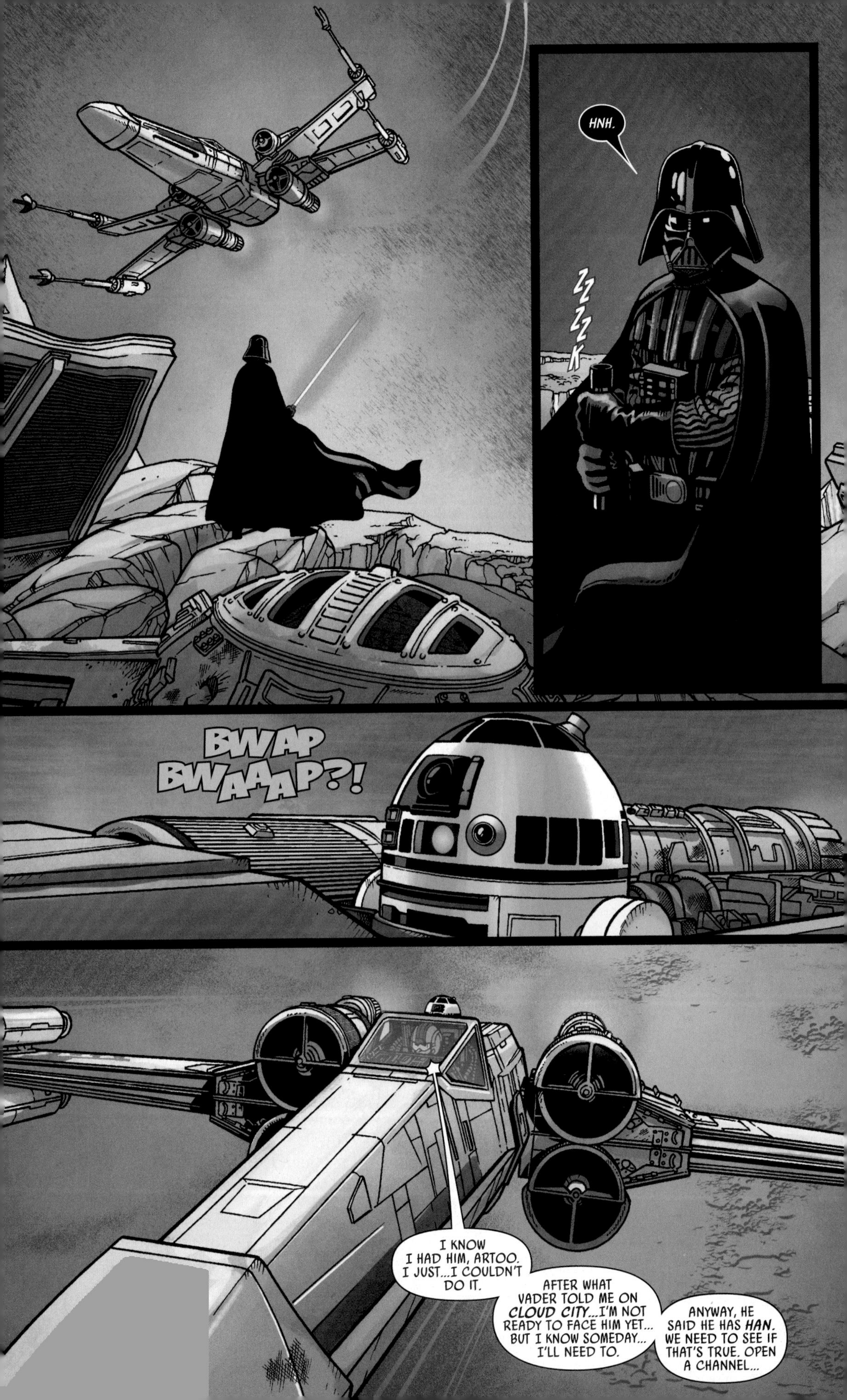
HNH.
ZZZK
BWAP BWAAAP?!
I KNOW I HAD HIM, ARTOO. I JUST...I COULDN'T DO IT.
AFTER WHAT VADER TOLD ME ON *CLOUD CITY*...I'M NOT READY TO FACE HIM YET... BUT I KNOW SOMEDAY... I'LL NEED TO.
ANYWAY, HE SAID HE HAS *HAN*. WE NEED TO SEE IF THAT'S TRUE. OPEN A CHANNEL...

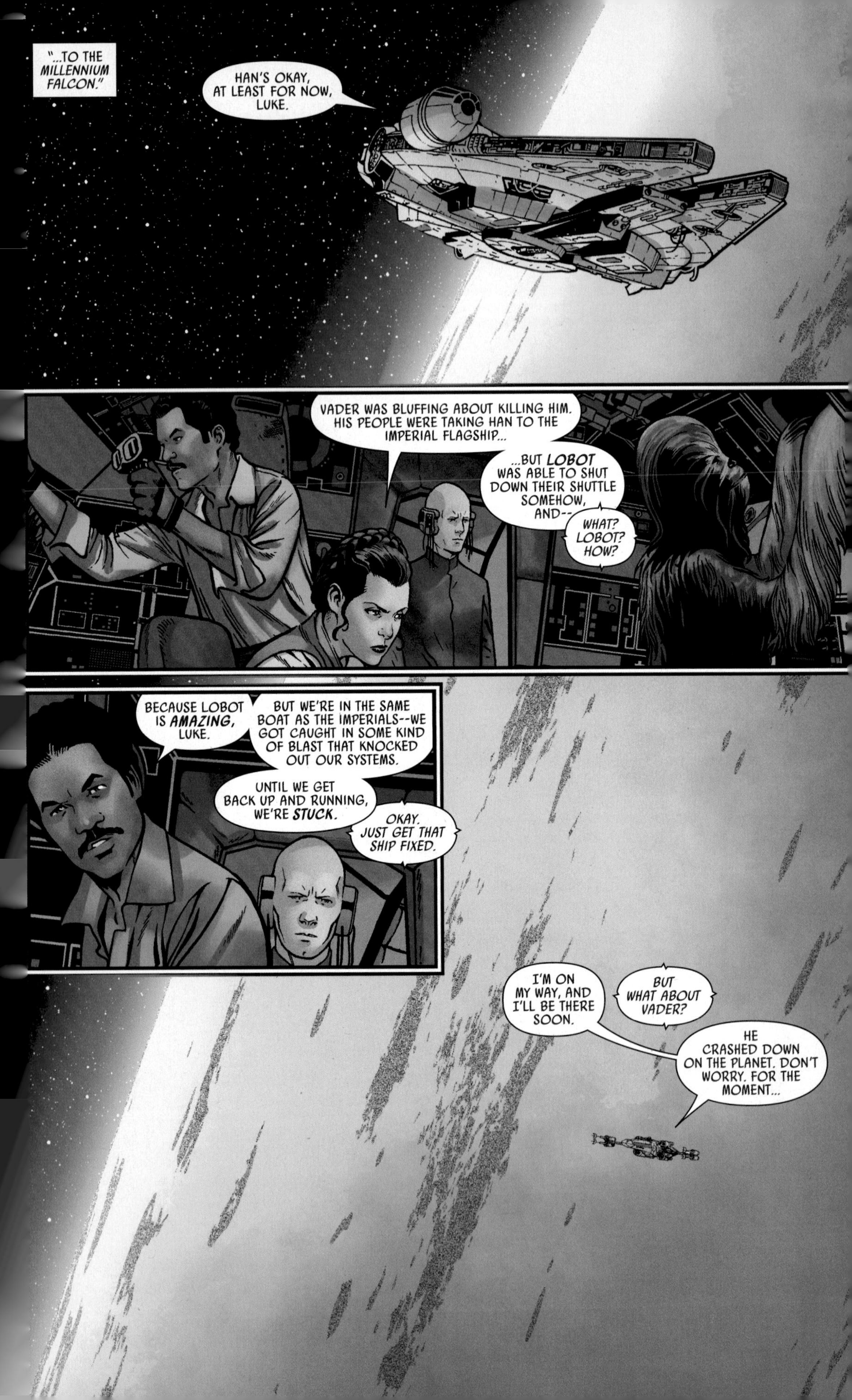
"...TO THE MILLENNIUM FALCON."
HAN'S OKAY, AT LEAST FOR NOW, LUKE.
VADER WAS BLUFFING ABOUT KILLING HIM. HIS PEOPLE WERE TAKING HAN TO THE IMPERIAL FLAGSHIP...
...BUT LOBOT WAS ABLE TO SHUT DOWN THEIR SHUTTLE SOMEHOW, AND--
WHAT? LOBOT? HOW?
BECAUSE LOBOT IS AMAZING, LUKE.
BUT WE'RE IN THE SAME BOAT AS THE IMPERIALS--WE GOT CAUGHT IN SOME KIND OF BLAST THAT KNOCKED OUT OUR SYSTEMS.
UNTIL WE GET BACK UP AND RUNNING, WE'RE STUCK.
OKAY. JUST GET THAT SHIP FIXED.
I'M ON MY WAY, AND I'LL BE THERE SOON.
BUT WHAT ABOUT VADER?
HE CRASHED DOWN ON THE PLANET. DON'T WORRY. FOR THE MOMENT...

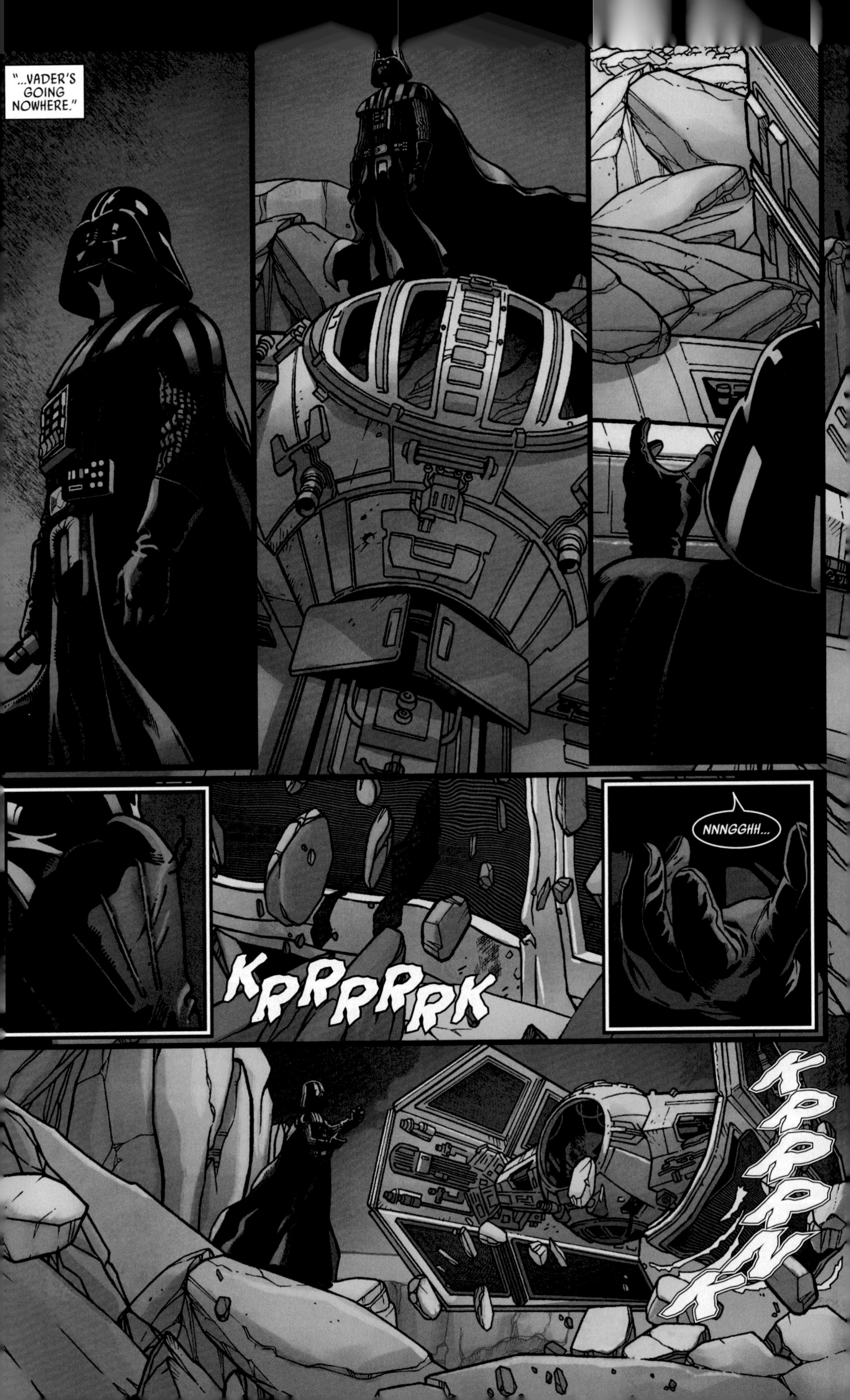
"...VADER'S GOING NOWHERE."
KRRRRRK
NNNGGHH...
KRRRNK

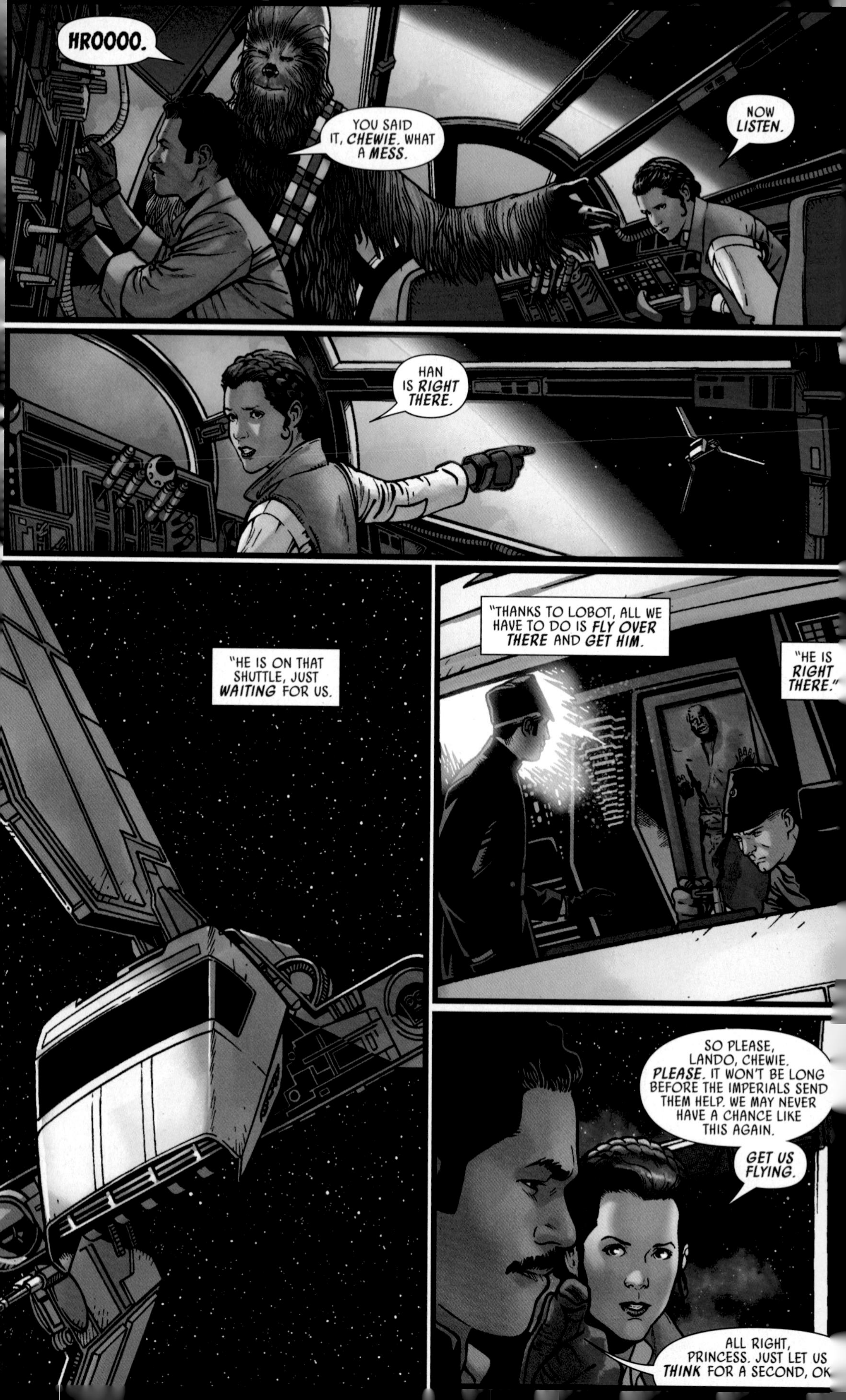
HROOOO.
YOU SAID IT, CHEWIE. WHAT A MESS.
NOW LISTEN.
HAN IS RIGHT THERE.
"HE IS ON THAT SHUTTLE, JUST WAITING FOR US.
"THANKS TO LOBOT, ALL WE HAVE TO DO IS FLY OVER THERE AND GET HIM.
"HE IS RIGHT THERE."
SO PLEASE, LANDO, CHEWIE. PLEASE. IT WON'T BE LONG BEFORE THE IMPERIALS SEND THEM HELP. WE MAY NEVER HAVE A CHANCE LIKE THIS AGAIN.
GET US FLYING.
ALL RIGHT, PRINCESS. JUST LET US THINK FOR A SECOND, OK

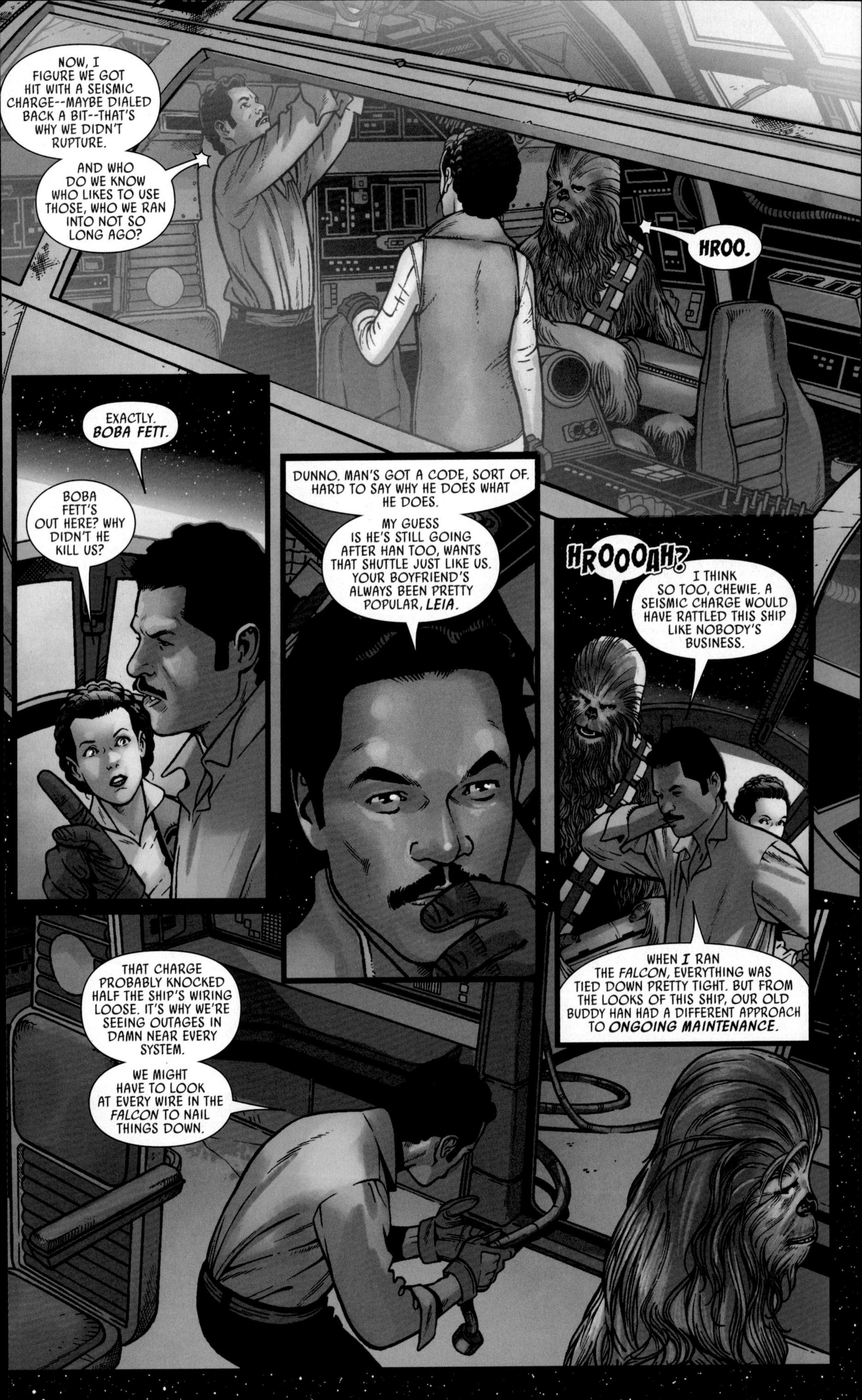
NOW, I FIGURE WE GOT HIT WITH A SEISMIC CHARGE--MAYBE DIALED BACK A BIT--THAT'S WHY WE DIDN'T RUPTURE.
AND WHO DO WE KNOW WHO LIKES TO USE THOSE, WHO WE RAN INTO NOT SO LONG AGO?
HROO.
EXACTLY. BOBA FETT.
BOBA FETT'S OUT HERE? WHY DIDN'T HE KILL US?
DUNNO. MAN'S GOT A CODE, SORT OF. HARD TO SAY WHY HE DOES WHAT HE DOES.
MY GUESS IS HE'S STILL GOING AFTER HAN TOO, WANTS THAT SHUTTLE JUST LIKE US. YOUR BOYFRIEND'S ALWAYS BEEN PRETTY POPULAR, LEIA.
HROOOAH?
I THINK SO TOO, CHEWIE. A SEISMIC CHARGE WOULD HAVE RATTLED THIS SHIP LIKE NOBODY'S BUSINESS.
WHEN I RAN THE FALCON, EVERYTHING WAS TIED DOWN PRETTY TIGHT. BUT FROM THE LOOKS OF THIS SHIP, OUR OLD BUDDY HAN HAD A DIFFERENT APPROACH TO ONGOING MAINTENANCE.
THAT CHARGE PROBABLY KNOCKED HALF THE SHIP'S WIRING LOOSE. IT'S WHY WE'RE SEEING OUTAGES IN DAMN NEAR EVERY SYSTEM.
WE MIGHT HAVE TO LOOK AT EVERY WIRE IN THE FALCON TO NAIL THINGS DOWN.

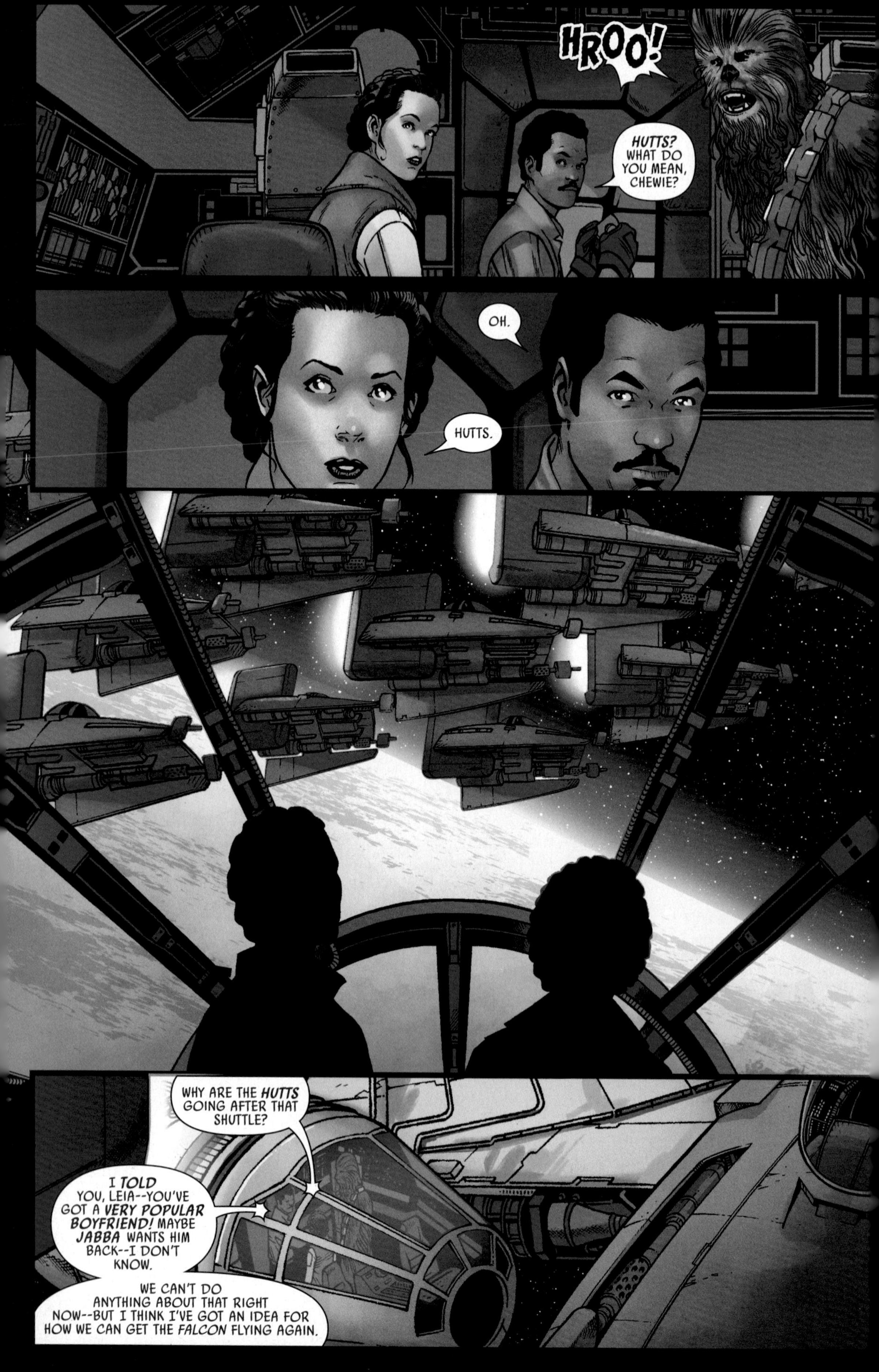

HROO!
HUTTS? WHAT DO YOU MEAN, CHEWIE?
OH.
HUTTS.
WHY ARE THE HUTTS GOING AFTER THAT SHUTTLE?
I TOLD YOU, LEIA--YOU'VE GOT A VERY POPULAR BOYFRIEND! MAYBE JABBA WANTS HIM BACK--I DON'T KNOW.
WE CAN'T DO ANYTHING ABOUT THAT RIGHT NOW--BUT I THINK I'VE GOT AN IDEA FOR HOW WE CAN GET THE FALCON FLYING AGAIN.

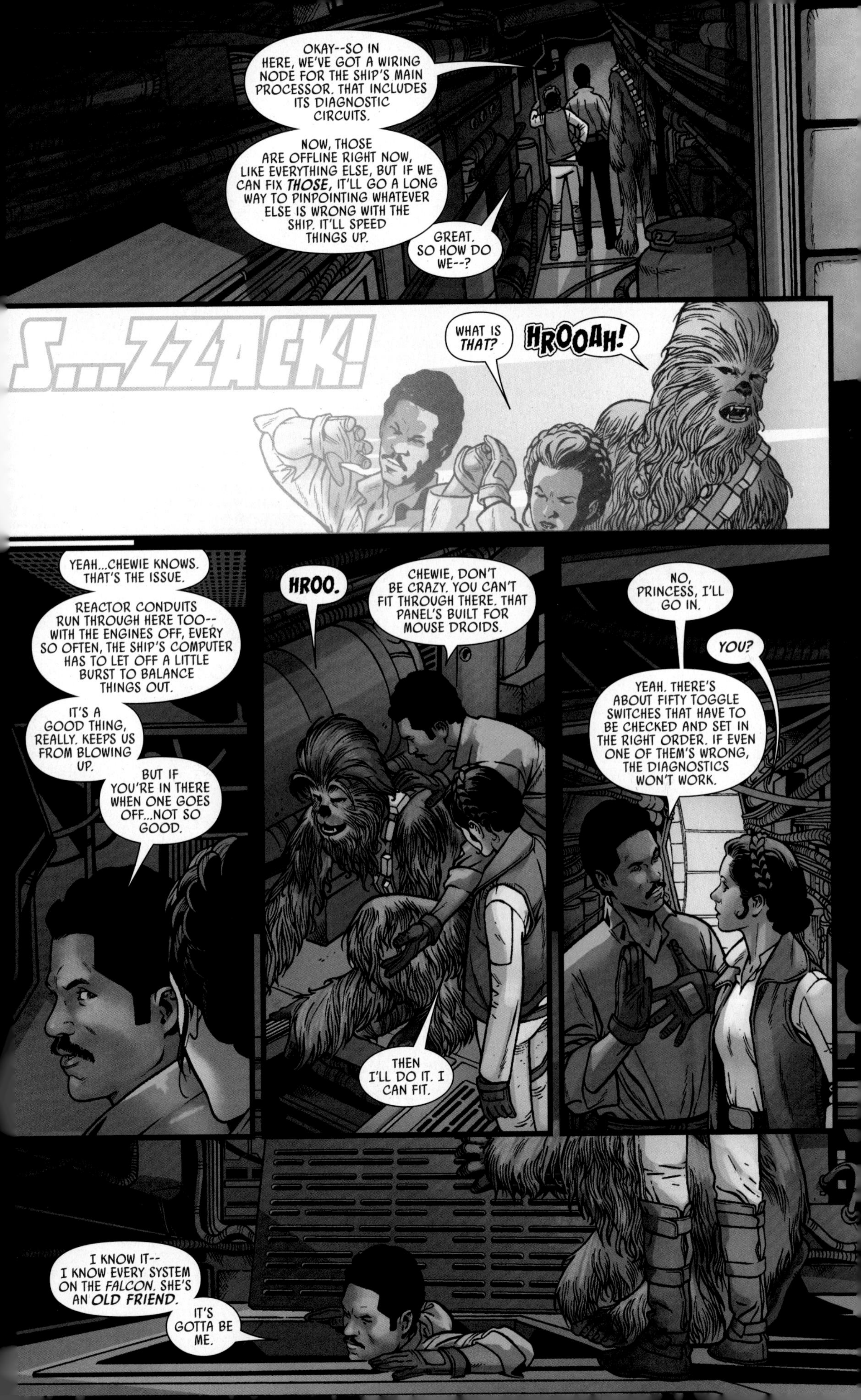
OKAY--SO IN HERE, WE'VE GOT A WIRING NODE FOR THE SHIP'S MAIN PROCESSOR. THAT INCLUDES ITS DIAGNOSTIC CIRCUITS.
NOW, THOSE ARE OFFLINE RIGHT NOW, LIKE EVERYTHING ELSE, BUT IF WE CAN FIX THOSE, IT'LL GO A LONG WAY TO PINPOINTING WHATEVER ELSE IS WRONG WITH THE SHIP. IT'LL SPEED THINGS UP.
GREAT. SO HOW DO WE--?
S...ZZACK!
WHAT IS THAT?
HROOAH!
YEAH...CHEWIE KNOWS. THAT'S THE ISSUE.
REACTOR CONDUITS RUN THROUGH HERE TOO--WITH THE ENGINES OFF, EVERY SO OFTEN, THE SHIP'S COMPUTER HAS TO LET OFF A LITTLE BURST TO BALANCE THINGS OUT.
IT'S A GOOD THING, REALLY. KEEPS US FROM BLOWING UP.
BUT IF YOU'RE IN THERE WHEN ONE GOES OFF...NOT SO GOOD.
HROO.
CHEWIE, DON'T BE CRAZY. YOU CAN'T FIT THROUGH THERE. THAT PANEL'S BUILT FOR MOUSE DROIDS.
THEN I'LL DO IT. I CAN FIT.
NO, PRINCESS, I'LL GO IN.
YOU?
YEAH. THERE'S ABOUT FIFTY TOGGLE SWITCHES THAT HAVE TO BE CHECKED AND SET IN THE RIGHT ORDER. IF EVEN ONE OF THEM'S WRONG, THE DIAGNOSTICS WON'T WORK.
I KNOW IT--I KNOW EVERY SYSTEM ON THE FALCON. SHE'S AN OLD FRIEND.
IT'S GOTTA BE ME.

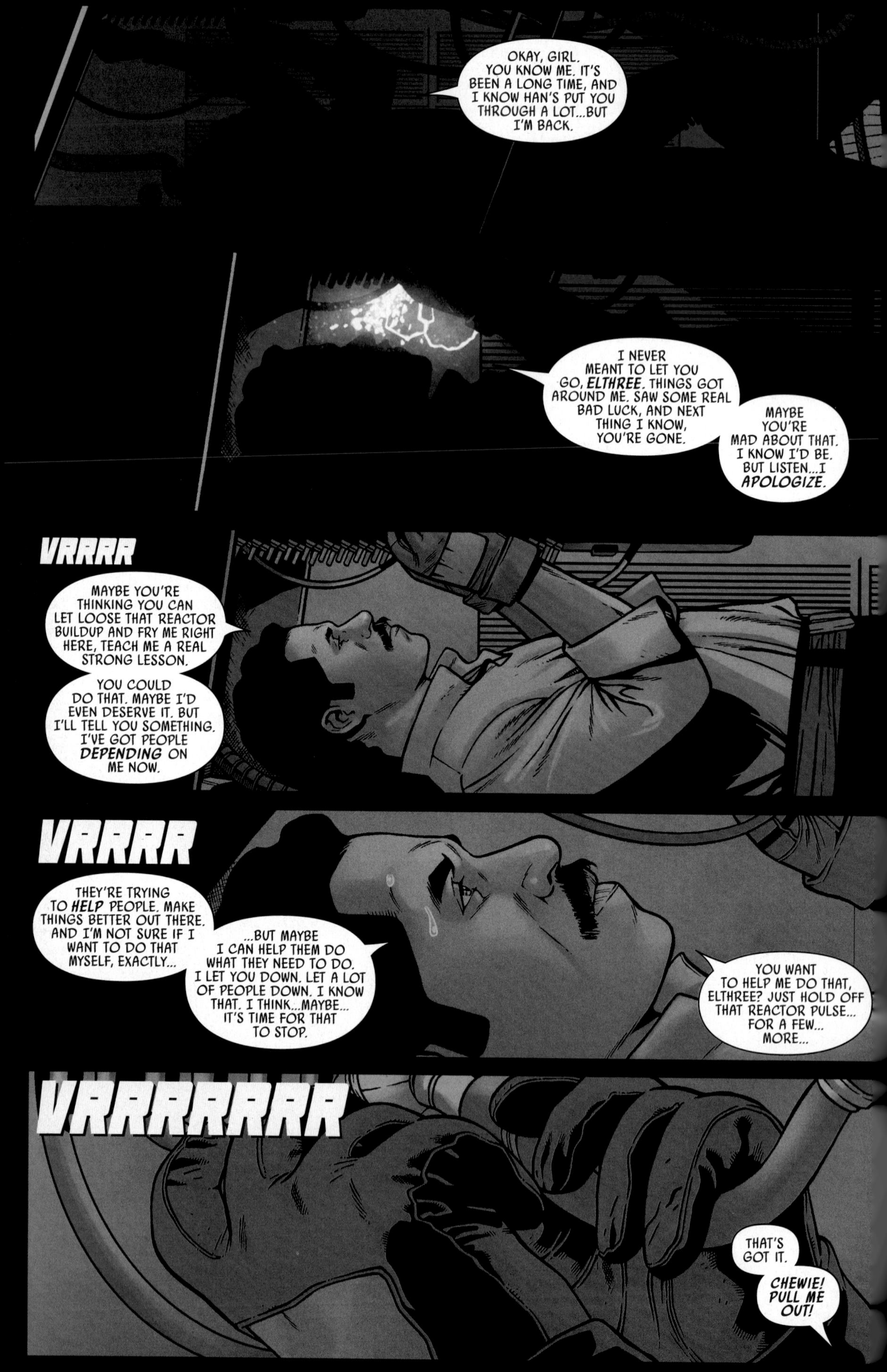
OKAY, GIRL. YOU KNOW ME. IT'S BEEN A LONG TIME, AND I KNOW HAN'S PUT YOU THROUGH A LOT...BUT I'M BACK.
I NEVER MEANT TO LET YOU GO, ELTHREE. THINGS GOT AROUND ME. SAW SOME REAL BAD LUCK, AND NEXT THING I KNOW, YOU'RE GONE.
MAYBE YOU'RE MAD ABOUT THAT. I KNOW I'D BE. BUT LISTEN...I APOLOGIZE.
VRRRR
MAYBE YOU'RE THINKING YOU CAN LET LOOSE THAT REACTOR BUILDUP AND FRY ME RIGHT HERE, TEACH ME A REAL STRONG LESSON.
YOU COULD DO THAT. MAYBE I'D EVEN DESERVE IT. BUT I'LL TELL YOU SOMETHING. I'VE GOT PEOPLE DEPENDING ON ME NOW.
VRRRR
THEY'RE TRYING TO HELP PEOPLE. MAKE THINGS BETTER OUT THERE. AND I'M NOT SURE IF I WANT TO DO THAT MYSELF, EXACTLY...
...BUT MAYBE I CAN HELP THEM DO WHAT THEY NEED TO DO. I LET YOU DOWN. LET A LOT OF PEOPLE DOWN. I KNOW THAT. I THINK...MAYBE... IT'S TIME FOR THAT TO STOP.
YOU WANT TO HELP ME DO THAT, ELTHREE? JUST HOLD OFF THAT REACTOR PULSE... FOR A FEW... MORE...
VRRRRRRR
THAT'S GOT IT.
CHEWIE! PULL ME OUT!

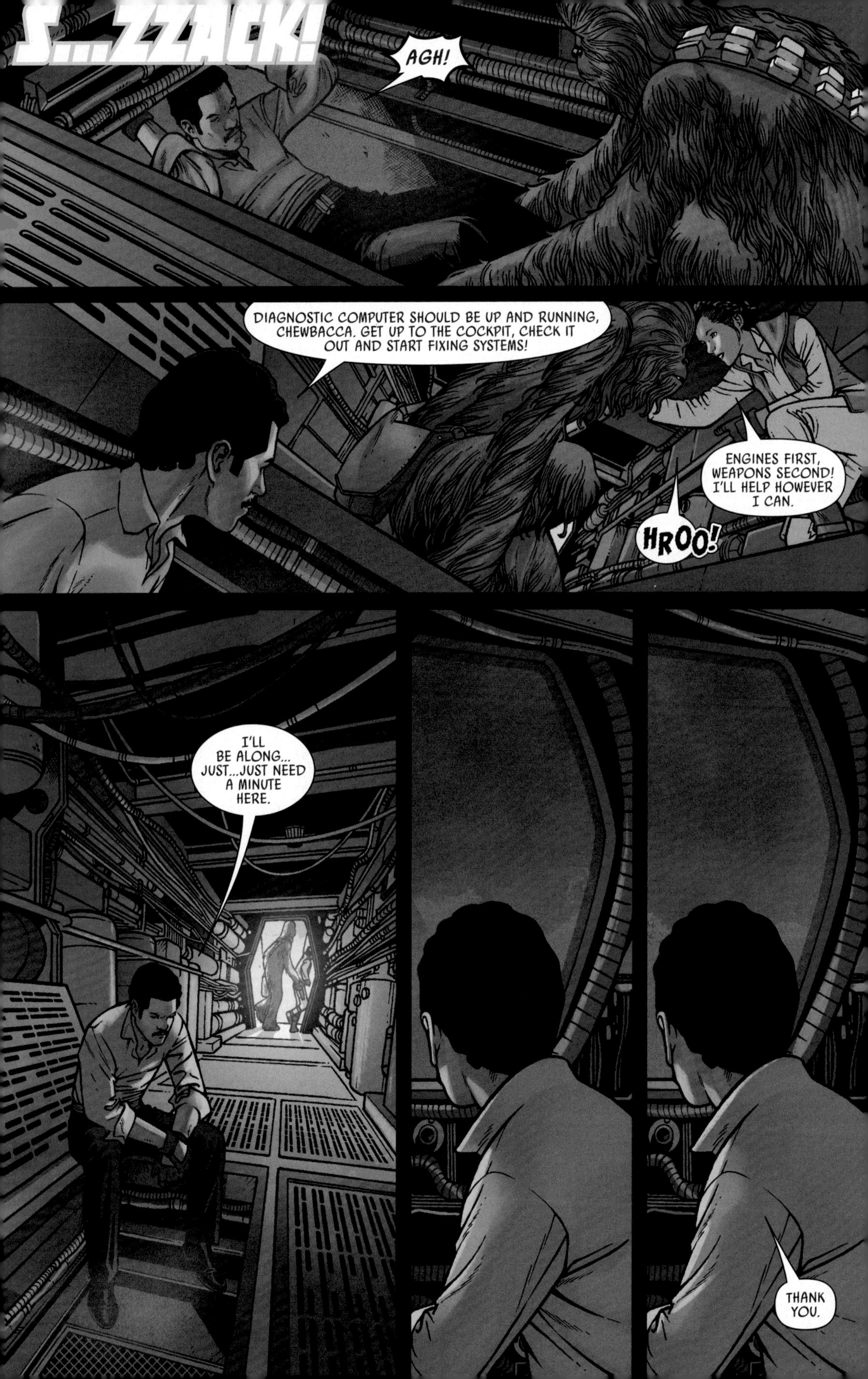

S...ZZACK!
AGH!
DIAGNOSTIC COMPUTER SHOULD BE UP AND RUNNING, CHEWBACCA. GET UP TO THE COCKPIT, CHECK IT OUT AND START FIXING SYSTEMS!
ENGINES FIRST, WEAPONS SECOND! I'LL HELP HOWEVER I CAN.
HROO!
I'LL BE ALONG... JUST...JUST NEED A MINUTE HERE.
THANK YOU.

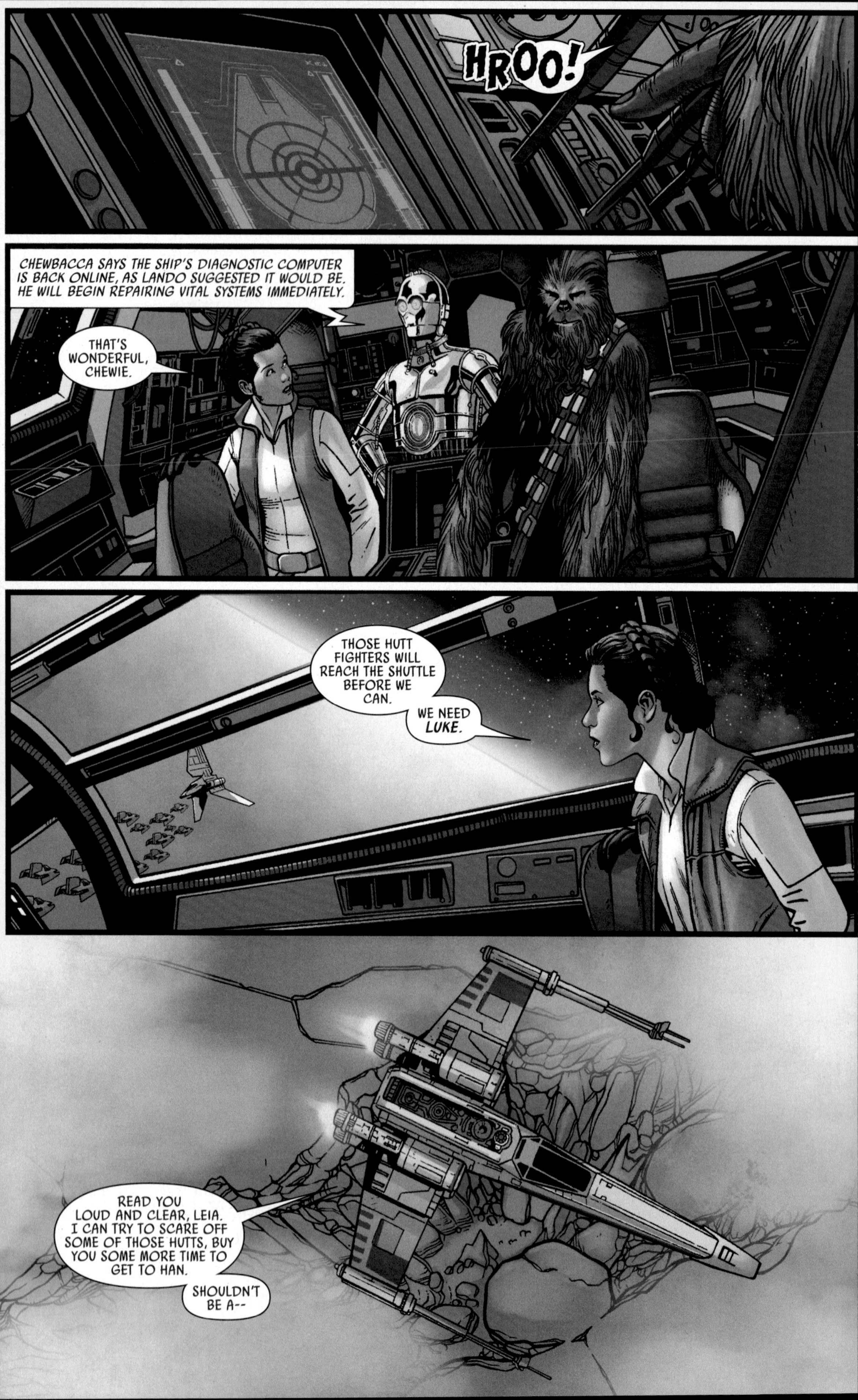
HROO!
CHEWBACCA SAYS THE SHIP'S DIAGNOSTIC COMPUTER IS BACK ONLINE, AS LANDO SUGGESTED IT WOULD BE. HE WILL BEGIN REPAIRING VITAL SYSTEMS IMMEDIATELY.
THAT'S WONDERFUL, CHEWIE.
THOSE HUTT FIGHTERS WILL REACH THE SHUTTLE BEFORE WE CAN.
WE NEED LUKE.
READ YOU LOUD AND CLEAR, LEIA. I CAN TRY TO SCARE OFF SOME OF THOSE HUTTS, BUY YOU SOME MORE TIME TO GET TO HAN.
SHOULDN'T BE A--

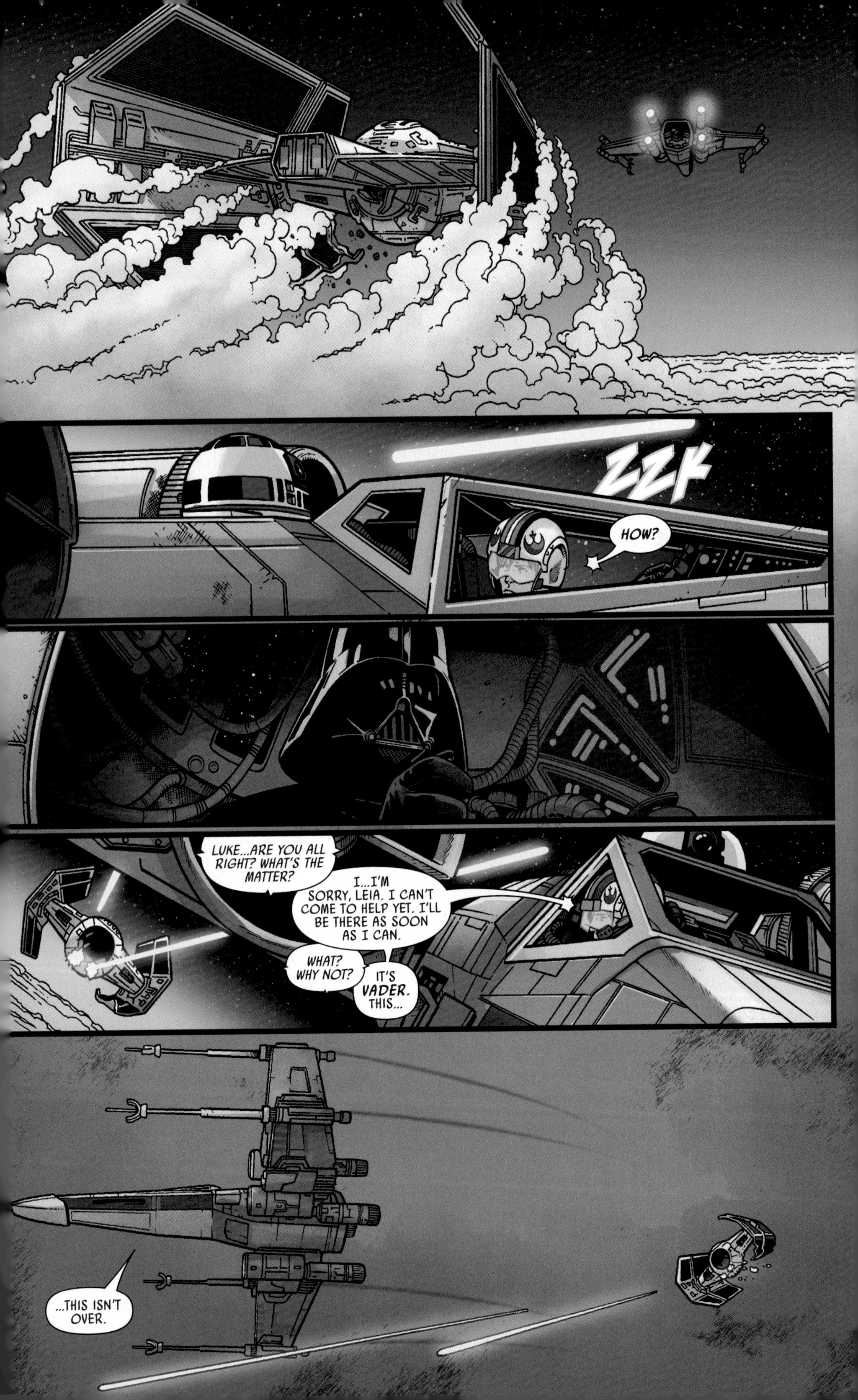
ZZK
HOW?
LUKE...ARE YOU ALL RIGHT? WHAT'S THE MATTER?
I...I'M SORRY, LEIA. I CAN'T COME TO HELP YET. I'LL BE THERE AS SOON AS I CAN.
WHAT? WHY NOT?
IT'S VADER. THIS...
...THIS ISN'T OVER.

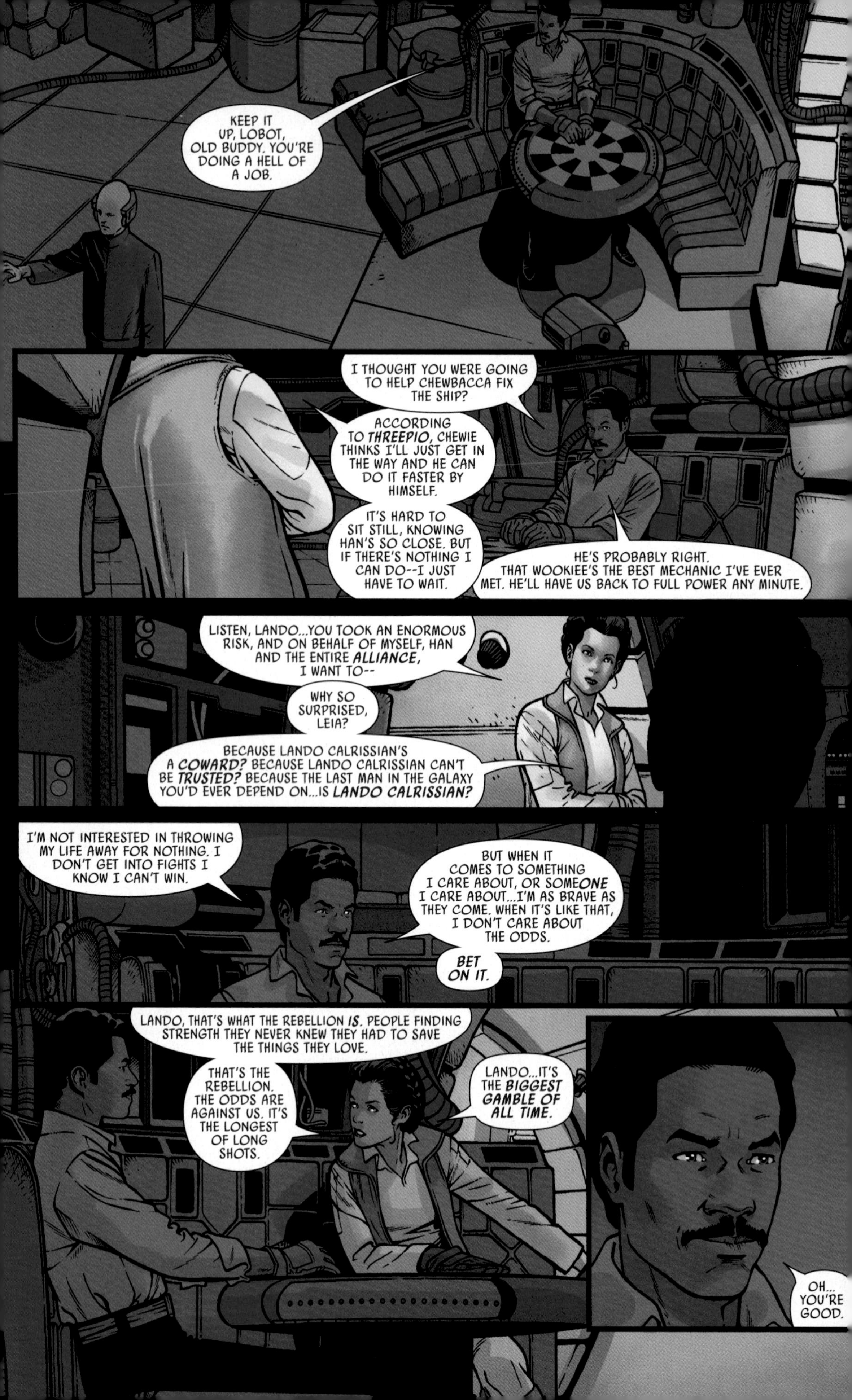
KEEP IT UP, LOBOT, OLD BUDDY. YOU'RE DOING A HELL OF A JOB.
I THOUGHT YOU WERE GOING TO HELP CHEWBACCA FIX THE SHIP?
ACCORDING TO THREEPIO, CHEWIE THINKS I'LL JUST GET IN THE WAY AND HE CAN DO IT FASTER BY HIMSELF.
HE'S PROBABLY RIGHT. THAT WOOKIEE'S THE BEST MECHANIC I'VE EVER MET. HE'LL HAVE US BACK TO FULL POWER ANY MINUTE.
IT'S HARD TO SIT STILL, KNOWING HAN'S SO CLOSE. BUT IF THERE'S NOTHING I CAN DO--I JUST HAVE TO WAIT.
LISTEN, LANDO...YOU TOOK AN ENORMOUS RISK, AND ON BEHALF OF MYSELF, HAN AND THE ENTIRE ALLIANCE, I WANT TO--
WHY SO SURPRISED, LEIA?
BECAUSE LANDO CALRISSIAN'S A COWARD? BECAUSE LANDO CALRISSIAN CAN'T BE TRUSTED? BECAUSE THE LAST MAN IN THE GALAXY YOU'D EVER DEPEND ON...IS LANDO CALRISSIAN?
I'M NOT INTERESTED IN THROWING MY LIFE AWAY FOR NOTHING. I DON'T GET INTO FIGHTS I KNOW I CAN'T WIN.
BUT WHEN IT COMES TO SOMETHING I CARE ABOUT, OR SOMEONE I CARE ABOUT...I'M AS BRAVE AS THEY COME. WHEN IT'S LIKE THAT, I DON'T CARE ABOUT THE ODDS.
BET ON IT.
LANDO, THAT'S WHAT THE REBELLION IS. PEOPLE FINDING STRENGTH THEY NEVER KNEW THEY HAD TO SAVE THE THINGS THEY LOVE.
THAT'S THE REBELLION. THE ODDS ARE AGAINST US. IT'S THE LONGEST OF LONG SHOTS.
LANDO...IT'S THE BIGGEST GAMBLE OF ALL TIME.
OH... YOU'RE GOOD.

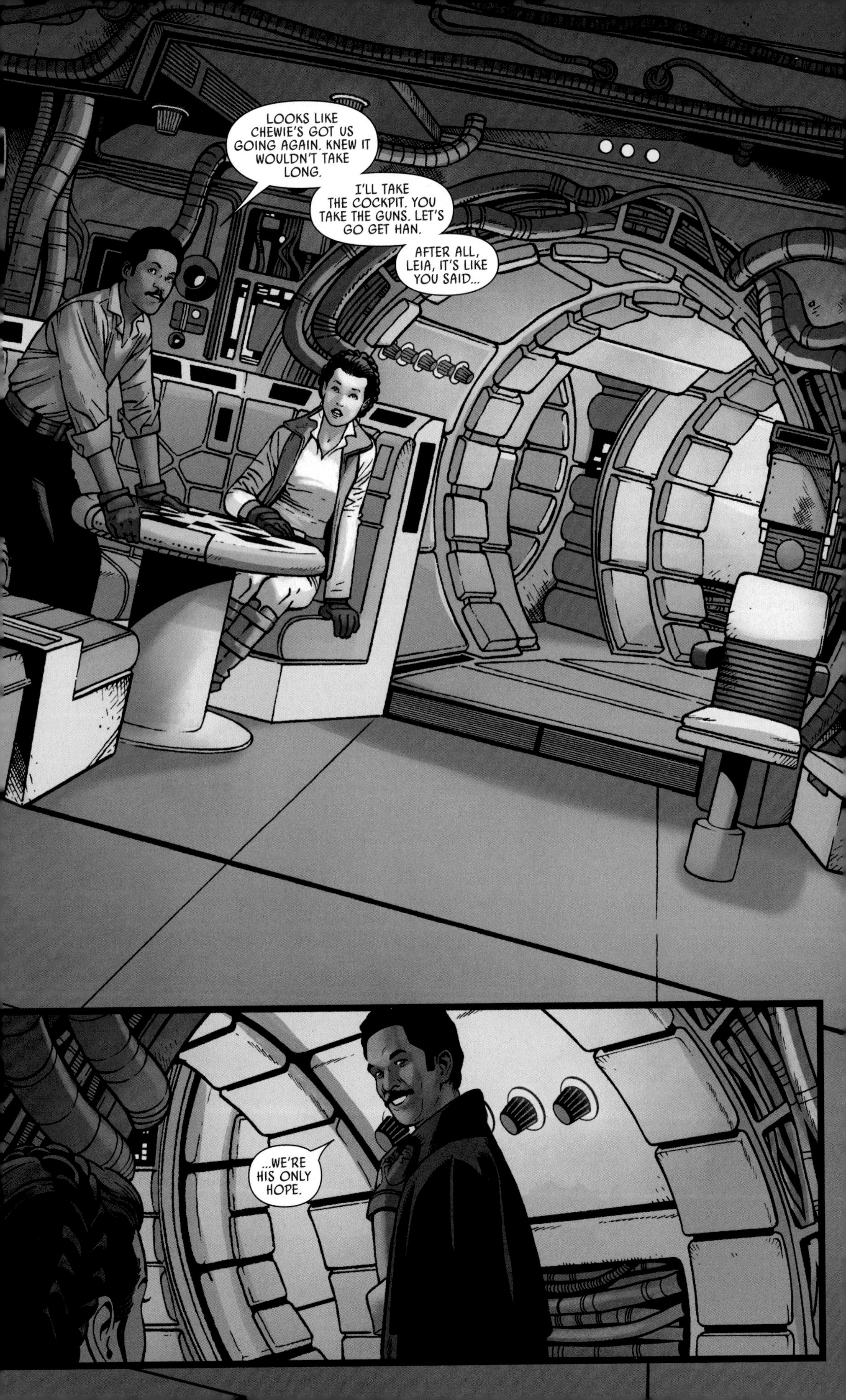
LOOKS LIKE CHEWIE'S GOT US GOING AGAIN. KNEW IT WOULDN'T TAKE LONG.
I'LL TAKE THE COCKPIT. YOU TAKE THE GUNS. LET'S GO GET HAN.
AFTER ALL, LEIA, IT'S LIKE YOU SAID...
...WE'RE HIS ONLY HOPE.

18 — COLLISION COURSE

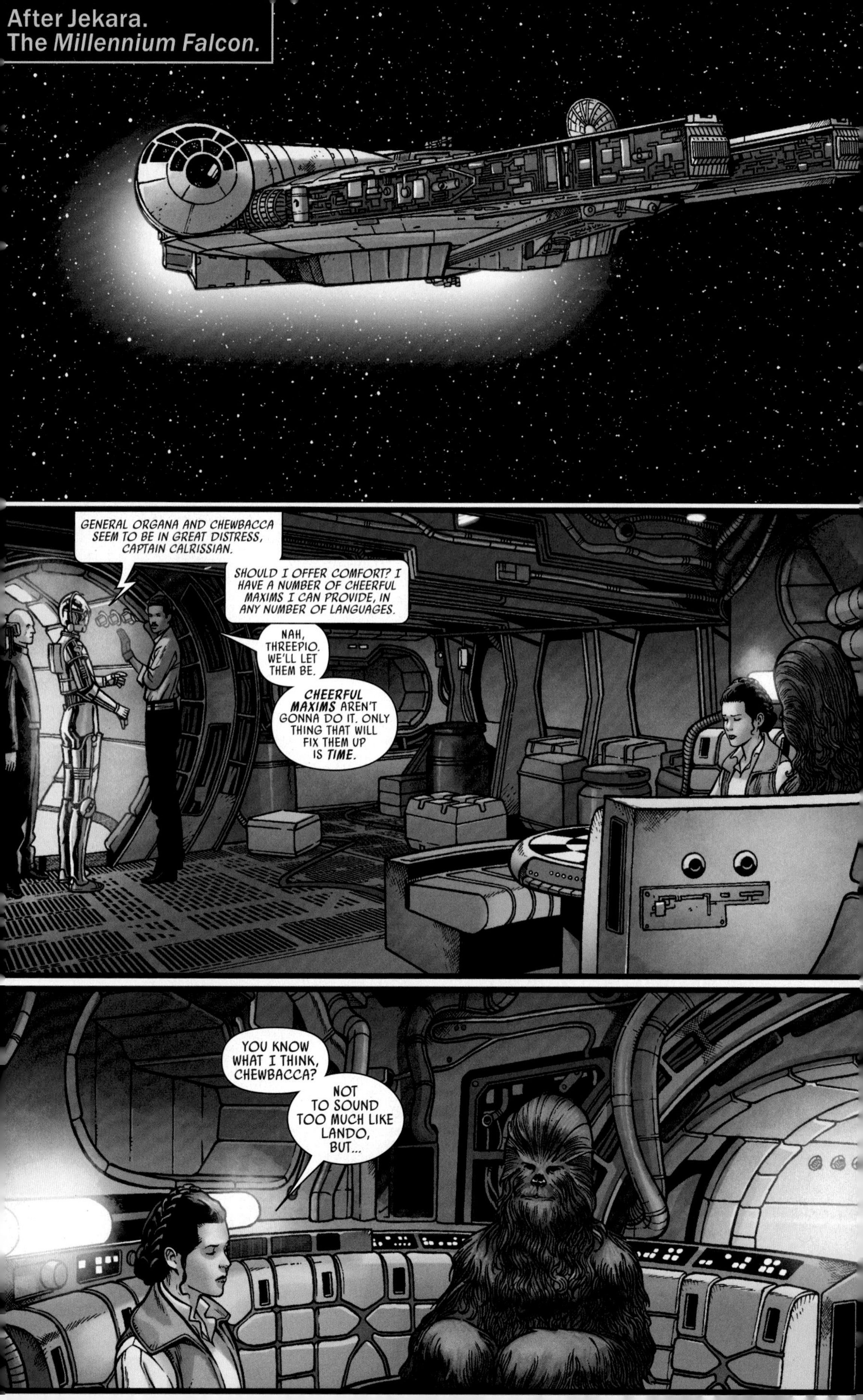

After Jekara.
The *Millennium Falcon.*
GENERAL ORGANA AND CHEWBACCA SEEM TO BE IN GREAT DISTRESS, CAPTAIN CALRISSIAN.
SHOULD I OFFER COMFORT? I HAVE A NUMBER OF CHEERFUL MAXIMS I CAN PROVIDE, IN ANY NUMBER OF LANGUAGES.
NAH, THREEPIO. WE'LL LET THEM BE.
CHEERFUL MAXIMS AREN'T GONNA DO IT. ONLY THING THAT WILL FIX THEM UP IS TIME.
YOU KNOW WHAT I THINK, CHEWBACCA?
NOT TO SOUND TOO MUCH LIKE LANDO, BUT...

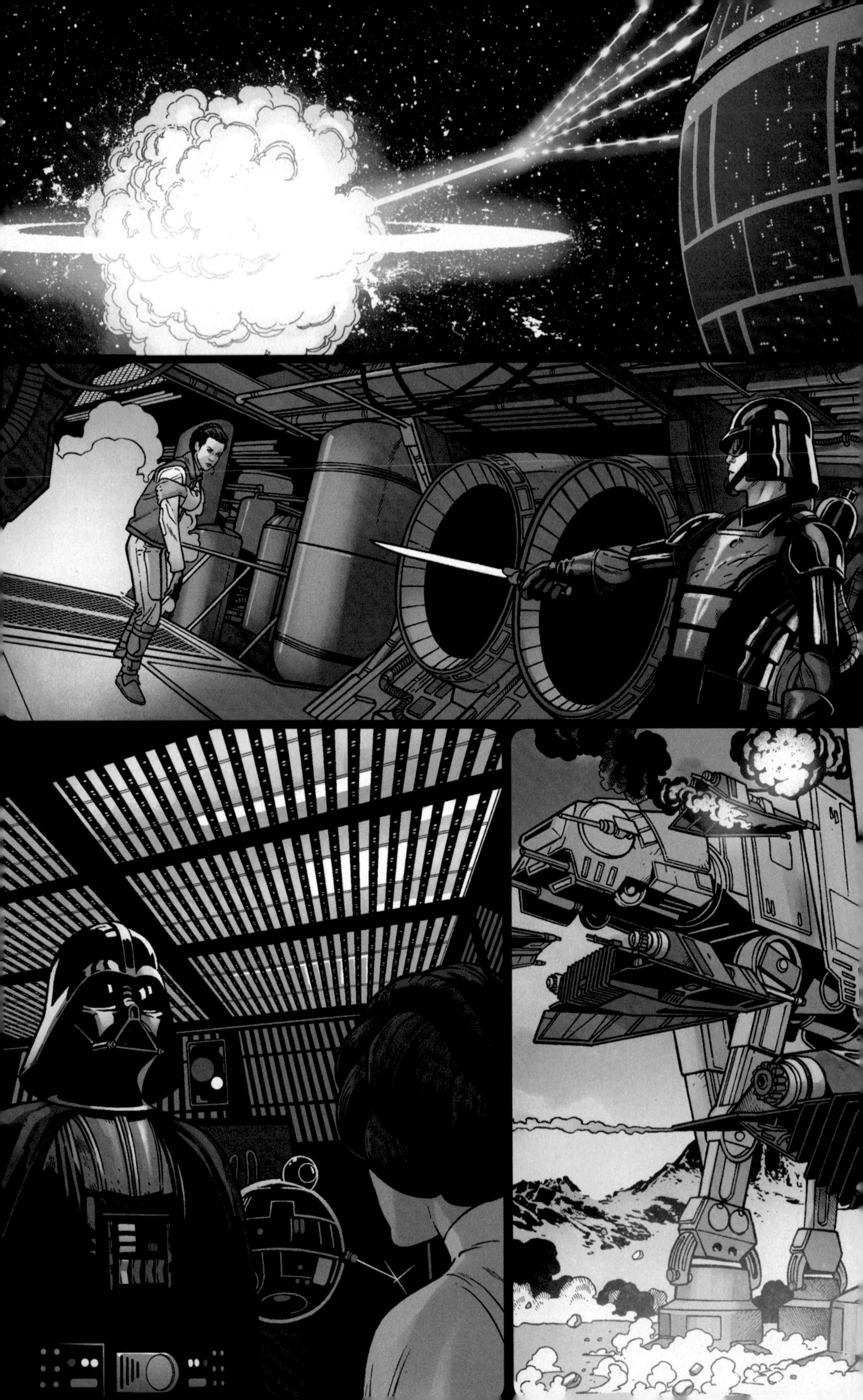

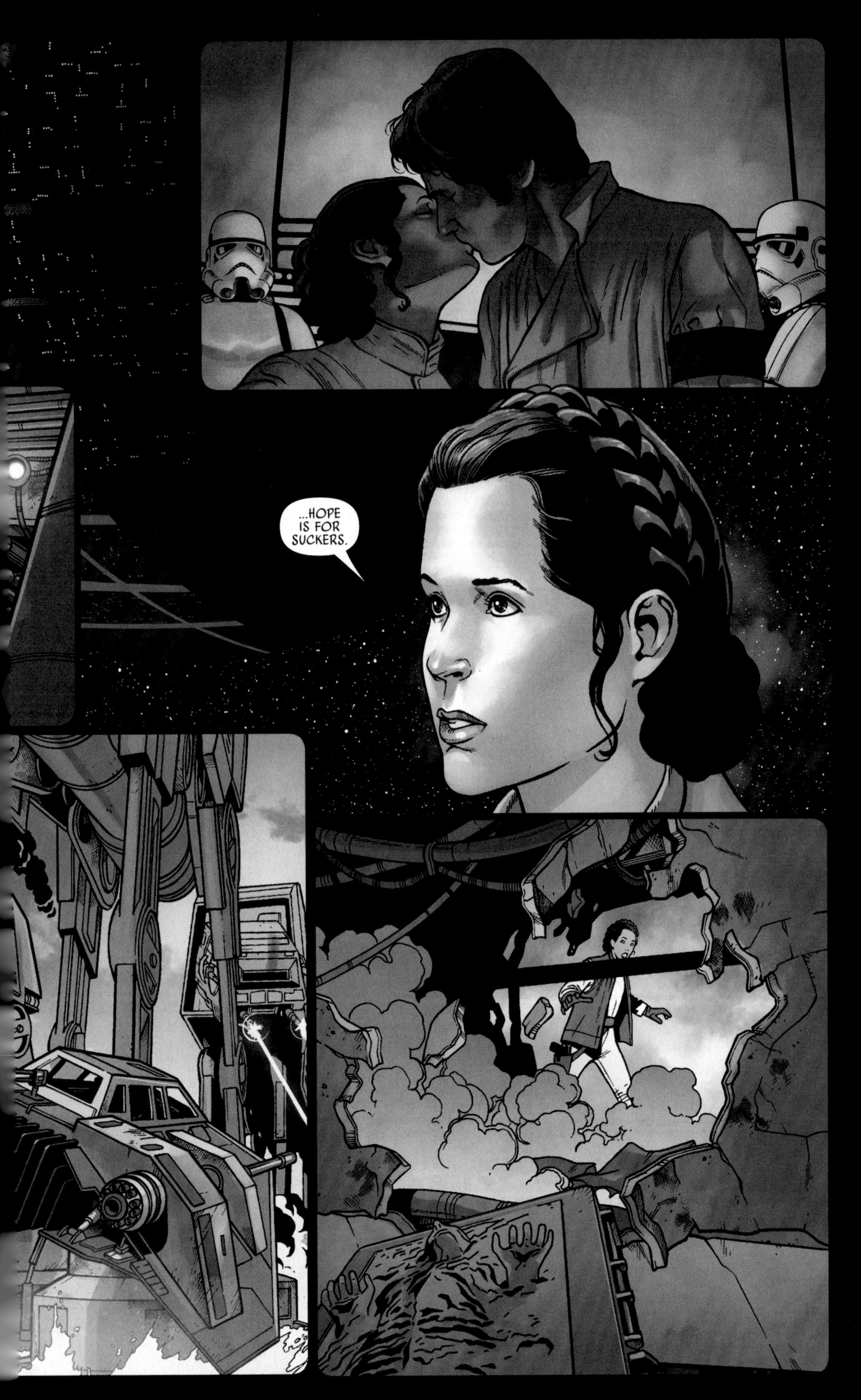
...HOPE IS FOR SUCKERS.

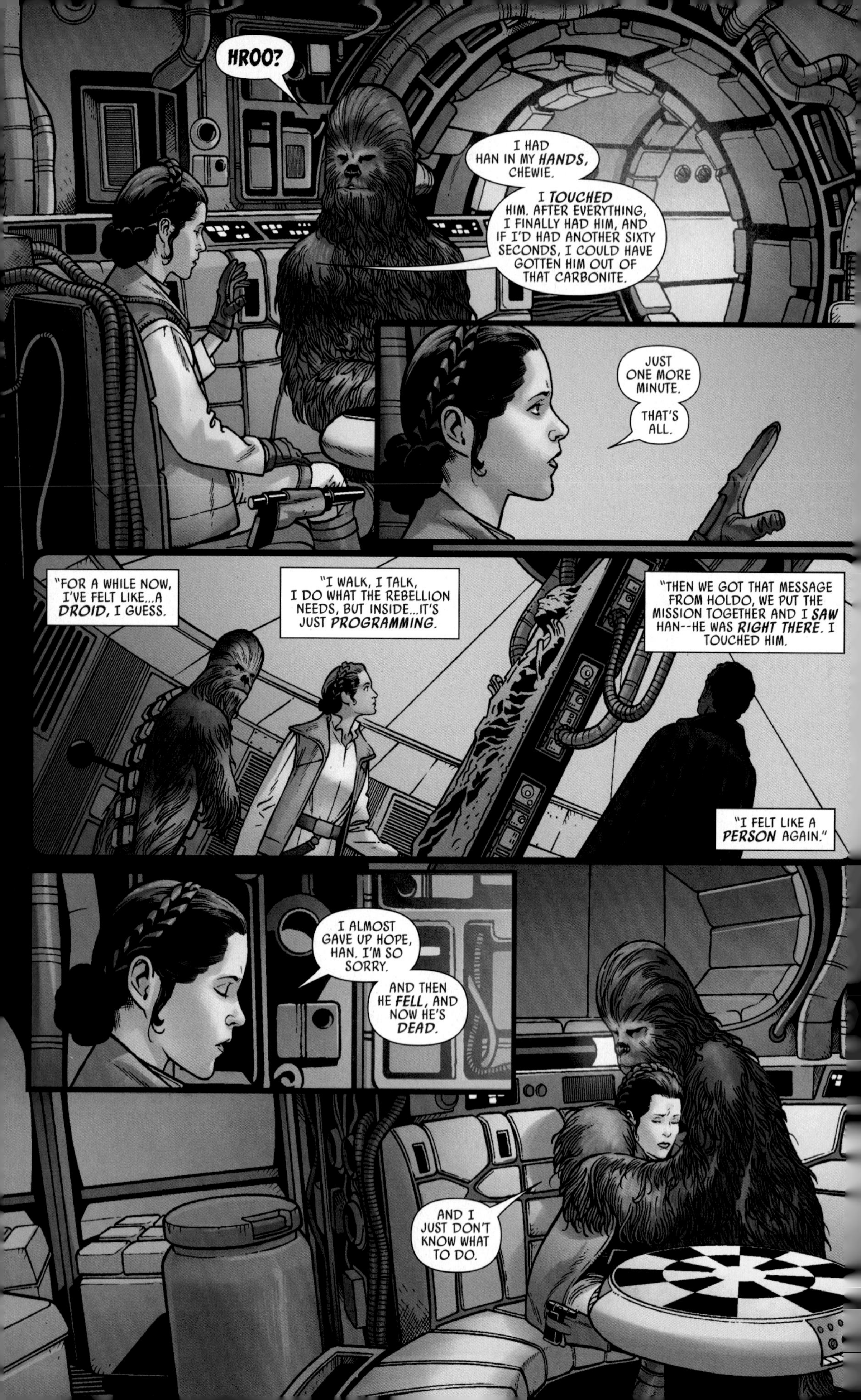
HROO?
I HAD HAN IN MY HANDS, CHEWIE.
I TOUCHED HIM. AFTER EVERYTHING, I FINALLY HAD HIM, AND IF I'D HAD ANOTHER SIXTY SECONDS, I COULD HAVE GOTTEN HIM OUT OF THAT CARBONITE.
JUST ONE MORE MINUTE.
THAT'S ALL.
"FOR A WHILE NOW, I'VE FELT LIKE...A DROID, I GUESS.
"I WALK, I TALK, I DO WHAT THE REBELLION NEEDS, BUT INSIDE...IT'S JUST PROGRAMMING.
"THEN WE GOT THAT MESSAGE FROM HOLDO, WE PUT THE MISSION TOGETHER AND I SAW HAN--HE WAS RIGHT THERE. I TOUCHED HIM.
"I FELT LIKE A PERSON AGAIN."
I ALMOST GAVE UP HOPE, HAN. I'M SO SORRY.
AND THEN HE FELL, AND NOW HE'S DEAD.
AND I JUST DON'T KNOW WHAT TO DO.

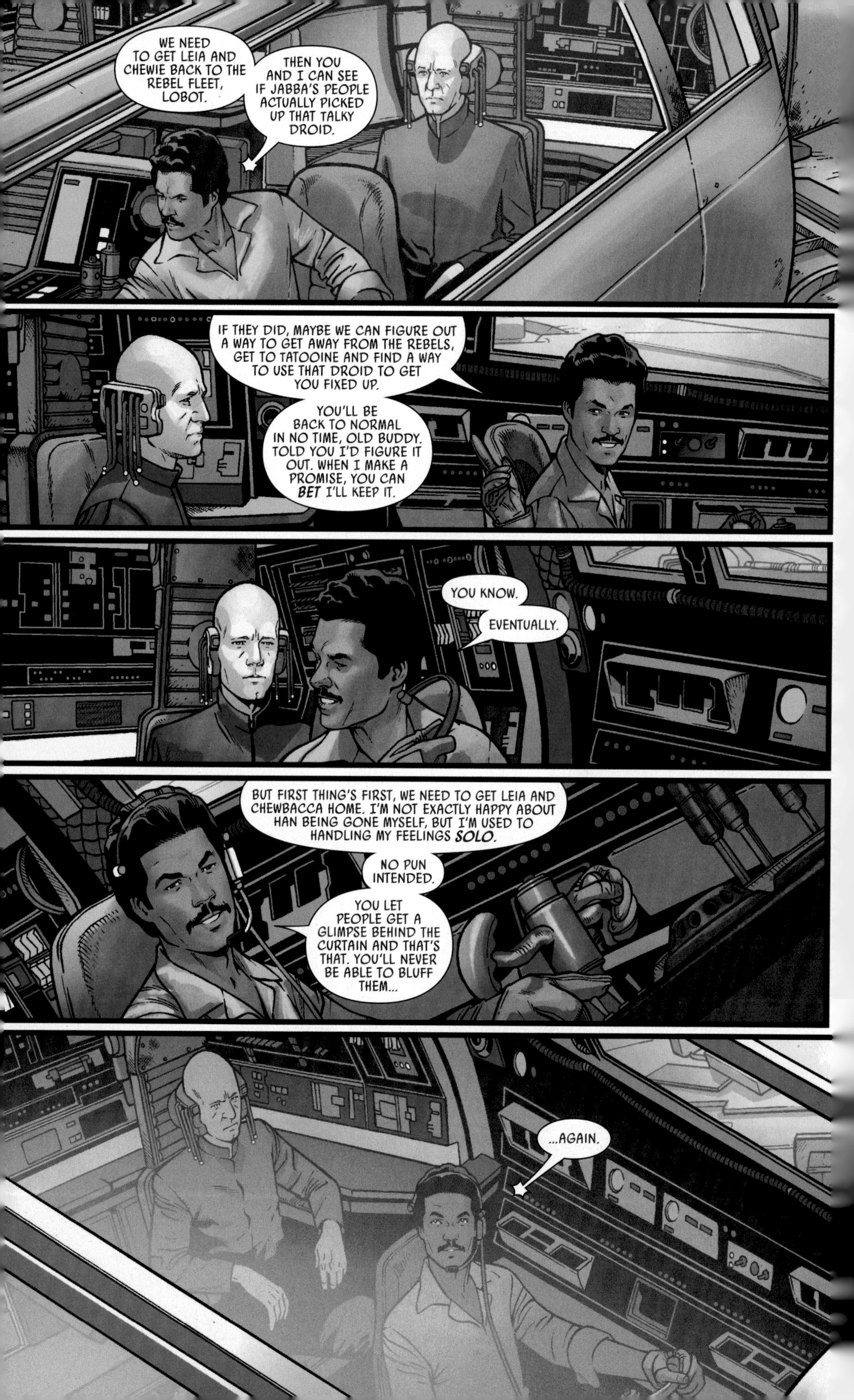
WE NEED TO GET LEIA AND CHEWIE BACK TO THE REBEL FLEET, LOBOT.
THEN YOU AND I CAN SEE IF JABBA'S PEOPLE ACTUALLY PICKED UP THAT TALKY DROID.
IF THEY DID, MAYBE WE CAN FIGURE OUT A WAY TO GET AWAY FROM THE REBELS, GET TO TATOOINE AND FIND A WAY TO USE THAT DROID TO GET YOU FIXED UP.
YOU'LL BE BACK TO NORMAL IN NO TIME, OLD BUDDY. TOLD YOU I'D FIGURE IT OUT. WHEN I MAKE A PROMISE, YOU CAN *BET* I'LL KEEP IT.
YOU KNOW.
EVENTUALLY.
BUT FIRST THING'S FIRST, WE NEED TO GET LEIA AND CHEWBACCA HOME. I'M NOT EXACTLY HAPPY ABOUT HAN BEING GONE MYSELF, BUT I'M USED TO HANDLING MY FEELINGS *SOLO*.
NO PUN INTENDED.
YOU LET PEOPLE GET A GLIMPSE BEHIND THE CURTAIN AND THAT'S THAT. YOU'LL NEVER BE ABLE TO BLUFF THEM...
...AGAIN.

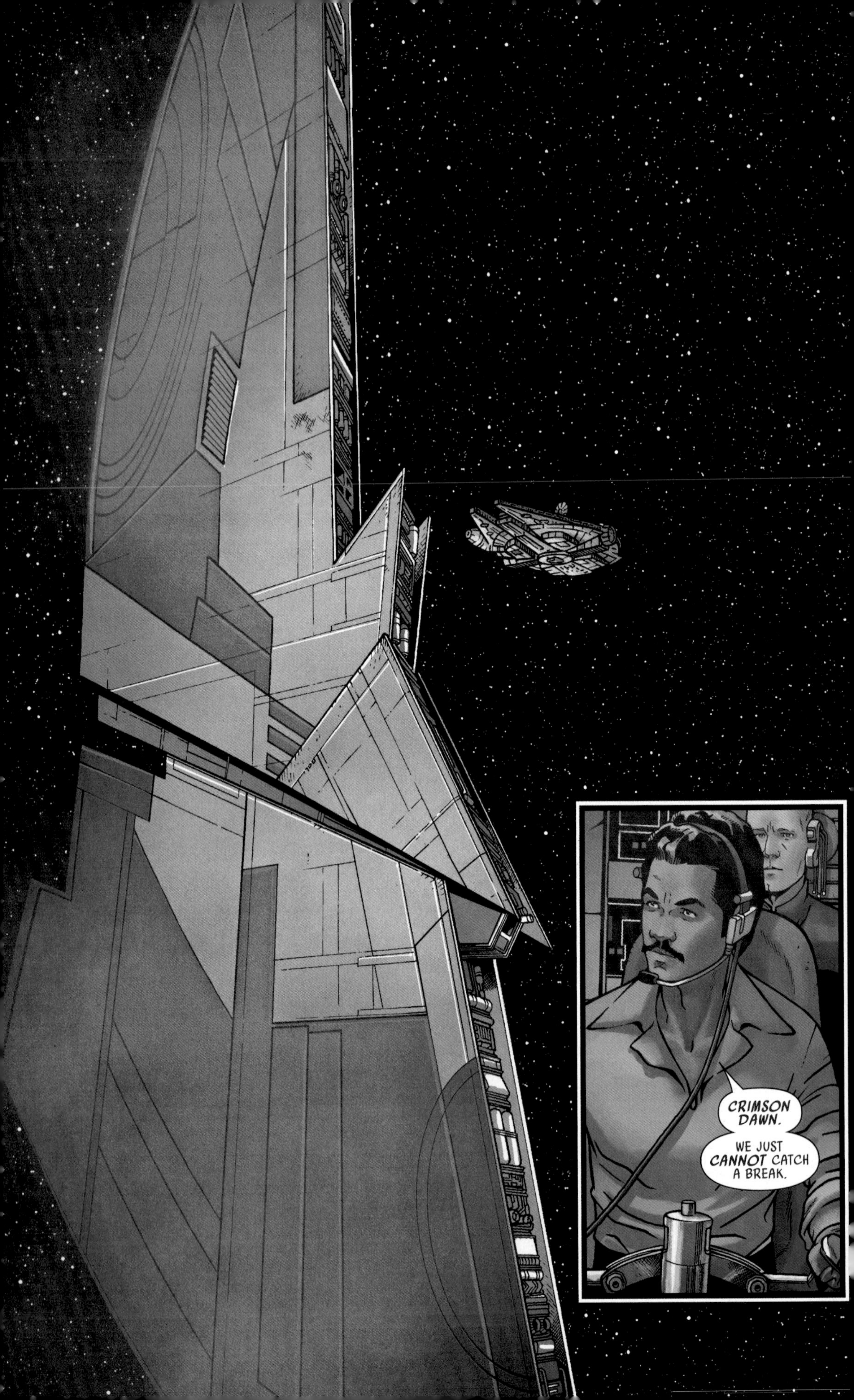
CRIMSON DAWN.
WE JUST CANNOT CATCH A BREAK.

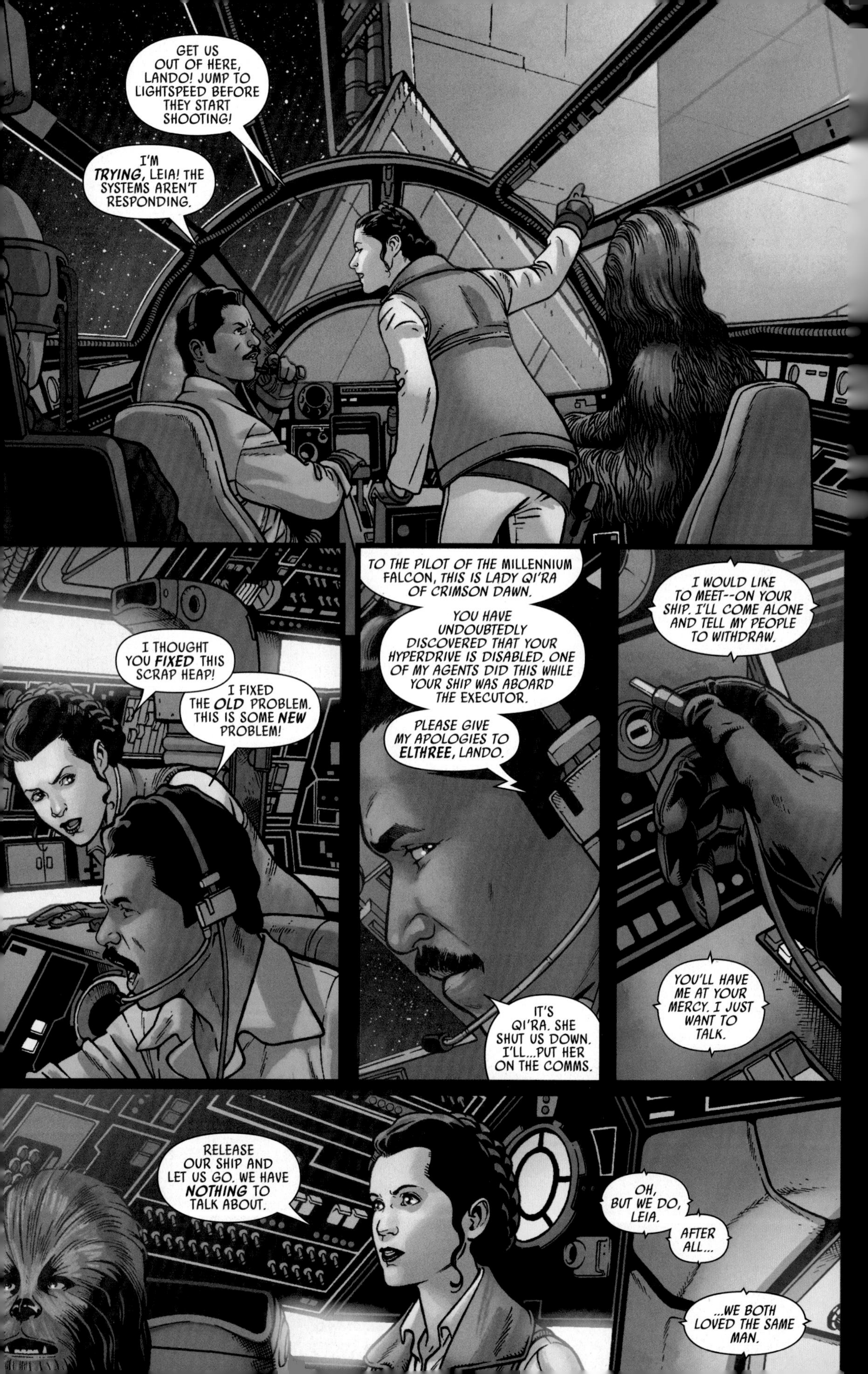
GET US OUT OF HERE, LANDO! JUMP TO LIGHTSPEED BEFORE THEY START SHOOTING!
I'M TRYING, LEIA! THE SYSTEMS AREN'T RESPONDING.
I THOUGHT YOU FIXED THIS SCRAP HEAP!
I FIXED THE OLD PROBLEM. THIS IS SOME NEW PROBLEM!
TO THE PILOT OF THE MILLENNIUM FALCON, THIS IS LADY QI'RA OF CRIMSON DAWN.
YOU HAVE UNDOUBTEDLY DISCOVERED THAT YOUR HYPERDRIVE IS DISABLED. ONE OF MY AGENTS DID THIS WHILE YOUR SHIP WAS ABOARD THE EXECUTOR.
PLEASE GIVE MY APOLOGIES TO ELTHREE, LANDO.
IT'S QI'RA. SHE SHUT US DOWN. I'LL...PUT HER ON THE COMMS.
I WOULD LIKE TO MEET--ON YOUR SHIP. I'LL COME ALONE AND TELL MY PEOPLE TO WITHDRAW.
YOU'LL HAVE ME AT YOUR MERCY. I JUST WANT TO TALK.
RELEASE OUR SHIP AND LET US GO. WE HAVE NOTHING TO TALK ABOUT.
OH, BUT WE DO, LEIA.
AFTER ALL...
...WE BOTH LOVED THE SAME MAN.

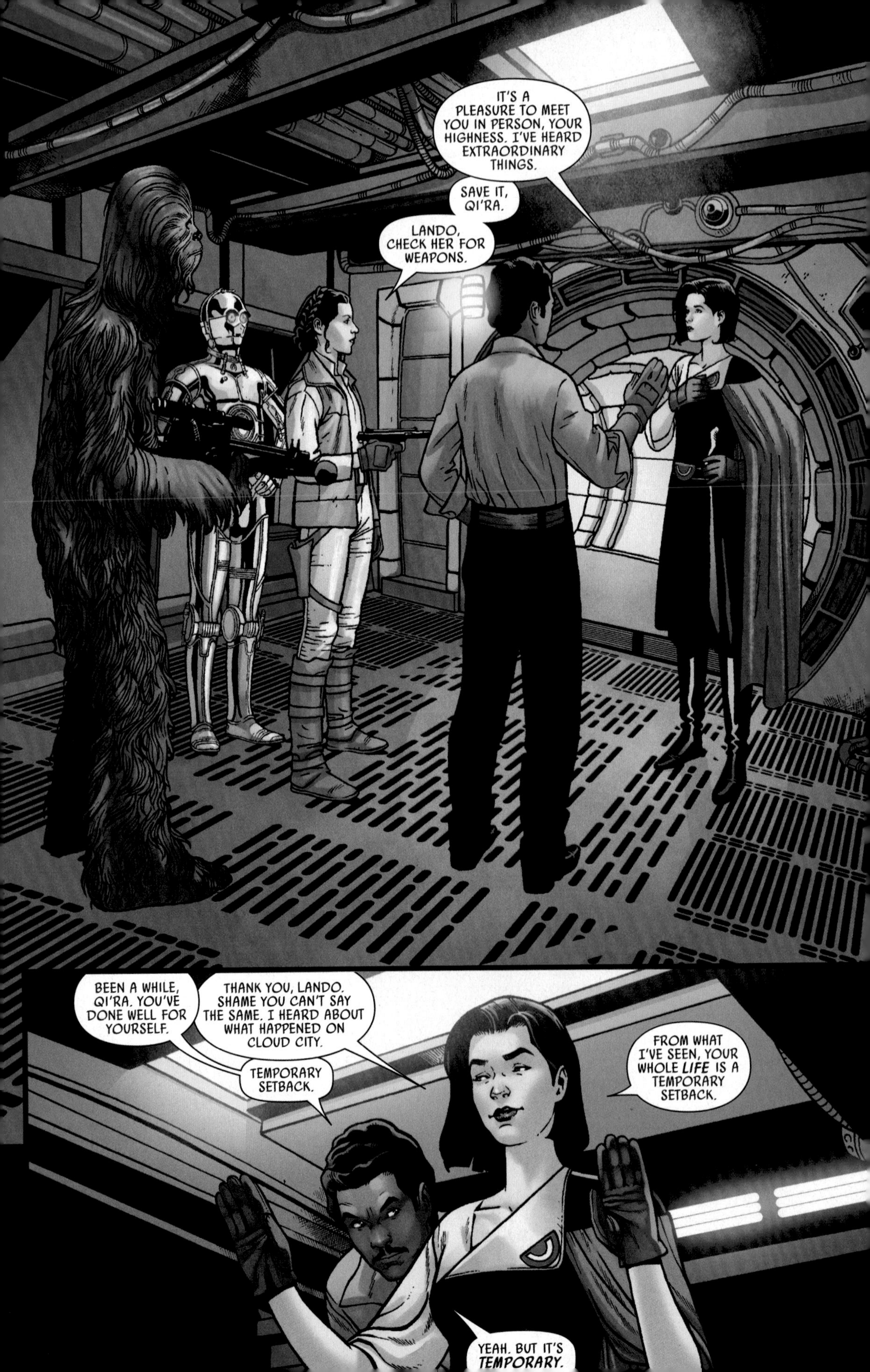
IT'S A PLEASURE TO MEET YOU IN PERSON, YOUR HIGHNESS. I'VE HEARD EXTRAORDINARY THINGS.
SAVE IT, QI'RA.
LANDO, CHECK HER FOR WEAPONS.
BEEN A WHILE, QI'RA. YOU'VE DONE WELL FOR YOURSELF.
THANK YOU, LANDO. SHAME YOU CAN'T SAY THE SAME. I HEARD ABOUT WHAT HAPPENED ON CLOUD CITY.
TEMPORARY SETBACK.
FROM WHAT I'VE SEEN, YOUR WHOLE *LIFE* IS A TEMPORARY SETBACK.
YEAH. BUT IT'S *TEMPORARY*.

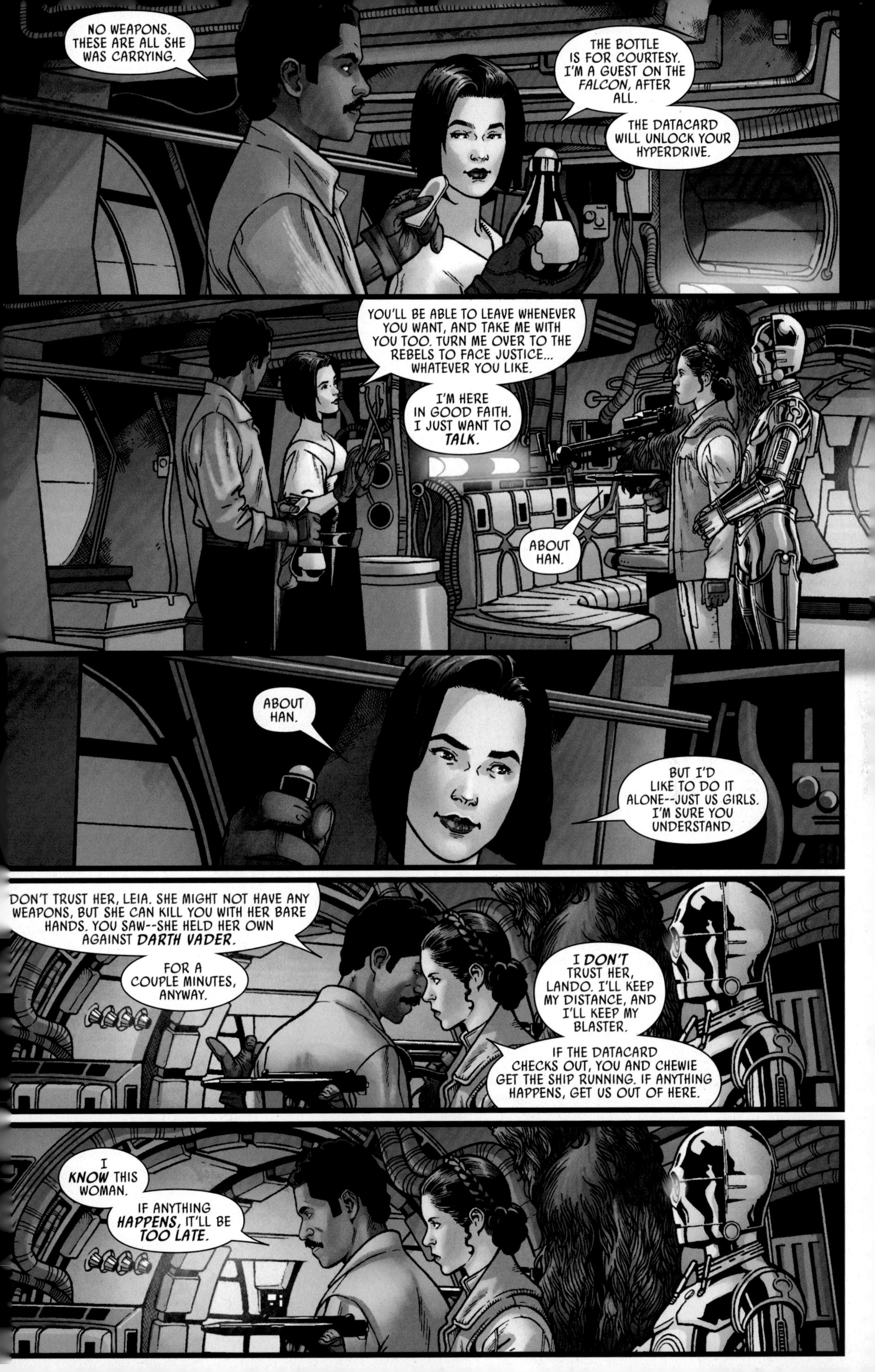
NO WEAPONS. THESE ARE ALL SHE WAS CARRYING.
THE BOTTLE IS FOR COURTESY. I'M A GUEST ON THE *FALCON*, AFTER ALL.
THE DATACARD WILL UNLOCK YOUR HYPERDRIVE.
YOU'LL BE ABLE TO LEAVE WHENEVER YOU WANT, AND TAKE ME WITH YOU TOO. TURN ME OVER TO THE REBELS TO FACE JUSTICE... WHATEVER YOU LIKE.
I'M HERE IN GOOD FAITH. I JUST WANT TO **TALK**.
ABOUT HAN.
ABOUT HAN.
BUT I'D LIKE TO DO IT ALONE--JUST US GIRLS. I'M SURE YOU UNDERSTAND.
DON'T TRUST HER, LEIA. SHE MIGHT NOT HAVE ANY WEAPONS, BUT SHE CAN KILL YOU WITH HER BARE HANDS. YOU SAW--SHE HELD HER OWN AGAINST **DARTH VADER.**
FOR A COUPLE MINUTES, ANYWAY.
I **DON'T** TRUST HER, LANDO. I'LL KEEP MY DISTANCE, AND I'LL KEEP MY BLASTER.
IF THE DATACARD CHECKS OUT, YOU AND CHEWIE GET THE SHIP RUNNING. IF ANYTHING HAPPENS, GET US OUT OF HERE.
I **KNOW** THIS WOMAN.
IF ANYTHING **HAPPENS**, IT'LL BE **TOO LATE**.

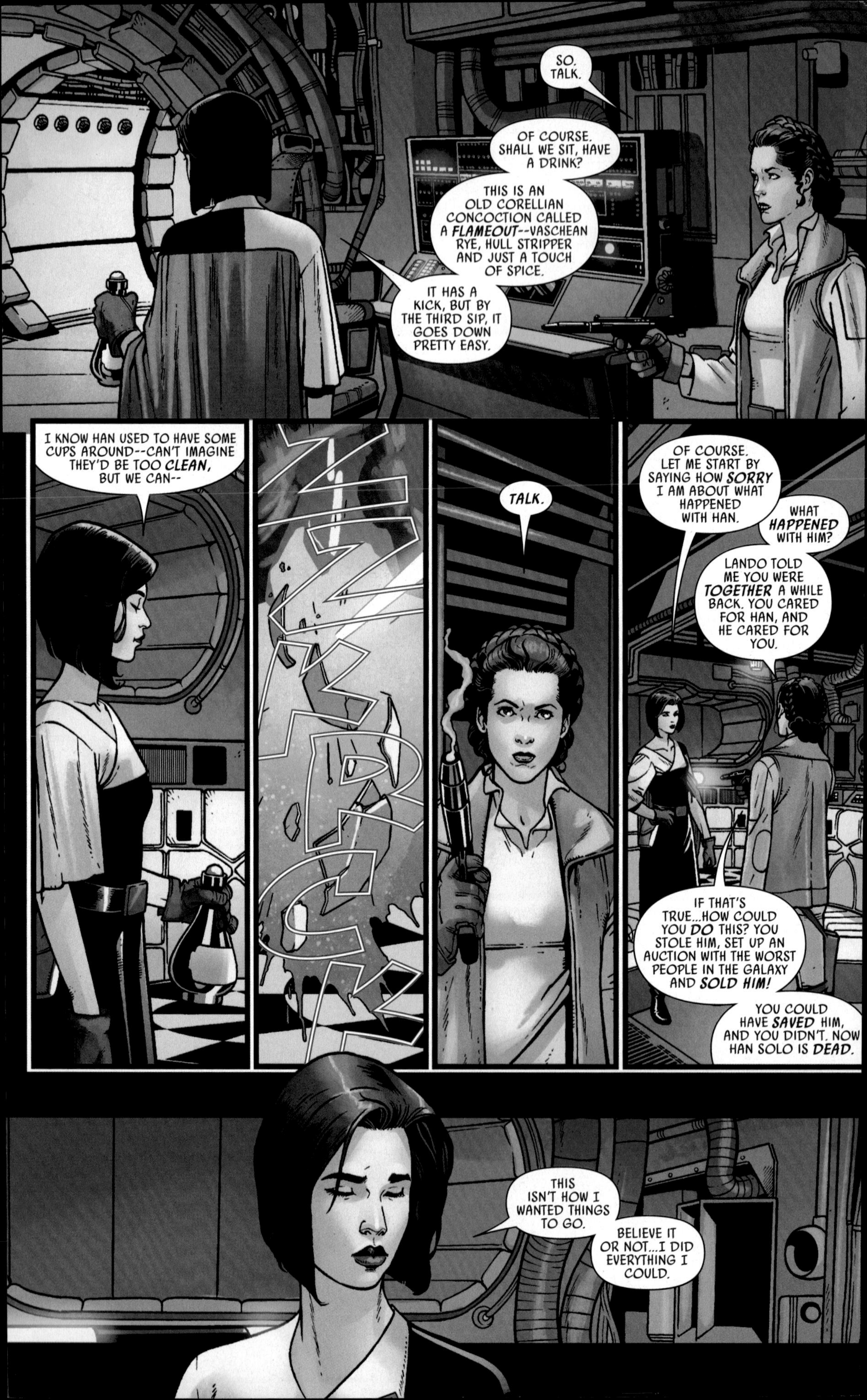
SO. TALK.
OF COURSE. SHALL WE SIT, HAVE A DRINK?
THIS IS AN OLD CORELLIAN CONCOCTION CALLED A FLAMEOUT--VASCHEAN RYE, HULL STRIPPER AND JUST A TOUCH OF SPICE.
IT HAS A KICK, BUT BY THE THIRD SIP, IT GOES DOWN PRETTY EASY.
I KNOW HAN USED TO HAVE SOME CUPS AROUND--CAN'T IMAGINE THEY'D BE TOO CLEAN, BUT WE CAN--
TALK.
OF COURSE. LET ME START BY SAYING HOW SORRY I AM ABOUT WHAT HAPPENED WITH HAN.
WHAT HAPPENED WITH HIM?
LANDO TOLD ME YOU WERE TOGETHER A WHILE BACK. YOU CARED FOR HAN, AND HE CARED FOR YOU.
IF THAT'S TRUE...HOW COULD YOU DO THIS? YOU STOLE HIM, SET UP AN AUCTION WITH THE WORST PEOPLE IN THE GALAXY AND SOLD HIM!
YOU COULD HAVE SAVED HIM, AND YOU DIDN'T. NOW HAN SOLO IS DEAD.
THIS ISN'T HOW I WANTED THINGS TO GO.
BELIEVE IT OR NOT...I DID EVERYTHING I COULD.

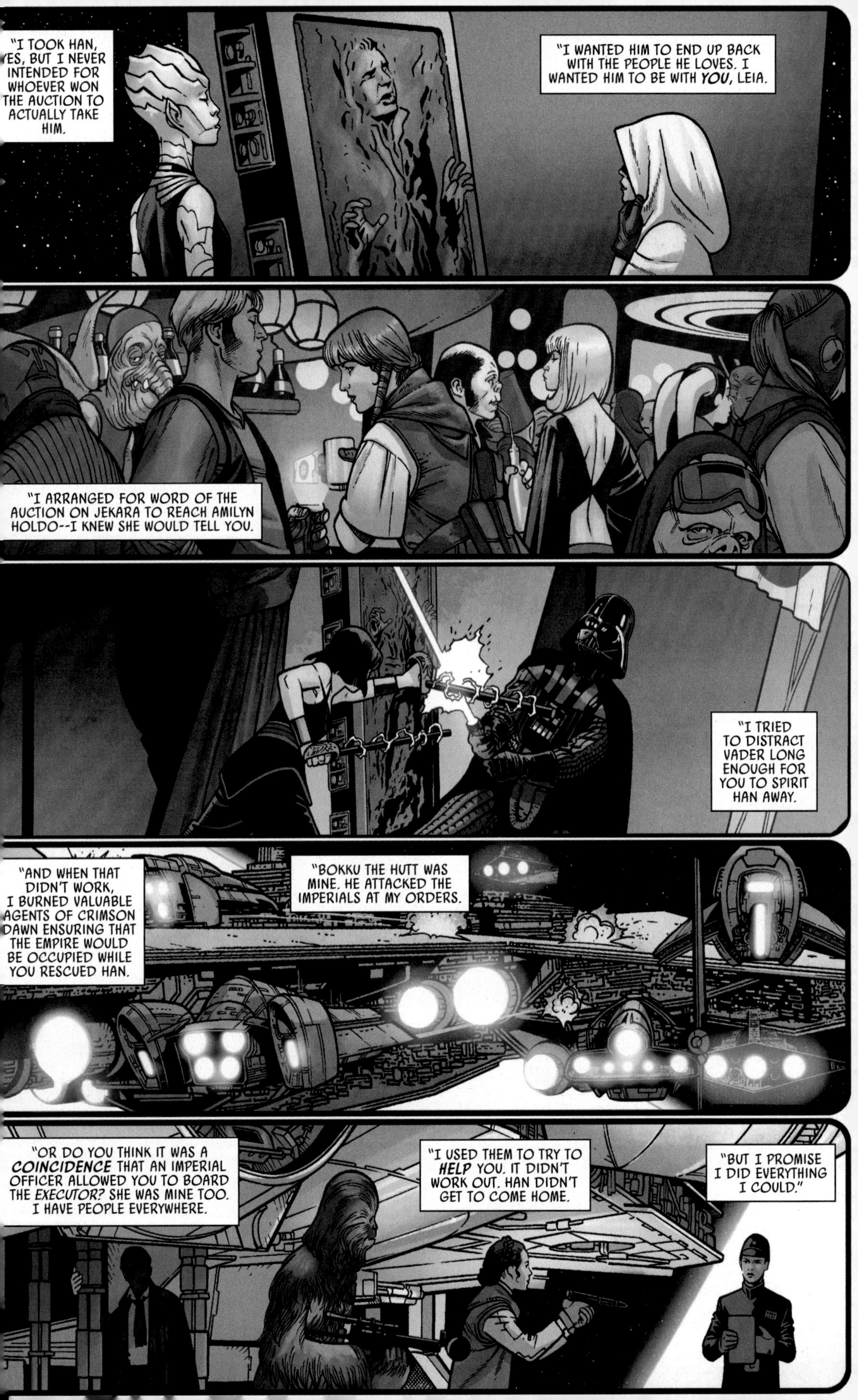
"I TOOK HAN, YES, BUT I NEVER INTENDED FOR WHOEVER WON THE AUCTION TO ACTUALLY TAKE HIM.
"I WANTED HIM TO END UP BACK WITH THE PEOPLE HE LOVES. I WANTED HIM TO BE WITH *YOU*, LEIA.
"I ARRANGED FOR WORD OF THE AUCTION ON JEKARA TO REACH AMILYN HOLDO--I KNEW SHE WOULD TELL YOU.
"I TRIED TO DISTRACT VADER LONG ENOUGH FOR YOU TO SPIRIT HAN AWAY.
"AND WHEN THAT DIDN'T WORK, I BURNED VALUABLE AGENTS OF CRIMSON DAWN ENSURING THAT THE EMPIRE WOULD BE OCCUPIED WHILE YOU RESCUED HAN.
"BOKKU THE HUTT WAS MINE. HE ATTACKED THE IMPERIALS AT MY ORDERS.
"OR DO YOU THINK IT WAS A *COINCIDENCE* THAT AN IMPERIAL OFFICER ALLOWED YOU TO BOARD THE *EXECUTOR*? SHE WAS MINE TOO. I HAVE PEOPLE EVERYWHERE.
"I USED THEM TO TRY TO *HELP* YOU. IT DIDN'T WORK OUT. HAN DIDN'T GET TO COME HOME.
"BUT I PROMISE I DID EVERYTHING I COULD."

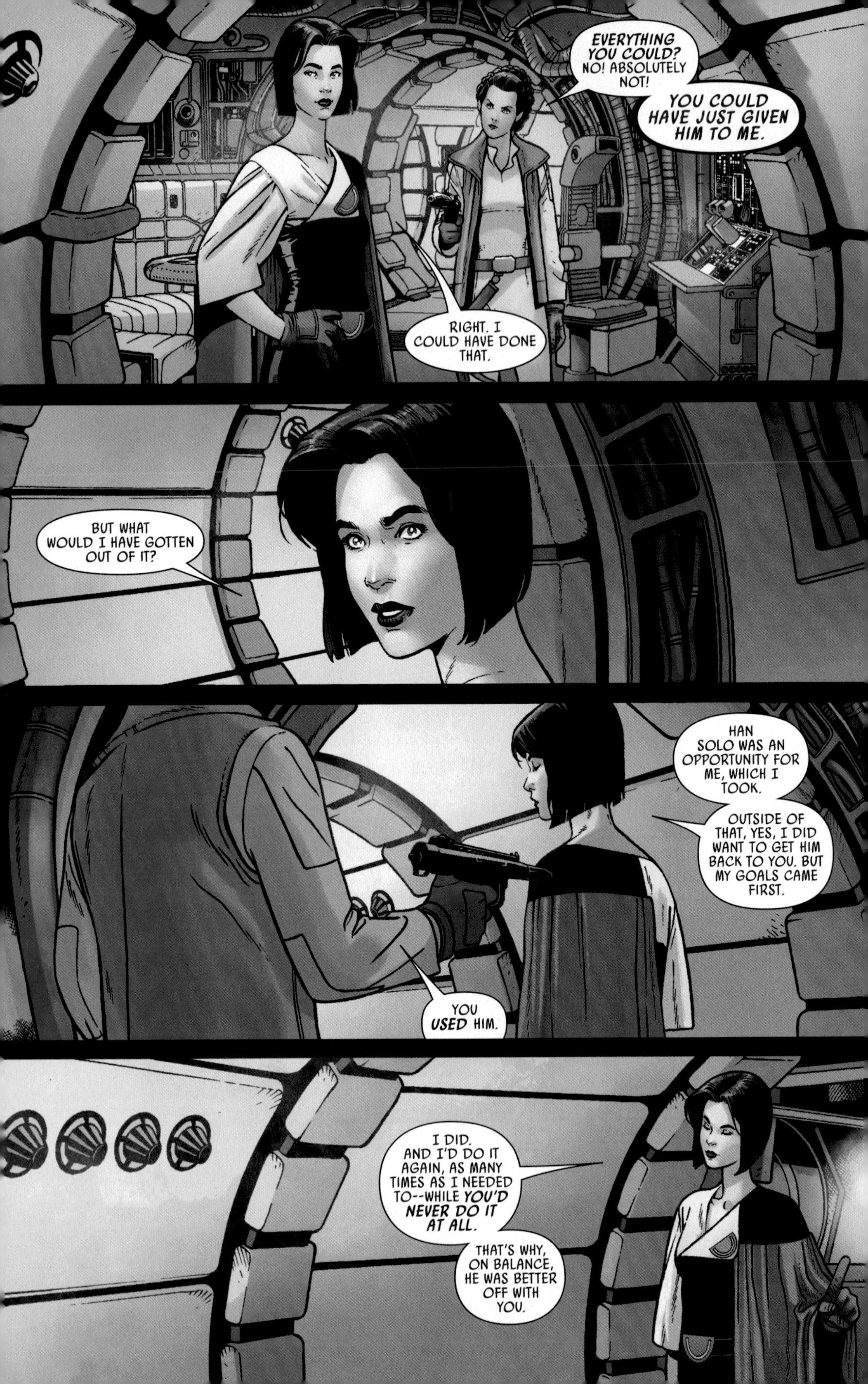
EVERYTHING YOU COULD? NO! ABSOLUTELY NOT!
YOU COULD HAVE JUST GIVEN HIM TO ME.
RIGHT. I COULD HAVE DONE THAT.
BUT WHAT WOULD I HAVE GOTTEN OUT OF IT?
HAN SOLO WAS AN OPPORTUNITY FOR ME, WHICH I TOOK.
OUTSIDE OF THAT, YES, I DID WANT TO GET HIM BACK TO YOU. BUT MY GOALS CAME FIRST.
YOU *USED* HIM.
I DID. AND I'D DO IT AGAIN, AS MANY TIMES AS I NEEDED TO--WHILE *YOU'D NEVER DO IT AT ALL.*
THAT'S WHY, ON BALANCE, HE WAS BETTER OFF WITH YOU.

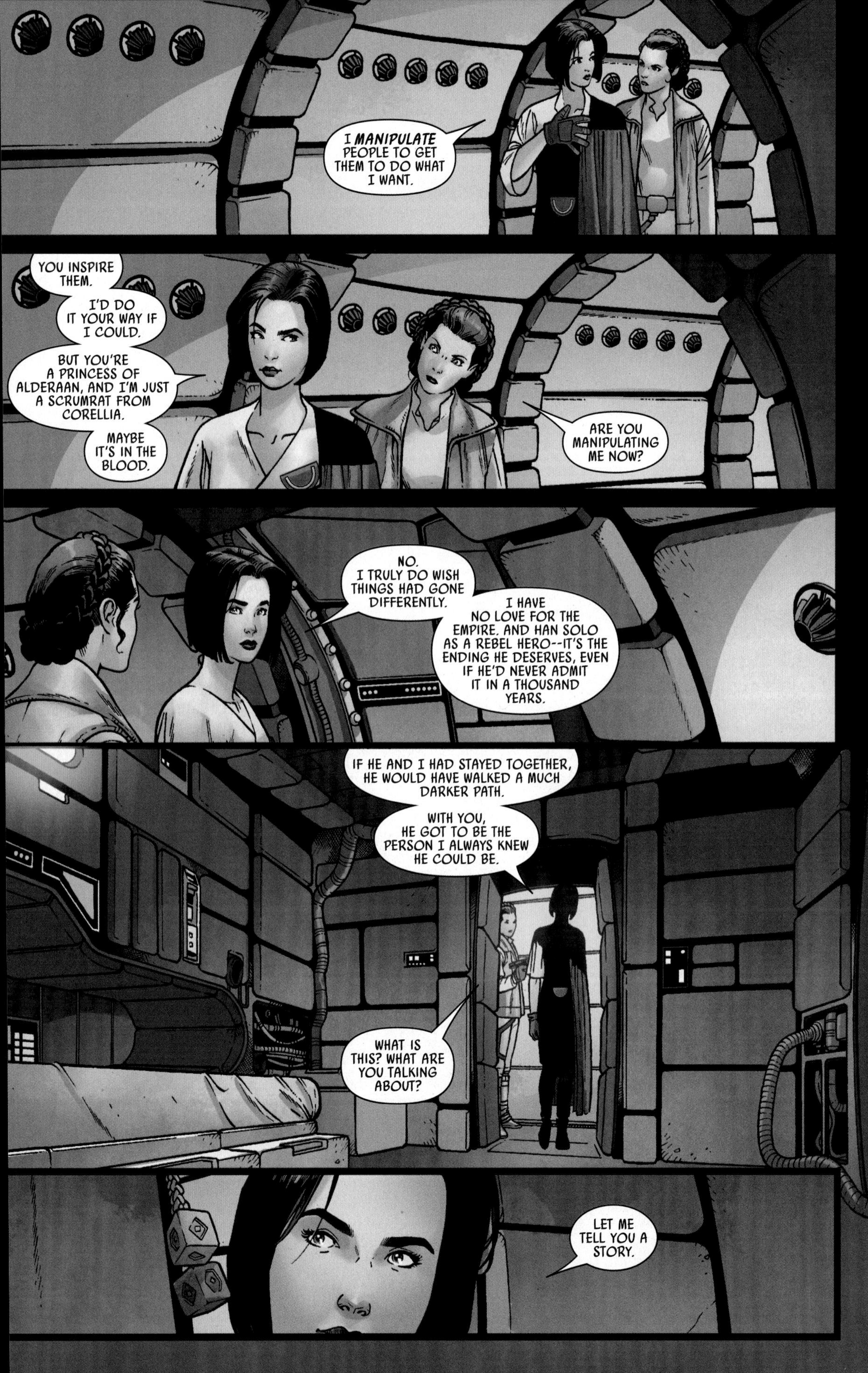
I *MANIPULATE* PEOPLE TO GET THEM TO DO WHAT I WANT.
YOU INSPIRE THEM.
I'D DO IT YOUR WAY IF I COULD.
BUT YOU'RE A PRINCESS OF ALDERAAN, AND I'M JUST A SCRUMRAT FROM CORELLIA.
MAYBE IT'S IN THE BLOOD.
ARE YOU MANIPULATING ME NOW?
NO. I TRULY DO WISH THINGS HAD GONE DIFFERENTLY.
I HAVE NO LOVE FOR THE EMPIRE. AND HAN SOLO AS A REBEL HERO--IT'S THE ENDING HE DESERVES, EVEN IF HE'D NEVER ADMIT IT IN A THOUSAND YEARS.
IF HE AND I HAD STAYED TOGETHER, HE WOULD HAVE WALKED A MUCH DARKER PATH.
WITH YOU, HE GOT TO BE THE PERSON I ALWAYS KNEW HE COULD BE.
WHAT IS THIS? WHAT ARE YOU TALKING ABOUT?
LET ME TELL YOU A STORY.

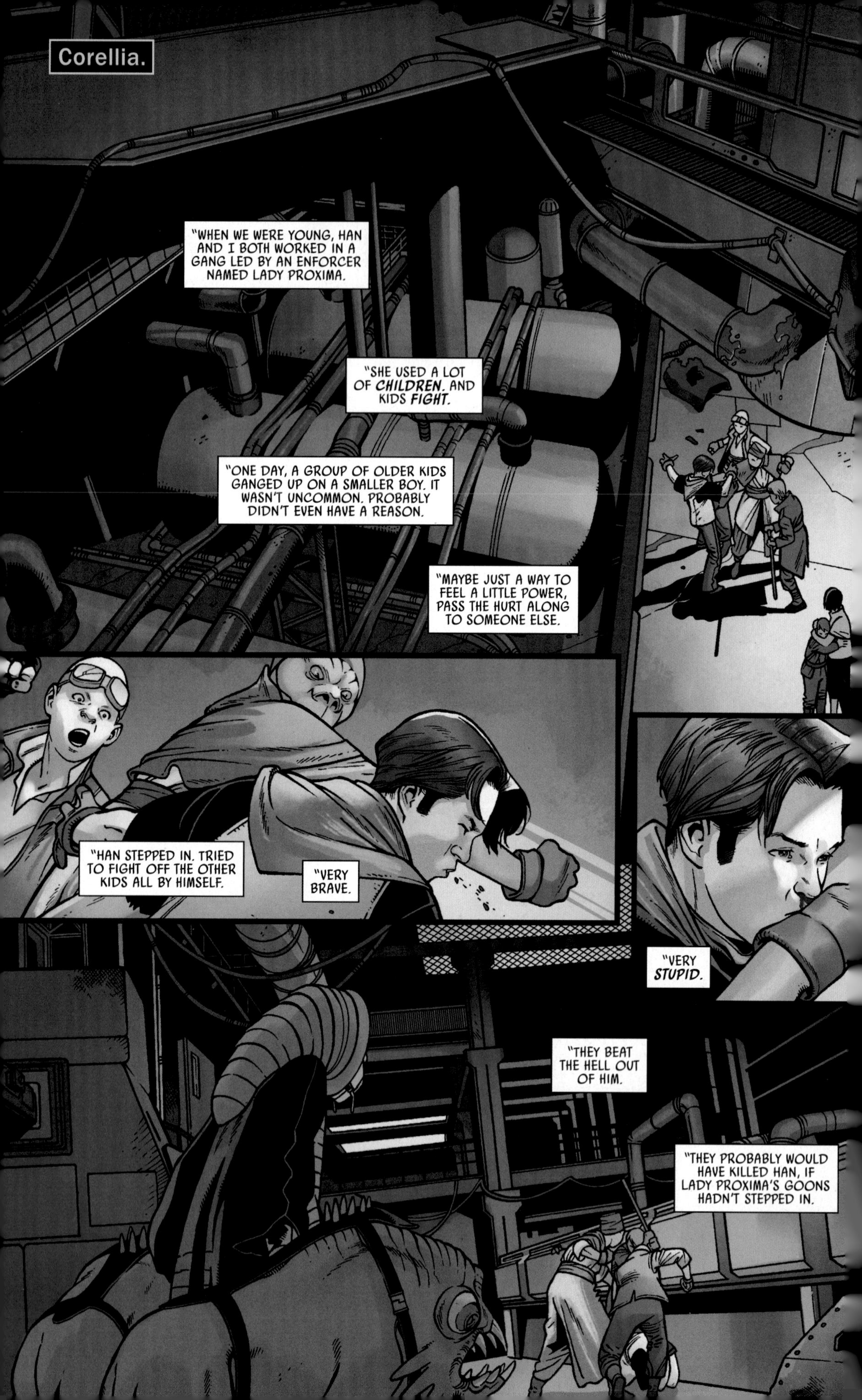
Corellia.
"WHEN WE WERE YOUNG, HAN AND I BOTH WORKED IN A GANG LED BY AN ENFORCER NAMED LADY PROXIMA.
"SHE USED A LOT OF CHILDREN. AND KIDS FIGHT.
"ONE DAY, A GROUP OF OLDER KIDS GANGED UP ON A SMALLER BOY. IT WASN'T UNCOMMON. PROBABLY DIDN'T EVEN HAVE A REASON.
"MAYBE JUST A WAY TO FEEL A LITTLE POWER, PASS THE HURT ALONG TO SOMEONE ELSE.
"HAN STEPPED IN. TRIED TO FIGHT OFF THE OTHER KIDS ALL BY HIMSELF.
"VERY BRAVE.
"VERY STUPID.
"THEY BEAT THE HELL OUT OF HIM.
"THEY PROBABLY WOULD HAVE KILLED HAN, IF LADY PROXIMA'S GOONS HADN'T STEPPED IN.

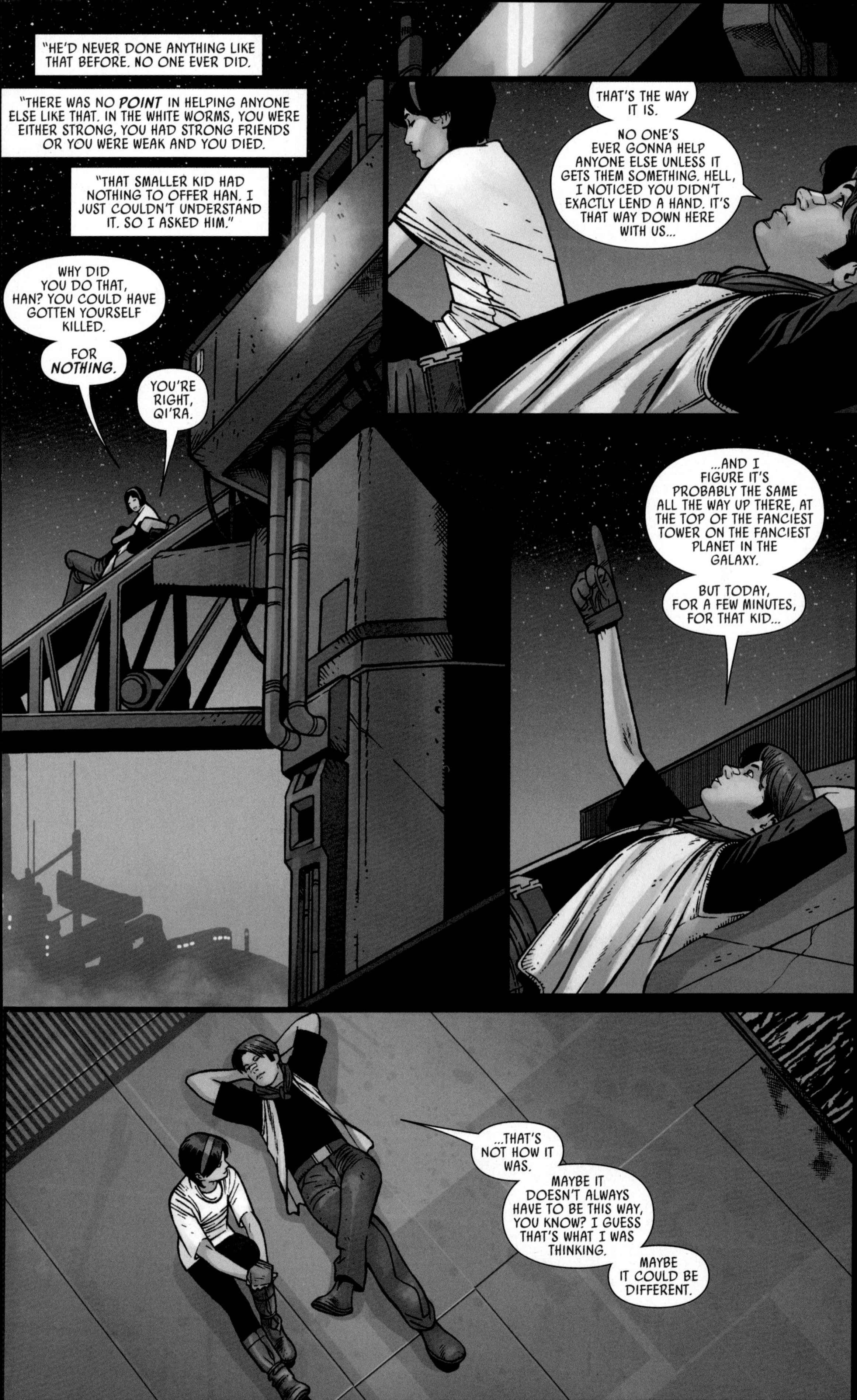
"HE'D NEVER DONE ANYTHING LIKE THAT BEFORE. NO ONE EVER DID.
"THERE WAS NO POINT IN HELPING ANYONE ELSE LIKE THAT. IN THE WHITE WORMS, YOU WERE EITHER STRONG, YOU HAD STRONG FRIENDS OR YOU WERE WEAK AND YOU DIED.
"THAT SMALLER KID HAD NOTHING TO OFFER HAN. I JUST COULDN'T UNDERSTAND IT. SO I ASKED HIM."
WHY DID YOU DO THAT, HAN? YOU COULD HAVE GOTTEN YOURSELF KILLED.
FOR NOTHING.
YOU'RE RIGHT, QI'RA.
THAT'S THE WAY IT IS.
NO ONE'S EVER GONNA HELP ANYONE ELSE UNLESS IT GETS THEM SOMETHING. HELL, I NOTICED YOU DIDN'T EXACTLY LEND A HAND. IT'S THAT WAY DOWN HERE WITH US...
...AND I FIGURE IT'S PROBABLY THE SAME ALL THE WAY UP THERE, AT THE TOP OF THE FANCIEST TOWER ON THE FANCIEST PLANET IN THE GALAXY.
BUT TODAY, FOR A FEW MINUTES, FOR THAT KID...
...THAT'S NOT HOW IT WAS.
MAYBE IT DOESN'T ALWAYS HAVE TO BE THIS WAY, YOU KNOW? I GUESS THAT'S WHAT I WAS THINKING.
MAYBE IT COULD BE DIFFERENT.

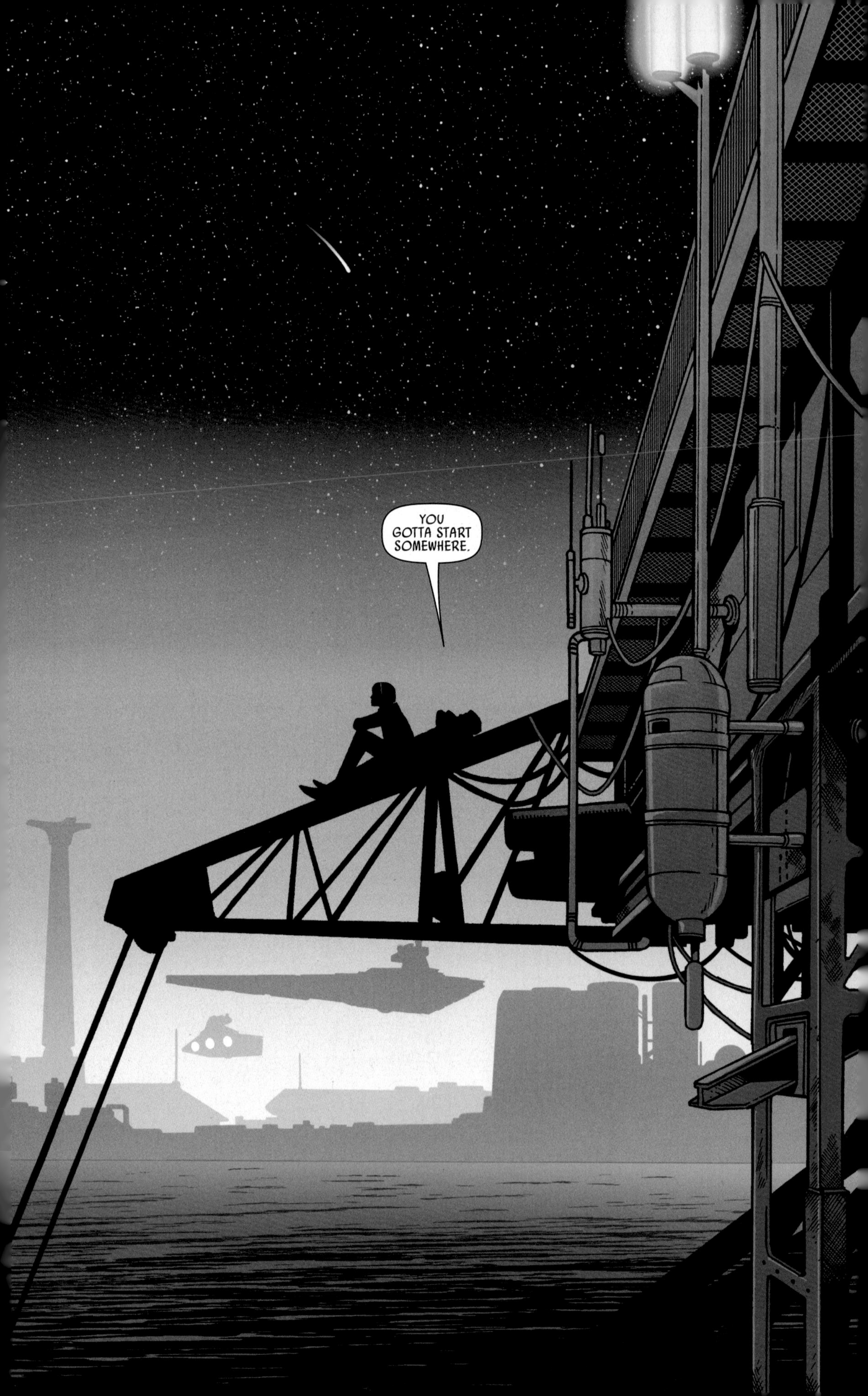
YOU GOTTA START SOMEWHERE.

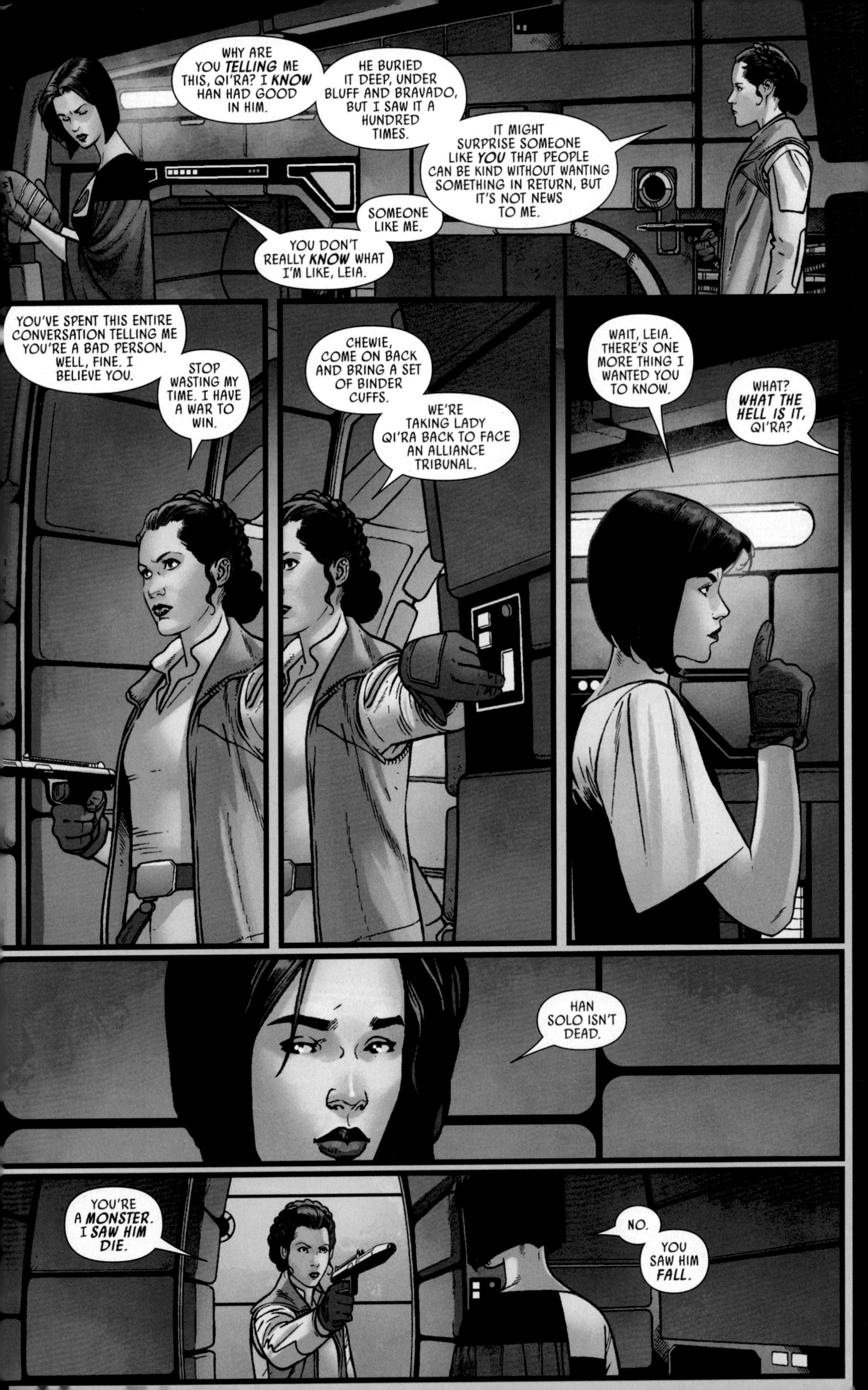
WHY ARE YOU TELLING ME THIS, QI'RA? I KNOW HAN HAD GOOD IN HIM.
HE BURIED IT DEEP, UNDER BLUFF AND BRAVADO, BUT I SAW IT A HUNDRED TIMES.
IT MIGHT SURPRISE SOMEONE LIKE YOU THAT PEOPLE CAN BE KIND WITHOUT WANTING SOMETHING IN RETURN, BUT IT'S NOT NEWS TO ME.
SOMEONE LIKE ME.
YOU DON'T REALLY KNOW WHAT I'M LIKE, LEIA.
YOU'VE SPENT THIS ENTIRE CONVERSATION TELLING ME YOU'RE A BAD PERSON. WELL, FINE. I BELIEVE YOU.
STOP WASTING MY TIME. I HAVE A WAR TO WIN.
CHEWIE, COME ON BACK AND BRING A SET OF BINDER CUFFS.
WE'RE TAKING LADY QI'RA BACK TO FACE AN ALLIANCE TRIBUNAL.
WAIT, LEIA. THERE'S ONE MORE THING I WANTED YOU TO KNOW.
WHAT? WHAT THE HELL IS IT, QI'RA?
HAN SOLO ISN'T DEAD.
YOU'RE A MONSTER. I SAW HIM DIE.
NO.
YOU SAW HIM FALL.

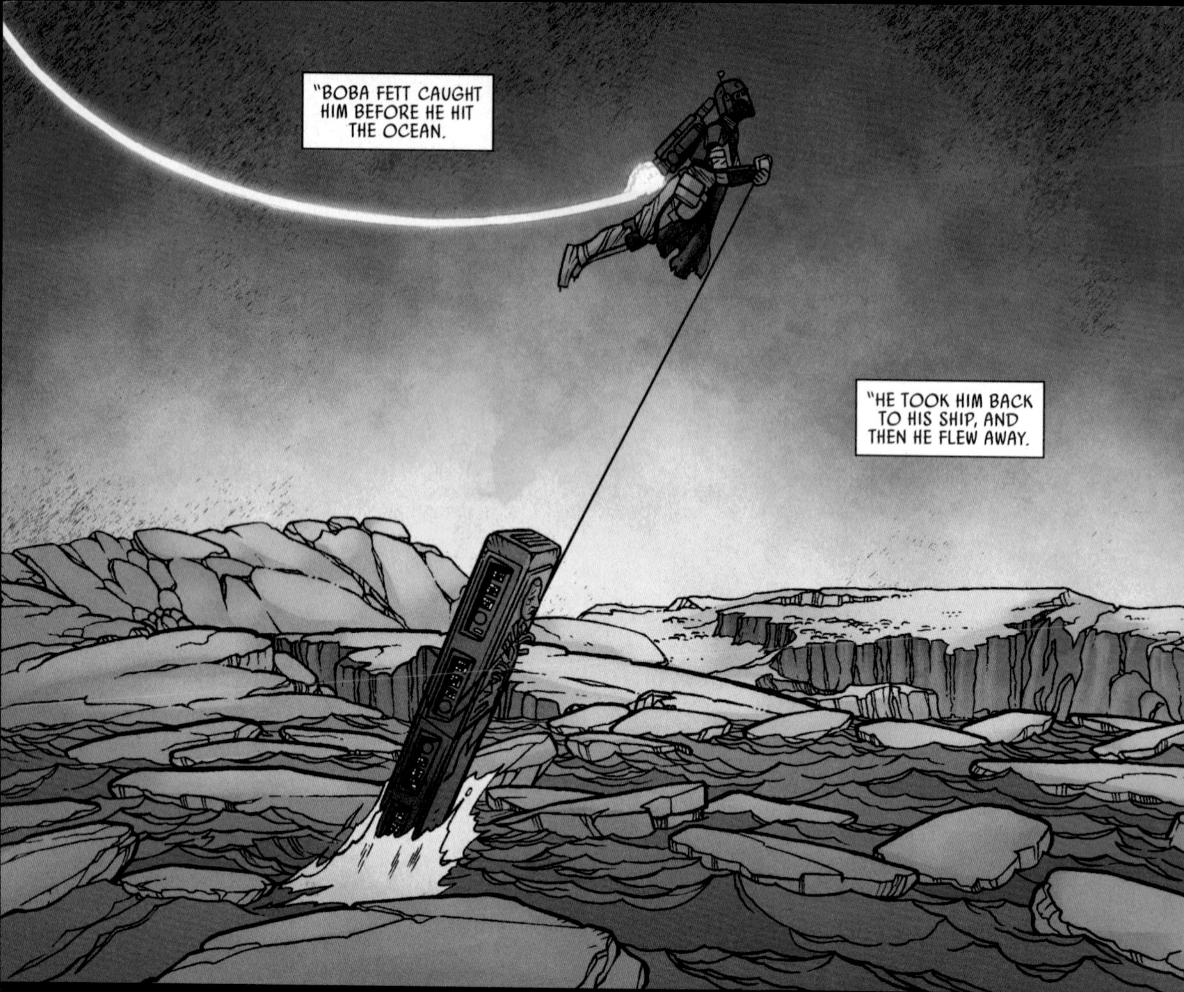
"BOBA FETT CAUGHT HIM BEFORE HE HIT THE OCEAN.
"HE TOOK HIM BACK TO HIS SHIP, AND THEN HE FLEW AWAY.

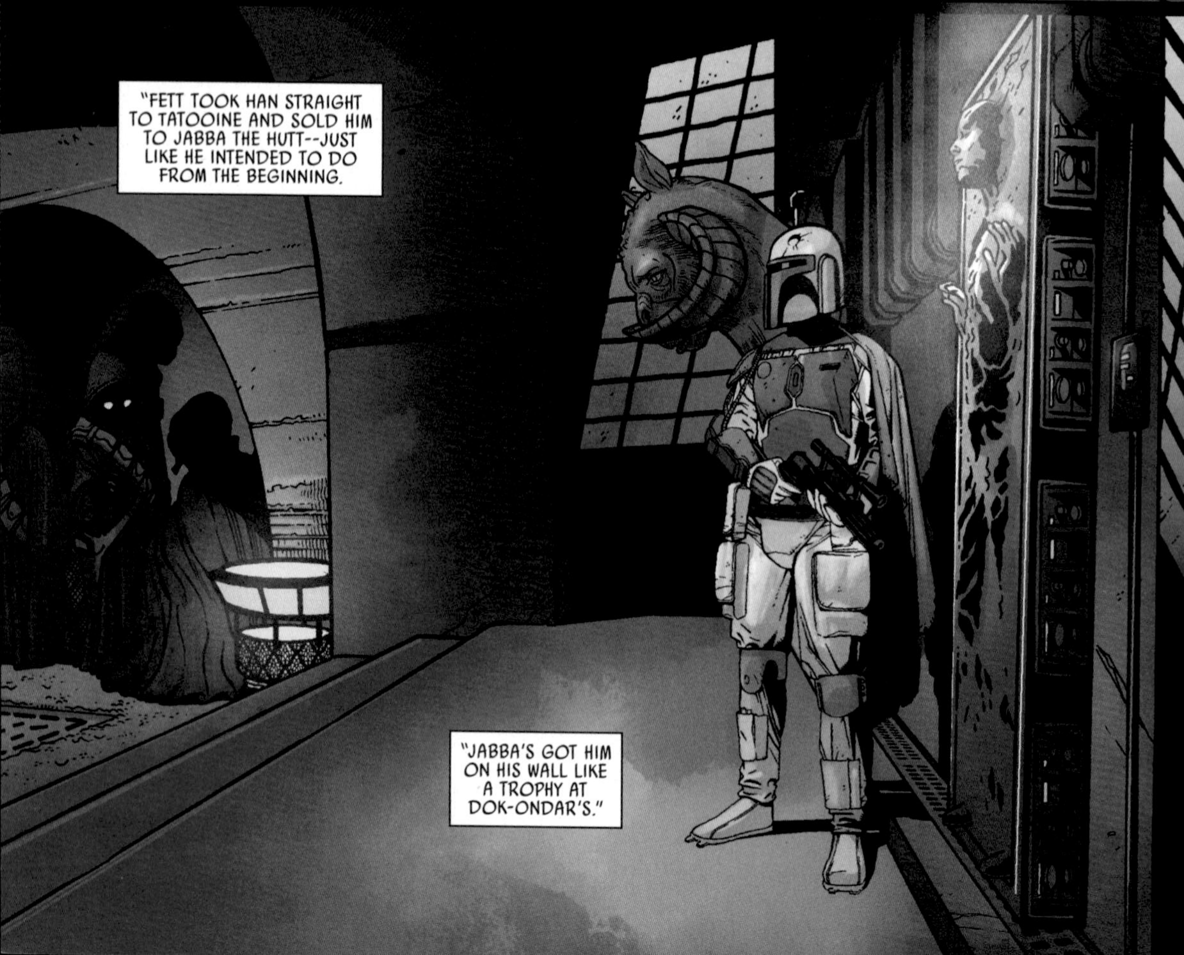
"FETT TOOK HAN STRAIGHT TO TATOOINE AND SOLD HIM TO JABBA THE HUTT--JUST LIKE HE INTENDED TO DO FROM THE BEGINNING.
"JABBA'S GOT HIM ON HIS WALL LIKE A TROPHY AT DOK-ONDAR'S."

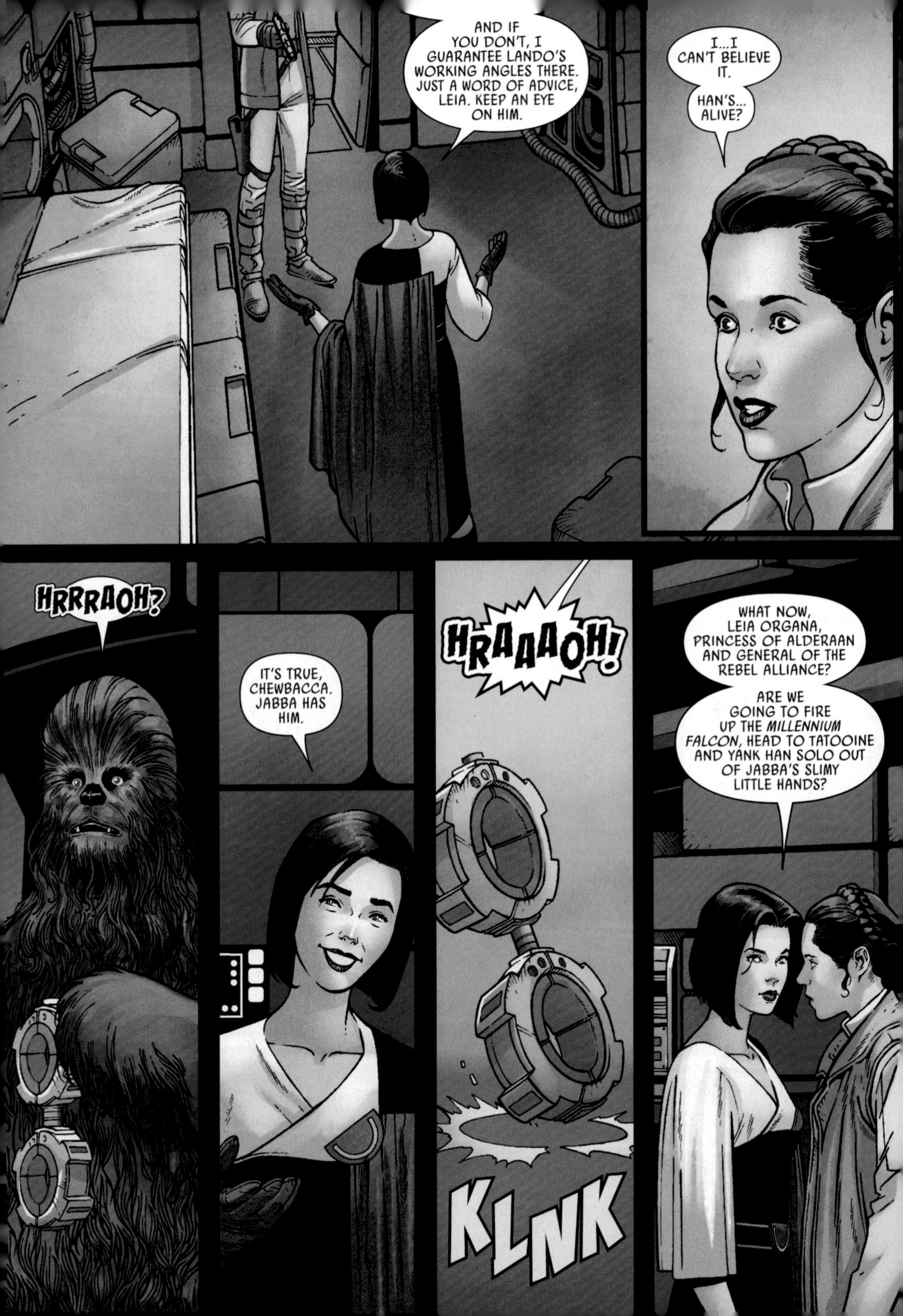
AND IF YOU DON'T, I GUARANTEE LANDO'S WORKING ANGLES THERE. JUST A WORD OF ADVICE, LEIA. KEEP AN EYE ON HIM.
I...I CAN'T BELIEVE IT.
HAN'S... ALIVE?
HRRRAOH?
IT'S TRUE, CHEWBACCA. JABBA HAS HIM.
HRAAAOH!
KLNK
WHAT NOW, LEIA ORGANA, PRINCESS OF ALDERAAN AND GENERAL OF THE REBEL ALLIANCE?
ARE WE GOING TO FIRE UP THE *MILLENNIUM FALCON*, HEAD TO TATOOINE AND YANK HAN SOLO OUT OF JABBA'S SLIMY LITTLE HANDS?

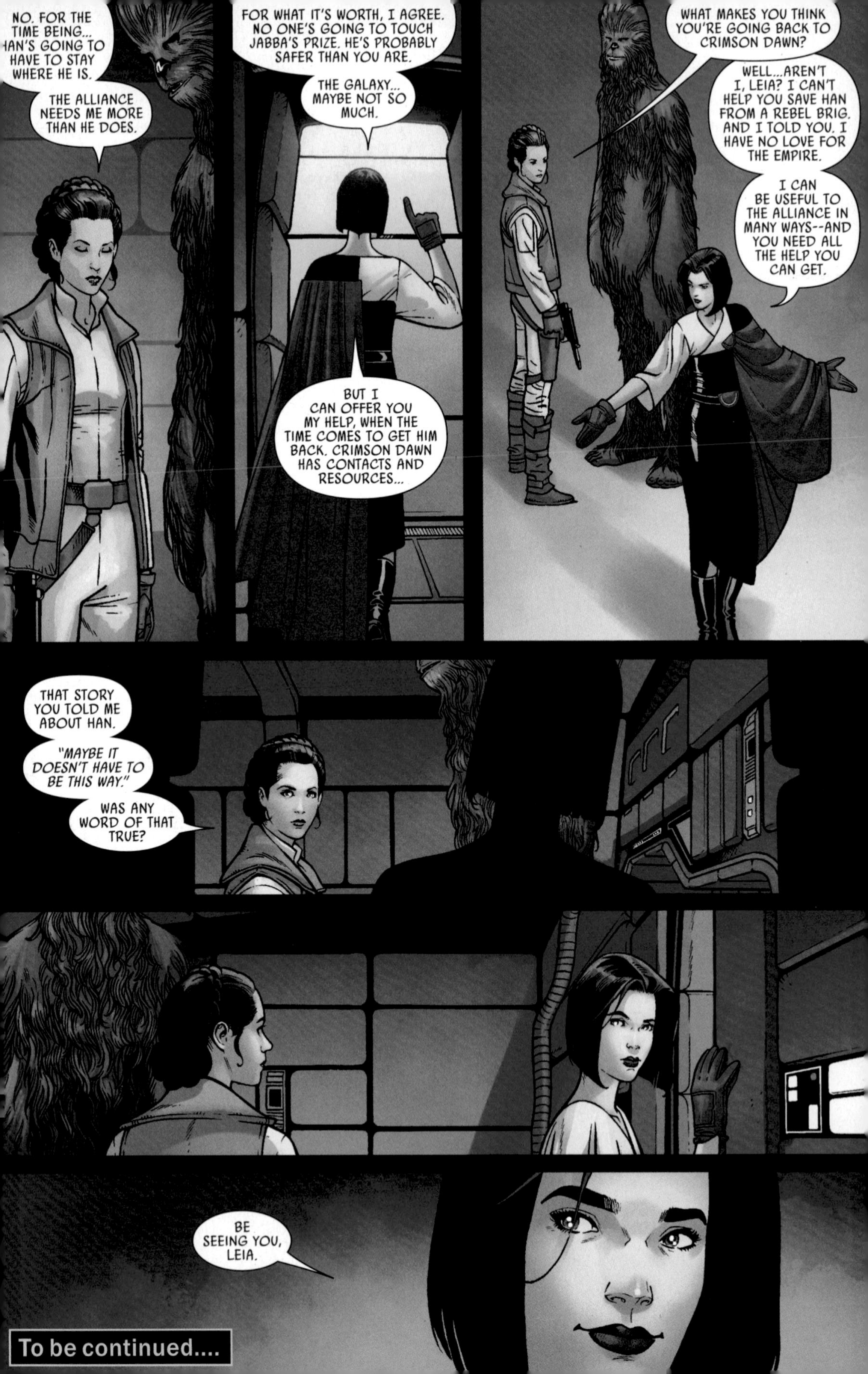
NO. FOR THE TIME BEING... HAN'S GOING TO HAVE TO STAY WHERE HE IS.
THE ALLIANCE NEEDS ME MORE THAN HE DOES.
FOR WHAT IT'S WORTH, I AGREE. NO ONE'S GOING TO TOUCH JABBA'S PRIZE. HE'S PROBABLY SAFER THAN YOU ARE.
THE GALAXY... MAYBE NOT SO MUCH.
BUT I CAN OFFER YOU MY HELP, WHEN THE TIME COMES TO GET HIM BACK. CRIMSON DAWN HAS CONTACTS AND RESOURCES...
WHAT MAKES YOU THINK YOU'RE GOING BACK TO CRIMSON DAWN?
WELL...AREN'T I, LEIA? I CAN'T HELP YOU SAVE HAN FROM A REBEL BRIG. AND I TOLD YOU. I HAVE NO LOVE FOR THE EMPIRE.
I CAN BE USEFUL TO THE ALLIANCE IN MANY WAYS--AND YOU NEED ALL THE HELP YOU CAN GET.
THAT STORY YOU TOLD ME ABOUT HAN.
"MAYBE IT DOESN'T HAVE TO BE THIS WAY."
WAS ANY WORD OF THAT TRUE?
BE SEEING YOU, LEIA.
To be continued....

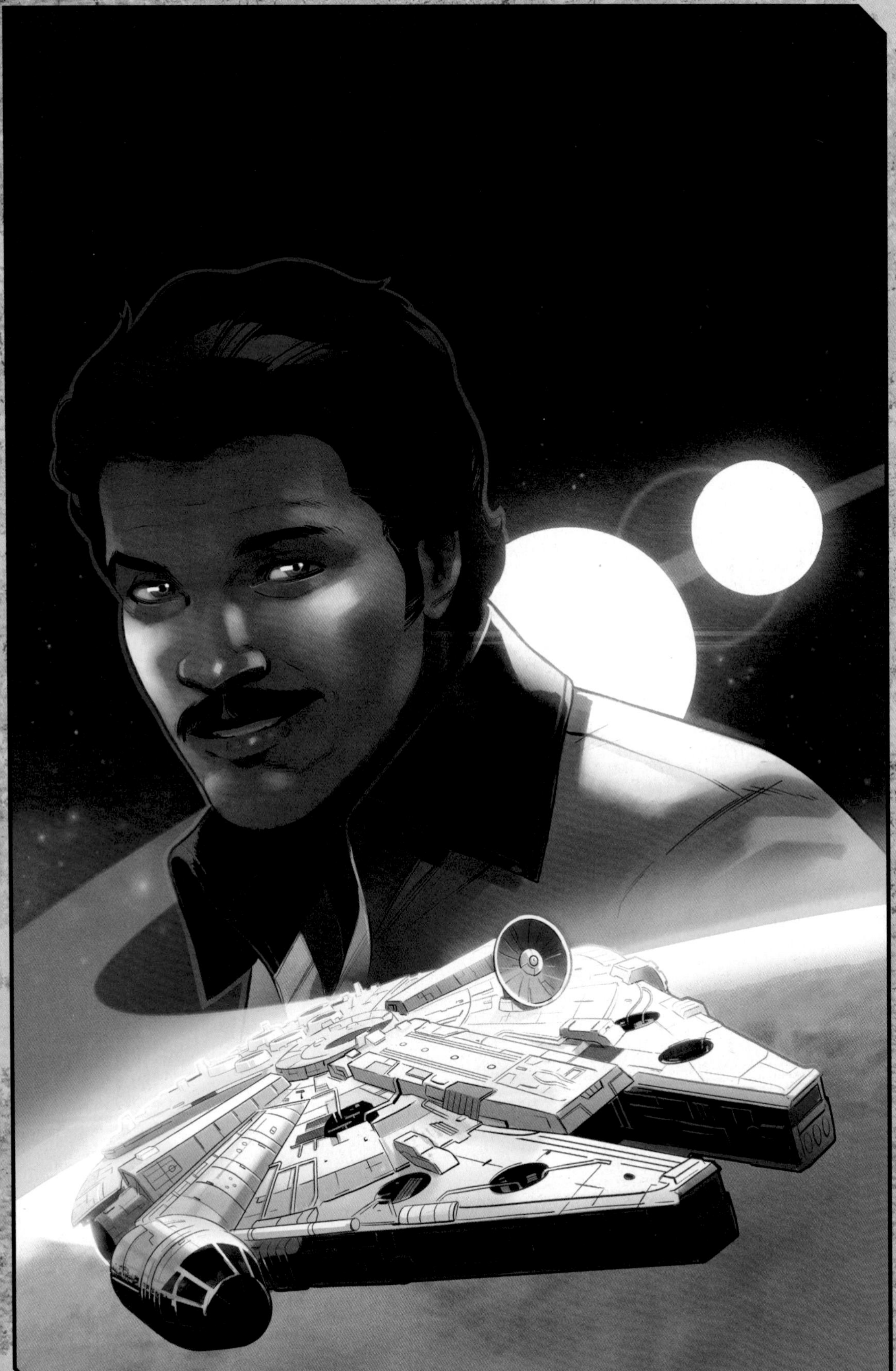

#14 Pride Variant by
STEPHEN BYRNE

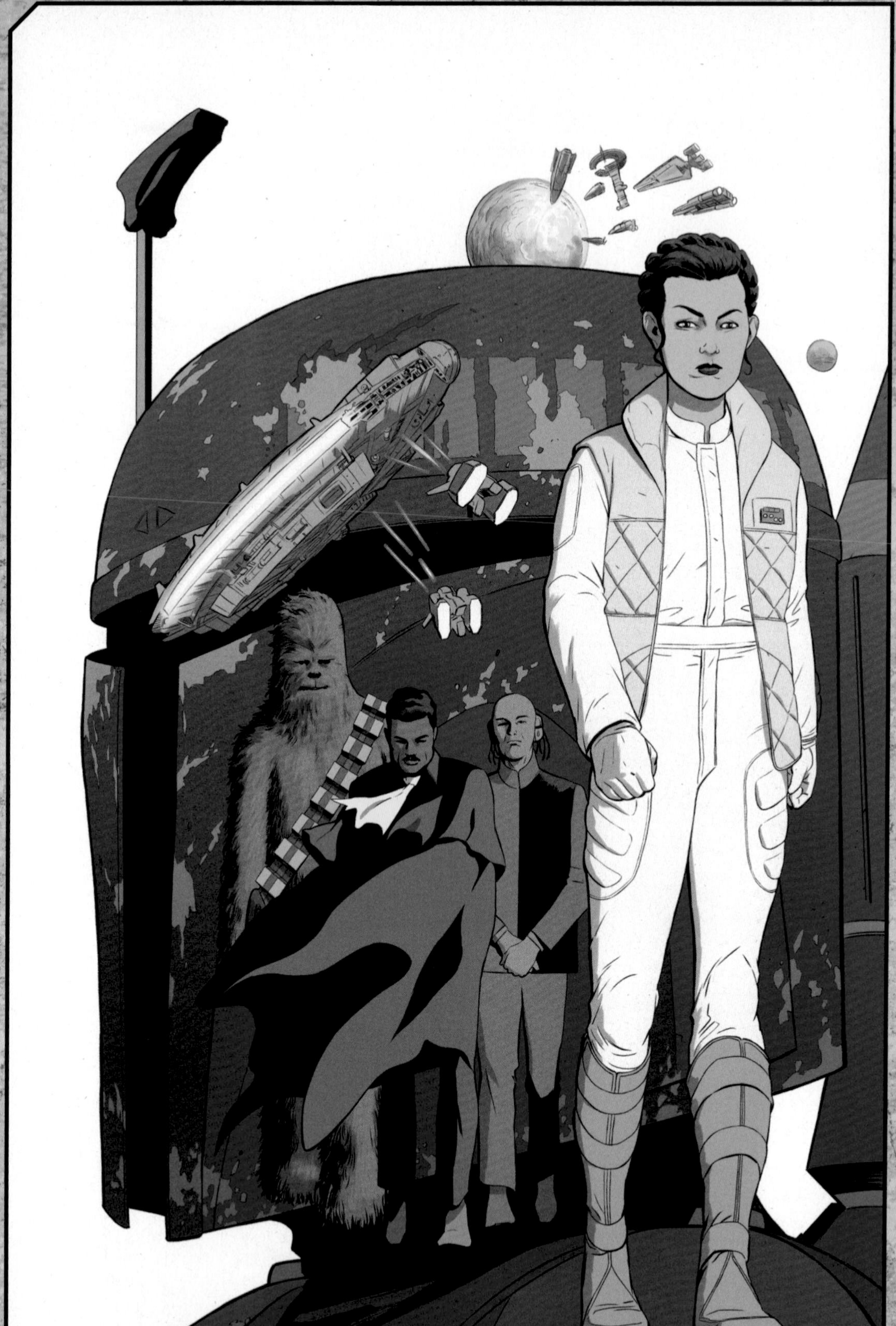

#14 Variant by
JAVIER RODRIGUEZ

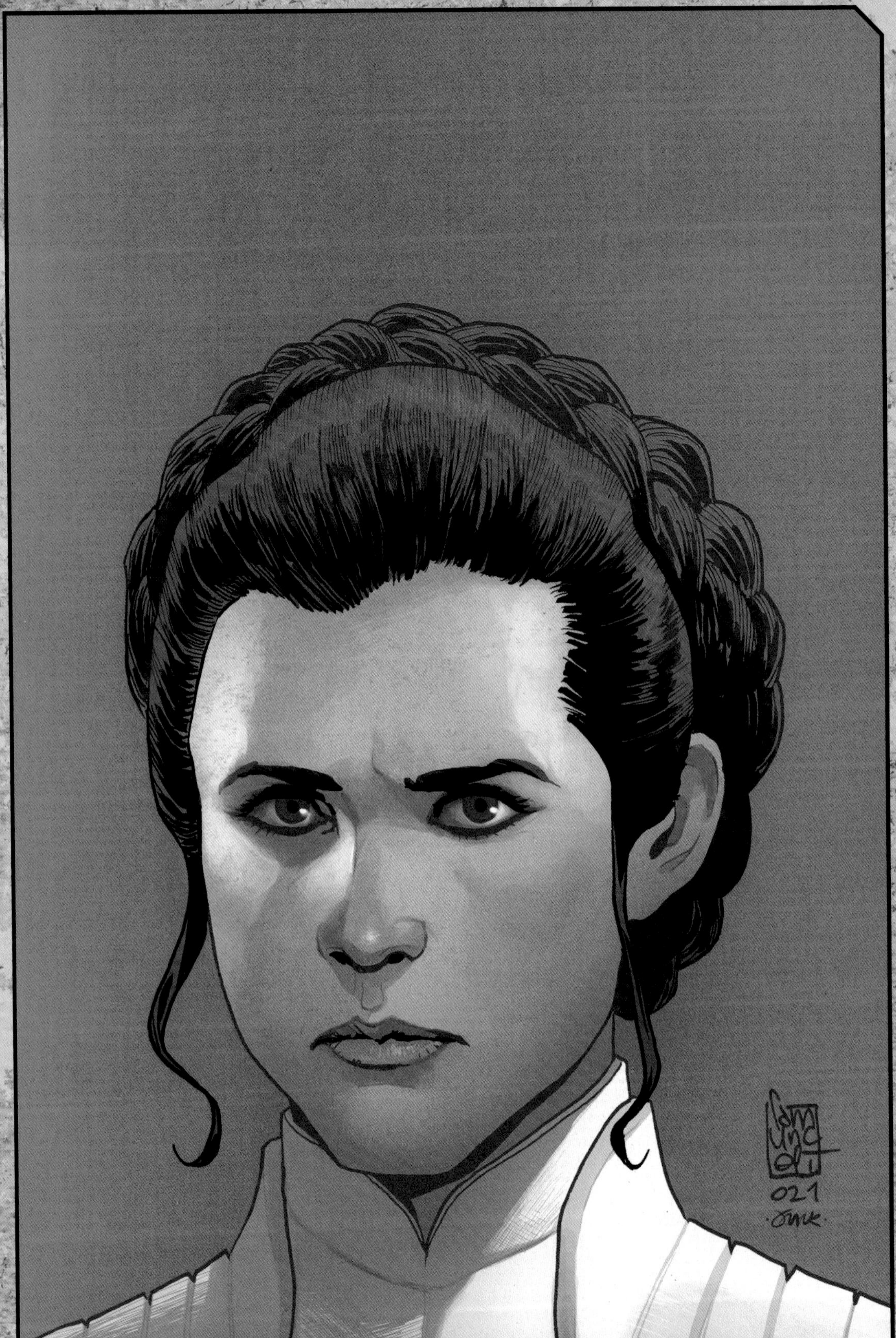

#15 Headshot Variant by
GIUSEPPE CAMUNCOLI & FRANK MARTIN

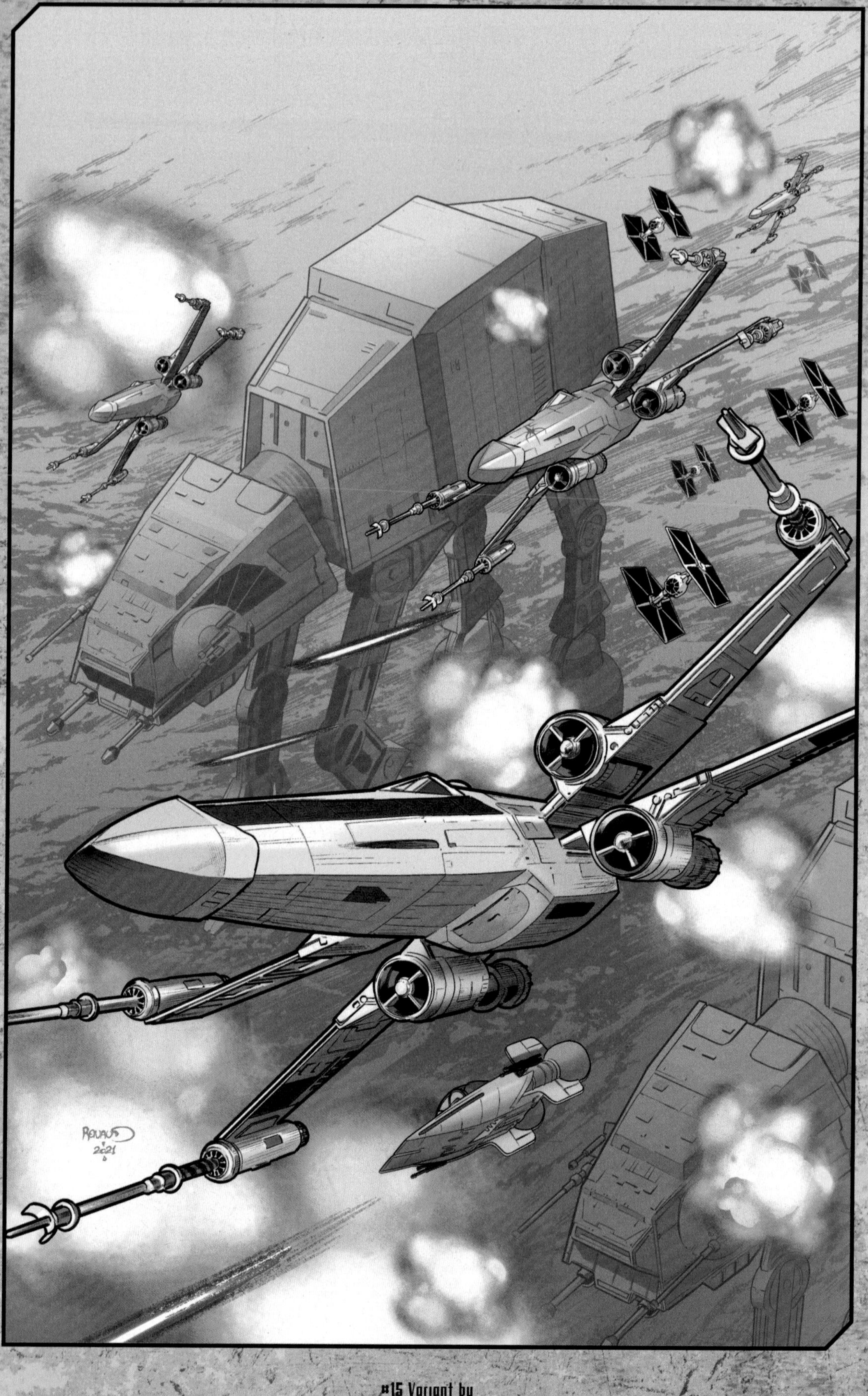
RENAUD
2021

#15 Variant by
PAUL RENAUD

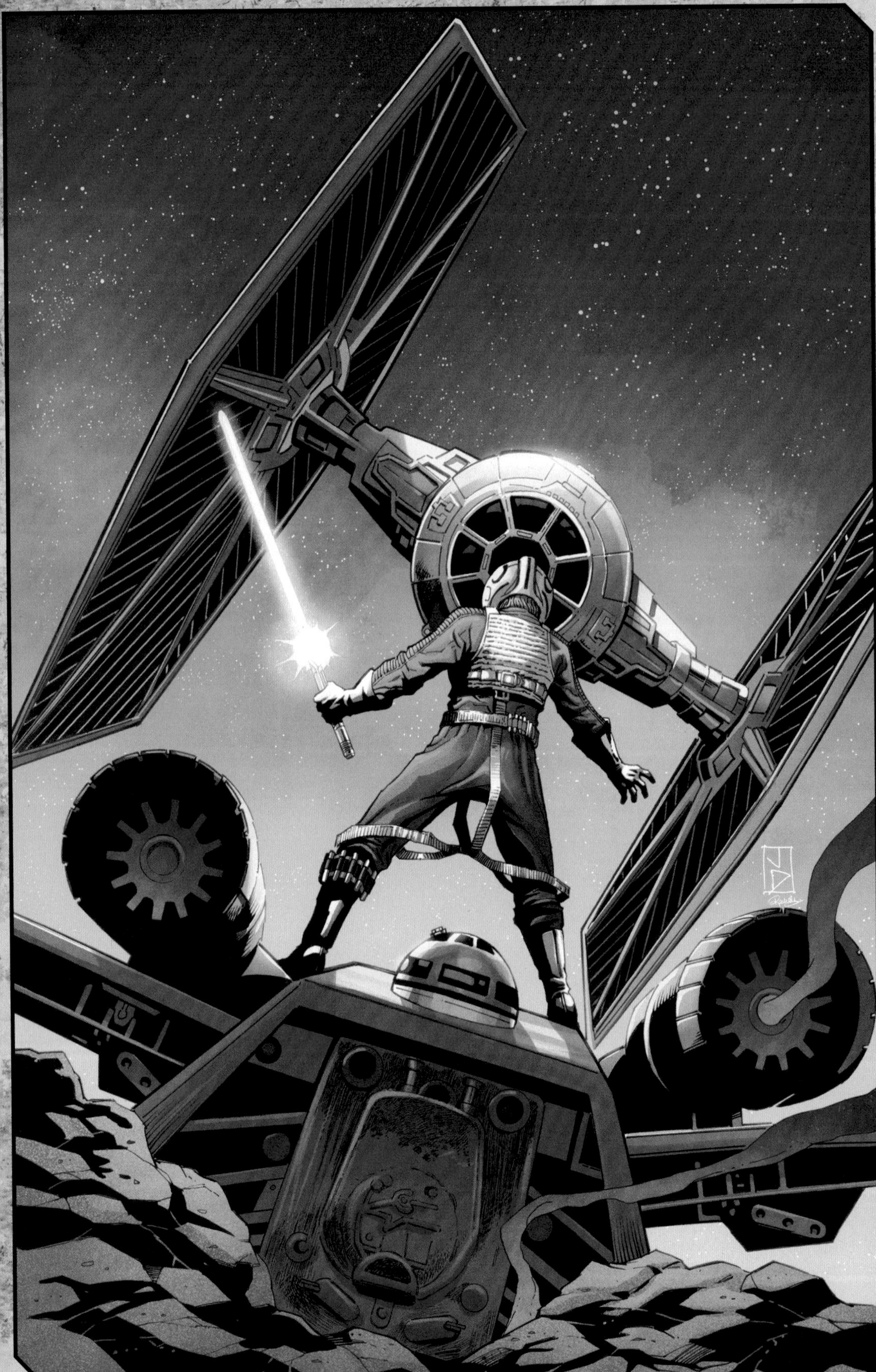

#16 Variant by
JAN DUURSEMA & RACHELLE ROSENBERG

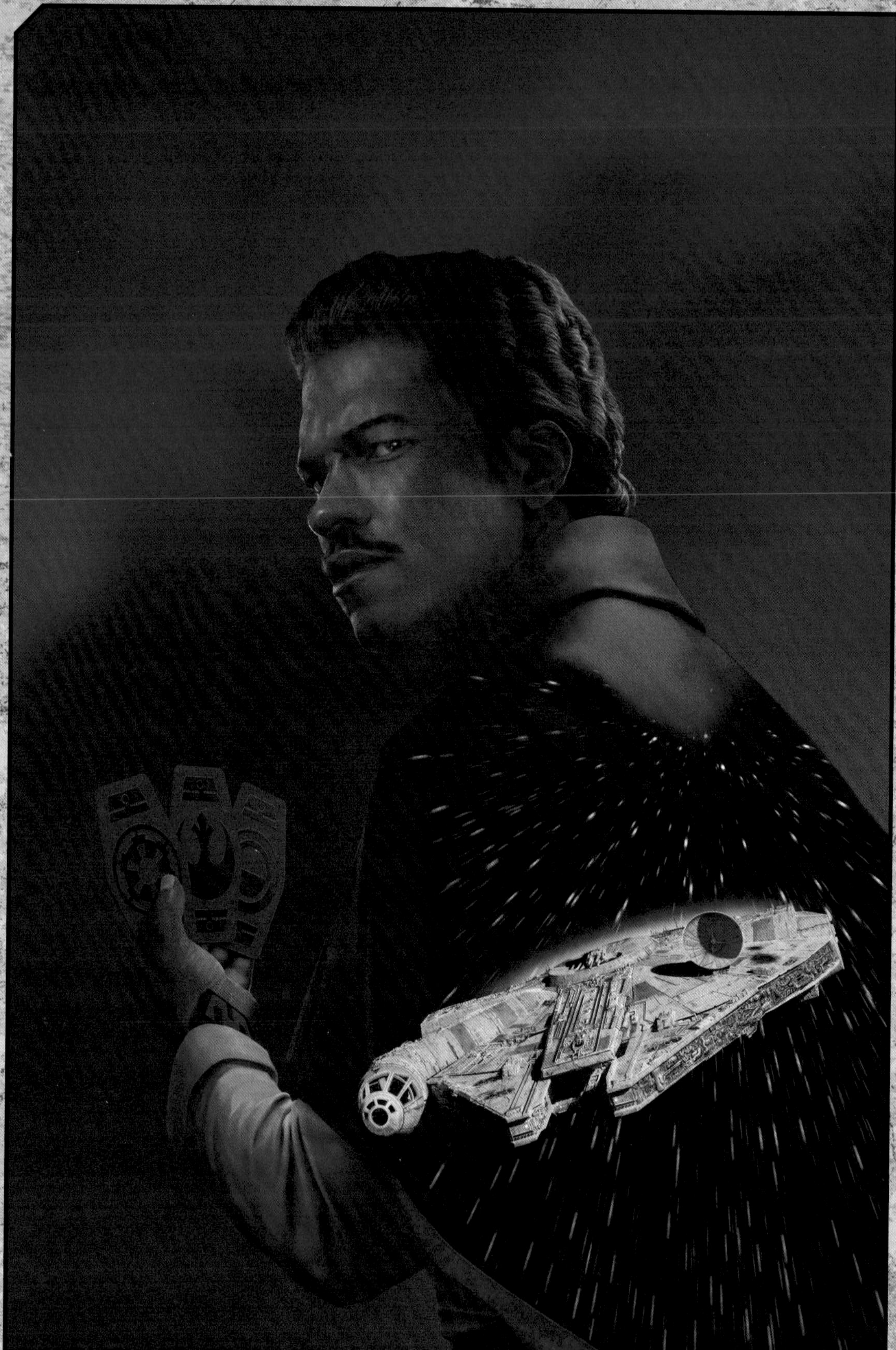

#17 Variant by
RAHZZAH

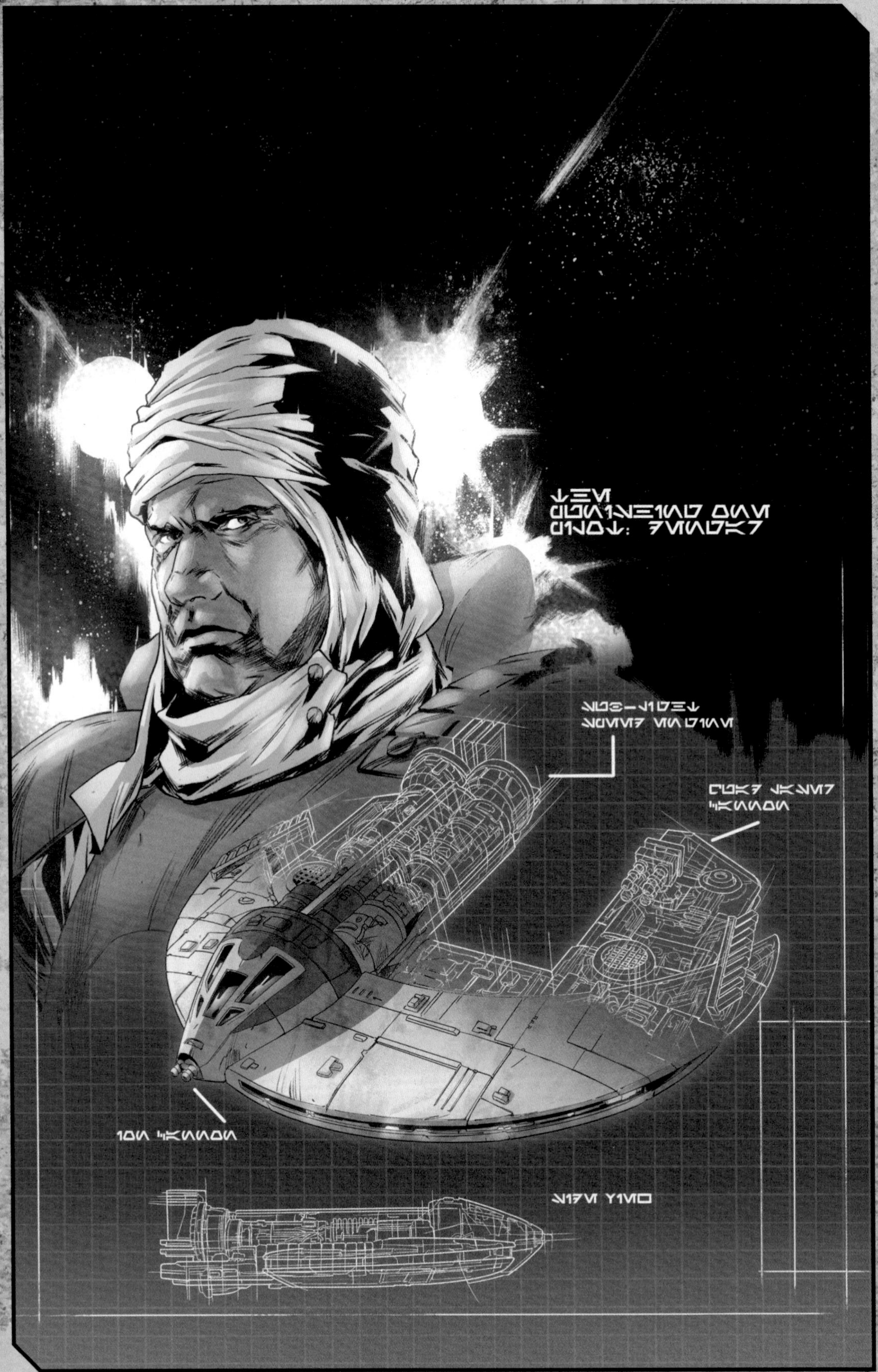

#17 Blueprint Variant by
PAOLO VILLANELLI & MATTIA IACONO

STAR WARS

WAR OF THE BOUNTY HUNTERS

STAR WARS

DENGAR

Homeworld: **Corellia**
Species: **Human**
First Appearance: ***Star Wars: The Empire Strikes Back***

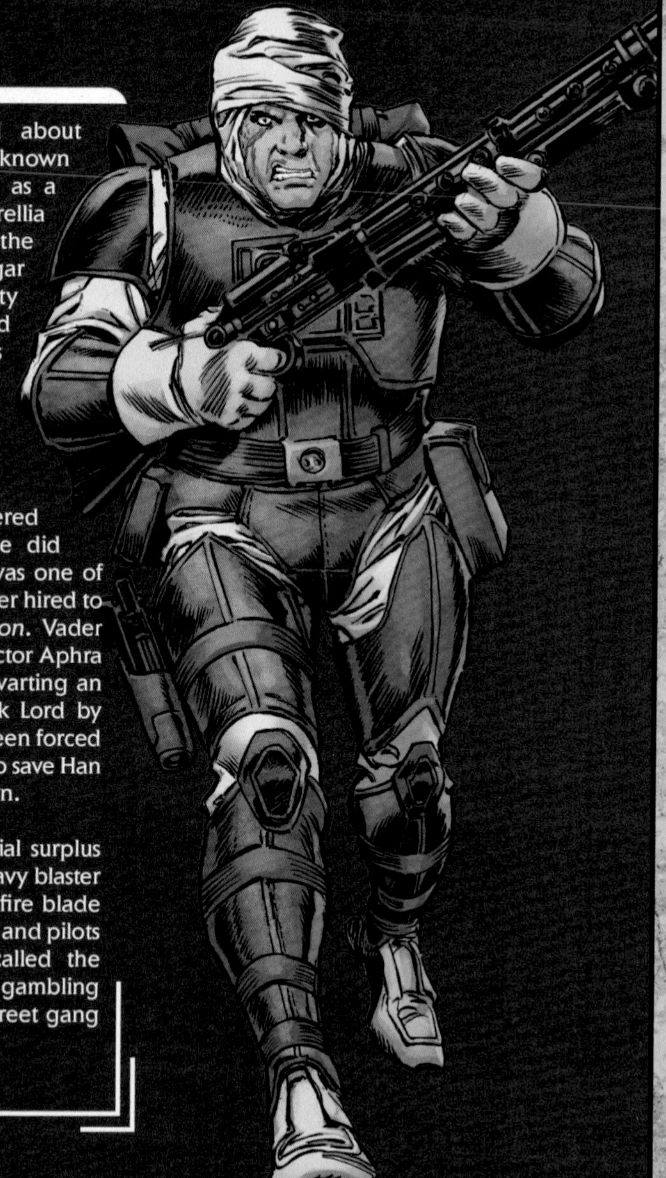

Not much has been revealed about Dengar's early life, but he's been known to brag about his alleged days as a professional swoop racer on Corellia during his youth. Operating since the early days of the Clone Wars, Dengar became a deadly and brutal bounty hunter whose career spanned beyond the Battle of Endor. He was sometimes associated with Boba Fett's syndicate, Krayt's Claw, and has worked for many other syndicates, including the Hutts.

Despite eventually being considered a grizzly vet past his prime, he did several jobs for the Empire. He was one of six bounty hunters who Darth Vader hired to track down the *Millennium Falcon*. Vader has also employed him to find Doctor Aphra and to serve as an informant, thwarting an assassination attempt on the Dark Lord by Beilert Valance. Since then, he's been forced to work with Valance in his quest to save Han Solo from the grips of Crimson Dawn.

Dengar's armor consists of Imperial surplus gear. He prefers using a DLT-19 heavy blaster rifle and is also equipped with a fire blade and an array of grenades. He owns and pilots a modified JumpMaster 5000 called the *Punishing One*, which he's lost to gambling debts to the smalltime Corellian street gang called the Sixth Kind.

#18 Handbook Variant by
RON FRENZ, TOM PALMER & NOLAN WOODARD WITH CARLOS LAO

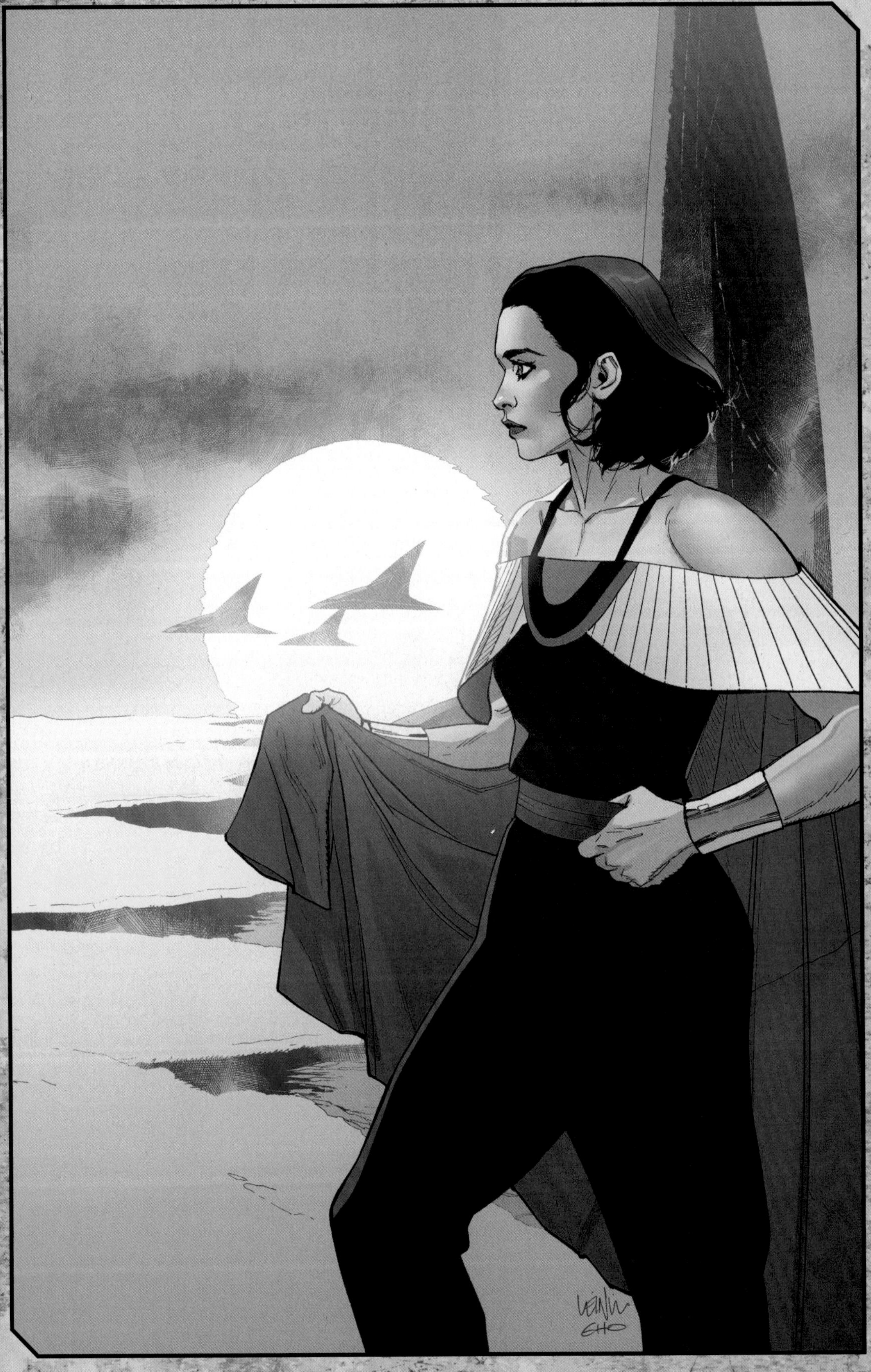

#18 Variant by
LEINIL FRANCIS YU & SUNNY GHO

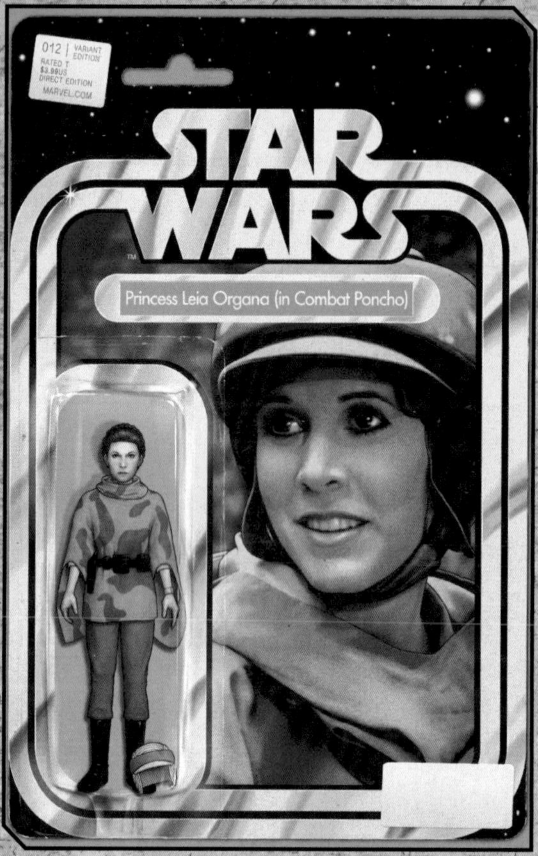
012 | VARIANT EDITION
RATED T
$3.99US
DIRECT EDITION
MARVEL.COM
STAR WARS
Princess Leia Organa (in Combat Poncho)

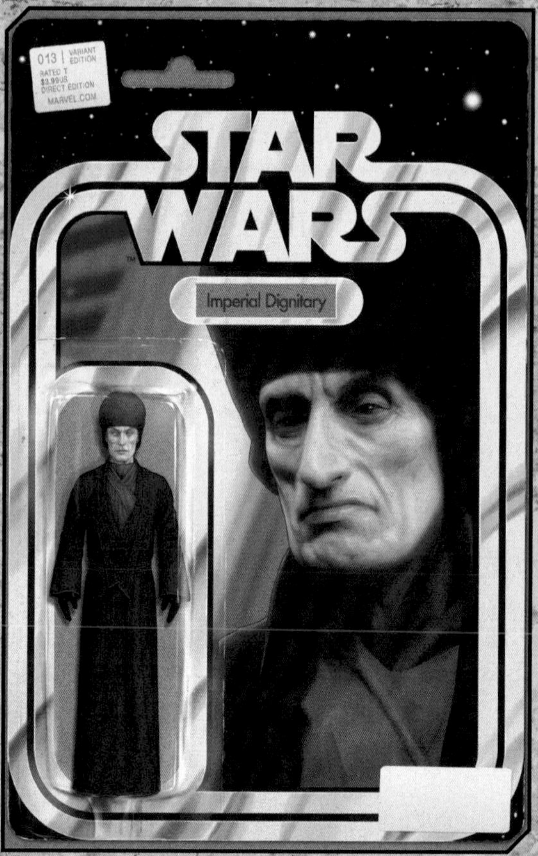
013 | VARIANT EDITION
RATED T
$3.99US
DIRECT EDITION
MARVEL.COM
STAR WARS
Imperial Dignitary

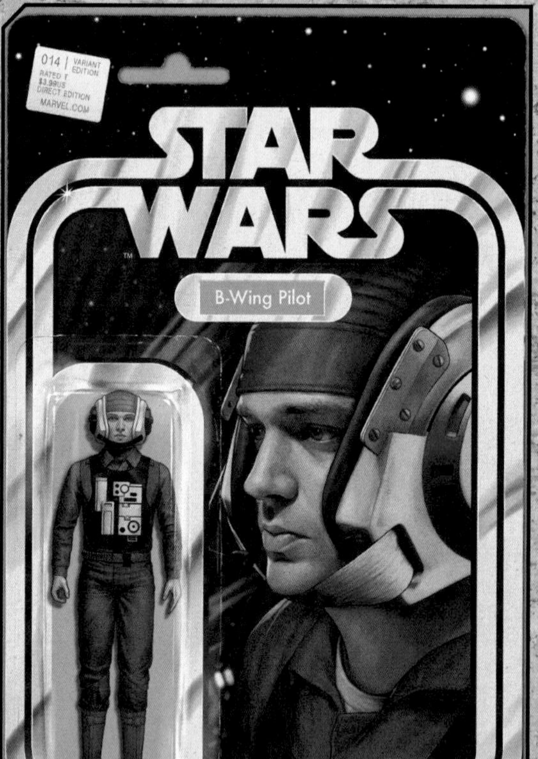
014 | VARIANT EDITION
RATED T
$3.99US
DIRECT EDITION
MARVEL.COM
STAR WARS
B-Wing Pilot

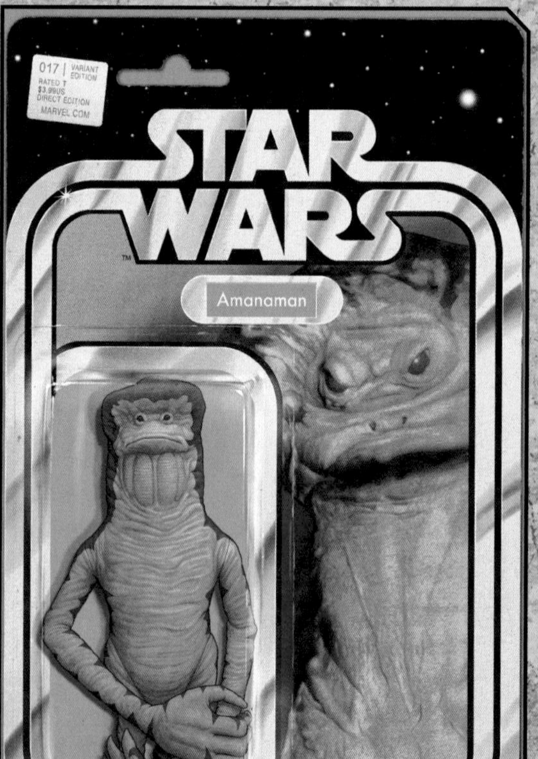
017 | VARIANT EDITION
RATED T
$3.99US
DIRECT EDITION
MARVEL.COM
STAR WARS
Amanaman

#12-14 & 17 Action Figure Variants by
JOHN TYLER CHRISTOPHER

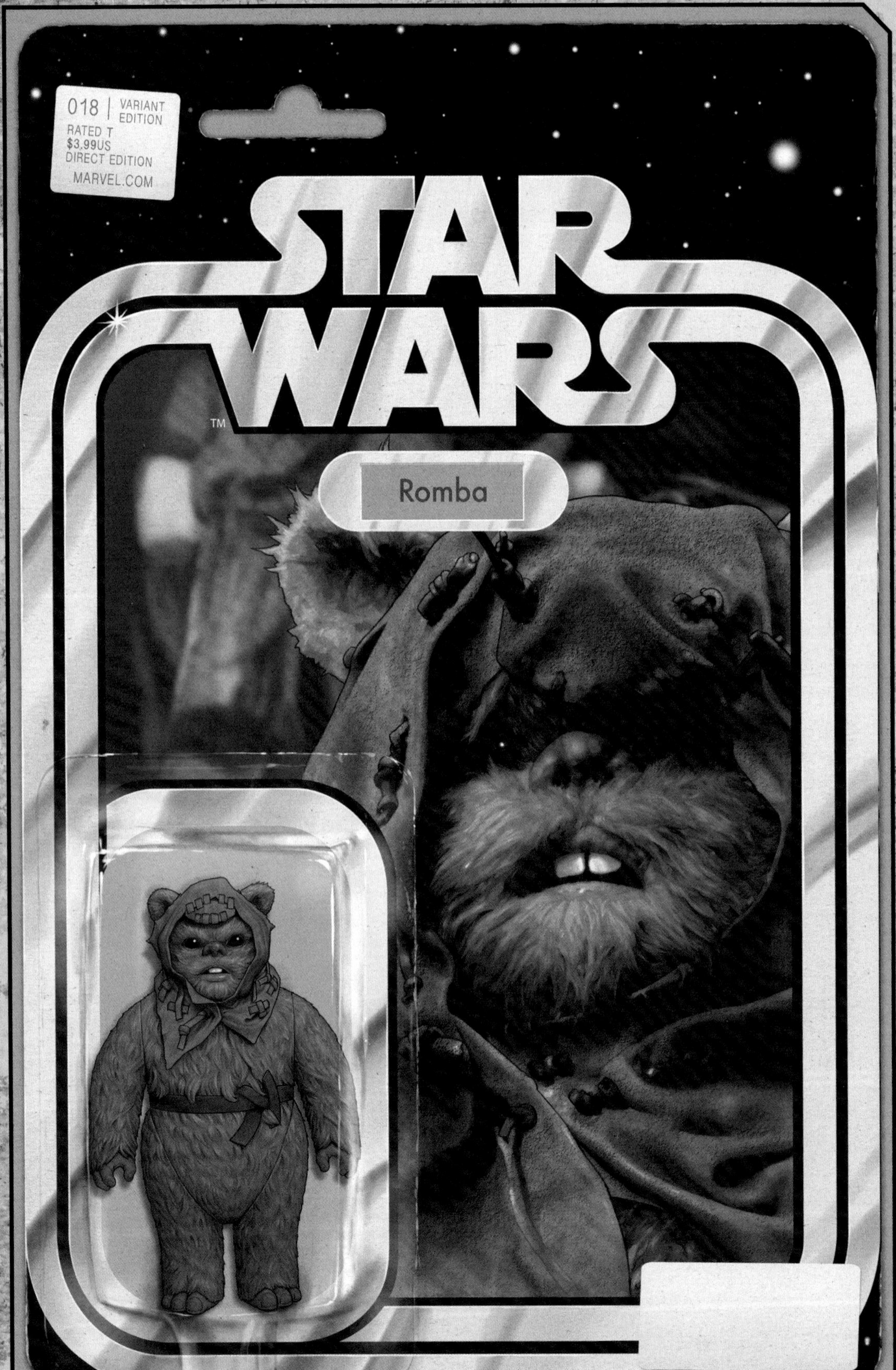
018 | VARIANT EDITION
RATED T
$3.99US
DIRECT EDITION
MARVEL.COM
STAR WARS
TM
Romba

#18 Action Figure Variant by
JOHN TYLER CHRISTOPHER

STAR WARS COLLECTED EDITIONS

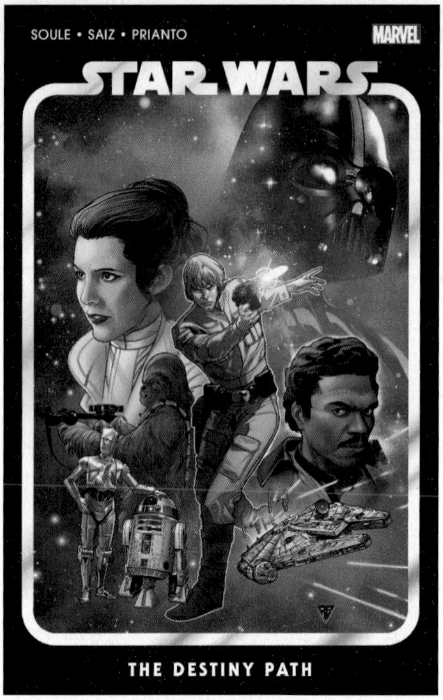
SOULE • SAIZ • PRIANTO
MARVEL
STAR WARS
THE DESTINY PATH

Star Wars Vol. 1:
The Destiny Path

ISBN 978-1-302-92078-4

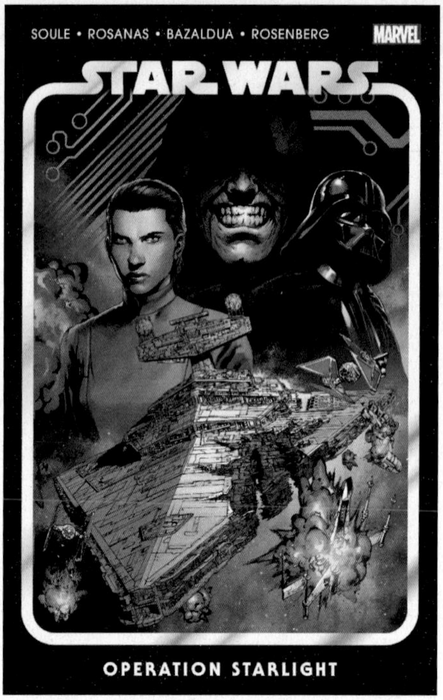
SOULE • ROSANAS • BAZALDUA • ROSENBERG
MARVEL
STAR WARS
OPERATION STARLIGHT

Star Wars Vol. 2:
Operation Starlight

ISBN 978-1-302-92079-1

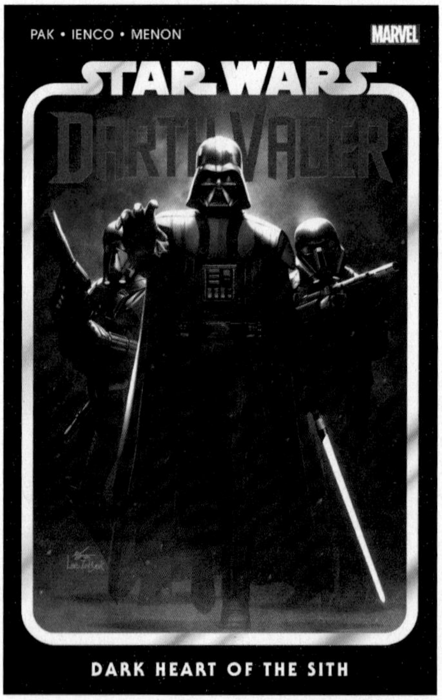
PAK • IENCO • MENON
MARVEL
STAR WARS
DARTH VADER
DARK HEART OF THE SITH

Star Wars: Darth Vader by Greg Pak
Vol. 1 — Dark Heart of the Sith

ISBN 978-1-302-92081-4

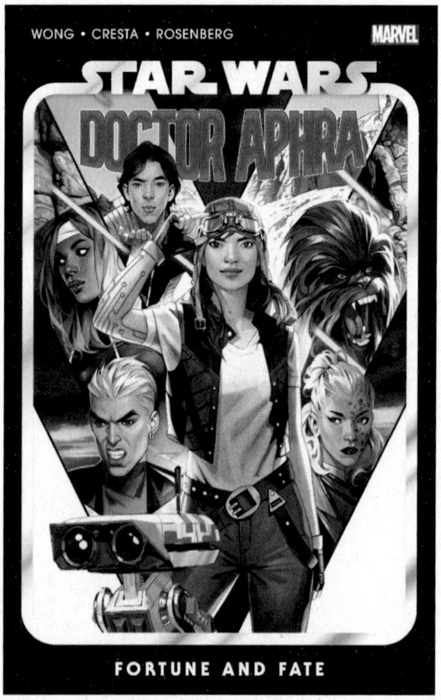
WONG • CRESTA • ROSENBERG
MARVEL
STAR WARS
DOCTOR APHRA
FORTUNE AND FATE

Star Wars: Doctor Aphra
Vol. 1 — Fortune and Fate

ISBN 978-1-302-92304-4

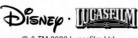

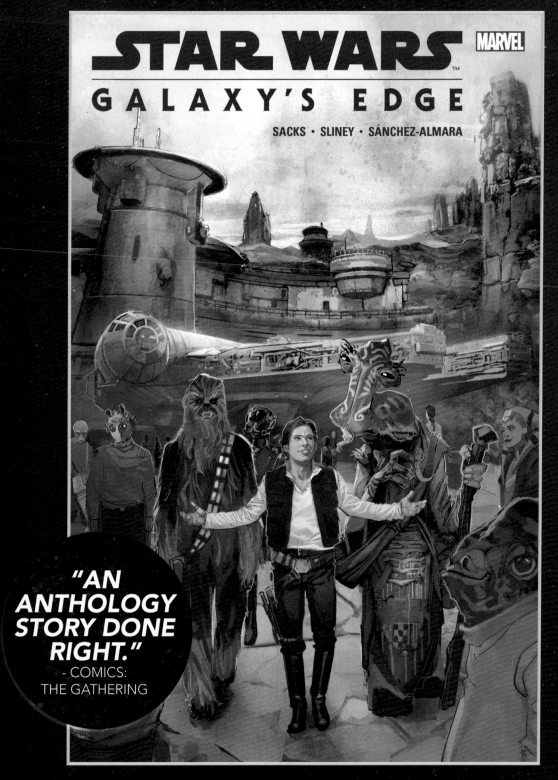